CALIFORNIA
BOUND

A FAMILY MEMOIR

CALIFORNIA
BOUND

PETER PIKE JR.

Printed by Gorham Printing, Inc., Centralia, WA

Book design by Kathryn E. Campbell

ISBN-13: 978-1-7321645-1-2

Library of Congress Control Number: 2018904210

To

Finn, Kai, Vincent, and Arthur

the next generation

CONTENTS

Part Three: Parents

List of Maps

Jacob M. Pike
b. 1831, d. 1916

Mary L. Howell
b. 1842, d. 1892

Asa M. Simpson
b. 1826, d. 1915

Sophie D. Smith
b. 1840, d. 1909

Married
1860
Copperopolis
California

Married
1875
Racine
Wisconsin

Roy M. Pike
b. 1878, d. 1949

Married
1910
San Francisco
California

Edith Simpson
b. 1881, d. 1977

Peter Pike
b. 1914, d. 1984

FAMILY

Frederick A. Cline
b. 1853, d. 1930

Frances E. Holmes
b. 1857, d. 1931

Walter J. S. McGavin
b. 1853, d. 1928

Kate Hinshelwood
b. 1856, d. 1921

Married
1880
St. Louis
Missouri

Married
1881
San Francisco
California

Married
1917
San Francisco
California

Alan P. Cline
b. 1885, d. 1955

Emilia H. "Dolly" MacGavin*
b. 1888, d. 1968

Married
1942
San Rafael
California

Catherine H. Cline
b. 1918, d. 1979

* Dolly spelled her last name "MacGavin," not "McGavin."

TREE

PREFACE

Who among us has not wondered about our parents' lives? What elements of chance and choice brought them together? How did our ancestors make their way into the world, and how did past generations weave themselves into a single family?

Six of my great-grandparents were born in the United States between 1826 and 1857. Mirroring the national divide, three were born in free states—two in Maine and one in Wisconsin—and three in slave states—one in Arkansas and two in Missouri. The two others were born in Scotland and France, both ruled by their sovereigns, Queen Victoria and Emperor Napoleon III, respectively.

All left their birthplaces and immigrated to California. One arrived as an eleven-year-old with her parents. Her future husband arrived at age eighteen. Four others arrived in their mid-twenties, the final two in their sixties. All died in the Golden State.

What drew them west? How did they earn a living? How did their children meet? And their children's children? This book answers many questions, but not all. Some can only be answered in our imaginations, and others will remain mysteries forever.

In family lore, no ancestor looms larger than Jacob Pike, who wrote a colorful memoir about his life in Gold Rush California. Jacob and my other paternal great-grandfather, Asa Simpson, both sailed from small towns on the coast of Maine, arriving in San Francisco in early 1850, unknown to each other. Jacob's wife, Mary Howell, arrived from Arkansas by covered wagon in 1853. Asa's wife, Sophie Smith, left Wisconsin and traveled by paddlewheel steamship, crossing the Isthmus of Panama in 1868.

My maternal great-grandparents, Frederick Cline and Frances Holmes, were from St. Louis, Missouri, the only two born and raised in the same city. They were also the last to arrive in California in 1919. My other maternal great-grandparents,

Walter McGavin and Kate Hinshelwood, were both born in Europe—Walter near Glasgow, Scotland, and Kate in Paris. Their romance blossomed when he visited her family on his way home from India. Soon he was off to California, and she followed a year later to marry him in San Francisco in 1881.

In lives filled with success and failure, joy and tragedy, and wisdom and folly, the Golden State bound these three generations together to produce me. This is their story.

—Peter Pike Jr.

California Bound
Great-Grandparents' Departure Ages and Dates

Jacob Pike, 17
Eastport, Maine
*1849: by sailing
ship via Cape Horn*

Asa Simpson, 23
Brunswick, Maine
*1849: by sailing
ship via Cape Horn*

Sophie Smith, 27
Racine, Wisconsin
*1868: by paddlewheel steamer
via the Isthmus of Panama*

Frederick Cline, 66
Frances Holmes, 62
St. Louis, Missouri
1919: by train

Mary Howell, 10
Russellville, Arkansas
1852: by covered wagon

ME
VT
NY
MN
WI
MI
IA
IL
IN
OH
WV
PA
MO
VA
KY
AR
TN
NC
SC
Atlantic Ocean
LA
MS
AL
GA
FL
Gulf of Mexico

N
W E
S
0   500 miles

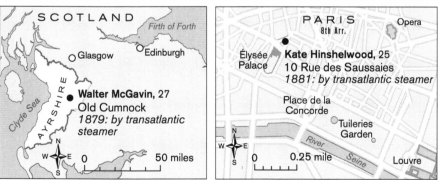

SCOTLAND
Firth of Forth
○ Glasgow   ○ Edinburgh

AYRSHIRE
Clyde Sea

Walter McGavin, 27
Old Cumnock
*1879: by transatlantic
steamer*

N
W E
S
0   50 miles

PARIS
8th Arr.
Opera

Élysée
Palace
Kate Hinshelwood, 25
10 Rue des Saussaies
1881: by transatlantic steamer

Place de la
Concorde
○ Tuileries
Garden ○

River
Seine

Louvre

N
W E
S
0   0.25 mile

Jacob M. Pike
b. 1831, d. 1916

Mary L. Howell
b. 1842, d. 1892

Asa M. Simpson
b. 1826, d. 1915

Sophie D. Smith
b. 1840, d. 1909

Part One

Great-Grandparents

Frederick A. Cline
b. 1853, d. 1930

Frances E. Holmes
b. 1857, d. 1931

Walter J. S. McGavin
b. 1853, d. 1928

Kate Hinshelwood
b. 1856, d. 1921

CHAPTER 1

Gold Rush Voyage

Jacob, 1831–1859

CALIFORNIA BOUND, the square-rigger *Nathaniel Hooper* was off the coast of Brazil on August 18, 1849, when trouble struck. "The Crew rose [up] and placed both the Captain and the First Mate prisoners in the forecastle," wrote Jacob Pike, my great-grandfather. "They then requested me to take the ship into [the] harbor, whereupon I changed the course of the ship for Rio de Janeiro."

Jacob was the second mate aboard the *Nathaniel Hooper*. On the day of the mutiny, he was seventeen years old, five days short of his eighteenth birthday. Five weeks earlier, his ship had left Eastport, Maine, on July 10 carrying 300,000 feet of lumber, 70,000 shingles, and five passengers, bound for the Gold Rush.

From the start of the voyage, the first mate had been a tyrant. "One day [the first mate] sent a sailor up to the main-top[mast] to perform some duty. It seemed that the sailor did not understand his order fully and made some little mistake. The Mate took a rope's end and went up the main-top and gave the sailor a hard whipping. This was what started an ill will among the sailors toward the Mate. Then there was hell-a-popping between the Mate and the Crew."

In the nineteenth century, brutality at sea was not unusual. "The line between enforcement of necessary discipline and tyranny," wrote one maritime historian, "was sometimes hard to distinguish, as was the line between sane, but severe, and psychotic captains and mates."

AS DOCUMENTED by the U.S. Consul, the mutiny started at 1:00 p.m. when Andrew Smith "came out of the forecastle, took hold of the [First] Mate, and confined him with a small rope that lay on the deck." Another seaman, Charles Riley, "assisted in tying him up." Simultaneously, other crew members surrounded the captain and marched him forward to the forecastle. John Stilson, one of the ringleaders, stated that the sailors "were afraid [for] their lives and were determined not to proceed on the voyage."

One of the passengers, L. H. Foster, painted a chaotic picture of the scene. "When I went forward, [I] found the Mate down and tied. I asked the men what they were doing. They said the Mate had come forward & threatened to stab them. I asked them why they were holding the Captain. They said they were holding him to prevent his going aft for his firearms as they were afraid for their lives."

Captain George D. Griffin was enraged to be a prisoner on his own ship. "The Capt. was remonstrating with [the mutineers] telling them they did not know what they were doing, and asked them to let him go. They refused to do so. The Capt. told them it was folly... as he had no intention of taking their lives."

Anxious to reach the California gold fields as soon as possible, the passengers spent two hours negotiating with the mutineers and the captain. Finally, the crew agreed to let Captain Griffin sail the ship to St. Catherine's, sixty miles south of Rio de Janeiro, provided that Jacob, who knew celestial navigation, confirmed that the ship was on its proper course. Later the crew released the first mate after the captain and passengers guaranteed that he would not use firearms against them.

Three days later, the *Nathaniel Hooper* arrived at St. Catherine's. "As soon as we dropped anchor in the harbor," Jacob wrote, "the Captain hoisted a signal for the American Consul to come aboard. He came aboard the ship with some... soldiers and took the Crew ashore and placed them in prison on a charge of mutiny."

After weeks of testimony and negotiation, Acting U.S. Consul, Robert J. Cathcart rendered his decision on September 15, 1849. The captain would pay a fine in order to legally discharge his crew ashore, and the crew would be released from jail. In turn, John Stilson and another ringleader, Andrew Smith, agreed "not hereafter, in any manner, to call on me as [the] U.S. Consul for any support from the Government of the United States."

One month after entering port, the *Nathaniel Hooper* cleared for San Francisco with eight new seamen and a stock of fresh provisions. Jacob reported that the first mate was a changed man. "After leaving St. Catherine's, the Mate behaved himself better. Doubtlessly, he thought that it did not pay to beat and bang men as he did at the commencement of the voyage."

BORN ON August 23, 1831, in Eastport, Maine, Jacob Mabee Pike was the middle child of five, all boys except the youngest. His father, Captain William Pike, drowned at sea when Jacob was five. To help support his widowed mother, Lydia Cutter, he went to sea at fourteen as a cabin boy for a Captain Dunham on a new bark, a small two-masted vessel.

On his first voyage, the bark loaded lumber in Eastport and sailed to Barbados, where it discharged its cargo. From Barbados, it sailed to the Bahamas and loaded salt for New York, returning to Eastport after two months. His wages were six dollars per month, and he had drawn four dollars during the voyage. So he was owed a net of eight dollars.

Paid off with fifty-cent pieces, he carried the coins home in his handkerchief and deposited them in his mother's lap. Jacob later recalled her reaction. "My son, I can buy all my winter's wood with that money." Over the next three years he made many more trading voyages to the Caribbean with Captain Dunham, who took an interest in him and taught him navigation.

When gold fever spread across Maine in 1849, Jacob signed onto the *Nathaniel Hooper* as an able-bodied seaman. Like the rest of the crew, he moved his baggage into the forecastle. By a stroke of fortune, he was soon promoted. "It seemed that the Captain had been told that I knew navigation and was a good sailor. So one day he called me aft, and asked me to take the position as Second Mate on the ship. I told him that I was pretty young to accept such a position. He said that I was fully capable of filling that position and that he wanted me to take it."

Magically elevated to a higher rank, Jacob moved his gear from the forecastle to the mate's cabin. From now on he would be "Mr. Pike" to the captain and the first mate, and "sir" to the crew. The three officers would mess together, although by tradition they rarely spoke during meals. Jacob would lead the starboard watch, the first mate the port watch.

RETURNING TO SEA after its forced stopover at St. Catherine's, the *Nathaniel Hooper* headed south toward Cape Horn. The change in climate was dramatic from balmy Brazil to the icy seas at the tip of South America. "We arrived off Cape Horn, were within sight of the Cape, and before we got around, we took a

southwest gale of wind which drove us to latitude 60° south in freezing weather."
This would have put them about 300 miles from Antarctica. Finally, the gale abated,
and the ship headed north into the Pacific with 7,000 miles remaining before its
landfall in California.

Seven months after departing Eastport, the *Nathaniel Hooper* sailed through
the Golden Gate on February 4, 1850, and anchored in San Francisco Bay in the
midst of hundreds of other ships. During the previous nine months, 805 vessels
had cleared customs into port, and most of them remained in the harbor, abandoned or converted into warehouses as storeships.

Before his ship dropped anchor, Jacob wrote, "I had already made up my mind
to run away from the ship and stay in the land of 'Gold.' You can imagine my surprise when the first man that I saw come over the ship's rail was my brother Sam,
who surely was a welcome angel." Truly a coincidence worthy of Charles Dickens.

When Jacob had sailed from Eastport, he left his oldest brother, Sam, behind.
Sam soon caught a bout of gold fever and decided that he, too, would seek his fortune in California. He took the faster steamer route via the Isthmus of Panama and
beat Jacob to San Francisco. The two brothers made an arrangement for Sam to
"hire a boat, and come under the ship's bow, and take me and my baggage ashore
that night." Sam did so and "away we went ashore, I being once more a free man."

THE BOAT CARRYING Jacob and Sam likely landed at the Central Wharf, which
one early resident described as the heart of the city. It "was the thoroughfare for
communication with vessels, and was crowded from morning 'til night with
drays and wagons coming and going; sailors, miners, and others of all nationali-
ties, speaking with a great variety of tongues, moved busily about; steamers arriving and departing; schooners were taking merchandise for the mines; boats were
crowding in here and there—the whole resembling a great beehive, where at first
glance everything appeared to be noise, confusion, and disorder."

After seven lonely months at sea, Jacob must have been thrilled and overwhelmed by the manic energy of the city. The population of San Francisco had
exploded from 2,000 people in February 1849 to 20,000 in February 1850. One
traveler wrote that half the population lived in tents and a third of the buildings
were saloons and gambling houses. "Gambling here is an occupation, day or night,
Sunday or any other time. The gray-haired father and the beardless boy are to be
seen side by side vying with each other to see who can win or lose the fastest, and

even beautiful women engage in these games with the same earnestness as the sterner sex, betting their last ounce."

After a few days in San Francisco, the two brothers headed for the foothills to search for gold. They booked passage on a steamer to San Joaquin City, a long-forgotten town near today's Tracy and walked fifty miles with blankets on their backs to Spark's Ferry on the Tuolumne River (near present-day La Grange). "We arrived there in a little less than three days. We were pretty well used-up boys. I had blisters on my feet three inches long."

STANDING ON the river bank, Jacob and Sam witnessed a scene they could hard-ly have imagined—thousands of miners frantically scrambling to extract as much gold as they could, as fast as they could, from the rushing river. William Perkins from Cincinnati, Ohio, remembered his first view of Woods' Creek, a tributary of the Tuolumne. "Here were real, live miners, men who had actually dug out the shining metal and who had it in huge buckskin pouches in the pockets of their pantaloons. These men were the awful objects of our curiosity. They were the demi-gods of the dominion.

"Their long rough boots, red shirts, Mexican hats; their huge, uncombed beards covering half the face; the Colt's revolver attached to its belt behind; the *cuchillo* [knife] stuck in the leg of their boot—all these things were attributes belonging to another race of men than ourselves, and we looked upon them with a certain degree of respect and with a determination soon to be ourselves as little human-like in appearance as they were."

By the spring of 1850, the day of the sole prospector with a pan was almost over. Companies of men now sought to divert entire rivers so that they could mine the riverbed where the gold lay. Jacob and Sam joined a company at Roger's Bar on the Tuolumne seeking to "turn the river." There were fifty members, mostly sailors from Maine and Nantucket.

"We had a big job ahead of us! A dam across the river to be built of logs and two-inch planks, and a canal to be dug through a bar of nearly solid rock, about four hundred feet long. It was a great mistake on our parts to have joined this company at all. Had we worked a rocker, washing the surface dirt from the bar, we would have made good money all summer. As it was, by the time we got the canal and the dam built so that the water could be held and carried, the fall rains came. It was very early that year and flooded us out. Thus, all of our summer work was lost."

ON SEPTEMBER 9, 1850, California was admitted to the Union as the thirty-first state. San Franciscans celebrated wildly after word arrived by steamer on October 18. In the foothills, the event went unremarked. "Humbug!" one miner exclaimed. "There is not one man in a hundred that cares a damn about it, one way or another. All they want is what gold they can get, and the state may go to hell, and they would vamoose for home."

Jacob's hard luck continued that winter at Big Oak Flat. "We built a log house and laid in our winter's grub. At this place you could not work without rain. We got all comfortably settled in our new log cabin and waited to see if the rains would come… [but] to our surprise and also our disgust, no rain came. We never mined a day that winter."

IN THE SUMMER of 1851, Jacob and Sam worked Stevens' Bar for two weeks until "One evening we heard of better diggings down at Morgan's Bar. So we packed up and started down the line. Night overtook us, and we camped at Hawkins' Bar. We asked the storekeeper if we might sleep on the grocery store floor. Permission was given, and so we turned in on our soft (!) beds."

That night disaster struck the sleeping Jacob. "All of the money we made at Stevens' Bar I had in a purse of leather in my pants pocket. There was $120 worth of gold dust in it. In the morning when I got up, I could not find my money. It had worked out of my pants during the night, and someone who saw it lying upon the floor picked it up. This left us without a cent."

Fortunately, the storeowner was a man from Maine and, hearing their tale of woe, gave the two brothers credit for "some grub and cooking utensils." He said to them, "You look like pretty nice boys, and by James Priestly Moses, you can have anything I have got in the store." At Morgan's Bar they staked a claim, and Sam built a rocker, or cradle, a device that extracted gold much faster than a pan.

The rocker was a wooden container four feet long with a removable box or hopper atop one end and a series of parallel cleats on the bottom level. As gold-bearing dirt was shoveled into the hopper and water poured over it, a perforated plate under the hopper held back the rocks, allowing the lighter material to fall through the grate and wash out, leaving behind the gold flakes caught behind the cleats. Sam rocked the cradle, and Jacob shoveled the dirt and poured the water. They had a good run for "three or four weeks and made quite a stake," enabling them to pay back the Maine storekeeper.

But soon their output dwindled to four or five dollars a day, not enough for two hungry men. So they abandoned their claim. "Just after we left, two men went into the hole that we had dug on the bar and struck it rich. They hit upon an old river channel running through there, and in a short time they were successful in working it into a rich claim. In about three months they took out about $70,000. It was surely too bad that we had not worked on our claim just a few days longer. If we had done so, all of that gold dust would have been ours."

JACOB NEVER did strike it rich as a gold miner. In 1854 he bought a store near Grand Bar on the Stanislaus River. "Beef, pork, beans, flour, potatoes, and coffee ranked high on miners' lists of provisions purchased," wrote one social historian. "In flush times, they might also have been able to buy onions, dried apples, or a head of cabbage, though fresh fruits and vegetables were the hardest items to find." Unfortunately, Jacob's store turned out to be a "bad place for hard characters," definitely not the type of customer interested in healthy eating.

The worst incident occurred on the Fourth of July 1855 when "two miners got to quarreling in my store. I got them outside, and as soon as I did one of them drew his six-shooter and the other one drew his knife. Then they both commenced—one shooting, the other cutting. They both fell dead in their tracks. It was the most desperate fight that ever occurred in that neighborhood. I was getting tired of taking so many chances with my life, so I concluded to sell my store."

One outraged minister visiting California in the 1850s wrote, "I have seen purer liquors, better segars [cigars], finer tobacco, truer guns and pistols, larger dirks and bowie knives, and prettier courtesans here than in any other place I have ever visited; and it is my unbiased opinion that California can and does furnish the best bad things that are obtainable in America."

Underneath Gold Rush mythology of youthful exuberance and derring-do ran a vein of unrestrained impulses and violent actions. More than half of the population of California was between twenty and thirty years of age. As late as 1855, only 10 percent was female, and mining camps were virtually all-male. Lamenting this imbalance, one lonely Forty-Niner wrote to his family, "This country cannot be a great country, nor the people a happy people unblessed by woman's society and woman's love."

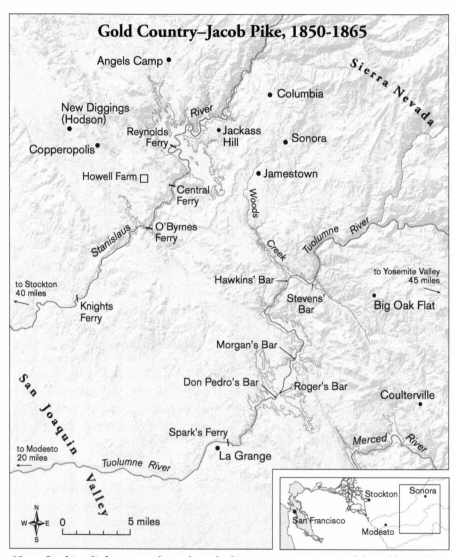

Gold Country–Jacob Pike, 1850-1865

Angels Camp •

New Diggings (Hodson) •

Copperopolis •

Reynolds Ferry

River

Columbia •

• Jackass Hill

• Sonora

Sierra Nevada

Howell Farm ▫

Central Ferry

O'Byrnes Ferry

Stanislaus

to Stockton 40 miles ←

Knights Ferry

Hawkins' Bar —

Stevens' Bar

• Jamestown

Woods Creek

Tuolumne River

to Yosemite Valley 45 miles →

• Big Oak Flat

Morgan's Bar

Don Pedro's Bar

Roger's Bar

• Coulterville

to Modesto 20 miles ←

San Joaquin Valley

Tuolumne River

Spark's Ferry

• La Grange

Merced River

N W E S

0   5 miles

Stockton   Sonora

San Francisco

Modesto

Note: On this relief map, gray lines show the historic river courses, and dotted lines show modern reservoirs. Along the Stanislaus River, Tulloch Lake now covers O'Byrnes Ferry and Central Ferry, and New Melones Lake covers Reynolds Ferry. Along the Tuolumne River, Lake Don Pedro now covers Don Pedro's Bar, Roger's Bar, and Morgan's Bar.

THE HANDMAIDEN to violence was vigilantism, and Jacob was a reluctant participant at a hanging in Coulterville. After hearing complaints of violence against Chinese miners, "We organized a committee [of merchants] to investigate and stop this robbing and killing. In a week we had two Mexicans arrested and evidence of their guilt. We had them tried and one was convicted of murder in the first degree. His sentence was to be hung immediately. This work was all done by our Committee, not by a Court of Justice. That is the way we used to do it in those days. Courts were too slow, and so seldom was a conviction procured.

"We rustled up a horse and cart, placed a board across the body of the cart and placed the prisoner on the board with his hands tied behind him. We drove him to an oak tree that we had selected and threw the rope we had procured over the limb. The next question was, 'Who could tie a hangman's knot?' The crowd was canvassed, and no one could tie a hangman's knot. I did not let anyone know I could tie one. Finally, I said that I could tie one, so I took the end of the rope and tied one, all hands looking on to see me do it and place the rope properly around the fellow's neck.

"The rope was pulled tight and made fast. When that was done, the prisoner, who was sitting back to the driver, turned his head around to the driver and said 'Pronto'; that, in Spanish means go ahead quick, so the driver drove out from under him." He died quickly. "The stand we took in this matter was the cause of all bad characters leaving Coulterville and the surrounding neighborhood, and from that day to this, there has not been any trouble in Coulterville of any serious nature."

IN THE SPRING of 1857, Jacob joined an expedition led by George Coulter, the founder of Coulterville, to Yosemite Valley. "We made a party of fourteen persons, two of whom were ladies, wives of two of the gentlemen in our party." One of the women was the wife of Coulter. "There were no wagon roads into the Valley at that time. We had to go in on an Indian trail…on horseback and packed our provisions…on mules." The journey to the valley took three days.

"[We] met a great many Indians, but all were friendly. Being well armed was a good conciliator. We treated them right and they were a good help to us while in the Valley, such as making trails and catching trout for our camp. You bet we lived high, as trout of the finest quality were in abundance there in all the streams."

The party camped on the Merced River at the eastern end of the valley. "Vernal Fall [was] located a short distance from our camp, and at that time of the year, there was a large quantity of water coming over it. At our camp all were anxious to go to the top of Vernal Fall, including the two women. So we concluded to give it a try. Next day we did, but only three of us and the two ladies would attempt it. We put up our lunch and started for our conquest.

"We got up to the bottom of the fall, as far from the water [on] one side as we could. I forgot to mention that we took our pack rope with us for fear we might need it. We examined the fall pretty thoroughly and concluded we had a very dangerous proposition before us. However, we tackled it. The distance we had to climb to the top was about fifty feet. We selected the most serviceable spot and started. What we had to climb was nearly perpendicular.

"We had made arrangements with the two ladies [that] if we got up safely, they would climb up as far as possible, and we would lower the rope down to them. They would tie it under their arms and we would pull them up. They said all right. They were as anxious to get on top of the fall as we were. It took us some time to get up. Oh, it was dangerous. We never could have accomplished it were it not for some strong brush growing out of the crevices of the rock. The ladies had climbed up twenty feet and could not climb any further.

"When they [saw] we were up all right, they commenced hollering for us to lower the rope and pull them up. We did as they commanded and pulled them up one at a time, not the worse for wear, but a little disfigured in the way of torn dresses. After that experience they were the heroes of the whole party. Surely they displayed nerve that you seldom see in ladies … Right here we sat down and took our lunch. We were as hungry as bears, after the great experience we had in climbing the fall … The scenery at the top of the fall and the pretty granite basin formed there by the continual action of the water was a sight well worth risking your life to see."

A year after Jacob's climb, a nearby hotel manager built a toll trail from the valley floor to the top of Vernal Fall, including "a pair of elongated wooden ladders, which provided a wet, rather scary passageway up the vertiginous cliffs alongside the fall." The charge for ascending the ladders was seventy-five cents. Today, 600 granite steps on the Mist Trail lead 371 feet up to Vernal Fall. The National Park Service warns hikers: *Prepare for slippery footing and a tremendous amount of waterfall spray in spring and early summer.*

Jacob's party decided their safest route home was not to climb back down the cliff. "We finally concluded to take a long way around the fall and make it that way if possible. It was worse for the ladies than the men. When we finally made camp, you ought to have seen us. We were the most pitiful looking group you ever saw. Our clothes were torn to threads by climbing over rocks and through bushes. A rougher country no one ever traveled through…They had our supper all ready, and it is enough to say we enjoyed it perfectly for, rest assured, we were hungry and tired from our day's trample and experience."

After three weeks in the valley, the Coulter expedition headed for home. One more surprise awaited Jacob. "Myself and one of our company were ahead on the trail. We were riding along leisurely. We came to the top of a rise, and there was a big grizzly bear lying right across the trail in front of us. He gave a snort as soon as he saw us and ran into the thick brush nearby. We followed him up to the brush, but we did not follow him into the brush. We thought best not to take any chances on Mr. Grizzly."

A YEAR LATER, Jacob did take a chance that almost cost him his life. In fact, the *San Joaquin Republican* erroneously reported his death in an article published on August 7, 1858, under the headline, "Dreadful Affair on the Stanislaus!—Two Men Killed." In the paper's account, Jacob was leading a posse chasing two murder suspects when "the pursued turned and commenced firing on the pursuers. Mr. Pike was instantly killed at the first fire."

Jacob documented the actual events in his memoir. The confrontation arose from a dispute between two gold mining companies. The older company was operating a water wheel to draw water from the river. The newer company of "Italians" built a dam downstream, which backed up the river and stopped the flow of water past the water wheel. In retaliation, the upstream company started to demolish the downstream dam.

When Jacob and a friend heard the commotion on the river, "We buckled on our guns and ran up to the dam…The Italians were in their tent and opened fire on the parties that had attacked the dam. There were three men. One was killed and another mortally wounded. This man died a few days after. One had buck shot in his legs. It surely looked like a battle field.

"Two of the Italians had crossed the river and gotten on top of a steep hill. Twelve of us formed a posse, and then the chase after the Italians began. At the top of the hill we concluded to divide our posse and take different directions. A man by the name of George Warren headed one party and followed up the river. I headed the other, and followed along the valley, inquiring at every house we came to if the two Italians had been seen…

"While resting, we heard the report of guns, and in a few minutes two of George Warren's party came running down the trail all covered with blood and said that they had met the Italians about a quarter of a mile above and that they had been shot by them. One of the men was shot through the breast, the ball lodging between the flesh and bone. The other had only a scalp wound. They both, however, got well very quickly."

Unfortunately, Warren had been shot dead. "It was a lucky thing that I did not go with George Warren's men as leader. If I had, I would have been served the same as he." Jacob had literally dodged a bullet. Alive and well, Jacob now entered the last chapter of his bachelorhood.

WHEN NEWSPAPERS reported a new gold strike in Salt Spring Valley, Jacob rushed to open a store there in 1859. His store was located in New Diggings, three miles from the future town of Copperopolis in Calaveras County. New Diggings would later be known as Hodson, a hamlet that pulsed to life briefly before disappearing off maps in the early twentieth century.

"Pike and his associates," noted a Calaveras County history, "were soon doing a brisk business with the store and blacksmith shop. His well-chosen location gave him the trade of miners, farmers, and settlers in and about the valley, as well as teamsters coming and going from the [river] ferries. Pike's store soon became the center of the New Diggings settlement, and several cabins and houses were built nearby."

SOME OF JACOB'S customers lived in mining camps near Jamestown, located higher in the Sierra Nevada. Each week Jacob drove his two-horse delivery wagon loaded with mining supplies to the Central Ferry on the Stanislaus River, a six-mile trip. About two miles before the river, the Central Ferry Road passed near a farm with a very attractive farmer's daughter.

"I had heard of his fine-looking daughter," Jacob wrote, "and later saw her several times, but did not get an introduction. I thought if I could get an introduction, I would be all right." The farmer was James Howell, and he and his family had traveled by covered wagon to the Golden State. We begin their story on the California Trail six years earlier.

CHAPTER 2

By Covered Wagon from Arkansas

Mary, 1842–1860

IN THE SUMMER of 1853, the Howell family faced their greatest challenge on the California Trail—crossing the Forty-Mile Desert in the future state of Nevada. They had reached the end of the Humboldt River, a river that shrank and disappeared into the Humboldt Sink unlike any river in their native Arkansas.

"One-half of it sinks into the sand; the other half rises into the sky," one pioneer wrote. "This is the end of the most miserable river on the face of the earth. The water of the lake, as well as that of the river for the last one hundred miles, is strong with salt and alkali and has the color and taste of dirty soap-suds. It is unfit for the use of either animals or human beings; but thousands of both have had to drink it to save life."

Eleven-year-old Mary Howell, my great-grandmother, would have understood the danger that her family faced as they set out across the Forty-Mile Desert, probably after dark to minimize exposure to the blazing sun. Her parents, James Howell and Sarah Bonds, must have looked anxiously at their oxen and wondered whether they could endure the hardship. Mary and her older sister, Nancy, thirteen, would have walked to reduce the burden on the animals. The four youngest children would have ridden in the wagon—Thomas, nine; Henry, seven; Arabella, five; and Vandalia, two.

Even at night, signs of tragedy might be visible. One pioneer party came upon two abandoned wagons in the desert. "We had candles with us, so, as there was not the least breeze, we lit one or two and examined. Everything indicated a complete breakdown, and a hasty flight. Some animals were lying nearly in front of a wagon, apparently just as they had dropped down, while loose yokes and chains indicated that part of the teams had been driven on, laden probably with some necessaries of life … at still shortening intervals, scenes of ruin similar to that just described kept recurring till we seemed to be but the last, little, feeble, struggling band at the rear of a routed army."

The next day, Mary would have looked across a desert wasteland strewn with all types of goods—dishes, bowls, utensils, boots, shoes, clothing, bedding, trunks, stoves, books, rifles, pistols, chains, chisels, saws, and wagons and live-stock stopped in their tracks. "As we advanced," another witness remembered, "the scenes became more dreadful. The heat of the day increased, and the road became heavy with deep sand. The dead animals seemed to become at every step of the way more numerous. They lay so thick on the ground that the carcasses, if placed together, would have reached across many miles of that desert."

THE HOWELL FAMILY had been moving west for generations. Mary's father, James, had been born in Tennessee. His father, English Jessie ("E.J."), had been born in Virginia, and his father, Amasa, in Delaware. E.J. migrated west from Tennessee to Arkansas Territory in the early 1830s with his wife and their seven children. James was the oldest, born in 1815.

E.J. bought land in Russellville along the Arkansas River, about seventy-five miles northwest of Little Rock. A few years after his arrival, Arkansas entered the Union in 1836 as a slave state, paired with Michigan, a free state, maintaining the legislative balance between North and South. E.J. prospered and, by 1850, the value of his farm placed him among the top dozen out of six hundred farmers listed in the Pope County Agricultural Census.

He owned 215 acres, of which 115 were improved, with a cash value of $2,000. He owned 8 horses, 2 mules, 4 cows, 11 oxen, 50 cattle, and 80 swine. In 1850 he produced 40 bushels of wheat, 1,500 bushels of Indian corn, 200 bushels of oats, 1,200 pounds of butter, and 21 bales of ginned cotton weighing 400 pounds each—more than four tons of cotton in total.

E.J. owned twelve slaves, making him one of the largest slave owners in Pope County. The 1850 Slave Census recorded only the age and sex of slaves, so we do not know their names or relationships. Four of E.J.'s slaves were men: 57, 20, 19, and 16. Three were women: 31, 28, and 18. Five were children: four boys, 12, 8, 7, and 2, and one girl, 4. As was common at the time in the South, the value of E.J.'s slaves vastly exceeded the value of his farm. In Pope County in the 1850s, a single male slave could be worth $1,000, a female slave $750, and even children were valued between $250 and $400.

Perhaps family discord factored into the decision of James to leave his home in Arkansas. An interesting speculation is that he had a contentious relationship with his stepmother, Elvira, who had married his father shortly after James's mother died in 1834. According to a Pope County history, when E.J. died intestate (without a will) in 1854, the stepmother and stepchildren "became embroiled in lengthy legal proceedings" over the division of E.J.'s "lands, slaves, and personal property." How his slaves might have been divided or separated is unknown.

NEWS OF the California Gold Strike spread to Arkansas via steamboat in the autumn of 1848. Soon Arkansan newspapers were stoking the imagination of readers with exaggerated and fabricated accounts of Gold Rush riches. "The whole of California is run wild at this time after a gold mine. If half we see is to be believed, every man, woman, and child there will be rich as cream a foot thick."

Promoters sprang into action. The first advertisement—"HO! FOR CALIFORNIA" —appeared in the *Arkansas Intelligencer* on January 27, 1849, announcing the springtime departure of a wagon train from Fort Smith, eighty miles upriver from Russellville on the edge of the Western frontier. Tempted though he might have been, James did not abandon his young family to search for gold. Although not nearly as wealthy as his father and stepmother, James was still a prosperous farmer, ranked in the top 10 percent in Pope County.

The 1850 Agricultural Census showed that he owned 40 improved acres and 280 unimproved acres with a cash value of $1,000. He had 6 horses, 8 cows, 2 oxen, 20 cattle, 20 sheep, and 80 swine. He produced 600 bushels of Indian corn, 5 bales of ginned cotton, and 600 pounds of butter. The Slave Census that year showed that James owned one fifteen-year-old male slave.

By late 1850, the reality that very few would ever strike it rich in California had percolated back to Arkansas. In a perfect echo of Jacob Pike's travails, the *Arkansas Gazette* published a letter from an Arkansan miner on the Tuolumne River: "We had our work completed, and were just about taking out the gold when it commenced raining, and made a complete wreck of all the dams on the stream. Hundreds of men are completely ruined—deeply in debt and out of funds." Another Arkansan wrote, "Thousands would most gladly return to the U.S., had they the means & opportunity of doing so, and are cursing their own folly for ever having left home."

Sobered by this reality, a new class of Arkansan immigrants emerged. No longer were they young men seeking a quick fortune, wrote one Arkansas historian. "The overwhelming characteristic of the 1852 emigrants was different; they were settlers. Many entire families were among those going West to buy land, to buy a home, or to work at steady wages."

ALL THAT we know for certain about Mary's covered wagon journey is contained in three sentences in Jacob Pike's memoir. "Mr. James Howell and wife and family started from Russellville, Arkansas, by ox team for California in 1852. Stayed all winter in Salt Lake. Arrived in California at Woodbridge about twelve miles east of Stockton, I think it was the latter part of 1853." Born Mary Lucy on January 26, 1842, she would have been ten when her family left Russellville.

"From what we can learn," editorialized the *Fort Smith Herald* on January 31, 1852, "there is a large number of persons getting ready for an overland trip to California in the spring…A great many…have determined to remove with their families to that country. The news from California, by those who have returned lately, has produced a great deal of excitement, and the fever begins to rage, almost equal to the spring of 1849, and threatens to carry off a large number of our best citizens."

Emigrants crossing the continent faced a harsh timetable. They could not leave until April or early May when "the spring grass had…come up, for grass was fuel in this age of animal power," wrote Keith Meldahl in *Hard Road West*. "On the far end of the journey, the Sierra Nevada had to be crossed before the first snows threatened to seal the high passes, which could happen as early as October." Essentially, they had a five-month window—May through September—unless they stopped in Salt Lake City.

On April 11, a company of families left Russellville for California. Perhaps the Howells joined this company. If so, it is possible that the Howells were included in the "fifty or sixty wagons" from Pope and Johnson Counties reported as passing through Tahlequah, the capital of the Cherokee Nation (modern Oklahoma), in early May 1852.

Once underway, their wagon train traveled through unorganized and ungoverned territory. James Howell and his fellow emigrants were subject only to the articles of association, which they had signed when joining their company. Emigrant companies were quasi-military organizations led by an elected captain and officers who

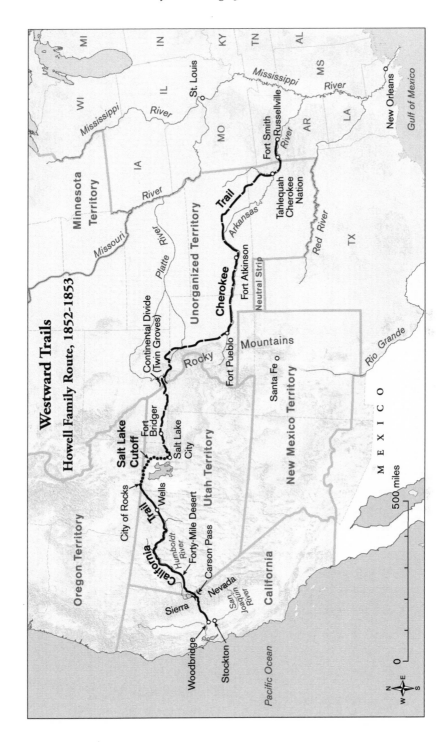

Westward Trails
Howell Family Route, 1852-1853

organized the wagon train, directed the order of march, and enforced discipline.

As a farmer, James Howell would have been well prepared for the journey west. He already owned a wagon and oxen to pull it, horses for exploring, and cows to produce milk for the children. For each adult, a family would typically have carried: "100 pounds of bacon, 150 pounds of flour, 20 pounds of coffee, 30 pounds of sugar, lard, 20 pounds of salt, pepper, crackers, pilot's bread (hardtack), rice, molasses, dried peaches, beans, tea, spices, baking powder, and vinegar." Fully loaded with housewares, tools, and bedding, James's wagon likely weighed about 2,000 pounds, one ton.

TRACKING THE Arkansas River westward on the Cherokee Trail, the Russellville company would have found ample water, grass, and wood—and if not actual wood, plentiful buffalo chips (dry dung). In 1852 buffalo roamed the Plains by the tens of millions. "Once women got over their initial aversion," wrote a Western historian, "they found that chips made a good fire and 'were much more satisfactory than one would think who had never tried them.'" One emigrant woman even found that the chips "made an excellent mosquito repellant. One or two lighted buffalo chips placed in the wagon, she reported, soon smoked the mosquitoes out, and 'we can stand it longer than they can.'"

Averaging fifteen miles per day, emigrants could have covered the first thousand miles in sixty-seven days, maybe longer after delays for river crossings, wagon breakdowns, and illnesses. "The marching itself was slow, at the pace of the slowest oxen, no more than two miles per hour," noted one writer. "All but the lead wagons choked on the dust…Women and children, who typically had expected to ride in the wagons, often abandoned their seats to escape the dust and walked well to the side of the trail."

Day after day, emigrants faced the same drill. "Rise before dawn, cook and eat breakfast, gather the animals, hitch up the wagons, head out, halt around midday, cook and eat dinner, march again to whatever camp the captain or scouts had discovered, undo what was done at dawn with the animals and wagons, cook, and eat supper, set guards on the stock, go to sleep under the stars or the canvas."

After almost a thousand miles on the flat plains, the next 300 miles over the Rocky Mountains in Colorado and Wyoming would be much harder. Their wagon train had to navigate narrow canyons and river crossings leading up to the Continental Divide at a place called Twin Groves, elevation 8,117 feet. Emigrants had a common expression for enduring the hardships they experienced on their westward trek. They called it "seeing the elephant," referring to the enormity of their challenge.

One woman who saw the elephant on Wyoming's high plains wrote, "I would make a brave effort to be cheerful and patient until the camp work was done. Then starting out ahead of the team and my men folks, when I thought I had gone beyond hearing distance, I would throw myself down on the unfriendly desert and give way like a child to sobs and tears, wishing myself back home with my friends and chiding myself for consenting to take this wild goose chase."

EMERGING FROM the Rockies, the Howell family arrived at Salt Lake City, which had been founded by the Mormons five years earlier in 1847 and was prized by emigrants as a place to resupply. In July 1852, a traveler from Virginia wrote the *Deseret News*, "I was never in better country or among a better people in my life. Every kind of grain and vegetables grow in abundance, and not to be surpassed in quantity or quality in any part of the United States."

Anxious to cross the Sierra Nevada before the winter snow, most emigrants paused for only a few days to resupply before pressing on. Why did the Howell family spend the winter in Salt Lake City? Did their wagon break down? Did a child get sick? Did James fall out with the captain of his company? After almost fifteen hundred miles of hard travel, social tensions between families would be expected.

"At this point, company organizations were broken up, almost without exception," wrote another pioneer in 1849, "and every man proceeded to make such arrangements as seemed best to himself and those belonging to the same wagon. In many cases, even those owning teams and wagons together, sold out and parted goods, each taking his own way...There was a general selling of tired out cattle, and buying of fresh."

Whatever the reason for stopping, the Howell family spent a long, cold winter in Salt Lake City. The *Journal History of the Church of Latter Day Saints* recorded the first snowfall on September 15, 1852 ("Snow fell on the Twin Peaks and the tops of surrounding mountains on the 15th instant, the first in sight this fall and continues to lie") and the last snowfall seven months later on May 1, 1853 ("After a storm of rain and snow in the night, the mountains around Utah Valley were covered with snow").

We can imagine the Howell family resuming their westward trek sometime in late May or early June 1853. They would have looped north around the Great Salt

Lake on the Salt Lake Cutoff and joined the California Trail at the City of Rocks, in southern Idaho. One hundred miles south of the City of Rocks, the trail bent westward around the future Wells, Nevada, the source of the Humboldt River.

For the next 350 miles, the Howell family followed the muddy, meandering, foul Humboldt River across Nevada—roughly parallel to modern Interstate 80. "One can get an idea of how it tastes," a pioneer wrote, "by making a strong solution of tepid water and bitter salts and adding several rotten eggs." Simply approaching the river could be dangerous to animals. "Livestock, desperately thirsty from hauling heavy wagons through the summer heat," noted Meldahl, "had to be stopped from charging headlong for the river, where they might mire down in the sloughs and drown. Instead, emigrants often had to fetch bucket after bucket of water and armloads of cut grass for the animals."

When the Humboldt River disappeared into the Humboldt Sink, the Howells, like tens of thousands of other immigrants, persevered and safely crossed the Forty-Mile Desert to the Carson River. "Its water was clear, cool, and pure, free from salt or alkali," one pioneer wrote, "as different from the Humboldt soap-suds [as day] is from night." They probably rested a few days along the banks of the Carson River under the shade of cottonwood trees, as they prepared to face their final ordeal on the California Trail—crossing the Sierra Nevada mountain range.

TOWERING ABOVE Mary and her family loomed 8,500-foot Carson Pass, their route to the Golden State. They began their ascent by climbing the "sheer-walled Carson Canyon, where the Carson River tumbles down a six-mile chain of foaming cascades," explained geologist Meldahl. "Boulders the size of bears and buses plug the canyon bottom…Where they could not go around the boulders, the men pried and pulled the wagons up and over with ropes, levers, and crowbars." One pioneer described the attendant noise as "the wildest hallooing, the loudest of whip cracking, and the most extraordinary profanity that ever saluted ears, whether of dumb beasts or men."

After a short break in Hope Valley, emigrant companies faced an even greater hurdle, a "fiendish scramble" up Devil's Ladder. "The route—thickly studded with pines clinging to cracks in fractured granite—is so steep in places that you can reach out and touch the rock in front of you without bending over…Up they went, using block-and-tackle strapped to trees, multiple teams of oxen, horses, or mules, and all hands pushing and turning the wagon wheels."

Once over the Carson Pass, pioneers found one final barrier. A few miles west of the summit "lay a set of impassable crags and cliffs called the Carson Spur. The only way around it was to go up and over yet *another* pass—9,500-foot West Pass." Although above the tree line and cold, the road over West Pass was not as difficult as the climb over Carson Pass.

At last California was truly downhill. For James Howell and other settlers, agriculture would be the gold of 1853. Farming was a growth industry in young California. The state's first census had tallied 264,435 residents in 1852. More than half were miners, and less than 5 percent were farmers. California would not be self-sufficient in food production until 1856.

James staked a claim to 160 acres in a small valley three miles south of the future Copperopolis. Modern topographical maps and aerial photography show about two-thirds of his farm as meadowland with the balance climbing the slope of Lightner Peak to the west. Campbell Creek runs down the middle, and hillside grasses grow among a checkerboard pattern of live oak trees and rocks.

WHEN JACOB PIKE opened his store in New Diggings six years later, he passed James Howell's farm on his weekly delivery run down the Central Ferry Road to the Stanislaus River. "Mr. Howell's house was right on the side of the road." Jacob longed to meet his daughter, Mary Howell, who turned seventeen in 1859, but he could not get an introduction until one fateful day that summer. Like most romantic encounters, Jacob's introduction to his future wife was part serendipity and part calculation.

"After I delivered my goods," Jacob wrote, "I had to drive up a very steep hill. Right at the top of the hill, one of my horses balked and would not move an inch. After a long time trying to make him go, he lay over on top of the wagon tongue and broke about three feet off the end of it. That made me red hot mad. I took the end of the tongue and hit him between the two eyes...and the blow killed the horse.

"The next question was, 'Where was I going to get another horse to work my wagon home?' The idea popped into my head in a moment to go to Mr. Howell's place about a mile away and borrow a horse. So off I started, thinking all the time that I might get an introduction to that pretty girl. So, I finally got to the house [and] knocked at the door...

"Mr. Howell came to the door and I commenced to tell him my tale of woe. He invited me to come in and sit down. I did not see the girl anywhere. We talked

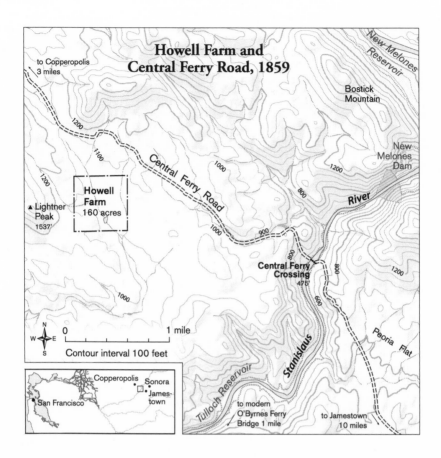

along, and finally, she came into the room, and I was introduced. I think the reason she did not come into the room sooner, was that she was trying to look nice when she came in. She surely accomplished her object, for I thought she was the sweetest-looking girl on earth. It was in the summertime, and she had a white dress on. Her hair was beautifully arranged and everything about her was perfection."

SIX MONTHS LATER, Jacob and Mary were engaged. Preparing for married life, Jacob built a cottage near his store in New Diggings, and furnished it with items bought at auction from neighbors vacating a nearby house. One item purchased was a self-rocking cradle. "It would wind up like a clock and run twelve hours. I thought it would be a good speculation on my part, so I bid on it and brought it home.

"You ought to have heard the joshing I got for buying a self-rocking cradle before I was married. At all events, it proved to be the best bargain I ever made in the way of furniture. When it was wound up, it clicked like a clock. Put the baby in it and start it to run and that click would put it to sleep right away. A marvelous assistance to the mother. It more than paid for all the joshing I got when I brought it home."

Jacob Pike married Mary Howell on Sunday, November 25, 1860, at her father's farm. He was twenty-nine; she was eighteen. We know nothing about the ceremony, but we do know a lot about the farm. Just three months earlier, the census taker had visited it to complete the Agricultural Schedule for the 1860 census. James Howell owned 8 horses, 60 cows, 8 working oxen, 40 other cattle, and 40 swine. We can imagine the odd "moo," "whinny," and "oink" punctuating the couple's marriage vows. Jacob simply wrote, "Had a great wedding and started in my buggy for Stockton. From there we took a steamboat for San Francisco."

JACOB AND MARY walked off the steamboat into a world apart from the Sierra foothills. Cosmopolitan San Francisco was the dynamic commercial, financial, and cultural center of the state. The city's population had almost tripled in the decade since Jacob's arrival to 56,802 in the 1860 census. Sacramento was the next largest city in the state at 13,785; the population of Los Angeles was 4,385.

A French traveler painted a vivid portrait of the street scene that greeted the honeymooners. "First come the Americans in hurried rows, just as it suits people who are at home. The French, English, Irish, Germans, and Italians are mixed with the Americans and are distinguished from the latter by type or by language. Then comes a strange mixture of Mexicans, the dispossessed masters of California, proudly draped in their serapes; Chileans covered by their brightly colored ponchos; Chinese men in round bonnets and silk pants, and Chinese women strangely dressed."

Perhaps the newlyweds stayed at the recently built Oriental Hotel on the southwest corner of Battery and Bush. "The Oriental was a two-story frame building with long galleries across the front," wrote Amelia Ransome Neville, who lived in the hotel for years with her husband. "Partitions between rooms were of cloth covered with paper, which necessitated the carrying-on of any intimate conversation in whispers. But in spite of these slight disadvantages, we were happy there, and found what was known as the elite of the city sharing the discomforts."

MEALS AT HOTELS in early San Francisco were included in the cost of lodging (the American Plan) and were served at long tables "each adorned with a center line of pies, broken by an occasional jelly cake in a high glass dish with glass cover." Neville wryly noted one memorable dinner companion. "Facing me was a stout elderly woman in a low-necked red velvet dress with a diamond necklace and fingers literally covered with rings set with every variety of precious stone. It was the custom for gamblers to invest their winnings in diamonds rather than hoard them in a bank. The lady had been lucky—or perhaps it was her husband."

If indeed the velvet lady's husband was a gambler, Neville would have spotted him. "A gambler in those days invariably wore a drooping mustache, wide felt hat, and Prince Albert coat, open to show a cable of gold stretched across a gorgeous waistcoat, to serve for watch-chain. Diamond shirt-studs flashed above the waistcoat of velvet or brocade, and usually a large solitaire was worn on the right hand in a perpetual state of display."

What entertainment did Jacob and Mary enjoy during their week in San Francisco? Did they attend a performance at Maguire's Opera House on Washington Street? Thursday's show included the first act of *Ernani*, the last act of *Rigoletto*, the Nightingale Polka, a Scottish Ballad, and the last act of *La Traviata*. Or perhaps the couple sought out lighter fare at the Lyceum Melodeon on Montgomery Street. The playbill for the week featured Elegant Modern Comedies, Roaring Modern Farces, and Ethiopian Interludes, starring Miss Belle Devine, Miss Nellie Brown, and Miss Rosina Shaw.

Did they ever catch sight of Emperor Norton, the self-proclaimed "Emperor of the United States and Protector of Mexico"? A delightfully deranged Englishman, Emperor Norton became the most beloved member of a colorful cast of eccentrics in early San Francisco. "His garb was of navy blue, cut in military style and profusely adorned with brass buttons. The shoulders were surmounted with massive gilt epaulettes." Always accompanied by his dogs, Bummer and Lazarus, Emperor Norton roamed the streets issuing wild-eyed proclamations to the citizens of "his realm."

HAPPILY IN LOVE as they wandered the big city, the last thing that Jacob and Mary likely thought about was national politics. Yet events on the other side of the country would dramatically alter the arc of their lives. After the election of President Abraham Lincoln three weeks earlier, war clouds had quickly gathered in the Southern states.

On the honeymooners' first day in San Francisco, the *Daily Alta California* printed a column of "Pony Express" news titled "The Secessionist Movement." At a rally in South Carolina, the paper reported, "a leading merchant declared himself ready to sacrifice all to the maintenance of the State's honor. When speakers declared the Union *dissolved*, the enthusiasm was wild. The *State* no longer doubts that South Carolina will secede."

Secession meant war, war meant munitions, and munitions meant copper—the primary element of brass and bronze. Copper had recently been found three miles from Jacob's store. The Union Army needed this copper. For more than a decade, Jacob had chased after riches in the Golden State. He would not miss the rush for copper.

CHAPTER 3

Boom and Bust

Jacob and Mary, 1861–1888

SEIZING HIS MAIN CHANCE, Jacob built the first store in the boomtown of Copperopolis in April 1861 and "had it stocked with general merchandise in thirty days." The *San Francisco Bulletin*'s correspondent reported on May 22 that "Pike and Brothers have a good store." The Pike brothers were Jacob, his older brother, Sam, and younger brother, William.

Within a year, one thousand copper miners were working in Copperopolis and the surrounding towns. "It is astonishing," one mining history noted, "how rapidly the new mining communities came into being, considering the remote location from the market and the incredibly difficult transportation." Hundreds of wagons, each pulled by teams of mules (sometimes as many as sixteen per wagon) hauled thousands of bags of ore on the forty-mile trip from Copperopolis to Stockton.

From Stockton, the ore was sent downriver by steamboat to San Francisco, where it was loaded onto sailing ships for delivery around the Horn to smelters in New York, Boston, and Philadelphia. Between February 1861 and July 1862, Calaveras County shipped more than six million pounds (3,050 tons in 57,721 bags) of copper ore east to support the Union war effort.

RECOGNIZED AS one of the founding families of Copperopolis, thirty-year-old Jacob and nineteen-year-old Mary were well-known figures about town. Jacob was appointed the first postmaster of Copperopolis and the local Wells Fargo agent. He wrote that his business flourished "right from the start … Being the first [store], I had the advantage, and being Postmaster and Wells Fargo's Agent gave me great prestige."

Most miners considered Wells Fargo's express service quicker and more reliable than U.S. Mail. "By 1858, Wells Fargo went everywhere," wrote one historian, "[and] did almost anything for anybody, and was the nearest thing to a universal service company ever invented. Next to the whiskey counter and gambling table, Wells Fargo's office was the first thing established in every new camp or diggin's."

"This community," raved a newspaper correspondent about Copperopolis in 1865, "is one of the most flourishing and active towns in the interior of the State—a town containing twenty-two saloons, three blacksmith shops, six stores, two druggists, three livery stables, two wagon-maker shops, four hotels, three restaurants, three schools, two churches, and a weekly newspaper—a town consisting of good buildings, some of them even elegant, having a population of nearly 2,000."

Less impressed was a young writer named Samuel Clemens ("Mark Twain"), who spent the winter of 1864–65 sharing a cabin with a friend on Jackass Hill, about ten miles away. On February 23, 1865, Clemens walked into Copperopolis, hoping to catch the next day's stagecoach to Stockton, only to find that the stage would not run for another day. In a foul mood, he wrote in his notebook. "D—n Copperopolis. Have lost my pipe, & can't get another in this hellfired town. Left my knife, meerschaum & toothbrush at Angels [Camp]...D—d poor hotel."

Did Clemens visit the J. M. Pike & Brothers store? A half-column advertisement in the *Copperopolis Courier* listed a bewildering supply of products offered by Jacob: "Groceries and Provisions, Hardware and Crockery, Mining Tools and Blasting Powder, Hemp and Manila Rope...Champagne and Wines, Ale and Porter...Assorted Syrups and Bitters, Sarsaparillas and Patent Medicines." Plus, "Gentlemen's Furnishing Goods...Dusters, Overshirts...White Linen...Shirts and Collars." For "Ladies, Misses, and Children...Boots, Shoes and Gaiters."

TO CELEBRATE the Union victory in the Civil War, the town planned an exuberant Fourth of July celebration, commencing with a one-hundred-gun salute at midnight, July 3, 1865. The *Copperopolis Courier* announced that J. M. Pike would be the Grand Marshall and lead the parade, which would feature a marching band, dignitaries, soldiers, and a final group of "Employees of Mining companies, invited guests, citizens on foot, citizens in carriages and on horseback."

So loud was the roar of the midnight barrage, wrote the *Copperopolis Courier* that "few could sleep. The firing seemed to serve as a signal to arise, for it brought out many of our patriotic citizens, whose shouts and songs were heard...The morning was cool and pleasant, and at an early hour the streets were alive with people. Flags floated over almost every house, and triumphal arches, adorned with flags and evergreens, gave the scene additional beauty." The day concluded with a "brilliant display of fireworks," and "the Union Guard gave a grand military and civic ball…The music at the ball was superb…The ladies were sweet and numerous, and the gentlemen agreeable and happy."

Sadly, this would be one of Jacob's last cheerful memories of Copperopolis. The end of the Civil War doomed the town, as the price of copper plunged from an all-time high of 55 cents a pound to 19 cents. "The Mines closed down," Jacob wrote, "and, in consequence, the whole town was busted, and it has never been anything since. I had a good deal of property in town, but it was worth nothing after the crash." For the first time—but not the last—Jacob was bankrupt.

SIXTEEN YEARS after arriving in San Francisco as an eighteen-year-old youth, Jacob returned to the city as a married man with a wife and three young children—Charles William, Laura Celia, and Jacob Mabee Jr. born respectively in 1861, 1863, and 1865. No more chasing lofty dreams of a rich strike, he now needed a steady salary. Jacob and Mary rented a house at 505 Greenwich between Grant and Stockton, at the time near the edge of the expanding city.

He started work as a drummer, or salesman, for B. C. Horn & Company, an importer and wholesaler of tobacco and cigars, at $125 a month. In 1866 he joined three other drummers representing different lines of goods on a sales trip by stagecoach from Sacramento to Portland, Oregon. "We drummed every town on the road, and there were many…We were about six weeks making it, and, when we arrived in Portland, we were a tired set of boys. We all did an excellent business, as we were the first drummers that ever took that trip straight through by stage."

The timetable for the California and Oregon Stage Company listed daily departures from Sacramento to Portland for a fare of $45.00. The distance was 642 miles, and horses would be changed "every twelve miles." Traveling twenty-four hours a day, the trip in the "Spring, Summer and Fall would be 5½ days and in the Winter 10 days." Meals cost an extra 50 to 75 cents. The stagecoach route generally followed later U.S. Route 99, up California's Central Valley to Yreka, over the Siskiyou Pass to Jacksonville, Oregon, and up the Willamette Valley to Portland.

Jacob and his companions rode in a Concord stagecoach, the classic red-and-gold, egg-shaped coach, suspended on bull-hide belts that cradled it like a

From l. to r., Jacob Pike (tobacco & cigars), Dick Brainard (drugs), Jim Riley (shoes), and Joe Schroder (hardware) on drumming trip by stagecoach from Sacramento, California, to Portland, Oregon, in 1866.

hammock, resulting in a swaying or rocking motion. The average speed of the Sacramento–Portland stage was about five miles per hour, faster on flat ground and slower in the mountains. The four drummers must have called on customers in all of the twenty-four towns listed in the timetable. Most remain well known to-day—Chico, Red Bluff, Shasta, Eugene, and Corvallis. Others—New York House, Louse Creek, and Coxton's—have disappeared off the map entirely.

One newspaper published a guide to stagecoach etiquette: "When a driver asks you to get off and walk, do it without grumbling. He will not request it unless absolutely necessary. If a team runs away, sit still and take your chances; if you jump, nine times out of ten you will be hurt… Don't growl at food stations; stage companies generally provide the best they can get… Don't smoke a strong pipe inside, especially early in the morning; spit on the leeward side of the coach… Never attempt to fire a gun or pistol while on the road; it may frighten the team… Don't discuss politics or religion, nor point out places on the road where horrible murders have been committed, if delicate women are among the passengers."

Traveling at night presented its own set of challenges. "Various devices and po-sitions," wrote one historian, "were contrived in an effort to obtain a longitudinal position: the top, if there was a rail guard; the boot, if not packed with baggage and mail; lengthwise on a seat, if not shared with others. But if the stage carried its full complement of passengers, there was nothing else to do but doze in a sitting position, let the head roll, allow oneself to be pummeled, pounded, and bruised, and await the morning cramps."

After a "good rest" in Portland, Jacob and his friends made sales calls farther north in Tacoma, Seattle, and Victoria, British Columbia, before taking a steamer home to San Francisco. "We were gone about two-and-a-half months on the trip. All the firms congratulated each one of their men for making a very successful and profitable trip." Unfortunately, Jacob's triumph did not translate into a higher salary. When he requested a raise, his boss refused to pay him more.

LUCKILY, Jacob's success came to the attention of Mr. Weil of Weil & Company, "the largest Tobacco and Cigar House in the city." Mr. Weil said, "I hear that you are the party who made a trip from Sacramento to Portland and had a profitable trip." Jacob replied, "Yes, we did very well." Mr. Weil offered Jacob a job at almost double his salary. "The Wholesale Merchants of this city are getting up a Board of Trade to go to Salt Lake City to solicit trade, and I will give you two hundred dollars a month and expenses to represent our house in the Salt Lake City Board of Trade." Soon Jacob was off on another long sales trip in 1870.

Welcoming the trade mission, the *Salt Lake Herald* wrote: "We take pleasure in noting the arrival in this city of a party of gentlemen representing the leading business houses … in San Francisco … San Francisco has, strangely enough, not made the efforts to secure the trade of this region which have been made by Eastern cities. Yet she possesses great advantages …" Among the dozen members of the trade delegation was "J. M. Pike, Esq., of Weil & Co., importers and manufacturers of tobacco and cigars."

Jacob boasted that the trip was both a commercial and a social success. "Brigham Young invited all of us to one of his balls and introduced us to his daughters, numbering about forty. With a few exceptions, all were fine looking. It is against their rules to dance round dances [ballroom dancing], so we were compelled to dance the old-fashioned Cotillions [square dancing], and you bet we made those Mormon girls fly around … It is putting it very mildly to say we had one hilarious time. All of us thanked Brigham Young for the honor he had bestowed upon us."

JACOB WORKED happily for Weil for two years. "They were fine people; I could not ask to have been treated better. Every Christmas I was with them, they gave me two hundred dollars." Mary must have liked the financial stability of her husband's steady salary. We might guess that she enjoyed city life and had developed a network of new friends. Perhaps she met other young mothers at Washington Square, two blocks away, or climbed Telegraph Hill with her children, one block away.

She and Jacob probably visited the new Woodward Gardens, a favorite excursion for San Francisco families. "The Central Park of the Pacific," blared one advertisement, "embracing a marine aquarium, museum, art galleries, conservatories, menagerie, whale pond, amphitheater, and skating rink. The Eden of the West! Unequaled and Unrivaled on the American Continent." Then on the outskirts of the city, Woodward Gardens occupied four acres bounded by Mission, Valencia, Thirteenth, and Fifteenth Streets.

Mrs. Neville fondly recalled the private park. "It covered a sloping hillside, the little valley, with gardens, artificial lakes and fountains, and an added zoo, was the delight of children. In a large tank, overlooked by a grandstand, were barking seals and sea lions whose feeding was the crowning event of the day... Men carrying great baskets of raw meat, and long pitchforks to toss it, passed through the grounds on their way to the tank and were followed like the Pied Piper of Hamelin by an ever-growing company."

Sadly, the 1870 U.S. Census recorded only two children living in the Pike household, Charles, now nine, and Laura, seven. Jacob Jr., born in Copperopolis in 1865, and Freddie, born in San Francisco in 1868, had died in infancy, aged two years and one year, respectively. On the date of the census enumeration, June 15, 1870, Mary was pregnant with her fifth child, James Howell, who would be born two months later, but he too would succumb within a year. Childhood mortality at the time was extraordinarily high by modern standards; in 1869 infant deaths averaged two hundred out of every thousand city births. Happily, Mary's last four children would all live into adulthood.

JACOB ENJOYED financial success over the next five years as a restaurateur. In 1871 he bought an interest in the New York Bakery and Restaurant at the corner of Kearny and Clay Streets. "We made money very fast, and, in a very short time, I made enough money to pay for my interest in the business. And shortly after, I bought out my partner."

San Franciscans patronized restaurants far more frequently than residents of other American cities. One city historian ascribed this proclivity to the city's "rapid growth, shortage of housing, high rents for available homes, lack of domestic servants, and a heavily male and often transient population." In 1872 San Francisco's adult white males outnumbered females almost two to one, 57,000 to 36,000.

Benjamin Lloyd, a contemporary chronicler of city life, explained the popularity of eating out. "Clerks, bookkeepers, printer-boys, and young men engaged in all the various departments of business; young mechanics and laborers, and many of the working females, occupy furnished apartments and board at restaurants. The restaurant fosters the lodging-house, and the lodging-house in turn furnishes the restaurants many patrons… Small families often secure furnished apartments, convenient to an eating-house, so as to be rid of the kitchen cares." Even those with "all the home-comforts in their residences" frequently patronized finer restaurants.

Jacob's business was so successful that he acquired a second restaurant, the United States Restaurant, at Clay and Montgomery in 1873. "My profit that year was sixty thousand dollars [$1,270,000 in 2017 dollars]. The business of both restaurants was enormous. Used to give out about five thousand meals a day. Made money very fast."

Lloyd documented Jacob's money-making machine. "Perhaps the most popular… [restaurant] patronized by all classes—rich as well as poor—is the United States Restaurant. The prices charged at this restaurant are presumably as low as good wholesome food can be furnished. One dish for fifteen cents, or three for twenty-five cents. Of course when extras are desired, a price in proportion to the rareness of the dish is had. For ordinary food, however, the above popular prices are maintained.

"It would be a matter of wonder and surprise to anyone unacquainted with the eating habits of San Franciscans, to spend a day inside this restaurant and observe the great number of persons that it feeds. A fair estimate of the number of meals served per diem at this one eating house would place the daily average at three thousand. The average daily receipts are $600 [$12,700 in 2017 dollars], which would make the average price per meal twenty cents."

Harkening back to his Maine roots, Jacob invested some of his profits in a ship-building venture. "A fine schooner was launched at Humboldt, November 27th [1875], for the coasting trade," reported the *Daily Alta California*, "and, as she slid gracefully down the ways, was christened…the *Laura Pike* in compliment to the daughter of our worthy townsman, J. M. Pike." Jacob commissioned W. A. Coulter, a young marine artist, to paint the *Laura Pike* under full sail in a spanking breeze off the Farallon Islands, a painting that remains in the possession of the family today.

BUOYED BY his good fortune, Jacob and Mary set out on a cross-country sojourn to visit their families—first, Mary's in Russellville, Arkansas, and then Jacob's in Eastport, Maine—before celebrating the Fourth of July in Philadelphia at the Centennial Exposition. They left San Francisco on May 1, 1876, with their two oldest children, Charles and Laura, now fifteen and thirteen. The two youngest, Willis and Thomas, Mary's sixth and seventh, born in 1872 and 1874, must have stayed behind with her family.

Consulting the *Travelers' Official Guide of the Railway and Steam Navigation Lines,* we can plot a two-thousand-mile, eight-day itinerary that they might have followed to Russellville. Six rail lines would have taken them through Omaha, Kansas City, St. Louis, and Little Rock. The family would have spent seven straight nights on a train and the last night in a Little Rock hotel. On their final morning, they would have risen early to catch the 6:30 a.m. train for the seventy-four-mile trip to Russellville on the Little Rock and Fort Smith Line.

In 1876 railroads had not yet adopted standard time. Nor did rail lines use common track gauges. There were no dining cars or vestibule passageways between cars. Overall, the Pike family would have spent about 146 hours on trains, traveling at an average speed of 13.2 miles per hour, including station stops.

WE CAN IMAGINE the emotion Mary felt alighting from the train in her hometown on May 9, 1876. Twenty-four years after leaving Russellville in a covered wagon as a ten-year-old girl, she returned as Mrs. Pike, a thirty-four-year-old mother of seven children, four of whom survived. She lived in the booming, cosmopolitan city of San Francisco, and her husband was a successful businessman, whose restaurants served thousands daily.

By contrast, Russellville's population totaled just 800 souls, served by fifteen stores, two cotton gins, and six doctors. Although growth had picked up when the railroad reached the town in 1873, Russellville's financial health rested firmly upon the state of the local agricultural economy.

The extended Howell clan—dozens of aunts, uncles, and cousins—must have welcomed the California couple into their homes with multiple family gatherings and celebrations. In return, Mary and Jacob must have regaled them with colorful tales of life out West. No embellishments needed, the truth would have been extraordinary.

One listener who was suitably impressed was the editor of the local newspaper, the *Russellville Democrat,* who wrote on May 18, "We had the pleasure of meeting Mr. Pike, of California, last week. Mr. Pike and family are kinsman of the clever Geo. Howell. They reside in the far western Golden State, and will visit Philadelphia, taking in the big show and other big cities and other watering places, before they return to California."

Did the Howells and Pikes ever talk about the Civil War? Arkansas had officially rejoined the Union in 1868, although the state remained in turmoil during the Reconstruction Era, which had ended only two years earlier when the antebellum Arkansas Democrats returned to power. Politics and family reunions rarely mix. Still, the ghosts of the bloody conflict might have been hard to ignore.

AFTER TWO WEEKS in Arkansas, Mary and Jacob were off to Washington, D.C., for three days of sightseeing. A contemporary tourist guide suggested visiting just six landmark buildings in the city: the White House; the Capitol (which included the Supreme Court and the Library of Congress); the new State, War and Navy Departments (today called the Old Executive Office Building); the Treasury Building; the Patent Office (which included the Department of the Interior); and the Smithsonian Institution.

Jacob did not mention meeting President Ulysses Grant in his memoir. But he could have. In those halcyon days, presidents received the public most weekdays in the East Room between noon and 3:00 p.m. A guidebook counseled the proper etiquette. "Persons simply wishing to pay their respects to the President should note on their cards, 'to pay respects,' and limit calls to two or three minutes…The address of the Executive, in conversation, is *Mr. President.*"

IN EARLY JUNE, the Pike family made their way to Boston for their steamer journey to Eastport. Perhaps they boarded the *New Brunswick,* which departed at 6:00 p.m. on Monday, June 5, for the overnight passage. The International Steamship Company ran "sea-going, substantial, and elegantly fitted steamers" to Eastport twice a week via Portland, Maine.

Landing at his hometown dock, Jacob must have experienced a range of emotions—pride, excitement, and nostalgia. Twenty-seven years after leaving Eastport as the seventeen-year-old second mate on the *Nathaniel Hooper,* he returned as a forty-four-year-old father and successful businessman in the dynamic city of San Francisco. Except for the embryonic sardine canning industry, little in Eastport had changed. The population had actually declined between 1850 and 1870 from 4,125 to 3,736.

Just as Russellville depended on agricultural production, Eastport depended upon the bounty of the sea. Five years later, in 1881, the *Maine Gazetteer* would write, "Catching and curing fish has been and is still the principal industry of the town. There are now thirteen sardine factories in full operation in Eastport, employing about 800 hands."

What a reunion Jacob must have had with his seventy-year-old mother, now the widow Lydia Matthews, who lived with his thirty-nine-year-old sister, Celia Paine, and her family. Imagine the wonderful stories they told each other while the cousins played nearby. The California Pikes were noted in the *Eastport Sentinel* on June 21, 1876: "Mr. Jacob Pike and family of San Francisco, formerly residents of Eastport, are visiting their relatives here." At the end of June, Jacob and Mary bade goodbye to family and friends and left for Philadelphia.

JACOB HAD RESERVED a hotel room for four weeks to attend the Centennial International Exposition, the first official World's Fair held in the United States. "We arrived there on July 2nd, got settled and commenced to take in the sights." As they toured the grounds, they might have seen a demonstration of Alexander Graham Bell's new telephone or Remington & Sons' new typewriter. They might have tasted new products like H. J. Heinz Company's tomato ketchup, Charles Elmer Hires' root beer, or a popular snack called popcorn.

But Jacob and Mary hated Philadelphia. "It was so hot, and there were so many people that I told my wife I would never be able to stay for four weeks." The *Philadelphia Enquirer* documented the city's brutal heatwave with its headline on July 10, "One Hundred and Four in the Shade, Numerous Deaths in the City." For the past twenty-two days "the mercury has not gone below 80°, while the average has been somewhere about 95°."

"I was never in such a jam of people," Jacob wrote, "and the hot weather both night and day was unbearable. My wife thought the same as I, for the poor thing would get up in bed all night and fan herself. We stayed there ten days. The last day I came very near having a sun stroke…We put out for home as fast as the good Lord would let us." San Francisco's fog had never seemed more inviting.

FINANCIAL DISASTER struck soon after Jacob and Mary returned home. "Just before I started on my trip," Jacob wrote, "I figured up what I was worth. It was $140,000, including real estate, stocks, the grocery business, two restaurants, and cash on hand [$3,300,000.00 in 2017 dollars]. When I returned, things were in pretty bad shape. The bottom had fallen out of the Restaurant business." Jacob regretted that he had not sold his restaurant earlier. "When we started for the East, I was offered twenty thousand for the U.S. Restaurant and declined to sell, which was another mistake of mine."

To add to Jacob's woes, the San Francisco stock market crashed in January 1877 when the Consolidated Virginia Mines of the Comstock Lode could not pay its normal monthly dividend. "A panic in mining stocks resulted," wrote financial

Jacob Pike, about 1876.

historian Ira Cross, "with prices tumbling headlong to the lowest recorded levels."

Unfortunately, Jacob owned a large number of shares of Nevada mining stocks. "I went to my Broker's office and requested them to sell every share of stock I had, but not in a day, for so large a block of stock would break the market... He sold it all in three days. A lucky thing I did, for in a few days it went much lower. After I got my statement from my broker, I figured up what I had lost in my stock dealings. I was a seventy thousand dollar loser" [$1,650,000.00 in 2017 dollars].

However, this was not the end of Jacob's financial troubles. "A short time after that, my broker failed; the stock market broke him flat. To make matters worse, I and another man were on his note for twenty thousand dollars in his bank. The other man... put his property out of his hand and left me to pay it all. I

Mary Pike, about 1878.

compromised with the bank by paying them ten thousand dollars."

Jacob was luckier than most. "I worked out of this scrape honorably and went to work vigorously to make more money...These were terrible times; a great many of my friends lost everything they had and never did recuperate, but such blows... always gave me more energy."

ONE YEAR LATER, Roy Melville Pike, my grandfather, was born on February 10, 1878. Roy was the eighth child born to Mary. Her ninth and last, Percy Mortimer, would be born in 1882, the same year that Jacob started his next business venture, a cigar manufacturing business at 324 Battery Street.

Operating as J. M. Pike & Son, Jacob took in his oldest son, twenty-year-old Charles, as his partner. Jacob drummed California and Oregon, and Charlie drummed Colorado and Texas. Unfortunately, Charlie's business judgment was poor, and his accounts did not pay their bills. Jacob wrote in his memoir, "That crippled me very much as my capital was small." Unable to pay his debts of $6,000, Jacob went broke—again.

The *San Francisco Chronicle* of January 20, 1888, reported that creditors were given the "power to dispose of all property, real and personal, belonging to Pike." "Father lost the home via mortgage foreclosure," Percy recalled in his memoir. "He moved the family...to a third-floor loft apartment over a restaurant at 636 Market Street opposite the Palace Hotel...I well remember Mother crying at the time of the move..." We can understand Mary's tears. For almost thirty years of her married life, she had watched her husband's fortunes soar, only to come crashing down time and again.

SIX BLOCKS AWAY on Market Street, Captain Asa M. Simpson occupied the opposite end of the financial spectrum, ruling over a vast shipping and lumber enterprise. Two decades hence, Asa's daughter, Edith, would marry Jacob's son, Roy, vaulting him into a life of wealth and privilege that he could only have imagined. We begin Asa's story four decades earlier on a schooner making a landfall on a desolate coast.

CHAPTER 4

Lumberman and Shipbuilder

Asa, 1826–1871

THE CAPTAIN SCANNED the shoreline for landmarks to fix the schooner's position off the mouth of the Umpqua River, Oregon Territory, in April 1851. Telltale breakers to the north and south bracketed a channel a hundred yards wide and thirteen feet deep between two sandy peninsulas. A sailing guide would later caution mariners, "This river is practicable for steamers, but dangerous to sailing vessels, unless under very favorable circumstances."

Crossing the Umpqua Bar would be the most dangerous part of the five-hundred-mile trip north from San Francisco for twenty-five-year-old Asa Simpson, my great-grandfather, and other passengers. Unlike most in Gold Rush California, Asa was prospecting for trees, not gold. "I made port and remained there two weeks exploring the Umpqua River," Asa later said. "I went up 25 to 30 miles" to present-day Scottsburg. "I had no motive for going except to explore the coast. It just shows the pioneering spirit in a man that would induce him to leave his business and go on a wild goose chase like this."

History would prove that this was no wild goose chase. Twenty-five years in the future, Asa would be hailed as the leading lumberman and shipbuilder in southern Oregon, and Simpson Lumber would cut 12.5 million board feet of lumber on the banks of the Umpqua River alone. (A board foot is one-foot by one-foot by one-inch.)

LIKE JACOB PIKE, Asa grew up in a small coastal Maine town. Born February 20, 1826, in Brunswick, Asa Meade Simpson was the eighth of thirteen children born to his father, Thomas, and his three wives—Margaret Pennell, Mary Wyer, and Elizabeth

Whitehouse. Asa's mother, Mary Wyer, died when he was three.

Asa had no memory of her, but was told by "neighbors and relatives that she was always a saintly woman…one of those puritanical New England women, earnest and fervent and always did what she thought was right." In a household teeming with children, "We were pretty constant workers, and every boy was expected to do his duty," Asa remembered. "The children were brought up according to the moral law and the Bible, as the world goes in a country place."

He had fond memories of his rural youth. "We were given our amusements. We had our guns; we were all good marksmen. We went gunning and fishing and had our ball games, and in the Winter went skating. Though we had to do considerable work, taking it all in we had fairly good times." Until he turned eleven, Asa went to school in both "Summer and Winter." Starting at age twelve, he worked in the summer and went to school for five months during the winter. At seventeen, he was apprenticed to his older brothers to learn shipbuilding.

IRONICALLY, Asa had spent his last year in school under the tutelage of "old Professor Pike" at the Pleasant Street Seminary studying "mathematics, algebra, geometry, etc." Professor Pike urged him "repeatedly and frequently to study for a civil engineer degree and to adopt civil engineering as a profession on account of my mathematical advancement." Forty-five years later, Asa reflected on his decision. "In my lifetime since I have regretted—not always, but at times—that I did not accept Professor Pike's advice."

Young Asa, however, marched to a different drummer. "I wanted to be a mechanic [a shipwright] and build ships like my brothers did—a boy's ambition." At twenty Asa was "well grounded in the principles of shipbuilding and had charge of a crew of men." By twenty-one, he was a "master mechanic," working with his oldest brother, Thomas Jr., also a "master builder," in nearby Bath, a major shipbuilding center.

But life in a shipyard on the coast of Maine was not enough for twenty-three-year-old Asa, who imagined a wider world for himself. Catching gold fever in 1849, he set his course for California. "My motive was to see the Pacific Coast and the wonderful climate that we had heard a great deal about and the great wonders of gold discoveries—to see if it was really true. The main impelling motive was curiosity—mainly curiosity—to see more of the world and possibly to make a fortune."

INVESTING ALL his savings, Asa bought a one-thirty-second interest in the square-rigger *Birmingham* and its cargo. The *Birmingham* carried "400 thousand feet of Lumber…21 House Frames and all the materials for erecting and finishing the same," noted a Portland newspaper, "100 thousand Bricks, 200 thousand shingles, 6 lighters, 3 wagons and a variety of other articles." The ship also carried twenty-seven passengers, including Asa and two of his brothers, Lewis and Isaiah.

Under the command of Captain Winchell, the *Birmingham* cleared Bath on November 4, 1849, and sailed south in the Atlantic. After rounding Cape Horn, the ship stopped for provisions in Valparaiso, Chile. Continuing north in the Pacific, the *Birmingham* arrived in San Francisco on April 7, 1850. About the passage, Asa simply said, "We were all well and enjoyed ourselves very well. It is rather monotonous to be confined to [the] narrow limits of a ship's deck [for] five months…We passed time in walking, talking, whistling, dancing, reading, eating, and sleeping."

Asa had sailed on the *Birmingham* as the supercargo, the person in charge of the ship's cargo and its sale at the end of the voyage. Unfortunately, the San Francisco market was glutted with goods from the hundreds of recently arrived ships. "The cargo of our ship was almost unsaleable, being nearly half lumber which could not be sold at that time. The next best thing was to go to the mines, as almost everyone did. We went to the mines."

ASA, HIS BROTHERS, and friends set out for Don Pedro's Bar on the Tuolumne River. (This was the same river that Jacob Pike worked, although they never met.) "We raised a tent and were ready for prospecting the next day. With bucket, pick, and shovel we started out, about as green a set of miners as could be found, but probably on a par with others in that respect." Luckily, the greenhorns struck gold, and, amazingly, Asa decided to quit while he was ahead, after just two weeks on the river.

Because he had paid the party's expenses for their mining venture, Asa retained the first proceeds, and he left with between "fifty and sixty ounces of gold dust." He walked to Sacramento in two days, camping under "an oak tree at night with gold dust for a pillow." Gold was worth about $16 an ounce, so fifty ounces would have been worth $800 ($25,900 in 2017 dollars).

On June 18, 1850, Asa happily wrote to his sister-in-law, Eliza Pennell Simpson, the wife of his older brother, Robert, who had recently arrived. "It is with the greatest pleasure that I take in hand my old gray goose quill (nature's noblest gift, that mighty instrument of little men) to talk a few moments to you…California, you are aware, is a great country… At one time, we were sitting down under the shade of a tree waiting for our team to come up, feasting our eyes on the beauty of the scenery around… So I began to pick and within my reach, and without moving, I picked a variety of some Five to Eleven distinct species of flower."

Ever the entrepreneur, Asa put his Tuolumne gold stash to work, lending thirty-one ounces to the builders of the *H. T. Clay*, a steamboat under construction, at an interest rate of 5 percent per month, the "prevailing commercial rate." Unfortunately, the builders' plan failed when new steamers arrived from around the Horn and reduced their projected revenues. Asa never saw a penny of his principal or interest. The final blow was delivered when a sneak thief stole the balance of his gold from his room on "Long Wharf" (another name for the Central Wharf). "Thus ended my gold mining adventure."

ASA EVENTUALLY succeeded in selling a quarter of the *Birmingham's* cargo, and, in the fall of 1850, he established a lumberyard in Stockton with S. R. Jackson, an acquaintance from Brunswick. Simpson & Jackson became "the pioneer lumber business of Stockton." This "was my first experience in the lumber business; I had never known anything of it before." Soon Asa expanded his operations to Sacramento and San Francisco. The demand for lumber was increasing due to the exploding population and the destruction of raging fires. One fire alone in San Francisco on May 4, 1850, engulfed twenty-two square blocks and destroyed a thousand buildings.

Over time, the supply of Eastern lumber was nearly exhausted, and Asa realized this created a business opportunity. "There were probably not more than a dozen mills on the whole coast at that time, and they were small." Asa decided that he would build his own sawmills where timber grew close to the ocean and where he could easily load lumber onto his vessels at coastal ports. This business model became the foundation of his lumber and shipping empire.

In 1852 he bought his first sawmill in Astoria at the mouth of the Columbia River. "Astoria was about the only decent place I could find for a mill location. The other places were perfectly wild, and at some of them were hostile Indians." The mill was "a primitive affair… I knew nothing about sawmills. I had to learn it by hard experience. The men that I employed knew less even than I did, if possible, so that was unfortunate." The capacity of the mill was between 10,000 and 15,000 feet of lumber a day, and the principal market was San Francisco, which needed pine lumber for street-planks.

IN FAMILY LORE, the spiritual home of the Simpson Lumber Company would always be Coos Bay, the largest harbor on the southwest coast of Oregon, forty miles south of the Umpqua River. When Asa first explored the Umpqua in 1851, he had heard of Coos Bay, "but no one had been there—the Indians had possession of it, and they were hostile."

On a second trip to the Umpqua the following year, Asa and two companions tried to walk south to Coos Bay, before turning back after confronting a group of Indians at Ten Mile Creek "with painted and tattooed faces and further adorned with plumes and feathers." He saw Coos Bay for the first time in 1855 when he hiked north from Port Orford forty miles through forests and along beaches. This time he was unhindered by Indians, whose population had been decimated by years of starvation, disease, and violence.

About this time, coal was discovered at Coos Bay, and Asa's ships began carrying it to San Francisco. "The object of building a mill at Coos Bay was to make deck loads for schooners that I was then assaying to bring coal in … it was a necessity to have a deck load [lumber carried on deck] as they were not fitted to carry coal without a deck load, and that was the inducement to build a mill."

Tragically, the *Quadratus*, the ship carrying equipment for the new mill, struck the bar at the entrance to Coos Bay. Asa's older brother, Lewis, was a passenger aboard. As the ship was pounded by waves, a woman named Mrs. McDonald screamed in panic at the captain and crew. Lewis volunteered to join the mate and to row her and her child ashore in a small boat. Her husband remained aboard the battered vessel.

Waves overturned the rowboat and all were lost, except the mate. The *Oregon Statesman* wrote that "Mr. McDonald saw his wife and child thrown out of the boat into the surf, but could render no assistance to them." Half-filled with water, the *Quadratus* was driven ashore, and those who had remained aboard were all safe.

LEWIS'S DEATH was a tremendous blow to Asa. "I searched the beach every day for a month looking for the body in hopes that it might be cast up, but never discovered it. This was the most serious knock-down I think I ever had because it was in the early days…There was not insurance, and I lost nearly everything I had. I did not, however, lose heart."

Three years earlier in 1853, Asa's younger brother, Isaiah, had also been lost at sea when the schooner *Machigone* vanished without a trace off the mouth of the

Columbia River. A marine history chronicled the *Machigone*'s mysterious disappearance: "She was deeply laden with lumber, and a terrible gale raged for several days after she left the river. The supposition is that she was battered to pieces and driven away from the track of vessels passing up and down the coast."

In memory of his deceased brothers, Asa erected a broken Roman column, symbolizing a life cut short at sea. Visible today in the Pine Grove Cemetery at Brunswick, Maine, the transcription under Lewis's name reads:

> He lost his life in the cause of humanity
> He sleeps where the coral grows
> And the sea kelp lines his tomb
> Where the mighty billows ebb and flow
> And roaring breakers speak his doom

ASA RECOVERED the boilers and engine from the wreck of the *Quadratus* and had his new mill completed by the end of 1856. "My operations have been a hard fight," he later recalled. "Accident and pioneering in new places where there were no facilities, with great expenses and small returns. Go into a place. Meet a lot of stragglers or people who have pioneered or emigrated, who have not a cent of money. The only thing you can do is to avail yourself of their labor—the most important thing. But I claim some credit for a little foresight, for a little enterprise."

A year later, in 1857, Asa built a shipyard adjacent to his Coos Bay mill. "This was deliberate," he said. "This was no blundering thing. I was a skilled man in the business—I had learned the shipbuilder's trade." Compared to Bath's shipyards where Asa had practiced his craft, his new shipyard was a primitive affair. "Very little power was used in Coos Bay shipyards at first," wrote one historian, "but later innovations included power drills, lathes, and steam-driven saws for all purposes. Steam cranes and derricks were used to hoist heavy timbers into position, and teams of horses or bulls furnished the power for moving loads around the yard."

As business boomed in Coos Bay, Asa built a company town for his employees, including a store, cookhouse, dormitory for unmarried men, and small dwellings for employees with families. He even recruited a baseball player from Washington to a "lucrative job" at Coos Bay to play for his sawmill team. Over time this settlement became known as "Old Town."

A Coos County history described how Asa's sawmill set the rhythm of daily life in Old Town. "During the next forty-odd years, the mill whistle continued to sound the time to get up in the morning, the time for dinner [lunch], and when to quit work at the end of each day." (Today Old Town is part of the city of North Bend and is known as Simpson Heights.)

AFTER LOSING more ships attempting to cross the Coos Bay Bar under sail, Asa acquired a steam tug in 1859. The appropriately named *Fearless* was the first bar tug on the Oregon coast. Built of teak in Calcutta, the *Fearless* had arrived in San Francisco under sail. Asa bought the boat and refit it with a steam engine, before sending it north to Coos Bay. If the bar was not breaking, the *Fearless* could safely tow ships through the narrow channel, and his shipping losses declined sharply.

Ten years later, Asa expanded his tugboat service to the Columbia River. Numerous shipwrecks at the mouth of the Columbia had finally prompted the Oregon legislature to offer a subsidy to a company that would maintain a tug at the bar for five years. Asa partnered with a well-known bar pilot, George Flavel, to build the steam tug *Astoria*, and they launched their service in December 1869. Asa would maintain his interest in bar pilotage on the Columbia for the next thirty years.

Seizing another business opportunity, Asa launched a line of Columbia River packets. (Packet was a term for a fast sailing vessel providing regular service between two ports.) The Portland *Oregonian* praised Asa's new service as an alternative to costlier steamships: "The country is indebted for the means of escaping the necessity of being at the mercy of the steamship line, in the matter of export freights." Eventually, Asa's line of packets included five ships, all flying the Diamond S pennant at the masthead (a white diamond containing an "S" set on a red background).

By the late 1860s, Asa's Coos Bay mill required a fleet of sixteen vessels shuttling back and forth to supply lumberyards in San Francisco, Sacramento, and Stockton, and he continued to acquire mills in other locations—Port Orford, Crescent City, and Santa Cruz. In 1869 his Coos Bay shipyard launched its thirteenth vessel, the *Webfoot*, a 146-foot, barkentine (a three-masted ship with square sails on the foremast and fore-and-aft sails on the other two masts).

Asa Simpson, about 1860.

WE KNOW LITTLE of Asa's social life in the 1850s and 1860s. He must have worked constantly, traveling frequently to his far-flung coastal outposts. When in San Francisco, he lived in a succession of hotels—Rassette House, the American Exchange Hotel, Russ House, and the Cosmopolitan Hotel, all well-known addresses. He would have taken his meals either at his hotel or nearby restaurants.

A staunch temperance advocate, Asa never visited saloons. "I recognize the drinking of intoxicants as the greatest of all evils." So he banned the sale of alcohol in his mill towns because, in his words, "The moment you see a young man go into the bar alone, he is in danger." Asa was particularly concerned about the wives and children who were the victims of dissolute husbands.

For reasons unknown, Asa moved out of the Cosmopolitan Hotel in 1870 and into Mrs. Kelsey's boarding house, unfashionably located at the southwest corner of Folsom and First over the Slosson Brothers grocery and liquor store. Why? The Cosmopolitan Hotel at Bush and Sansome would have seemed a perfect fit for a wealthy and peripatetic businessman like Asa. The first-class Cosmopolitan, touted one city guide, "reposes in elegant dignity, very much in accord with the tastes of gentlemen inclined to the old school style."

Asa was a rich man. That year he had told the census enumerator that he owned real estate worth $200,000 and personal property worth $300,000, for a total of $500,000 ($9,690,000 in 2017 dollars).

"LIVING IN a first-class hotel," wrote a contemporary social critic, "is a strong presumption of social availability, but living in a boarding house … is to incur grave suspicions that you are a mere nobody. But even in a boarding house

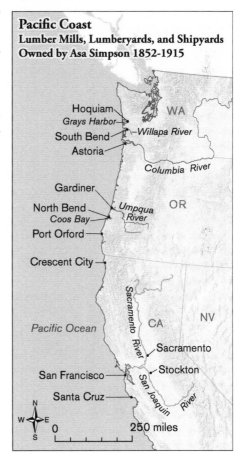

Pacific Coast
Lumber Mills, Lumberyards, and Shipyards
Owned by Asa Simpson 1852-1915

Hoquiam
Grays Harbor
WA
Willapa River
South Bend
Astoria
Columbia River
Gardiner
North Bend
Umpqua River
OR
Coos Bay
Port Orford
Crescent City
Sacramento River
Pacific Ocean
CA
NV
Sacramento
San Francisco
Stockton
Santa Cruz
San Joaquin River
N
W E
S
0   250 miles

the lines may be drawn between those who have a single room and those who have a suite."

Mary Kelsey was a forty-one-year-old Canadian widow living with her three children and two other children, perhaps cousins, ranging in age from twelve to twenty. Two Chinese servants helped Mrs. Kelsey. Six single men and three single women made up the balance of the seventeen occupants enumerated by the census taker on August 1, 1870. The men listed a variety of occupations—a dry goods clerk, a bookkeeper, and a clerk in a harness store.

All the residents at Mrs. Kelsey's would have dined at a common table. Did Asa enjoy their company? The short answer is yes—at least in the case of one resident, a thirty-year-old music teacher named Sophie Smith, whom he would marry five years hence.

ALTHOUGH THEIR COURTSHIP will forever remain a mystery, one intriguing clue remains with the family—an invitation to a masked ball that Sophie kept all her life. The envelope was addressed to "Miss Sophie D. Smith" and enclosed a printed invitation to the Second Annual Masquerade Ball of the San Francisco Bachelors' Club on February 17, 1871. "Dancing at 8½ o'clock."

The event was held at the Pacific Hall on the second floor of the magnificent California Theatre building on Bush Street. Built two years earlier, its opening "was a grand gala occasion; an evening of light and color, laces and flowers...The city's wealth, beauty, and fashion were all there...The guests arrived in carriages, their horses' hoofs clattering on the cobblestones."

We do not know what costume Sophie wore to the Masquerade Ball. San Francisco women were noted for their elegant dress, leading a visiting newspaper editor to write, "Perhaps in no other American city would the ladies invoice so high per head as in San Francisco, when they go out to the opera, or to a party, or a ball. Their point lace is deeper, their moire antique stiffer [a French silk technique], their skirts a trifle longer, their corsage an inch lower, their diamonds more brilliant—and more of them—than the cosmopolite is likely to find elsewhere."

By tradition, Sophie and Asa would have removed their masks at midnight, but the party continued well into the early hours of the morning. "The fun was kept up with renewed vigor," reported the Daily Alta California, "until about the time the milkmen were going on their rounds." While we can imagine the younger crowd enjoying music, laughter, and dancing until the crack of dawn, it is harder to imagine temperate, workaholic, forty-five-year-old Asa relishing the scene.

WHATEVER TIME the couple returned to Mrs. Kelsey's boarding house, Sophie must have remembered the night fondly. Was this their first date? Their first kiss? We will never know. We do know that Sophie was an independent woman, determined to chart her own course, and we begin her story with the fraught capture of a runaway slave before the Civil War.

CHAPTER 5

An Educated Woman Heads West

Sophie, 1840–1895

THE POSSE CREPT toward the isolated cabin on the cold winter night of March 10, 1854. The sound of their footsteps crunching in the snow was muffled by the rapids of the Root River. They knocked loudly, rushed in, and subdued their target, Joshua Glover, a runaway slave living on the outskirts of Racine, Wisconsin. Quickly hustling Glover onto an open wagon, they set out on a nighttime journey to Milwaukee, twenty-five miles north.

News of Glover's capture electrified Racine the next morning. Summoned by the courthouse bell, an angry crowd, the largest in Racine's history, assembled in Haymarket Square (modern Monument Square) demanding the release of Glover. Thirteen-year-old Sophie Smith, my great-grandmother, and her family lived three blocks away and must have joined the demonstration. Almost all Wisconsinites were staunch abolitionists.

Meanwhile in Milwaukee, citizens rallied to their courthouse to demand justice. Fiery rhetoric drove some protestors into a frenzy, and they broke into the jail, freeing Glover. Waving his hat to thank his liberators, Glover was spirited off to a series of safe houses on the Underground Railroad and eventual freedom in Canada.

News of Glover's freedom was celebrated that night in Racine. "One universal expression of satisfaction burst forth" reported the *Racine Advocate*, "and cannons were fired, bonfires were lighted, bands of music patrolled the streets and every demonstration was made … at the triumph of humanity over the brutality of the slave driver's power."

We can imagine Glover's capture and escape galvanizing young Sophie's abolitionist views. Ten years later, in the middle of the Civil War, she would deliver a fiery speech to the female alumnae of Racine High School on July 3, 1864: "Put back your woman's tears. With a steady hand and a brave heart, buckle on your sword. With words of cheer, bid your dear ones forth to battle for the rights of all. Be a Spartan mother, a Spartan wife, a Spartan sister."

All citizens, she said, had been summoned to this struggle by the "sounding notes of woe & bitter sadness. Every whizzing ball & shrieking shell, every cannon's boom & muffled drum, every orphan's cry & widow's moan, the same crimson beat of the blood of thousands now gazing out so still." The *Racine Advocate* praised her speech as a "jeweled frame of words."

SOPHIE'S FATHER, Eldad Smith, and his first wife, Sophia E. Dwight, had emigrated from Massachusetts to Wisconsin Territory in 1835 and built a log cabin near Racine. After her death, he married Harriet A. Underwood, and their first child, Sophia (Sophie) Dwight Smith, was born on October 17, 1840. In 1841 the Smiths moved to the village of Racine, building a house at the northeast corner of Barnstable (later renamed College Avenue) and Eighth Street. Two younger sisters, Harriet and Eliza, followed in 1845 and 1847.

Sophie graduated from Racine High School in 1859, earning special recognition in English, French, and philosophy. At a time when less than 2 percent of eighteen-year-olds earned a high school diploma, she would have been considered a highly educated woman. In the 1860 census, she listed her occupation as "Teacher at a Common School" (a public school), where she taught second grade. Over the next decade, teaching and tutoring would enable Sophie to live a more independent life than most single women her age.

WHEN THE Civil War began in April 1861, the citizens of Wisconsin rallied strongly to the Union cause. Recognizing the importance of women in the war effort, Wisconsin Governor Alexander Randall proclaimed: "It is your country and your government, as much as theirs, that is now in danger, and you can give strength and courage and war sympathies and cheering words to those who do battle for all that is dear to us."

Embracing this spirit, Wisconsin women "knitted mittens, scraped lint, wrote letters, made bandages, organized aid societies, and sometimes even encouraged

Sophie Smith, about 1860.

men to enlist," noted one historian. Just ten blocks south of Sophie's house, a thousand Union soldiers of the Fourth Wisconsin Regiment mustered at Camp Utley. Now Sophie and other women could directly aid the war effort by cooking meals or simply wearing a pretty dress.

One Camp Utley soldier wrote home, "We marched along Racine's most aristocratic streets, and every man did his best, for the walks were filled with the belles of that fair city." Another raved about a Thanksgiving feast prepared by Racine women: "We had cold turkey, roast chicken, apple, pumpkin, and mince pies, sponge cake, pound cake, and, above all, the ladies seemed to take a special delight in smiling upon us, while we were eating."

Did Sophie form an attachment to a Union soldier? Possibly. One hundred years later Sophie's daughter, Edith, would write about her mother, "This was Civil War time, and I vaguely remember whispers of a man who went to war. Whether he was killed or just never came back, I have no idea." The disappearance of a Civil War soldier was not unusual. "Nearly half the dead remained unknown," wrote historian Drew Gilpin Faust. For hundreds of thousands of Americans, "the unknown fate of missing kin 'left a dread void of uncertainty' that knowledge would never fill."

SOPHIE TURNED twenty-five in 1865 and dreamed of a more exciting life. "I was anxious, when I had finished my studies in Racine, to become self-supporting, and my parents yielded to my ambition." Put more bluntly, Edith stated that her mother was "quite bored with the role of spinsterhood" and wanted out of Racine, "the sooner the better and the further away the better still." In family lore, Sophie probably left home for the Pacific Coast in 1868.

"I came out by steamer via Panama and went to Portland," she later said. "I did not know a soul in that city nor on the steamer, but I found valuable lady friends." The Pacific Mail Steamship Company operated a fleet of paddlewheel steamers connecting New York to San Francisco, via the Isthmus of Panama, in just twenty-two days.

Perhaps Sophie boarded the *New York*, a paddle wheeler almost three hundred feet long, powered by a single-cylinder, coal-fired steam engine driving two wooden side wheels, each thirty-five feet in diameter, turning at ten revolutions per minute, delivering a speed of about 12 miles per hour. Three decks accommodated 870 passengers (200 in first class, 170 in second, and 500 in steerage). We might guess that her earnings from teaching enabled her to purchase a first-class ticket.

One traveler described her fellow passengers as "male and female adventurers, farmers, merchants, officers, laborers, mechanics, loafers, thieves, and pickpockets, and some of the latter did not wait until their arrival in California to ply their avocation." The great California historian Hubert Howe Bancroft remembered the ravages of seasickness on his steamer. "It prostrates pride, purges man of his conceit, makes him humble as a little child; it is especially conducive to repentance and after repentance, resignation. I know of nothing, after the first fear of death has passed away, that makes one so ready to die."

Arriving at Panama, passengers disembarked at Aspinwall (modern Colón) and boarded a special train for the forty-six-mile trip to Panama City on the Pacific Coast. If the tides were right, they could then re-embark on a California-bound steamer the same day. John Muir, who also crossed the Isthmus in 1868, wrote, "Never shall I forget the glorious flora, especially for the first fifteen or twenty miles along the Chagres River. The riotous exuberance of great forest trees, glowing in purple, red, and yellow flowers, far surpassed anything I had ever seen, especially of flowering trees…I gazed from the car platform enchanted."

IF SOPHIE ARRIVED in San Francisco at night, she might have shared the observation of an English traveler who wrote, "Seen as I saw it for the first time, the appearance of San Francisco is enchanting. Built on a hill slope, up which many streets run to the top, and illumined as these streets were with innumerable gas lamps, the effect was that of a huge dome ablaze with lamps arranged in lines and circles."

Once ashore, the scene was rather less enchanting. "The din and bustle soon recall the errant mind from aerial flights of fancy to the harsh realities of terrestrial life. A Babel of tongues rises from the crowded landing-stage as soon as the steamer has been moored. Hardly has the passenger set foot on shore than he becomes the prey of men intent upon earning a gratuity by doing or professing to render him a service."

Perhaps Sophie's "valuable lady friends" helped her navigate this mob, and maybe one of them hired Sophie to tutor her children. All we know for certain is that Sophie soon left for Portland, where she gave private lessons to a family for the next eighteen months.

IN 1868 Portland was a small town with a population of 2,700, about a quarter of the size of Sophie's native Racine. She was two thousand miles from home, about as far as she could get in the continental United States. Without family and friends close by, she could relish a personal sense of freedom and independence for the first time in her life.

Our only direct knowledge of Sophie's life in Portland is the draft of a letter that she wrote on August 2, 1869, to "My Dear Ones at Home." "I have a little leisure this evening, and I will try to give you a faint idea of my delightful trip to the 'The Dalles'" (a town on the Columbia River).

Sophie was escorted on her river excursion by a Major Dallas and other soldiers stationed at nearby Fort Vancouver on the Columbia River. Major Dallas called at Sophie's rooming house at 4:00 a.m., alerting her to get ready for the departure of their boat. Then a few minutes later, he returned to say that the boat would leave earlier than expected. After the first warning, she was "progressing on her toilet and had gotten on my button boots and corsets." After the second warning she had "to hurry, slipping on my shirts, dress, and hat, leaving my hair hanging & crowding the rest of my necessary articles into my jacket, we started on the run…We ran four blocks & I laughed."

It turned out that the party had fifteen minutes to spare before the *Cascade*, a 150-foot sternwheeler, left the dock at 5:00 a.m. for the sixty-five-mile trip to the Cascades, an unnavigable stretch of rapids on the Columbia River. After leaving Portland, the *Cascade* steamed down the Willamette River for twelve miles before heading east on the Columbia River. Sophie was well-attended by Major Dallas, "who kindly placed at my disposal a fine field glass [telescope], so I was able to enjoy everything that good eyesight with the aid of a good glass could find."

The *Cascade* stopped briefly at Fort Vancouver, which she called, "the favorite military post on this Pacific Coast…the Garrison is beautifully situated & very commodious." After passing miles of shoreline with "trees in countless numbers [rearing] their tall unbending forms upward," Sophie saw "a strange shaped mass, called Rooster Rock…which to me appeared more like some mammoth camel crouched with head & long neck raised up." Originally noted by Lewis and Clark in 1805, Rooster Rock was a large natural obelisk or monolith. (Today Rooster Rock is an Oregon State Park.)

Here Sophie's letter and our knowledge of her river cruise ends abruptly. If Sophie really did continue on to The Dalles, she would have debarked at the Cascades for a six-mile portage on the Cascade Railroad to connect with another paddle wheeler to take her the last fifty miles upriver to The Dalles. Perhaps more likely, she returned to Portland that afternoon on the *Cascade*. What an adventure for a single woman with new friends in a new land. She was one week shy of her twenty-ninth birthday.

FATE AND a wealthy banker eventually drew Sophie back to San Francisco. D. O. Mills, a legendary financier and founder of the Bank of California, hired Sophie to tutor his twelve-year-old daughter, Elisabeth, and her cousin, Jennie Easton. He owned "Millbrae," a palatial estate south of San Francisco (today the city of Millbrae). The name came from a combination of his last name and the Scottish word for rolling hills (*brae*).

Set on 1,500 acres and surrounded by gardens and lakes, the forty-two-room mansion featured an art gallery with works of well-known artists, including Albert Bierstadt, the famed painter of Western landscapes. The second story contained the family's bedrooms and day rooms, where Sophie might have instructed her charges. Like other Gilded Age mansions, the third floor was devoted to servants' quarters.

Sophie probably tutored the young girls in English, French, and music. Eighteen years older than Elisabeth, Sophie and her pupil developed a lifelong bond. Decades in the future, Elisabeth would recommend a finishing school for Sophie's own daughter in New York City.

WHEN SOPHIE met Asa remains a mystery. All we know for certain is that the census taker recorded both living in Mrs. Kelsey's boarding house in August 1870. Asa had turned forty-four that February, and she would turn thirty that October.

They would not marry until 1875. Why did their courtship last five years? Was she still heartbroken over the loss of a Civil War beau? Or was their courtship simply the natural growth of their mutual affection?

We do know that Sophie valued her freedom. In her talk to Racine alumnae years earlier, titled "Painting & Sculpting," she had urged her audience to treat life as a work of art: "You yourselves are in truth the real painters. Will & thought your brush, the soul your canvas of life, its everyday deeds your colors."

In 1873 she found a new job teaching English and music at Académie Parisienne, "in order to perfect myself in the … language." The Académie Parisienne was an all-girls school located on Sutter Street near Leavenworth in San Francisco. "The method of instruction will be essentially the European," boasted the school catalog. "The government will be mild and impartial, but firm; prompt obedience and lady-like deportment will be required of all. Special attention will be given to the physical development and the moral and social culture of the pupils." Sophie was helping refine the next generation of San Francisco's roughhewn upper crust.

ASA FINALLY proposed and Sophie accepted in 1874. Upon hearing the news, her parents, Eldad and Harriet Smith, insisted that she give up her work and return home before her wedding in 1875. "When I started west from Racine, my father gave me two $100 U.S. Bonds that, in case I got stranded, I could be sure of transportation back home. I did not spend them. My work was not always agreeable, but I was cheerful and got on well and had a small bank account when I became engaged … I was proud that I could put these two bonds back into his hands."

How thrilled Sophie must have been to introduce Asa to her family when he arrived in Racine. They were married on June 24, 1875, at St. Luke's Episcopal Church. "The church was crowded with the *elite* of the city," wrote the *Racine Weekly Journal*, "mainly ladies, who brought out fashion in beautiful array. The altar was crowned with bouquets, showered from the many friends of the bride in this city. The bride was attired in white silk, trimmed with tulle and orange-blossoms, and a white lace veil reaching to the bottom of the dress, looped with orange-blossoms, and diamond ornaments."

Asa's wedding present to Sophie was "a pair of elegant diamond ear-rings." For their honeymoon, the couple headed off for "an extended tour to eastern cities." Perhaps they even visited Asa's home in Brunswick, Maine. Then it was back to Racine for another reception at her parents' house and off to California. Sadly,

Sophie Smith Simpson in 1875, about the time of her wedding.

this would be the last time that Sophie would see her father, who would die six months later on Christmas Day 1875, at age seventy.

ARRIVING HOME in San Francisco, it was time for the couple to move out of Mrs. Kelsey's boarding house. Where to go? Possibly the last place on earth that Asa would have chosen to raise a family was the city of San Francisco with its ubiquitous saloons, gambling halls, opium dens, and worse. He did not smoke, gamble, or drink, yet debauchery was never far. The notorious Barbary Coast on Pacific Avenue was only blocks from Asa's office at 44 Market Street.

In 1873 a reporter for the *Daily Alta California* walked through the heart of the Barbary Coast. "The whole street, for half a dozen blocks, is literally swarming with the scum of creation. Every land under the sun has contributed toward making up the crowd of loafers, thieves, low gamblers, jay-hawkers [robbers], dirty, filthy, degraded, hopeless, bummers…From the 'deadfalls,' as the low beer and dance cellars are designated…come echoes of drunken laughter, curses, ribaldry, and music from every conceivable instrument."

The leafy suburb of Oakland and its environs across the bay beckoned. Benjamin Lloyd, the contemporary chronicler, raved about the area. "As places for family residence, Oakland and Alameda are unsurpassed in California; and there are few more lovely abiding places on the face of the continent. Indeed, it would seem that anyone ought to be happy and perfectly content, if he is the fortunate possessor of a pleasantly situated home in Oakland or Alameda, with a sufficient income to maintain it properly."

SOPHIE'S DAUGHTER, Edith, remembered the family's Oakland house on half of a city block on Grove Street (modern Martin Luther King Jr. Way). "A large square…Sixteenth and Grove St. was divided into two plots. One half was the Kellogg house, the other the Simpson house. The Kellogg place had an artesian well in the back. We had stables and horses and a large, wooded drying yard and place for laundry which was always done at home…You entered the big curving gate and drove around a rose garden. Large lawns and trees in front and the back…"

When Asa and Sophie moved to Oakland, their home was three blocks from the edge of the built-up city (today's San Pablo Avenue). For a lifelong bachelor, Asa showed a surprising domestic touch. When Sophie showed an acquaintance around her new Oakland home, her friend observed "the furniture, carpets, etc.," and asked, "Who looked after this?" After Sophie answered that "her husband attended to many things," her surprised friend said, "I thought Asa Simpson was all sawmills and lumber. This is a revelation. He evidently knows other things as well."

SOPHIE'S FIRST two children, Louis Jerome and Edgar Meade, arrived in 1877 and 1879. Two surviving letters from Asa to his (again) pregnant wife—warm, playful, and businesslike—provide a poignant look at their newly married lives. Both were written on Sundays a week apart, October 31 and November 7, 1880, from the tiny town of Gardiner on the Umpqua River in Oregon.

Asa underlined his important words: "My Dear Wife—Again I have the pleasure of writing to you from this burg and of course it's raining...I am in the Counting room off the store alone & have just cooked and ate my lunch and a good one it was too. Can you guess...three baked soda crackers & one immense big pear makes me a sumptuous lunch." Asa and his crew of fifteen were building a new lumber mill, which was "up and shingled so that we have lots of work now under cover and will make speedy work of finishing the mill."

A week later, Asa wrote, "My Dear Wife—Sunday and raining of course as it is wont to do in these parts in wintertime. I sent my Coos Bay gang home this A.M. and have the new mill pretty well along—smokestack up, etc....Your last letter 21st ultimo [last month] was duly rec'd and very welcome. I am glad to know that you are well and enjoying yourselves so much." Ever the workaholic, Asa regretted that he could not get home sooner. "After I begin a job, I hate to quit until it's satisfactorily done. Therefore I have given this one more time than I expected and would like to give it one month more if I could..."

His second letter ended on a tender note that would resonate with any parent. Many of the children in Gardiner had whooping cough, and the streets resounded with the barking sound of coughing. Asa admired the seven-month-old boy of his mill manager, Mr. Emerson, "quite a sufferer, poor little fellow nearly chokes to death, but bears it with great patience and does not cry, in fact he is quite a wonder in that respect..."

Five months later, Sophie delivered her third child and only girl, Edith, my grandmother, on March 27, 1881, and two years after that her last child, Harry, in 1883. Asa may have been away frequently on business, but Sophie was well attended. She later recalled that her husband was happy to provide employment to laboring people. "He enjoys having more servants about the house and grounds than we actually require. He says, if we can find something for them to do, this is about as wholesome a form of charity as any other."

THE SIMPSON HOUSEHOLD was attended to by at least six servants, three young Irish women who appear in the 1880 census and three others whose names do not appear—a Japanese butler, a gardener, and a coachman. "Dan was in charge of the carriages and stables," according to Edith, "and did all of the driving. He took father every morning to the [train] station [for the ferry] to the 'The City.' He took Harry and me to Miss Dyer's Kindergarten on Alice Street and later took me to Miss Horton's School...Dan used to drive mother to market in her little Victoria where the man used to come out to the carriage to take her order."

While Asa liked to employ servants, he did not enjoy their personal attention "I never allow them to black my shoes. I do it myself. Once in a while they steal them away, but I would much rather do it myself. I pay these men the biggest kind of wages, and they are faithful and perfectly willing to do anything. But I don't want anybody to wait on me at all; I would rather take care of myself. When I go home, I take my own coat off and brush it myself, and, if one of the girls in the house volunteers to do it, I say, 'No, it is only a minute of work and I prefer to do it myself.'"

Asa Simpson with three of his children in Oakland, 1889.
Edgar, ten, on horseback; Edith, eight, and Harry, six, in the carriage.

The same applied to his personal grooming. "I think I have been once inside a barber's shop in the last two years, and only three times in ten years, and then because I hadn't my valise with me. I can shave myself in two minutes. I cannot bear to be talked to death, and fumbled over, and fingered for a quarter of an hour." Nor did Asa seem overly attentive to meals prepared by his servants. According to Sophie, "If he is late and the dinner is cold, you would not know, but he enjoys it just as well; and to the extent that eating has to do with the mind, I believe he does."

EDITH WARMLY REMEMBERED family vacations as a young girl. "In summers we all went to Skaggs' Springs. This was a great day. Sarah [Hannon, the governess] and us four children took the train to Cloverdale where we got off and changed to a stage with four horses and drove up the little mountain road to the Springs. I can't remember how long it was, but it seemed hours. Skaggs' Springs was on a little river which gave us much fun. The stage splashed over a wide crossing to the hotel." (Located nine miles west of Geyserville, Skaggs' Springs today would be covered by Lake Sonoma.)

Hardworking Asa joined the family on weekends, traveling by train and stage. If the stagecoach was full, Asa walked. "I don't rush for the stagecoach like some people, but take the last seat...When I see them rush as though they hadn't a minute to live, it disgusts me... Skaggs' Springs is a favorite place of mine and I often go there. I have walked from there to the station twice. The coach would be filled and crowded

Edith Simpson, about 1891.

and I would say, 'Alright go ahead, I would sooner walk'...The people of Maine and the Scotch people from whom I am descended are all strong robust men and great walkers."

STRONG AS HE WAS, Asa's constitution was not unbreakable. "When I feel that I have overdone the thing, I call a halt right there and just walk right out and buy a ticket and get away. These trips are my safety valve." He reached such a point in early 1888. George Sanderson, his friend and the mayor of San Francisco, agreed: "[Asa] attended strictly to business, too much so. In fact, [he] broke himself down and had to take a trip to Europe to get entirely away from his business and find the rest he needed." Both Asa and Sophie would spend that summer abroad.

We do not know their itinerary. Most Americans on the Grand Tour were intent on covering as much ground in as short a time as possible. These travelers were well served by W. Pembroke Fetridge, an author of popular guidebooks. For a tourist with "limited time" (three months), Fetridge suggested an itinerary that allowed for "twenty days for crossings, one month for a survey of the British Isles, ten days to 'do' Paris, and 30 days for a sweep of 27 continental cities." This, said Fetridge, was "sufficient time."

How much ground did Asa and Sophie cover? On July 11, 1888, the Simpsons applied for an Emergency Passport in Rome. We do not know why. In the application, Asa stated that they had left the U.S. on May 26, six weeks earlier. Maybe Rome was the midpoint of a three-month Grand Tour. We can guess that they might already have "done" London and Paris.

THE SIMPSONS ARRIVED back in Oakland in the late summer of 1888, perhaps about the same time that Sarah and the four children returned from Skaggs' Springs. We can imagine that home life returned to normal, as Edith and her brothers started school again in the fall. But the Simpsons' neighborhood was changing. Between 1880 and 1890, the population of Oakland had increased by 40 percent from about 35,000 to 49,000. No longer was their Grove Street location quite so bucolic. According to Edith, "Father decided this was too close to 'in town' and expanding Oakland. So he bought a place on Vernon Heights [at the corner of Vernon and Perkins streets] on the other side of town."

Vernon Heights was a tract of estates in the hills north of Lake Merritt. Ever mindful of the dollar, Asa acted as his own contractor. At least, this is what his daughter remembered. "Having built so many ships, Father did not see any reason why he should not build a house, so he proceeded to do so." It would be fascinating to know what materials he used to finish the interior. Asa was not known for his extravagance. "Whatever he does in the way of expenditure for his family and himself," Sophie recalled, "is done with reference to what is useful, necessary and comfortable. He is liberal to this end, but he would not invest a dollar in display of any kind for effect nor in anything that is useless."

THE FAMILY probably moved into their new home in 1893, but they only remained there two years. Edith thought that the daily commute had become too tiring for her sixty-nine-year-old father. "The great decision was made to leave Oakland and settle in San Francisco." On November 25, 1895, the *Oakland Tribune* noted that "Mrs. A. M. Simpson, formerly of Vernon Heights, has issued cards for an afternoon reception at her home on Pacific Avenue, San Francisco."

Twenty-seven years after landing in San Francisco as a single woman with a superior education and a determination to forge her own course, Sophie returned as a wealthy, married woman widely recognized by society. She was fifty-five years old; her husband was sixty-nine. They had arrived. But he would not rest.

CHAPTER 6

Building an Empire

Asa and Sophie, 1874–1900

"THE SPIRIT of his energy was the love of progress and improvement. Idleness, which is synonymous with retrogression, he could not have endured, yet he was not a slave to business. He was endowed with a faculty that many ambitious men fail to utilize, or else do not possess; that is, common sense... His career and personality... should teach young men who have their own way to make, the value of industry and perseverance, temperance and economy, courage and integrity."

This was the portrait of Asa Simpson painted by Hubert Howe Bancroft in his *Chronicles of the Builders of the Commonwealth*, a seven-volume "Historical Character Study" of one hundred prominent Californians. "[Asa] stood in the lead in shipping and lumbering, and for several years probably employed more men than any other one person in California... In the midst of reverses such as would have overwhelmed many another, he presented an admirable spectacle of self-control, acquiescing in the inevitable without bitterness or lamentation. Laboring on with philosophical composure, he rebuilt ruin after ruin."

If these words smack of hagiography, that was the whole point. Bancroft's *Chronicles* were sold by subscription to the *Builders* themselves. This was not an unusual arrangement at the time. "From the pattern standardized and especially popular in the field of local history," wrote Bancroft's biographer, "the *Chronicles* deviated only in requiring fees considerably above the average in amount." Asa paid $1,500 for his subscription and was the subject of a twenty-one-page chapter ($41,700 in 2017 dollars).

Bancroft employed a team of researchers, writers, and editors to produce his works. We are fortunate today to have their field notes in the Bancroft Library at the University of California in Berkeley. Asa's collection includes typed manuscripts of two interviews with him in 1890 and 1891, along with interviews of his wife and three of his friends as character references. These interviews fill eighty-one legal-size pages. While Asa may have paid for the privilege, we can treasure the results—his unfiltered words about his life and times.

Although Bancroft's *Chronicles* extolled Asa's composure when facing his losses, the transcribed interviews captured him railing against shipmasters who had abused his trust and taken unnecessary chances. "Risk, risk, risk, gambling, it comes natural to some men. They will go right to the stock-board and gamble their last dollar away, when they know, if they lose, they cannot buy themselves a meal.

Steel-cut engraving of Asa Meade Simpson, in 1892,
from Hubert Howe Bancroft's *Chronicles of the
Builders of the Commonwealth.*

"Shipmasters are no more exempt than anyone else, and it is a most difficult thing to confine him and make him realize the responsibility...I have lost by shipwreck 34 different vessels that I either owned or had a large interest in. The total value of these losses is over $500,000" [$13.9 million in 2017 dollars].

NO LOSS stung like the wreck of the *Western Shore*, the only clipper ship ever built on the Pacific Coast. Launched at Coos Bay in 1874, the *Western Shore* was 183 feet long—208 feet, if you included the bowsprit. It set eighteen square sails from its three masts with the mainmast soaring a hundred feet above the deck.

Lewis & Dryden's Marine History of the Pacific Northwest would record, "No sailing vessel set afloat on the Coast made such a remarkable record for speed." In 1875 the *Western Shore* beat the side-wheel steamer *Oriflamme* on a run from San Francisco to Astoria, Oregon, a distance of 562 miles, in just over two days. The *Western Shore* set sailing records to Europe that stand to this day—in 1876 from Portland to Liverpool in 101 days and in 1877 from San Francisco to Liverpool in 103 days.

The end of the *Western Shore's* short life came near midnight on July 9, 1878, when the ship struck Duxbury Reef off Bolinas, just north of the Golden Gate. The *San Francisco Chronicle* reported, "The disaster is difficult to account for, as at the time the ship struck, both the Farallon and Point Reyes lights were plainly visible; and although there was a stiff breeze blowing, the weather was not unfavorable. At the time of the disaster, the ship with all sails spread was speeding before a good strong wind at the rate of twelve knots."

The unspoken truth was that the ship's captain was drunk. Twelve years later, Asa still raged, "That fellow should have been sent to prison for ten years...His instructions were not to make landfall at night under any circumstances. To these he paid no respect. Not alone the loss of the money. She was a pride. It was a perfect knock down to me when I learned that man had lost her...He was drunk, and, when a man gets two glasses of whiskey into him—some men...think they could...sail right over Niagara Falls...We did not know he was a drinking man, but found it out later."

No wonder that Asa boasted of his resilience in the face of misfortune. "It is indomitable perseverance that will surmount all difficulties. If you are knocked down, get up. Don't be discouraged...That is literally and exactly what I have done. I would never yield to temptation, always had self-control and a determination to do the right what ere betide. Self-confident with an abundance of hope, even temper, never rattled by reverses, nor elevated by success."

"YEAR BY YEAR, Simpson expanded his operations," wrote historian Thomas R. Cox, "until by the early 1880's, taken together, they represented the largest lumbering enterprise along the entire 900 miles of forested coastline that stretched southward from Puget Sound and the Strait of Juan de Fuca [to San Francisco]...It was an old-fashioned business empire consisting of a maze of proprietorships and partnerships...Simpson owned seven sawmills...These mills supplied Simpson's yards with all the major varieties of lumber marketed on the West Coast: Douglas fir and spruce from the northern mills, Port Orford cedar from Coos Bay, redwood from Crescent City, and pine from Boca [a town in the Sierras]...

"More than a quest for increased sales lay behind the growth of the house of Simpson. Equally important was the captain's desire to free his enterprises of dependence on others...He acquired sawmills to supply his lumberyards; he acquired a fleet of vessels to link the two. Knowing replacements and additions would have to be made to his fleet, he established shipyards to furnish them... Realizing that steam tugs were necessary if entry into the harbors of the coast were to be made safe...Simpson acquired tugs and put them to work...In the terminology of a later generation, Simpson was integrating his holdings both vertically and horizontally."

By reputation, Asa was a hard taskmaster, a micromanager with a legendary temper. "Even his sons had to be wary when the director of the Simpson companies came to town," wrote historian Stephen Beckham. "L. J. [Louis] Simpson's secretary at North Bend at the turn of the century, Mrs. Frances McLeod, more than once had to flee the office when word came from the lower bay that Captain Simpson had been sighted on an incoming vessel. Louis would say to Mrs. McLeod, 'Get out quickly!' And in a frenzy to clear the decks and leave everything in the office quiet and orderly, the secretary dumped her papers, account books, and letters into drawers and scurried away for a holiday until the old captain left town."

ONE WRITER described a famous dispute between Asa and K. V. Kruse, his shipbuilder, about where to locate the head [toilet] on a new schooner. "A. M. Simpson, a very dignified man who was always formally attired, came aboard in his usual dress and told Kruse that they would put the crew's head under the forecastle deck instead of in the forward deckhouse... Squatting down, [Asa] backed into the space, but was unable to lower his trousers. He crept into the open and stood erect to half-mast [lower] his nether garment [underwear] and again backed under the forecastle.

"This time his head hit a deck beam with a resounding crash... Early the next morning he went aboard the new vessel with an axe and notched the offending beam himself." At the time, Asa was seventy-five-years old, still wielding an axe just as he had as an apprentice in Bath sixty years earlier. Asa's formal dress led to his nickname, "Stovepipe" Simpson, because of his habit of wearing the fashionable top hat of the era, even when visiting his logging camps.

REMARKABLY, Asa understood that managing his empire as a one-man band was near impossible. "I have been drawn into my large business gradually; sometimes accidentally and sometimes necessity has compelled me to take hold, when I would much rather not," he told Bancroft's researcher in 1891.

"I have a great deal more to attend to than I can comfortably handle. One of my mills is quite enough for any one man to manage, and yet I now have some six mills and their attendant shipping which require special care. I have to engineer, plan, see to the construction and repairs, and provide a market for the output. If I had not had so much to do, I could have taken more comfort in life. I got into this business accidentally and now I have to stay with it."

ONE CLOSE OBSERVER of Asa was a bookkeeper named Peter B. Kyne, at his mill in Hoquiam, Washington. Kyne later penned a series of popular novels featuring a protagonist called Cappy Ricks, a character inspired by Asa. "[Kyne] saw Captain Simpson as a crusty but lovable shipping tycoon engaged in battles of wits not only with rival shipping interests," wrote one historian, "but with henchmen within his own firm, among them his own shipmasters... Kyne not only patterned the famed Cappy after his boss, but also drew many of the incidents and true-to-life facts of his novels from affairs around [Hoquiam]."

His first novel, *Cappy Ricks, or The Subjugation of Matt Peasley*, began, "A psychologist would have termed Alden P. Ricks an individualist, but his associates in the wholesale shipping and lumber trade of the Pacific Coast proclaimed him a character... Since he was what he was—a dapper, precise, shrewd, lovable little old man with mild, paternal blue eyes, a keen sense of humor and a Henry Clay [upturned] collar, which latter, together with a silk top hat, had distinguished him on the 'Change [Merchants Exchange] for forty years—it was inevitable that along the Embarcadero and up California Street he should bear the distinguishing appellation of Cappy."

Kyne also met a fellow Simpson employee at Hoquiam named Ralph E. Peasley, a ship captain, who would later become the fictional Matt Peasley. The real Peasley "was a rangy Yankee whacked from the very sailing heart of Maine," wrote a local newspaper editor, "his ready smile, a walrus mustache bracketing his lips, the tail of a black coat whipping about a generous length of shin." Both the fictional Peasley and the fictional Cappy were equally strong-willed, and their volcanic clashes—over money, cargo, and Cappy's daughter—animated the novel. Spoiler alert: Peasley marries Cappy's daughter, Flora.

CAPTAIN RUDOLPH SMALE was a real captain who wrote about his fifteen years sailing for Asa in his autobiography, *There Go the Ships*. Smale called on ports up and down the Pacific Coast between Alaska and Mexico and made long passages across the Pacific to Vladivostok (Russia), Hakodate (Japan), and Haiphong (Indochina).

When ordered to sail the *Gleaner*, a three-masted barkentine, to Sydney, Australia, with a cargo of lumber, Smale determined to make a special request. "I succeeded, to the surprise of not a few, in prevailing upon my reluctant chief owner, hardboiled Captain A. M. Simpson, to give his consent for me to carry my wife with me on this voyage. The letting down of the bars created quite an astonishment."

Homeward bound, the *Gleaner* was struck by a South Pacific hurricane east of Tonga, which he described in terrifying detail: "The vessel, now lying on her beam-ends with the lee side of the top deckload even with the water, was out of control and unmanageable. It was a physical impossibility to face the fury of the wind standing up, so the men were lying flat on the deckload, holding on to the deck lashings for dear life as the seas broke over them…We were facing a condition absolutely beyond human possibility to combat. The limits of our resources had been reached and exhausted, so whatever was ahead of us—well, we simply had to take it and take it like men…

"The *Gleaner*'s sails gone, her rudder useless, she was now but a fragment of flotsam, subject to the mad, chaotic sweep of the elements. Standing near the man at the wheel, who was lashed to it so he could not be washed overboard, I more than once was almost carried over the lee rail by the heavy seas breaking over her... And as one green wall of water after another swept over us, the question in my mind now uppermost, was not, will she hold out, but for how long?

"The gigantic roar overhead and the shrieking of the gale through the rigging made it impossible to converse with each other, and really there was no need to do so..." Periodically, Smale would return to his cabin to check the barometer. "Again I stood with eyes blurred and inflamed from the driving salt spray, staring into the face of that little instrument fastened to the wall in my cabin below, and—could I, did I dare believe my eyes? I looked and looked again. Yes, it had actually risen a hairsbreadth above the last reading an hour ago... I turned to my wife, and said, 'Girl, the worst is over, the battle won!'"

Before widespread use of radiotelegraphy, Smale and the *Gleaner* were totally cut off from society. "Sailing ships in their days took us completely out of the world. It became a dead issue as soon as we saw the old familiar coastline disappearing beneath the horizon." Asa's San Francisco headquarters knew nothing of his voyage until he arrived at a port where he could send a telegram home after months at sea. Reflecting back decades later, Smale recalled, "A shipmaster was master of the ship in the full sense of the word, and not, as he is today, a mere coach driver, subject only too often to contrary orders from inexperienced, so-called efficiency experts warming swivel chairs in some uptown office."

ONE SWIVEL-CHAIR jockey who greatly irritated Asa Simpson was George Emerson, the manager of his mill at Hoquiam. Their dispute was about whether to buy new equipment for the mill and where to sell the lumber. In short, Emerson wanted to invest for the future, and Asa wanted to spend as little money as possible. The result was a succession of heated letters bouncing between Washington and San Francisco for years.

Emerson argued that his mill's lumber should only be cut to order, so as to reduce inventories and the need for large storage yards. In 1895 he warned Asa, "The day of sawing lumber other than to order has in the main gone by... old mills and old methods are out of the competition." In 1897 Emerson told Asa that shipping lumber from his mill to an oversupplied San Francisco market was like, "throwing a large portion of their cut into the San Francisco lumber cesspool."

Two years later, he echoed the same theme. "I consider that San Francisco stands in the same position to the lumber business that a Fire-pit stands to the old-time mill. The question is into which of the two furnaces you will throw your refuse." We do not have Asa's side of the exchange, but it is safe to conclude that he fired back with gusto, just as the fictional Cappy Ricks did.

Emerson's final salvo sent May 2, 1899, began, "Dear Sir: The subject of my salary is one upon which I am hardly able to write to you civilly. To my suggestion of necessities last fall I received an insolent reply... During the eighteen years I have been at Hoquiam I have never received compensation for services from any source except the North Western Lumber Company [owned by Asa], because I could not promise attention to any other business.

"During that entire time, your agreement with me, under which I came here, has been broken and the subject has been a sore one and one I have been ashamed of before the world. Had you treated me fairly, I should not owe you a cent today and should stand before the world a man among men, instead of a failure." After rehashing a litany of injustices over the years, Emerson concluded his letter with a flat declaration that he would increase his salary to $300 per month ($9,150 in 2017 dollars) effective immediately and would expect another increase next year from the company's directors. We do not know Asa's reaction. We do know that Emerson was not fired and that he did not quit.

No doubt reflecting local gossip, Coos Bay's *Harbor* newspaper noted Asa's fabled irascibility: "Captain Simpson's well known conservatism is proverbial. In plain truth he is known as a bear on almost everything. He does not enthuse; he never dreams...Temperance in all things has been his motto...He says he has lived all his life on half rations. People, he thinks, eat too much, especially meats."

SOPHIE DID NOT think her husband was a bear, although she was aware of his public reputation. "Mr. Simpson is a man who is not generally understood," she told one of Bancroft's researchers. "He is retiring, makes no show of himself or his affairs, so that he cannot be fairly judged by those who take only a superficial view of him... He is self-contained, self-controlled to a remarkable degree and is very even tempered.

"He does not love money for money's sake and he uses it freely in doing good. If successful he is not exhilarated, nor is he depressed unduly if unsuccessful... I do not think it ever occurred to him to make a fortune because he would enjoy the reputation of being a rich and prominent man or because he takes much pleasure in the power and influence derived from riches.

"He has a fine appreciation of what is beautiful and good. His nature is essentially tender. When we are travelling on the railroad and the cars stop, it is his delight to go out and find a twig in the rocks or a spray of wild flowers and bring them in for me to admire and enjoy."

Asa agreed that people did not really understand him. "I am going to say something that I have said many times before," he told Bancroft's researcher, "and I am perfectly willing to swear to it. It may perhaps be a little surprise to some people who don't know it: I never have been ambitious to get rich. I have done business and been impelled on but never because I was ambitious to get rich...I do business because I like to do business...I cannot be idle, and I am always anxious to find employment for all the men I can, and to do my best by the world."

SOPHIE SHARED Asa's imperative to do good. "We are, to some extent, trustees of our fortune and we should prize riches mainly for the use we can put them to in relieving and making less fortunate people comfortable and happy. I admire my husband, perhaps, you may say too much. But if you knew him familiarly you would observe how unselfish he is and how considerate."

Although her own children had attended Miss Dyer's, a private kindergarten, Sophie supported the new Free Kindergarten, serving Oakland's less fortunate population. The *Oakland Tribune* of December 1, 1888, noted that "The ladies of the Free Kindergarten completed arrangements for their fancy dress ball, and it will be given at Cavalry Hall on the 13th day of the present month. While fancy dress will be in order, it is not imperative, and it is hoped that many will attend, both from their interest in such a worthy cause and the more selfish motive of enjoying the pleasant occasion." On a list of eleven ladies with tickets, the name of "Mrs. A. M. Simpson" appeared first.

What motivated Sophie to help those less privileged? Could it have been the capture of a runaway slave in Racine? Could it have been her work as a low-paid tutor in the rich household of D. O. Mills? Or her lifelong interest in education?

DID SOPHIE'S social conscience extend to women's suffrage? When the family moved to San Francisco in 1895, she lived only a block away from her sister-in-law, Mary Simpson Sperry, an ardent suffragette. Mary was the widow of Austin Sperry and heir to the Sperry Flour fortune. After her husband's death, she had successfully managed the flour milling company, and Asa considered his sister "a fine businesswoman."

Mary was the prime organizer of the Susan B. Anthony Club in California and hosted its first meeting at her house in 1896. Did Sophie attend? Did Asa agree with his sister's political views? The answers are buried in the sands of time.

When Mary Sperry later met Phoebe Hearst, the first woman regent of the University of California and the mother of William Randolph Hearst, she wrote a warm note. "My dear Mrs. Hearst: I wish to acknowledge the pleasure it gave me at our recent Club meeting, when you told me that you favored 'Votes for Women.' Perhaps you do not realize how much it means to me, who has worked for it so long, to know that women like you are on our side…We need financial aid in this campaign, but far more than that, we need the public utterance of women beloved and respected by all for great goodness and helpfulness—Your influence, dear Mrs. Hearst, will be of untold assistance."

In 1911 California voters narrowly approved Proposition 4, amending the State Constitution to enfranchise women, and Mary cast her first vote on March 28, 1912. The *San Francisco Call* captured the moment in a picture labeled: "Prominent society woman casting her vote…Mrs. Mary Simpson Sperry."

AT THE DAWN of the twentieth century in 1900, Asa would be seventy-four, and Sophie sixty. He would live another fifteen years, she only nine. But nothing would change. He would remain in command until the day he died, and she would be his loyal wife into their twilight years.

We now turn our attention to my four maternal great-grandparents, born a continent apart and a world away from San Francisco. We start our journey in Missouri before jumping across the Atlantic Ocean to France and Scotland.

CHAPTER 7

St. Louis Roots

Frederick and Frances, 1853–1870

ONE MONTH after the bombardment of Fort Sumter, the Civil War arrived in St. Louis on May 10, 1861. Marching west up Clark Avenue, a column of Union soldiers crossed South Fourteenth Street, less than a block from the home of Frederick Cline, my great-grandfather. We can imagine that seven-and-a-half-year-old Frederick was thrilled by the sight of a thousand armed men passing by, prepared for battle.

Missouri was a slave state, but the city of St. Louis was staunchly pro-Union. Thousands of German immigrants, solidly Republican and rabidly anti-slavery, had enlisted in the Union army. A fifteen-year-old student witnessed another column of Union troops nearby. "They were Germans and had no uniforms, were not very orderly, were very much excited and frightened... held their arms 'at the ready'... There was no music and everything was oppressively silent, nothing being heard but the shuffling of feet, or now and then an officer's command, or a taunt from the dogging crowd."

Missouri's governor, Claiborne Fox Jackson, and the state legislature strongly supported the Confederacy. Hoping to capture the trove of weapons in the United States Arsenal, Jackson had sent the Missouri National Guard to St. Louis. This state militia, largely drawn from Southern planter families, was now encamped on the western edge of the city in tree-shaded Lindell Grove. Camp Jackson had a relaxed atmosphere with young ladies visiting their beaux and mothers bringing hampers of food to their sons. "Could anything equal this gathering for harmony of color," wrote one observer, "the beauty of youth, aristocratic breeding, clannish pride, courage, audacity, and contempt of the northern Abolitionist?"

Eight thousand Union troops in seven columns, under the command of Captain Nathaniel Lyon, converged on Camp Jackson that afternoon. Surprised, surrounded, and outnumbered eight to one, the Missouri National Guard peacefully surrendered to the Union soldiers. But as the prisoners were marched away, someone opened fire—no one ever knew who fired the first shot—and nearly three dozen spectators, militiamen, and soldiers fell dead or mortally wounded.

What became known as the Camp Jackson Affair marked the first blood spilled in Missouri, a border state sandwiched between the Union North and the Confederate South. In the words of Civil War historian Bruce Catton, "The fighting in St. Louis was clear warning that the middle of the road was no path for Missourians. No longer would carefree militiamen lounge picturesquely in a picnic-ground camp...Now they would fight, and other men would fight against them, and no part of the United States would know greater bitterness or misery."

FREDERICK'S FAMILY was of German descent, but they were not recent immigrants to America. Both his great-grandfather and his grandfather were born in Pennsylvania. After descending the Ohio River on a flatboat, the family settled near Cincinnati in Warren County, Ohio, where Frederick's father, George Washington Cline, was born. George trained as a lawyer in Ohio before moving to St. Louis in the late 1840s.

Ethnic tensions between Germans and Southern planters in St. Louis had brewed for years. Immigrants from Europe found economic and political freedoms in their new country for the first time in their lives. Many of them saw in Missouri's slaveholding class "exactly what they had come to escape: a swaggering clique of landed oligarchs [and] boorish aristocrats obstructing the forces of modernity and progress," wrote one historian. Conversely, Southern planters and slaveholders considered the Germans a godless people. "One need only walk downtown on a Sunday afternoon to see them drinking beer, dancing, and flocking to immoral plays—flagrantly violating not just the commandments of God but city ordinances of St. Louis."

WE CAN BE fairly certain that George Cline would have violated the Sabbath. His name was mentioned in the diary of whiskey merchant, Joseph Mersman, who wrote on Thursday, August 16, 1849: "Monday, Tuesday, and this evening until 10 o'clock passed in Thompson's and Cline's office. They are both young Buckeye Lawyers. Very agreeable companions." George and his partner, Alexander Thompson, practiced law at 92 Chestnut Street, near the Old St. Louis Courthouse.

Mersman was a whiskey rectifier. In the nineteenth century, farmers frequently made alcohol from surplus corn. After retaining a few barrels, they sold the balance to rectifiers who "distilled it a second time, occasionally added other ingredients, converted it to a palatable beverage, and marketed it to the public." We can imagine that Mersman provided the evening's refreshments and that twenty-six-year-old George Cline was not averse to imbibing.

THREE YEARS later in 1852, George married Livonia Dodds, also from Warren County, Ohio, and so perhaps a family friend. Their first child, Frederick Addison Cline was born November 16, 1853. When the family moved to Clark Avenue and South Fourteenth Street in the late 1850s, they lived near the western edge of the city, surrounded by a patchwork quilt of open fields, factories, and rows of houses. The steeples of churches were the highest points on the landscape.

In the 1850s, St. Louis was "a city in motion," wrote historian James Neal Primm. "Always a trader's city, it would remain so; but industry was stirring too… its sewage was still running in open gutters; its water supply was untreated and its delivery uncertain… its fire and police protection was largely voluntary and unprofessional… To counter these liabilities, the city was bursting with vitality; it was a promised land for a diligent, determined, intelligent, and self-disciplined people… To its residents, to the thousands who came every year, and to most visitors, it was an exciting place of unlimited opportunity."

BETWEEN 1860 AND 1870, the population of the city doubled from 160,000 to 310,000, making it the fourth largest city in the nation. St. Louis was the dominant commercial center of the western states during the heyday of river steamboats. An average of 2,675 steamboats landed at the city every year between 1866 and 1870.

We can imagine teenaged Frederick occasionally walking the fifteen blocks from his home to the Mississippi River waterfront. A contemporary reporter painted a vivid scene of the bustling river port with its "mile of steamboats [and] hundreds of drays, wagons, and carriages rushing along at all speed. Thousands of men jostling each other." Another observer claimed that "he could walk the length of the wharf over piles of produce."

For passengers who could afford cabins on the upper deck, "steamboats brought together western farmers, southern planters, merchants, politicians, artists, theatrical companies, titled Europeans, writers, speculators, preachers, slave traders, gamblers—the rich and not so rich (not the poor, they were on the main deck) in a grand social mix," wrote Primm. "Professional gamblers were good customers, lavish tippers, and free spenders at the bar; and captains seldom expelled any except flagrant cheaters. When they were thrown off the boat, usually at the demand of the shorn lambs, they were left on the first convenient sand bar."

ALTHOUGH SLAVERY was legal in Missouri, free blacks in St. Louis outnumbered slaves in 1860—1,755 to 1,542—due partly to manumission (the act of freeing a slave). In 1856 Frederick's father witnessed a Deed of Manumission that freed a "Negro Philip aged about forty-three years, Jemima aged about forty years [and five children, ages nineteen, fourteen, nine, five, and three]." However, "Even free blacks were only half-free," wrote Primm. "They could not live in the city without a license, testify against a white person in court, or vote."

FREDERICK'S FUTURE wife, Frances Emily Holmes, my great-grandmother, was born in St. Louis on March 20, 1857. Her parents, Robert Holmes and Charlotte Powell, lived on South Fifth Street (modern Broadway) between Walnut and Elm. Frances was the fifth of their six children, three of whom survived into adulthood. The Holmeses were an old St. Louis family. Robert had arrived in 1838 from Pennsylvania and Charlotte one year earlier in 1837 from Maryland. Robert became a wealthy lumber merchant and for many years was considered "a prominent citizen of Missouri, as well as a public-spirited St. Louisan."

The Holmes's residence occupied prime downtown real estate, close to the steamboat landing. The area between their house on Fifth Street and the Mississippi River was filled with hotels, boarding houses, and businesses that catered to the river traffic. Two blocks away was the Old Courthouse, where Joshua Glover, the runaway slave captured in Racine, had been sold on New Year's Day 1850 and where the last slave auction would be held January 1, 1861, on the eve of the Civil War.

GUNFIRE BROKE OUT less than a block away from the Holmes's residence on May 11, 1861, a day after the Camp Jackson Affair. As a column of Union soldiers returned from a drill, a crowd of "angry secessionists first jeered the predominantly

German recruits, then threw dirt and stones at them. Suddenly a pistol shot rang out." Some thought the shots were fired from the steps of the Second Presbyterian Church, which the Holmes's family attended, at the corner of Fifth and Walnut.

"The surprised recruits returned fire wildly, firing at the church, at the houses, at bystanders, and even into their own ranks. When the firing stopped, eight people were dead and a ninth lay mortally wounded." Some of the dead and wounded may have been neighbors of Robert Holmes, who was a staunch Unionist and had contributed $100 to buy arms for the city's Home Guard before the outbreak of war ($3,040 in 2017 dollars).

THE FIRST major engagement of the Civil War west of the Mississippi was the Battle of Wilson's Creek in southwestern Missouri in August 1861, resulting in a decisive Confederate victory. By one account, "Almost a thousand of the dead and wounded on the Union side were St. Louis volunteers, and probably several hundred of the casualties on the Southern side were from St. Louis." Robert Holmes certainly would have known some of the casualties.

The shock of the Confederate victory at Wilson's Creek echoed across the state of Missouri. "When hostilities arrived," wrote one historian, "they did so with intense savagery... Sixty percent of Missouri's eligible men served in the war, with nearly three-fourths of them fighting for the Union. Beyond formal encounters between Federal and Confederate forces was a second kind of conflict, a guerilla action which devastated entire counties and left perhaps 27,000 citizens dead."

Outside of St. Louis, another historian wrote, "Missouri would be the scene of atrocities unlike any seen elsewhere: ceaseless guerilla warfare that erased distinctions between soldier and civilian almost entirely; violence with no greater strategic purpose than avenging the violence that had come before; in a few notorious instances, hundreds lined up and executed in cold blood."

THE HOLMESES were remembered decades later for their humanitarian efforts in St. Louis: "During the Civil War, Mr. and Mrs. Holmes were active in efforts to relieve the necessities of the sick and wounded soldiers who filled the hospitals and... Mrs. Holmes devoted much of her time to relief work generally in the interest of Union soldiers in the field."

"Unionist refugees from southwest Missouri and Arkansas had streamed into the city," wrote Primm. "Confederate prisoners, wounded soldiers, escaped slaves, and impoverished southern Unionists were discharged from riverboats by the tens of thousands…Volunteers such as the Ladies' Union Refugee Aid Society took care of them, but as the guerilla persecutions increased, the incoming tide of refugees overwhelmed their resources."

FRANCES'S OLDER SISTER, sixteen-year-old Belle, was elected Corresponding Secretary of the St. Louis Ladies' Union Aid Society in 1861, which provided services to soldiers, refugees, and escaped slaves. "Soldiers' families had…to be assisted," noted a later account. "Widows and orphans to be visited and cared for; rents, fuel, clothing, and employment to be provided, and the destitute relieved, of whom there were thousands whose husbands, sons, and brothers, were absent fighting the battles of the Union."

In January 1865, twenty-year-old Belle Holmes married Norton P. Chipman, a Civil War hero, at her mother's home. Perhaps eight-year-old Frances was a flower girl in her sister's wedding party. Colonel Chipman had achieved fame at the Battle of Fort Donelson in 1862 where he was wounded as he led a charge of his men. During later service in the War Department, he accompanied President Lincoln to Gettysburg and stood on the platform as Lincoln delivered the Gettysburg Address in 1863.

FREDERICK AND FRANCES probably started public school at age six—Frederick in 1859 and Frances in 1863. Education was important to both families. George Cline hoped that his firstborn would become a lawyer and someday join him in his law practice, a dream that would be fulfilled. Frances's father, Robert Holmes, was president of the St. Louis school board in 1862 and 1863.

At the time, public schools in St. Louis separated students according to their abilities. "When bright scholars are kept back for dull ones, they acquire loose, careless habits of study," noted a local history. "When the pupils of slower temperament are strained to keep pace with quick and bright ones, they become discouraged and demoralized." Frederick must have been one of the brighter students in his class, and at some point, perhaps in the ninth grade, he entered the private Smith Academy.

Run by Washington University, Smith Academy was a preparatory school for college. In 1871 a newspaper editor lauded this unique feature of education in St. Louis. "This system has two branches, Washington University and the public school organization... It is really a completely organized system of semi-private schools... They have now succeeded in building up an educational organization quite without parallel... in any other city in America."

FREDERICK ENTERED Washington University as a freshman in the fall of 1869, shortly before his sixteenth birthday. The university did not provide any student housing, so all students lived off campus. Frederick must have lived at home. "Here the daily routine of coming and going is so nearly that of a [high] school," one Washington University student observed, "that Freshmen and Sophomores do not feel that they have left... preparatory class and entered upon their college life."

At the time, rote learning, in the form of a daily recitation, dominated college classrooms. "It was a protracted oral quiz," noted the university history, "conducted by the professor for the purpose of discovering whether the student had memorized the textbook lesson assigned the day before."

"We had lessons to learn and recite," one student remembered. "Everything was prescribed; education was disciplinary; we were studying Latin and Greek, not for the beauty of their literature, but to train the memory and to sharpen our wits; we [memorized]... rules of grammar, long lists of exceptions; and anyone who could conjugate a verb in nineteen seconds was that much better than he who took twenty."

FREDERICK MUST have conjugated verbs at lightning speed. Two years later he would seek admission to Yale College in Connecticut. For her cultural refinement, Frances would attend Miss Porter's School, an exclusive girls' boarding school, also in Connecticut.

CHAPTER 8

Eastern Schools and Western Lives

Frederick and Frances, 1871–1902

AT NINE in the morning on July 14, 1871, Frederick Cline presented himself at the door of Alumni Hall at Yale College to take the entrance examination. He gave his name to the official seated at a long table and handed him an envelope testifying to his general morality signed by William Greenleaf Eliot, Chancellor of Washington University. He entered the examination room and took his seat at a small octagonal table, one of dozens arranged in rows of four. On the table he found a blank form, which he filled out in pencil with his name, birthplace, birthdate, the place of his preparatory study, and his chief instructor (also William Greenleaf Eliot).

A contemporary graduate, Lyman Hotchkiss Bagg, recalled the anxious scene in the room as each candidate was tested: "...an examiner approaches...hands him a text-book, and points to a marked passage within it, or leaves him a mathematical paper; then departs. In five or ten minutes—the time occupied in examining another candidate—the examiner returns, and, if our friend signifies his readiness, he recites, in a low tone of voice, still sitting at his table. A few hieroglyphics are marked in the score-book of the examiner, and he is again left alone, to reflect that for good or ill at least one step has been taken."

Candidates prepared for Yale's examination by memorizing long passages from classical works and modern texts, including the "seven orations of Cicero...the first six books of the *Aeneid* of Virgil...the first three books of Xenophon's *Anabasis*...Loomis's Algebra, to quadratic equations, and the first two books of Playfair's Euclid...Sufficient knowledge of English is, of course, indirectly shown in passing muster on the Latin and Greek grammars," Bagg wrote.

"The candidate is called upon for only a few lines from the author, but upon his knowledge of the few lines, the examiner bases his verdict of his knowledge of the entire [work]; and, as the passages are selected at haphazard, the many hundred lines must be prepared as carefully as if they were all to be recited." Seventeen-year-old Frederick mastered his recitations. The chief examiner acknowledged his success and laid a sheet of white paper at his table indicating Frederick's admission as a sophomore to Yale College, class of 1874.

"If the [examinee] doesn't turn a somersault and fling his cap to the ceiling with a yell of delight," Bagg remembered, "if, instead of this, he simply picks up his precious certificate and quietly withdraws from the inquisitional hall, followed by the longing glances of the poor wretches who are still at work; if he makes no outward demonstrations of his joy; it is not because he does not esteem that moment the happiest moment of his life."

How did Frederick develop an interest in Yale? Perhaps the name Chauvenet offers a clue. When Frederick attended Smith Academy, William Chauvenet was the esteemed chancellor of Washington University. A mathematician and astronomer of national repute, Chauvenet was Yale class of 1840. Fifteen years in the future, Frederick would choose Chauvenet as the middle name of his second son.

ARRIVING AT the New Haven train station in September 1871, Frederick would have been swarmed by members of the three freshman societies competing for new pledges. "They jump upon the platforms of the moving cars," Bagg wrote, "they fight the brakemen, they incommode the travelers, they defy the policemen— but they *will* offer the advantages of 'the best freshman society' to every individual 'candidate.'" Although he entered Yale as a sophomore, Frederick was treated like a freshman. He pledged Kappa Sigma Epsilon.

Frederick made his way to 90 York Street, a block west of the Old Campus, where he had engaged a room. He probably paid about $3.25 a week for his room and an additional amount required for "fire," "light," and "washing." For his meals, he would have joined an "eating club." Bagg provided an unflattering portrait of such an arrangement: "The steward, usually a poor man, engages some woman, accustomed to the business, to supply a dining room, dishes, table furniture, and waiters, and to do the cooking for his proposed club. For this he agrees to pay her a certain price per plate—not including his own, which is free…The steward occupies the 'head of the table' and does the carving whenever necessary."

YALE'S SCHOOL DAY began with chapel at 7:45, six days a week. The first recitation followed chapel from 8:30 to 9:30; the second from 11:30 to 12:30. The third was from 5:00 to 6:00, except Wednesday and Saturday. All students attended two church services on Sunday at 10:30 and 2:30. Frederick was one of thirteen new sophomores joining the class of 1874, which numbered 137; total enrollment at Yale College was 532 students.

Names were drawn randomly for classroom recitations. "The reciter is expected simply to answer the questions," Bagg remembered, "which are put to him, but not to ask any questions of his instructor or dispute his assertions." Years later, Frederick's classmate, John Seymour Wood, published a novel, *College Days: Or, Harry's Career at Yale*, in which the narrator disparages this rote method of instruction: "It was before the days of electives, and it was not considered that the brain of one boy differed much from another…The object of education was 'mental discipline,' not culture…'Drill' was the work, and mental gymnastics the object of recitations."

Frederick's first term at Yale covered "Isocrates…the first two *Olynthiacs* of Demosthenes (Champlin's)… In Latin, Horace was completed, by the reading of most of his satires and letters, at the rate of 50 lines a day. In mathematics…the first three books, 80 pages, of Trigonometry (Loomis's) were recited. In Greek tragedy, the *Oedipus Tyrannus* of Sophocles (Crosby's) was read, with a single omission of 100 lines."

IN SHARP CONTRAST to this academic world of order, discipline, and regimentation stood a freshman's campus life of abuse, cruelty, and brutality. "The regular time for pillaging the Freshmen," wrote Bagg, "is when they are absent at recitation…Sophomores proceed to the Freshmen's rooms, in parties of three or four, and carry off anything they find there likely to please themselves or, by its loss, to inconvenience the owner."

But nothing compared to the harsh initiation practices of a freshman's society. Bagg provided a semi-terrifying example: "A red devil…assisted by a living skeleton redolent of phosphorus, quickly blindfolds [the initiate], and he is hurried upward…Someone jostles him, and down, down, down he falls until he strikes—a blanket, held in readiness for him. Then up he flies into the air again, amid admiring shrieks of…'Shake him up!'…He is rolled in an exaggerated squirrel wheel, a noose is thrown around his neck, and he is dragged beneath the [mock] guillotine…Being thus executed, he is thrust into a coffin."

HAPPILY, these initiation practices ended during Frederick's time at Yale. Recognizing this change, Wood even set his novel "at the close of Yale's barbaric era." The alumni notes of the class of 1874 recognized this transition. "Hazing, the terror of timid parents, has received its death-blow during our stay here. We were the last class, really, to enjoy the benefits and pleasures of that 'time-honored' institution. No more shall those good old days occur, and our Annual Rush alone will remain as the landmark of the ancient college customs."

However, to modern ears, the Annual Rush still sounds pretty barbaric. Like a medieval battle scene, the freshman and sophomore classes formed opposing columns, five persons wide and thirty ranks deep. "The heads of the two columns slowly and with terrible earnestness came together," wrote Wood, "moving like two huge leviathans on the green, close-cut turf. As the ranks came within talking distance they jeered and taunted and threatened each other with instant annihilation.

"They came within five feet, three feet, then an impulse from both sides and from behind, and they were pressing each other's life out…The front rank were carried up in the air off their feet; the next rank could just touch their toes to the ground; the third rank had the hardest squeeze, and all the while each side behind these ranks were shouting cries of defiance and pushing like oxen." When the columns disintegrated, a general melee ensued.

AT THE END of every year, Frederick and his classmates took their "Annuals," a series of four examinations over ten days, covering all recitations of the year. Two daily sessions began at 9:00 a.m. and 3:00 p.m. in Alumni Hall, the same location used for the entrance examination.

Bagg described the process: "An entire class go in together, and are seated alphabetically at the little octagonal tables, no two of which are placed within eight feet of each other. An ink bottle, fixed in a square standard of cork, a blotter, and a dozen or twenty half-sheets of quarto post lie upon every table. Pen and penholder each man brings for himself." After the tests were distributed, students had three hours to complete their work.

Frederick Cline at Yale College in 1874, age twenty-one.

Chosen the Class Odist, Frederick wrote the Parting Ode for Class Day (the day before his graduation). Sung to the tune of "Auld Lang Syne," the lyrics began:

> Once more we meet as classmates true,
>> Once more our voices raise,
> But sad the strain—we chant the dirge
>> Of happy college days.
> We now must part from thee, Old Yale,
>> The echoes fade away
> In halls deserted, for, alas!
>> We leave these scenes to-day.

The 123 graduates of the class of 1874 must have felt immense pride when they received their diplomas on June 25, 1874. Although Frederick would live far away from the campus and from most of his classmates, he would always feel a strong connection to Yale. He attended the Triennial (1877) and Fortieth (1914) Class Reunions, and, when he did not attend, he faithfully reported his life events and accomplishments to the class secretary.

WE DO NOT know the year or years that Frances Holmes attended Miss Porter's School in Farmington, Connecticut, forty miles north of New Haven. In an era with few women's colleges or coeducational colleges, "women's seminaries, including Miss Porter's, were respected as institutions of higher education where women could receive an advanced liberal arts education," noted one school history. Most students came to Miss Porter's "at fifteen and stayed from one to three years." If true for Frances, her first academic year would have been 1872–73, coinciding with Frederick's second year at Yale.

Headmistress Sarah Porter "exclusively emphasized women's usefulness within the home, which she saw as a setting both for the raising of children and for the mother's intellectual and moral growth. [She] hoped to prepare her students for a lifetime of intellectual development through their independent study of literature, history, art, music, and nature...a secular form of spiritual growth that Victorian educators called 'culture.'"

Miss Porter's students could choose from a variety of courses, including Chemistry, Composition, French, Geography, Geology, German, History, and Music.

Practicing domestic skills, the girls did needlework while listening to their teachers read from novels.

ALL BOARDERS followed a strict set of house rules. "Bed clothes laid neatly back in the morning. All things neatly put up in readiness for the chambermaids who will be directed to lay in a mass in the halls all things left out of place…Rooms will be inspected three times daily and a report be made weekly."

With military precision, Miss Porter issued detailed Dress Regulations: "During May, the early part of June, September and October, for School, two worsted dresses, or one worsted and two calico dresses; and for other occasions, two dresses of worsted or silk; if of silk, to be made simply, with skirts untrimmed, and unless of black silk, not more costly than $1.50 per yard" ($38 in 2017 dollars).

Regarding headwear, "For summer and autumn, straw hats for school; straw bonnets or hats for church, trimmed in summer with white or with blue, and in autumn with black velvet or bright ribband. In winter, one hood or thick hat for school; and a velvet, silk, or beaver hat or bonnet for church." For footwear, the girls prepared for muddy walks: "One pair of India rubber boots, one pair of India rubber shoes, one pair of thick leather boots, two pairs of gaiter boots, and one pair of slippers; and for winter one pair of woolen leggings."

GIVEN THE inherent conflict between Miss Porter's severe nature and the affluence of some of her charges, she fought a constant battle against ostentation. In an 1873 letter, she sternly warned her students, "During the last year, the dress of some of my pupils has been more elaborate and costly than before…Our simple mode of life makes no demand for any other than a simple toilet…articles of dress should…be simply made…dresses should be so short as not to trail in walking.

"Silk dresses are not necessary and, if sometimes worn, should be rather inexpensive than rich, and jewels and costly laces, as well as their showy imitations, should be inadmissible. I shall be happy if these hints should remove the impression that elaborate dress is desirable in my school, and should repress any tendency towards it."

Might Frances have been one of the girls to whom Miss Porter's admonitions were directed? She was wealthy. When her father, Robert Holmes, died unexpectedly at age forty-seven in 1863, he left a fortune in lumber and real estate interests. Frances's mother told the census enumerator in 1870 that she and her three children each owned real estate worth $45,000 and a personal estate of $5,000 ($872,000 and $96,900 in 2017 dollars, respectively).

WE HAVE no record of Frances's thoughts about her experience at Miss Porter's School. But we do have letters home from another western student, Julia Anna Clark of Dubuque, Iowa, who was acutely aware of the cultural differences between New England and the West. Easterners might naturally have wondered—if Iowa bordered Dakota Territory and Missouri bordered Indian Territory (future Oklahoma)—how civilized could Westerners really be?

"I don't wonder that eastern people don't like western society with all its peculiarities," Miss Clark wrote. Likewise, she found a social chasm between Miss Porter's students and Farmington's townspeople. After spending the evening with a local family, she wrote to her sister, "They behaved just as Dubuque girls do; you can imagine how that was. I was very glad to get home."

Miss Porter sought to instill in her charges a sense of social, moral, and intellectual values above the common. "Avoid slang expressions, ungrammatical phrases, calling each other by disagreeable names." "None should run up or down stairs and all should walk lightly at all times." "There may be dancing in the back room of the wing, but Miss Porter wishes that there should be no waltzing." Boys were especially dangerous. "None may introduce any to boys. Waving of handkerchiefs, making or returning any signals to young men or boys is an offence that will demand dismissal from school."

Did Frances ever meet Frederick on the long train rides between St. Louis and Connecticut? If so, we can imagine that she felt blessedly free of Miss Porter's shackles. Assuming that Frances spent two years at the school, she would have been seventeen when she finished in 1874, the same year that Frederick graduated from Yale. He would turn twenty-one later in the year. How their courtship bloomed, we have no idea. All we know is the date of their marriage, six years hence.

BEFORE FREDERICK could marry, he would need to earn a living. That meant he would have to choose a profession, an easy decision for him to make. He would become a lawyer, like his father and like almost 40 percent of his Yale classmates. In the fall of 1874, he entered St. Louis Law School, today the Washington University School of Law.

The idea of training lawyers in an academic setting was relatively new at a time when most young lawyers still apprenticed themselves to a practitioner. "The LL.B. curriculum" a law school history noted, "was only two years long. Study for the law, moreover, was a part-time pursuit. The annual term lasted only six months, and

Frederick Cline, about 1880.

classes met only an hour a day in the late afternoon five times a week ... Many of the students filled their days by reading law in the offices of practitioners, and for them law school merely supplemented their apprenticeships."

Frederick graduated in 1876, one of nineteen who received law degrees. He proudly announced to his Yale classmates that he had won "the prize for best legal thesis." Graduation exempted him from the bar exam, and on March 10, 1876, Frederick was admitted to practice in the United States District Court in St. Louis.

He started his legal career at his father's firm, Cline, Jamison & Day, at 417 Pine Street near the Old Courthouse and lived at home with his mother and father and two younger brothers at 840 South Eighth Street, about a half mile away. Surrounded by three senior partners, we can imagine Frederick cramming his brain full of legal knowledge, learning both the letter of the law and its practical application.

FREDERICK MARRIED FRANCES on February 4, 1880, at the home of her mother, Charlotte Holmes. On their wedding day, Frances was twenty-two and Frederick twenty-six; both would celebrate birthdays later in the year. The newlyweds moved to a house at 2712 Chestnut, where they employed two Irish servants, Ann Reilly, thirty-eight, a housemaid, and Ann Coulon, twenty-six, the cook. Reflecting the wealth and prominence of Frances's family, the *St. Louis Post-Dispatch* recorded the Clines' summer escape from the sweltering St. Louis heat in August. "Frederick A. Cline and wife returned this week from a month's visit to Nantucket."

Their first three sons arrived annually—Frederick Holmes in 1881, Louis

Frances Holmes, about 1880.

Chauvenet in 1882, and John Holmes in 1883. Two years later, Alan Purnell Cline, my grandfather, was born on August 15, 1885. By now, we can be sure that the Cline household did not, in any way, resemble the subdued atmosphere at Miss Porter's School. Indeed, what rule of etiquette would not have been broken by four rambunctious boys?

Alan Cline, about 1895.

We know little of Frederick's professional life during the 1880s. After his father retired, he mostly practiced solo, except for a brief partnership with Hugo Meunch as Meunch & Cline. He and Frances moved three times as their family grew, before settling into a large two-story house at 4321 Olive Street in 1891, where they would remain for nearly three decades. Their last child, Isabel Violet, was born in 1894, the same year that Frederick's legal career reached its zenith.

"NEW JUDGES," headlined the *St. Louis Post-Dispatch* on November 11, 1894. "These nine new justices…will be looked upon as judges of the people-at-large in all minor disputes growing out of property rights, contracts, civil wrongs, and injuries…Some of these are old in the business, while others are about to don the judicial ermine [a symbol of incorruptibility] for the first time"—like Frederick Cline.

"Cline's selection," the paper noted, "gives general satisfaction to members of the bar, many of whom speak very highly of his legal ability." He would receive an annual salary of $2,500, "besides certain fees and perquisites," which could raise his salary to $3,000 ($88,200 in 2017 dollars).

Frederick's court had jurisdiction over all civil cases up to $500 ($14,700 in 2017 dollars). The *St. Louis Post-Dispatch* covered numerous cases in his courtroom over the years. A woman contested a bill from her dressmaker for a garment not delivered in time ("it was wanted for a special occasion"). A church declined to pay for a typewriter that was stolen ("Judge Cline said the introduction of religious differences into the controversy was sheer foolishness"). Perhaps most interestingly, Judge Cline seated the first all-black jury in the city's history ("the case involved the possession of some billboards").

Unfortunately, on November 4, 1902, Frederick's eight-year term came to an abrupt and unhappy end when he lost his reelection bid, along with almost every other Republican candidate city-wide up for election that year. Commenting the next day on the Democratic landslide, the *St. Louis Post-Dispatch* wrote, "The judiciary, both criminal and civil, in all their branches is today the official property of the dominant party."

Alleging "illegal registration and voting" violations, Frederick sought to reverse his defeat by proving that fraud had been committed. But six months later, he dropped his suit after the Missouri Supreme Court ruled that "ballots in the boxes could not be compared with the registration lists." Out of a job at age forty-nine, Frederick would return to private practice, although in family lore he would always remain "Judge Cline."

Frederick Cline, age fifty-six, for his
thirty-fifth Yale College reunion in 1909.

After his retirement in 1919, Frederick and Frances moved to Los Angeles to live with their daughter and son-in-law, Isabel and Gerald Harney. A photograph captured the family celebrating the Fourth of July 1922 at Ocean Park Beach in Santa Monica. Dressed in formal attire, Frederick and Frances sat on the sand—he wearing a coat and tie and a straw boater, she wearing a long dress and a fancy hat—enjoying the California sun.

Frederick Cline, 1922

WE NOW TURN to my other set of maternal great-grandparents, Walter McGavin and Kate Hinshelwood, whose daughter, Emilia, would marry the Clines' son, Alan. Our story begins in Paris, which is surrounded by the Prussian army poised to bombard the city.

CHAPTER 9

City Lights and Country Life

Walter and Kate, 1853–1875

THE FIRST PRUSSIAN SHELL landed on the Left Bank on January 5, 1871, the 109th day of the Siege of Paris. After months of trying to starve the city into submission, Chancellor Otto von Bismarck chose this "psychological moment" to launch a campaign of terror. The daily bombardment usually started after 10:00 p.m. and lasted four hours with three hundred shells or more landing on the city.

Thirteen-year-old Kate Hinshelwood, my great-grandmother, and her British expatriate family, including her beloved godfather, Dr. Drummond MacGavin, lived near the Élysée Palace on the Right Bank beyond the range of Prussian artillery. But they would have heard the bombardment and seen the flight of refugees across the Pont de la Concorde and other bridges over the Seine.

Six months earlier, Emperor Napoleon III had launched the disastrous Franco-Prussian War on July 19. After he was captured at the Battle of Sedan, the Prussian army marched on Paris, surrounding the city on September 20. Two million residents, including four thousand British subjects, were trapped behind the Paris Wall, a twenty-mile, thirty-three-foot-high structure, bordered by a ten-foot moat (today's Boulevard Périphérique).

The French government had tried to stock Paris with enough food and fuel for a long siege. Flour and corn stocks would last eighty days. Forty thousand oxen and a quarter million sheep were herded into the Bois de Boulogne. Coal supplies were sufficient for seventy-eight days. That was the plan. The reality was far different. The American ambassador, Elihu Washburne, wrote in his diary on just the fifty-ninth day of the Siege, "Fresh meat is getting almost out of the question, that is, beef, mutton, veal, pork. Horse meat and mule meat is very generally eaten now, and they have commenced on dogs, cats, and rats." Fresh vegetables and milk simply disappeared.

Compounding the city's misery, heavy rains in October turned to sleet and snow, and temperatures in December were mostly below freezing, sometimes plunging as low as five degrees above zero. The Seine was covered with ice. Desperately short of fuel, residents burned their furniture and cut down trees, stripping the Bois de Boulogne and the Champs Élysée of foliage.

BEFORE THE SIEGE, young Kate had known only the glory of the Second Empire under the reign of Emperor Napoleon III. Born Katharina Hinshelwood on October 3, 1856, she was the youngest of six children. Her parents, James Hinshelwood and Margaret Mary Coker, lived at 320 Rue Saint-Honoré near the Tuileries Garden. They were British citizens and had married in London in 1844. At the time, James was a tea broker and Margaret a clerk in a lace shop.

They moved to Paris, probably in 1847, where James listed his profession as a man of letters (in French, *homme d'lettres*). Perhaps he taught English to support his family. James and Margaret may have loved Paris, but they did not love each other. In family lore, James abandoned his wife and children, who then moved to Neuilly-sur-Seine, a middle-class suburb west of the Paris Wall.

In 1861 Margaret was enumerated in the departmental census of Hauts-de-Seine as Marie Hinshelwood, the sole head of household, at 189 Avenue de Neuilly (today Avenue Charles de Gaulle). Intriguingly, her occupation was listed as *rentière*, roughly translated as a person of private means, indicating that she may have lived off income from taking in boarders.

DURING THE 1860s the Hinshelwood family must have marveled at the changing cityscape of Paris under the direction of Georges Haussmann, Napoleon's master organizer. Most visibly, Haussmann rammed new boulevards and avenues through crowded *quartiers* and disease-ridden slums, replacing winding lanes, dark alleys, and open sewers with the modern street grid of Paris. He created seven new *arrondissements*, demolished 20,000 houses, and added 40,000 new ones.

"Along the great boulevards," David McCullough wrote, "new apartments would rise—whole apartment blocks of white limestone—none more than six stories high and in a uniform Beaux-Arts style, with high French windows and cast-iron balconies. Sidewalks were to be widened. Streets and boulevards would be lined with trees and glow at night with 32,000 new gas lamps. Gaslight everywhere would turn night into day, making Paris truly *la ville lumière.*"

To celebrate his re-sculpted city, Louis-Napoléon Bonaparte hosted the World's Fair of 1867, the biggest and most spectacular world's fair yet. A vast elliptical glass building, 1,500 feet long, set in a filigree of iron-work, housed thousands of exhibits on the Champ-de-Mars, where the Eiffel Tower stands today. "The displays of novel manufactured items," McCullough noted, "included an almost overwhelming array of things large and small, things almost unimaginable—magnificent locomotives, steam engines, a feather-weight metal called aluminum... and a new kind of brass horn, *le saxophone*, devised by Napoleon III's official instrument maker, Adolphe Sax."

Kate and Dr. MacGavin must have been among the fifteen million visitors to attend the fair. She turned eleven a month before the Exposition closed, old enough to be impressed by the swarms of street performers, the wandering exhibitors dressed in native costume, and the unending display of household goods from around the world. (Another eleven-year-old visitor to the fair was John Singer Sargent, later the famous American painter, whose life would intersect with Dr. MacGavin's almost two decades hence.)

DR. DRUMMOND MACGAVIN occupies an exalted place in family lore as the benefactor of Margaret Hinshelwood and the guardian of young Kate, who was an infant when her father disappeared. Historical evidence suggests that Dr. Mac-Gavin lived in Neuilly during the 1860s, perhaps as a permanent boarder in the Hinshelwood household. Sadly, we know this because he witnessed the deaths of three of Kate's older sisters—eighteen-year-old Laura in 1864, sixteen-year-old Augusta in 1868, and eighteen-year-old Camilla in 1869.

We have no idea of the cause of their deaths. Typhoid fever, pneumonia, and smallpox, among many other diseases, were common and often fatal at the time. Whatever the cause, the deaths of three older sisters must have taken an emotional toll on Kate, who would have turned eight, twelve, and thirteen in these years. We can imagine that Dr. MacGavin was a great source of emotional stability and financial support.

He was born John Drummond McGavin in 1821 in the village of Sorn, county of Ayrshire, Scotland. At age fifteen in 1836 he matriculated at the University of

Glasgow where he studied medicine, graduating eight years later with an M.D. in 1844. After college, he was an assistant at the Glasgow Lunatic Asylum before his appointment as superintendent of the Montrose Lunatic Asylum, Scotland's oldest asylum for the insane. Sometime in the 1850s, he went abroad to continue his medical education. *(This is when he added an "a" to his last name.)*

Recommending Dr. MacGavin for membership in the Royal College of Physicians of Edinburgh in 1859, one doctor wrote, "He is highly educated, both professionally and otherwise; a sound Christian and a gentleman. He has been resident for some years past on the Continent, and has further extended his professional acquirements by studying at the Schools of Paris, Vienna, and Berlin."

During the Siege of Paris, Dr. MacGavin and the Hinshelwoods had been forced to evacuate their home outside the Paris Wall in Neuilly and to relocate into the city proper. They moved to an apartment with enough space for Dr. MacGavin's medical office at 10 Rue des Saussaies on the Right Bank. Outside of his own practice, Dr. MacGavin treated wounded French soldiers as a member of the British Ambulance, one of the many volunteer field hospitals. In recognition of his service, the Third Republic awarded him the Legion of Honor, a rare accolade for a non-French citizen.

THREE WEEKS after the Prussian bombardment began, the French government surrendered on January 27, 1871, the 131st day of the Siege. If the Hinshelwoods hoped to return to Neuilly after the Siege, their hopes were quickly dashed when the *commune* (the city council) seized control of Paris on March 18, triggering a French civil war between the Paris Commune and the French national army, which encircled the city. Just seven weeks after the Prussian Siege was lifted, Parisians were once again trapped behind the Paris Wall.

As the federal troops battled their way into the city, they laid waste to Neuilly. "Every single tree is cut in pieces," one witness remembered, "and the ground is covered with grape, canister, shot and broken shells and flattened bullets. I entered what had been beautiful houses, with floors wobbling and held up only by a side, utterly wrecked, billiard tables, looking-glasses, sofas, and costly furniture all smashed to pieces... Bedding and furniture all piled up into barricades..."

By the end of May, the national army had regained full control of Paris after weeks of fighting that left tens of thousands dead. Ambassador Washburne wrote to the American secretary of state, "The reign of The Commune... pursuing its career of murder, assassination, pillage, robbery, blasphemy, and terror, finally expired in blood and flame."

We have no record of the Hinshelwood family at this time. But as expatriate British citizens, they would have been relatively safe from the internecine warfare that pitted Frenchman against Frenchman. Whatever their circumstances, we can be certain that fourteen-year-old Kate would have witnessed harrowing street scenes and heard tales of great suffering.

ACROSS THE ENGLISH CHANNEL, the man Kate would marry ten years in the future lived in London, seat of the vast British Empire. He was an eighteen-year-old Scot, whom she had met a year earlier when he visited Paris. His name was Walter McGavin, and, not coincidentally, he was Dr. MacGavin's nephew, the son of his older brother, William. (*The two brothers spelled their last names differently.*)

William was the miller at Green Mill in Old Cumnock in the county of Ayrshire, south of Glasgow. He and his wife, Helen Samson, had eight children. Walter James Samson McGavin, my great-grandfather, was their sixth child, born April 27, 1853.

The *New Statistical Account of Scotland* painted an idyllic picture of Old Cumnock. "The parish is partly flat and partly hilly, so as to present to the eye a very pleasing undulating surface, finely varied and adorned by numerous belts of wood, intersecting in all directions, and giving a peculiarly rich and cultivated appearance to the entire landscape." Grouse, partridge, and pheasants were abundant. The nearby lakes were filled with pike, perch, and eels. The River Lugar contained plenty of trout.

IN 1850, three years before Walter's birth, the South-Western Railway had connected Old Cumnock to Glasgow, forty-nine miles to the north. To promote tourism, the railroad published a guidebook extolling the scenic beauty of Ayrshire. "Little are the inhabitants of our crowded cities and towns aware of the enjoyment of which they may avail themselves, at a trifling expense, by paying a visit to our Southern Highlands." One of the highlights in the guide was the viaduct over the River Lugar at Cumnock. "The scenery down the Lugar, as seen from the bridge, is varied and beautiful in the extreme."

By 1861, the year that Walter turned eight, the population of the parish of Old Cumnock totaled 3,700 people. The bustling town boasted three banks, three grocers, a printer, and a stationer. A distant relative, John McGavin, operated a bakery that made the "famous Cumnock tarts," according to a local history. Gas lighting would come to Cumnock in 1866 and running water in 1869.

WALTER McGAVIN'S NAME first appeared in the historical record as a seven-year-old "Scholar" in the 1861 Scotland Census. Students of any age were designated as "Scholar" in the census, which was recorded April 7, three weeks before Walter's eighth birthday. Perhaps he attended the parish school, which was administered by the Church of Scotland, a Presbyterian denomination. All schools in Scotland were sectarian, and each day began with a prayer. Walter would have been taught the core subjects of English, Writing, Arithmetic, and Latin.

We can imagine that his education emphasized rote learning and firm discipline. But all students would have eagerly anticipated New Year's Day. On this day, students brought their teacher presents like "cakes, parcels of tea, and sugar," according to a local history. In return the teacher handed out treats like "apples, oranges, cookies, and sweets."

Cumnock celebrated four village fairs each year: the Race Fair in March, the May Fair in May, the Scythe Fair in July, and the Harvest Fair in October. What fun young Walter must have had scampering about the fairgrounds with his friends and staring in wide-eyed amazement at the jugglers, acrobats, and carnival barkers. He must have watched a puppet show and visited the stalls filled with sweetmeats and toys.

WALTER'S FATHER, the town miller, would have been a prominent figure in Old Cumnock. "The central importance of the corn [grain] mill to the traditional Scots' community," wrote one historian, "is not easily grasped until it is understood that the mill used to be the supplier of almost every mouthful of food…For most people…food was meal, ground from their own grains and pulses."

Above all, farmers trusted the miller to be honest. He picked up the farmer's grain with his horse and cart; milled the grain to the customer's specifications, which varied depending upon its use, and returned the finished meal to the customer. Carefully segregating and tracking one farmer's grains from another required constant diligence and detailed recordkeeping as the miller monitored the grinding process and collected payments for the finished product.

Green Mill was located within a loop of the River Lugar. A weir, or low dam, diverted water into a lade, the channel that delivered water to the millwheel. The mill is clearly visible on the 1857 Ordnance Survey map of Old Cumnock. Scaled at twenty-five inches to a mile, each building and landscape feature is distinct. Fence lines enclose backyards, and trees delineate property boundaries. The cottage at Bridgend, where Walter was born, is outlined, and we can imagine Walter and his siblings playing for hours in the fields and woods nearby.

ROBERT BURNS, Scotland's poet and Ayrshire's native son, referred to the Lugar in his love song, "My Nanie, O," in which a young lad longs for his lassie.

> Behind yon hills where Lugar flows,
> 'Mang [among] moors an' mosses many, O,
> The wintry sun the day has clos'd,
> And I'll awa to Nanie, O.

In 1788 Burns himself had stopped in Old Cumnock, just long enough to dash off a letter to a paramour. "I am here, returning from Dumfriesshires, at an inn, the post-office of the place, with just so long a time as my horse eats his corn to write to you." His love for this Edinburgh lady would never be requited.

As Walter reached his teenage years, he must have helped his father around the mill. Like all Scots, he would have loved Burns's poetry, and we can imagine that Walter particularly appreciated his poem, "Hey, the Dusty Miller," about a young lass who steals a kiss from a miller.

> Hey, the dusty Miller,
> And his dusty coat,
> He will win a shilling,
> Or [before] he spend a groat [four pence]
> Dusty was the coat,
> Dusty was the colour,
> Dusty was the kiss
> That I gat frae [got from] the Miller.

But Walter had larger ambitions than the life of a country miller—like another young Scot, James Lyle Mackay, who fled his small town in 1871. "Ambition begat discontent," Mackay's biographer wrote. "[He] looked...for new and wider fields. The strange restlessness of the Scotsman was upon him and, excited by the advertisements which he read in the newspapers, he set his heart on London." Walter also left his home in Scotland and moved to London. (Within a decade, he and Mackay would cross paths in a far corner of the British Empire.)

WALTER McGAVIN WAS ENUMERATED in the 1871 England Census as living at the home of his older, married sister, Catherine McGavin Hair. The Hair household included her husband, Robert, their five children, two boarders, and two servants. The family was solidly middle class residing at 30 Offord Road in the parish of Islington on the northern edge of the city.

London had doubled in size to almost four million people in the previous twenty years. It was the largest city in the world, three times larger than New York. Listed in the census as a "Commercial Clerk," Walter worked for Smith, Fleming & Company, an East Indian mercantile house owned by John Fleming of Glasgow. The offices of Smith, Fleming & Company were at 17 Leadenhall Street in the City of London—three miles south of his sister's residence.

Over one hundred thousand clerks managed the enormous paper flow among merchants, bankers, and customers in London. Mail was collected ten times a day and delivered within one-and-a-half hours. "As postal communications improved, more clerks were needed everywhere. Every business letter had to be painstakingly written, copied, filed, and posted by hand. Every entry in a ledger had to be written legibly by hand," wrote Liza Picard in *Victorian London*.

"Traffic jams were appalling. Omnibuses from the residential quarters barged their way to the Bank of England, cutting across the streams of animals...The crowds of clerical workers employed in the City walked in from the suburbs. They walked astonishing distances, come rain or shine. In 1854 it was officially estimated that 200,000 people walked into Central London every day."

If Walter walked to his office, he navigated streets of gelatinous mud. "This was not the mud of the field or the stable-yard," noted one writer. "For a start, although largely composed of horse dung, it was black. The capital's sooty atmosphere tainted everything it touched, even the dirt on the streets. London mud was also terribly sticky, 'enough to suck off your boots.'"

If Walter decided instead to take a horse-drawn omnibus to work, he faced two unpleasant choices—to ride inside or outside. If inside, passengers "had the benefit of straw on the floor, to keep their feet dry and warm, but this got progressively filthier as a wet day wore on," wrote Picard. "Another disagreeable aspect of inside travel was other travelers. Omnibuses were a favorite haunt of pickpockets.

"A respectable-looking female sitting necessarily close to another passenger might appear to have her gloved hands modestly clasped in her lap, but one might be false, while her real hand was busy in her neighbor's pockets. Another risk was, of course, fleas." If Walter rode outside, he "sat back-to-back on a bench, called a 'knife-board,' along the middle of the roof, with nothing to hold onto and no protection from the weather."

Notorious fogs offered yet another challenge. "In December 1873, a dense haze settled on London for five days," wrote one historian. "Pedestrians feeling their way blindly along pavements…crossed roads at their peril. In central London… one might meet an enterprising youth with a flaming torch, willing to offer safe conduct in return for a few pence."

Although we would consider Walter a white-collar worker today, he probably thought of himself as a "top-hat-and-black-coated" worker. As Picard wrote, "The Victorian middle-class urban male wore a tall hat, a coat, waistcoat [vest], and trousers, with an overcoat in cold weather. Any picture of a crowd is punctuated by these black cylinders…They were hot, uncomfortable, and unpractical." However, they would have immediately distinguished Walter from manual laborers commuting to their jobs.

AS A LIFELONG BACHELOR, Dr. MacGavin seems to have taken a special interest in his bright young nephew. Perhaps the good doctor saw something of himself in the boy who dreamed of the world beyond his Scottish roots. Evidence that Dr. MacGavin invited Walter to visit him in Paris is contained on a *carte de visite* of Walter in Neuilly.

Commonly used to document family occasions in the nineteen century, a *carte de visite* was a photograph pasted on thick paper. In the picture Walter appears to be a teenager of middle years. On the back is printed the name and address of the photographer: Adolphus Pepper, 60 Avenue de Neuilly. Walter's name is also handwritten on the back, maybe by Dr. MacGavin himself.

Walter McGavin, about 1870 in Paris.

It seems logical that this *carte de visite* was produced when the Hinshelwood family also lived in Neuilly. We might guess that Walter visited his uncle in the spring of 1870 before the Siege. At that time, Walter would have been seventeen years old. Kate, whom he probably met for the first time, would turn fourteen later in the year (during the Siege).

THE EXCITEMENT of visiting a foreign country must have stimulated Walter's interest in living abroad, particularly when contrasted with the drudgery of his clerkship in fog-bound London. When Paris roared back to life after the Siege, Dr. MacGavin might have further whetted Walter's appetite with glamorous tales of life during the Belle Époque. In April 1874, Dr. MacGavin attended the annual ball of the British Charitable Fund, along with honored guests, including the British and American ambassadors, Lord Lyons and Elihu Washburne.

"The display of female grace and beauty was extraordinary," gushed *Galignani's Messenger*, an English language newspaper for expats, "and the English and American ladies may rest well satisfied with their rivalry of all foreign beauties. Then, the toilettes [coiffures], so fresh, so rich, so original, may vie with those of any entertainment of the season... As the number of musical pieces to be given during the night was 28, we can imagine the ball terminating about half-past four in the morning."

WHETHER BY SERENDIPITY or by calculation, Walter's dream of a life abroad came true in 1875 when he was sent to Bombay (modern Mumbai), India. He would work for W. Nicol & Company, a Scottish trading company related to his original employer, Smith, Fleming & Company. That November twenty-two-year-old Walter boarded the *Mongolia*, a P&O steamship, for the month-long, 8,000-mile voyage to India via the Suez Canal. He carried a Bible with the inscription: "Presented to Walter J. S. McGavin by his affectionate Mother on his going out to India, 19th October 1875."

CHAPTER 10

Scotland Woos Paris

Walter and Kate, 1875–1893

DISEMBARKING IN BOMBAY on December 1, 1875, Walter entered a new world. "A tide of seething Asiatic humanity ebbs and flows," wrote a contemporary traveler, "up and down the Bhendi bazaar and through the chief mercantile thoroughfares. Nowhere could be seen a play of livelier hues, a busier and brighter city life! Besides the endless crowds of Hindu, Gujerati, and Mahratta people coming and going—some in gay dresses, but most with next to none at all—between the rows of grotesquely painted houses and temples, there are to be studied here specimens of every race and nation of the East.

"Arabs from Muscat, Persians from the Gulf, Afghans from the Northern frontier, black shaggy Biluchis, negroes of Zanzibar, islanders from the Maldives and Laccadives, Malagashes, Malays, and Chinese throng and jostle Parsees in their sloping hats, with Jews, Lascars, fishermen, Rajpoots, Fakirs, Europeans, Sepoys, and Sahibs…The motley population lives its accustomed life in the public gaze, doing a thousand things in the roadway, in the gutter, or in the little open shops, which the European performs inside his closed abode."

Yet Walter would also have found himself strangely at home. "British metropolitanism," noted a city historian, "was, in the 1860s, 70s and 80s, imported into Bombay, complete with water pipes, gas pipes, paving authorities, sewage disposal authorities, tramlines, parks, apartment blocks both grand and squalid, and every other amenity of western civilization." Mail was delivered six times daily at 8:00, 10:00, and 11:30 a.m., and 12:30, 2:00, and 5:00 p.m. The offices of W. Nicol & Company were located on Elphinstone Circle, which featured gently curved, four-story office blocks surrounding a lovely city park, echoing the design of an English spa town.

Walter's employer was a long-established mercantile firm and the Bombay agent for the British India Steam Navigation Company. Like other mercantile houses, Nicol & Company earned commissions as agents for British manufacturers and traded locally on their own account. That Walter was of Scottish descent was not a coincidence. Similar overseas firms were "largely the work of family and clan groups," wrote one maritime historian, "among whom the Scots were particularly prominent."

A YEAR AFTER Walter landed on the subcontinent, Queen Victoria proclaimed herself Empress of India, "the jewel in the crown" of the British Empire. Encompassing the modern countries of India, Pakistan, Bangladesh, and Sri Lanka, the British Raj ruled over 255 million people, more than eight times the combined populations of England, Scotland, and Ireland.

The declaration ceremony was orchestrated by Lord Lytton, the Viceroy of India. "At his invitation, over 400 Indian princes and their retinues converged on Delhi during the closing weeks of 1876 for a dazzling display of imperial theater," wrote one historian, "devised to show them the majesty, permanence, and sheer strength of the Raj. There were 15,000 red-coated British soldiers, the muscle of the empire and its brains, the immaculately uniformed, plumed and bemedalled British officials and officers."

In a deft display of rhetorical contradiction (to modern ears), the British Viceroy read the queen's telegraphic message to the assembled multitude in January 1877: "We trust that the present occasion may tend to unite in bonds of close affection ourselves and our subjects; that from the highest to the humblest, all may feel that under our rule the great principles of liberty, equity, and justice are secured to them; and to promote their happiness, to add to their prosperity, and to advance their welfare, are the ever present aims and objects of our Empire."

EVEN A CLERK like Walter was a member of a privileged class and would have enjoyed an exceedingly comfortable lifestyle in colonial Bombay. Servants were plentiful and cheap by English standards—in fact, sometimes too plentiful. "It was a perennial complaint of the British in India," observed a writer, "that each class of servant had his specialty—cooking, sweeping, water-bearing, care of horse, etc.—and that none would perform anything but his function."

Walter, who was a lifelong fitness enthusiast, joined the Bombay Gymkhana, a local athletic club. Cricket and lawn tennis were his favorite sports. In August 1876, his name was listed in *The Times of India* as a member of the "All Comers" side in a Gymkhana cricket match against the "Lawyers and Soldiers." In September 1878, he played in the Gymkhana tennis doubles tournament, which included a peculiarly British rule for the match: "A ball attempted and not taken, though it fall out of [the] court, shall count in favor of the striker."

Later that month, Walter dressed as "Jack Tar" (a common expression for a British sailor) to attend the Calico Volunteers Ball on September 28. *The Times of India* raved, "During the forty odd years that have elapsed since the Bombay Town Hall was built, there have been many highly imposing ceremonials and picturesque gatherings within its walls; but we doubt very much if there has been any more interesting sight than that which was witnessed on Friday evening on the occasion of the Volunteer Ball."

The *Times* printed the names of all 355 guests and the costumes they wore, which ranged from the obvious (Court Jester, Little Bo-Peep, and Romeo) to the exotic (Nine of Clubs, Venetian Courtier, and Knight of Malta) to the obscure (Night, Snow, and The Starry Firmament). Based upon the twenty dances that the band of Her Majesty's 21st Regiment would play (quadrille, waltz, galop), the *Times* estimated the ball would terminate "shortly before three."

How happy and confident Walter must have been. He was twenty-five years old, handsome and fit. After almost three years of residency in Bombay, he was a member of society. But within days of the Calico Ball, Walter's world was rocked by a financial earthquake. The collapse of a Scottish bank delivered a mortal blow to his employer, W. Nicol & Company.

WHEN NEWS of the failure of the City of Glasgow Bank reached India on October 3, 1878, "It produced a profound impression in Bombay," *The Times of India* wrote, "and led to something very like a panic. Ugly rumors concerning one or two firms were at once circulated…business was at a complete standstill. The connection of Messrs. W. Nicol & Company with the City of Glasgow Bank was the absorbing topic of conversation, and it was fully anticipated on Thursday evening that they would be compelled to close their doors on Friday morning."

This is exactly what transpired the next day. The *Times* reported: "Messrs. Nicol & Company issued a circular stating that owing to the failure of the City of

Walter McGavin as "Jack Tar," at the Calico Volunteers Ball
in Bombay, September 27, 1878.

Glasgow Bank they were compelled to suspend payment and were summoning a meeting of their creditors at three o'clock...The meeting...was very influentially attended, and the heartiest sympathy was expressed for misfortunes which have so unexpectedly and undeservedly overtaken them through the failure of a bank that was supposed to stand as high as any in Scotland."

Walter must have been shocked by this sudden turn of events, just like the editors of the *Glasgow Herald* who railed against the management of the city's bank. "The light thrown day-by-day on the conduct of the directors puts a blacker aspect on their culpability. They have made a shipwreck of a noble institution; they have recklessly divided the plunder among themselves and their friends; and they have inflicted misery and ruin on thousands of innocent sufferers." Investigators soon linked the collapse to disastrous speculation and fraudulent reporting over many years.

THE LIQUIDATION of Nicol & Company placed the fate of Walter and other employees in the hands of another Scottish trading firm, Mackinnon Mackenzie & Company of Calcutta. Mackinnon Mackenzie had pounced on the opportunity to acquire the Bombay agency and quickly dispatched James Lyle Mackay, the same restless Scotsman whom we met earlier, to the city.

Mackay, who would later became Lord Inchcape and a towering figure in British maritime commerce, wrote of his new assignment, "I found the work quite interesting and had no trouble...within a few weeks I had surrounded myself with an efficient European and Indian staff." We can imagine that Mackay and Walter, as two young Scotsmen, would have been compatible and that Walter remained employed as one of the "efficient" members of Mackay's staff, at least for a short time.

Exactly how long Walter worked for Mackinnon Mackenzie we do not know. *The Times of India* reported that he returned to Bombay from Karachi on October 28, 1878. He may have been sent there to look after Fleming & Company, another Scottish trading firm in liquidation after the failure of the City of Glasgow Bank. This would be the last mention of Walter's name in the *Times*. Within months, he had left Bombay and sailed for home, although we do not know the precise date of his departure.

IN FAMILY LORE, Walter stopped off in Paris, fell in love with Kate, and found a job in California. The precise details of his movements are lost in the sands of time. But we might guess that he arrived in Paris in the spring of 1879, his first visit since

1870. Kate was no longer a shy thirteen-year-old girl, but a confident twenty-two-year-old woman. Walter was no longer a slight seventeen-year-old teenager, but a strapping twenty-six-year-old man.

Perhaps after a welcome dinner, Kate and Walter went for a walk and ordered coffee at a sidewalk café. He told her tales of colonial Bombay, and she told him stories of the Siege of Paris. He spoke English with a Scottish burr. She spoke English with a French accent (French was her first language). Sparks flew and a romance blossomed.

Whatever actually transpired on his visit, Walter eventually left Paris and made his way home to Cumnock that summer. We have a photograph of him and his parents along with other family members dated July 18, 1879. Later that fall he sailed to the United States and crossed the country by train. We have another picture of him and two companions inscribed "Xmas Day 1879, Virginia City, Nevada." By January 1880, we know that he had started work at the Nevada Bank in San Francisco.

HOW DID a recently unemployed Scotsman from Bombay land a job in California? Again, Dr. MacGavin probably played a critical role in Walter's life. Recognized in Baedeker's guidebook as one of the "eminent" doctors in the city, Dr. MacGavin was well-known to the expatriate British and American community and had been appointed physician to the American Embassy.

So it seems logical that he might have socialized with a wealthy American couple, John and Louise Mackay (no relation to the Bombay Mackay). Mackay was one of the Silver Kings of the Consolidated Mines in Nevada. The company's four founders—two saloon keepers and two engineers—had struck an enormous vein of silver 1,200 feet below Virginia City. Over the years, Mackay and his partners took out $400 million in silver ore, worth billions today. Mackay used part of his personal fortune to found the Nevada Bank, which was headquartered in San Francisco.

Mackay's wife "had no qualms about transforming herself into a worldly woman," noted one writer. "The family built homes first in Virginia City and then in San Francisco. They then moved to New York and Paris to try and break into the ranks of high society." That desire is what led the Mackays into the same social orbit as Dr. MacGavin. Another writer put it more plainly: "John Mackay commuted between his Nevada silver mines and his wife's Parisian salon, networking at Franco-American banquets."

Perhaps Dr. MacGavin suggested to Mackay at one of these banquets that his nephew, recently employed by a Bombay mercantile firm, would make an excellent bookkeeper at his bank in California. Walter's obituary would say simply that "he became associated with John Mackay, the bonanza king, who installed him in the old Nevada Bank as a bookkeeper." However it happened, Walter was hired and started his new job at the Nevada Bank in San Francisco on January 29, 1880.

WE CAN IMAGINE Walter walking to work on his first day filled with determination and excitement. The bank's headquarters were located at Pine and Montgomery. As he entered the main banking hall, he would have noticed the walls of pristine marble and the ceilings adorned with mahogany. Soon, he would find out that some offices on the floors above had fireplaces with mantels of quartz inlaid with gold.

On that first January day, Walter could not possibly have dreamed that he would retire forty-three years hence as the bank's longest serving employee. Yet over the many decades ahead, Walter would retain the confidence of management as the bank acquired new owners (1890), secured a national charter (1897), and merged with Wells, Fargo & Company (1905) to become the Wells Fargo Nevada National Bank—and much later, simply, Wells Fargo Bank.

ALMOST TWO YEARS elapsed between Walter's arrival in California and his marriage to Kate on December 1, 1881, at the Trinity Episcopal Church in San Francisco. Does this gap indicate her hesitation to move to a new country? His desire to establish himself first in a new city? Or the natural progression of their courtship? We do not know.

Neither bride nor groom had any family nearby, so the wedding must have been small with only a few of Walter's friends witnessing the ceremony. He was twenty-eight, and she was twenty-five. They moved into an apartment at 910 Taylor Street, and a year later their son, John Drummond, arrived in December 1882. Named after Dr. MacGavin, both would always be Drummond to the family, not John. Their second and last child, Emilia Helen McGavin, my grandmother, would be born six years later on February 25, 1888, named after Kate's older sister. (*To honor their great-uncle, both siblings would alter the spelling of their last name to MacGavin.*)

Walter and Kate thrived during the 1880s both professionally and socially. Walter appeared regularly in the annual editions of the *San Francisco City Directory* ascending the corporate ladder—clerk, teller, and assistant accountant. Kate's name was first mentioned on the society page of the *San Francisco Chronicle* in April 1884. "Mrs. McGavin contributed some delightful music, singing several French airs and giving selections of sacred music." Two years later, she performed at a benefit for the surgical ward of Children's Hospital. "Each participant was well received and encored," the *Chronicle* wrote. Kate and tenor Ugo Talbo sang a duet from Verdi's opera, *I Masnadieri*, "Qual Mare, Qual Terra" (What Oceans, What Mountains).

IN MAY 1886, the McGavin family left for a four-month trip to Europe to visit relatives in London, Old Cumnock, and Paris. Such an extended vacation might suggest that Walter had become a valued employee at the bank after five years of service. In any event, he was no longer a clerk. The *San Francisco City Directory* in 1886 listed his position as "teller."

The Scottish McGavin clan must have been thrilled to meet Kate for the first time and to celebrate Walter's return after an absence of six years. His father had died, but his mother, Helen, lived in town with her two youngest daughters and their families. So there would have been a slew of cousins to shepherd three-and-a-half-year-old Drummond about the village of Cumnock.

Walter would have shown Kate around Green Mill and the River Lugar where he spent his youth. At crowded family gatherings, we can imagine Kate listening intently, trying to decipher the thick Scottish brogue as Walter's relatives swapped family gossip.

When Walter and Kate arrived in Paris, they would have been proud to show off Drummond to his namesake, Dr. MacGavin. Kate's sister, Emilia, still lived with Dr. MacGavin in his new apartment at 4 Rue St. Philippe du Roule in the Eighth Arrondissement. A lifelong spinster, Emilia Hinshelwood would be known to future generations as "Little Auntie."

NOW IN HIS MID-SIXTIES, Dr. MacGavin was a prominent figure in the Parisian medical community. So it was logical that *Galignani's Messenger*, the city's leading English-language newspaper, had turned to him two years earlier for advice after an outbreak of cholera. "Dr. MacGavin stands in the front rank of the medical profession," boasted the newspaper, "and his views will be received as entitled to the highest respect and confidence." Sadly, his advice on how to avoid cholera reflected old-fashioned and even dangerous thinking.

By 1884 medical research had definitively linked cholera to contaminated water.

Walter and Kate McGavin with son Drummond, age three, in Paris, 1886.

Yet Dr. MacGavin suggested that Parisians could avoid cholera by following a few lifestyle rules. "Be moderate in eating and drinking, and let both food and drink be simple and of the best quality, avoid all damaged articles of diet, unripe or un-wholesome fruits; above all keep a cheerful mind and banish fear, face your daily duties bravely, as if no such disease existed, and I promise you that you will not easily fall a victim either to cholera or any other contagious or infectious disease."

A week later the *British Medical Journal* blasted Dr. MacGavin for ignoring "the whole scientific and social history of the question...Neither a good heart nor a cheerful mind will avail against cholera-poisoning, if the unfortunate victim happens to imbibe it, either in food or in water." The real problem was "the foul water-supply and imperfect drainage of Paris houses…We hope that English science and English courage have not yet fallen so low, but that some of the English physicians in Paris may find courage to tell the Parisians the truth."

PERHAPS DR. MacGAVIN was esteemed more for his social prowess than for his medical knowledge. But one American who did value his healing skills was a twenty-eight-year-old expat named John Singer Sargent. Whatever his illness and whatever Dr. MacGavin's cure, Sargent was so pleased that he painted his portrait in 1884, inscribing across the top, "To my friend Dr. MacGavin, John S. Sargent."

In his waist-high portrait, Dr. MacGavin appears as a white-haired, whiskered gentleman with arms folded, dressed in a black coat with a red Legion of Honor ribbon in his buttonhole. Under his bald pate, his eyes look straight ahead over a long nose. He wears an engaging expression, as though he might be listening before thoughtfully responding to a question. Two years later, this portrait hung on the wall of Dr. MacGavin's apartment when the San Francisco McGavins visited.

Now with their young son, Walter and Kate must have revisited scenes from their Paris romance six years earlier—walking the tree-lined boulevards, drinking coffee at sidewalk cafés, and playing with Drummond in city parks. Both Walter and Kate would always feel strongly attached to their British and French roots, and neither would ever become a naturalized American citizen. Nevertheless, they loved San Francisco and must have been glad to arrive back home in September 1886.

TENNIS WAS Walter's passion, and, in family lore, he was one of the founders of the California Tennis Club in San Francisco. At the time, tennis was called "lawn tennis," a relatively new sport in California, and Walter's obituary would later recognize him as the "father of lawn tennis on the Pacific Coast." Beyond physical fitness, tennis would have offered Walter the opportunity to meet new friends and make social connections, important for a young banker on the rise.

Six months after his arrival in the city, Walter's name first appeared in the *San Francisco Chronicle* in July 1880 when he finished second in the San Francisco Lawn Tennis Club tournament. Although he lost in the final, the reporter was impressed. "This tie [match] eliciting some very fine playing on both sides drew frequent rounds of applause from the spectators. Mr. McGavin's service and returns were very sure."

In September 1887, the *San Francisco Chronicle* published a long article extolling the virtues of the sport under the headline "Why Lawn Tennis is Very Fashionable—No Broad-Chested Athletes or Tasteless Politicians Wanted." Tennis was a game for high society. "It is a matter of notoriety that within the past four years the taste for athletics has increased wonderfully among the better classes of men." At a gala to celebrate the game of tennis, Walter played the "Highland bagpipes" in a trio with a mandolin and a lute as part of the musical offering. (If only we had a recording of that mashup.)

The *Chronicle* praised thirty-six-year-old Walter in 1889 as "the only old-timer whose game has kept up to the standard, and there are but few players on the coast who can beat him." A year later, the newspaper again lauded his skill: "Some of the alleged judges of tennis are trying to make it appear that McGavin is a back number and is about to retire from the tennis arena. The fact is, McGavin is far superior to most of the players...Mac is still in it." (Walter's son, Drummond, would also become an excellent tennis player and win the Pacific Coast Championship in 1904.)

Dr. John Drummond MacGavin,
John Singer Sargent, 1884.

KATE AND HER CHILDREN, Drummond and Emilia, made two more trips to Europe in 1890 and 1893, spending, respectively, seven and five months abroad. Possibly one reason for the length of each trip was to immerse Drummond in the French language at a young age. In 1890 he was seven and in 1893 ten, good ages for learning a foreign tongue, and he did become fluent in French for the rest of his life. Emilia at ages two and five did not retain any fluency.

On their first European trip in 1890, Kate left San Francisco

Emilia "Dolly" MacGavin, age five, in Paris, 1893. Sargent's painting of
Dr. MacGavin hangs on the wall. Her mother wrote, "This picture gives a
mistaken impression of Dolly—who has ever seen her so quiet?"

in March and returned home in October. She might have visited Cumnock in Scotland, although we do not have any evidence of it. She must have spent most of her time in Paris with her sister, Emilia, and their beloved Dr. MacGavin. She had no way of knowing it, but this would be the last time she would be together with her benefactor.

She sailed for home from Le Havre in first class on *La Champagne*, owned by the Companie Générale Transatlantique, which touted its "Fast Steamers from Paris to New York in 8 Days." Interestingly, the passenger list recorded Kate and her two children all as British citizens, even though Drummond and Emilia had been born in the United States. She arrived in New York on October 25, passed through Chicago on October 27, and landed in San Francisco probably on October 30.

Three years later, Kate must have received an urgent telegram from her sister that Dr. MacGavin was gravely ill. She made hurried travel arrangements to be with him in Paris, but did not arrive in time. Unfortunately, he had died on April 19, 1893, the day after she and her children had left San Francisco by train.

NOTING HIS DEATH, *Galignani's Messenger* wrote that "one of the oldest and most honored members of the British colony in Paris died of pneumonia yesterday in his seventy-second year. Dr. MacGavin will be regretted by a wide circle of friends, as well as by numbers of his poorer fellow countrymen resident in this city, among whom his unostentatious kindness was proverbial."

Dr. MacGavin's memorial service was held at the Anglican Church on the Rue d'Aguesseau, where 400 people heard the Reverend H. E. Noyes deliver the eulogy: "We mourn one today whose kindness and skill have brightened many a home and eased many a shoulder—one whose presence inspired confidence, and whose cheery words ever gave encouragement and hope. There is one class amongst us who will more than miss his kind offices—the struggling and [the] poor, both those who had been reduced in circumstances and the working class. These ever found in Dr. MacGavin a true and generous friend. He would place his skill at their service without fee or reward, and often providing the necessary medicines. All he has done in this way cannot be told."

When Kate arrived in Paris a few weeks after the service, we can imagine that she and her sister fell into each other's arms and wept at the loss of their beloved guardian. The good doctor who had been a father figure to them all their lives was gone, and the two sisters, the last of the Hinshelwood family in Paris, were alone.

Kate and her children remained in Paris for four months until early fall, when she booked passage back across the Atlantic, this time joined by her sister Emilia, probably making her first trip to America. Their ship, *La Gascogne*, arrived in New York on October 8, and less than a week later Walter would have held them in his arms again for a joyous and bittersweet family reunion.

WE NOW TURN to the story of my four grandparents, the next generation of our family tale. We begin in Dawson City, Yukon Territory, with a dire warning.

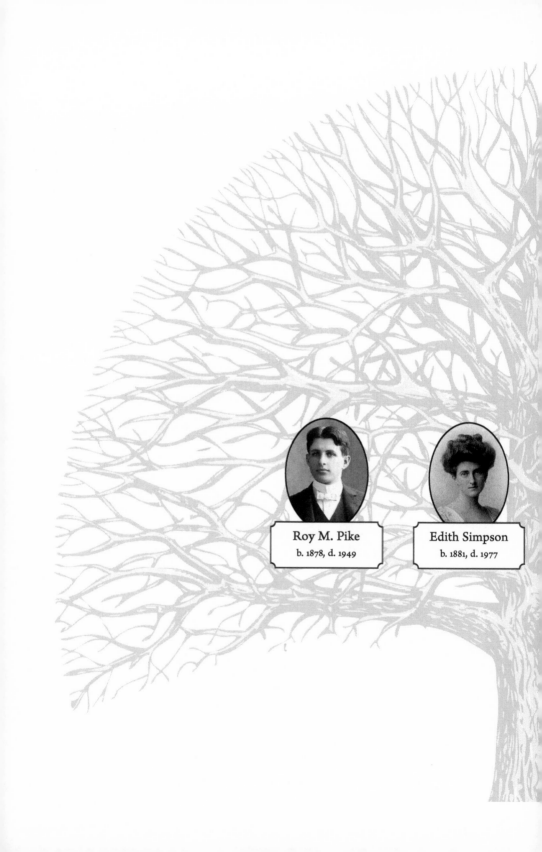

Roy M. Pike
b. 1878, d. 1949

Edith Simpson
b. 1881, d. 1977

Part Two

Grandparents

Alan P. Cline
b. 1885, d. 1955

Emilia H. "Dolly"
MacGavin*
b. 1888, d. 1968

* *Dolly spelled her last name*
"MacGavin," not "McGavin."

CHAPTER 11

A Go-Getter
Seeks His Fortune

Roy, 1892–1909

"GO! GO! FLEE FOR YOUR LIVES!" shouted Captain J. E. Hansen, assistant superintendent of the Alaska Commercial Company, as he ran up and down Front Street in Dawson City on October 1, 1897. The North West Mounted Police warned, "For those who have not laid in a winter's supply [of food], to remain here any longer is to court death from starvation, or at least a certainty of sickness from scurvy and other troubles."

The population of Dawson City, located at the junction of the Yukon and Klondike Rivers, had exploded from a few dozen prospectors to a town of thousands after gold was struck nearby in August 1896. Within a year prospectors had mined millions of dollars of gold ore. Unimaginable fortunes flowed into the pockets of the first to stake claims.

Too many gold rushers now threatened to exhaust the town's food supplies, and ice was already running in the Yukon River. When the river froze solid, Dawson would be cut off from the outside world for six months, and resupply would be impossible. The last chance to escape would be on the paddle wheeler *Bella*, scheduled to depart that afternoon at four o'clock.

One person who would not starve that winter was nineteen-year-old Roy Pike, my grandfather, a clerk in the Alaska Commercial store at Forty Mile, located forty-eight miles downriver from Dawson. A year earlier, Forty Mile was described by a traveler as "a collection of eighty or ninety dismal-looking log huts on a mud-bank … Huge placards with the words 'Hotel,' 'Saloon,' and even 'Opera House' (the latter a dive of the lowest description) adorn some of the larger dwellings where, though bread is often lacking, whiskey is never scarce."

ROY PIKE WAS NOT a Klondike gold rusher. He had landed in Forty Mile by historical accident. The decade of the 1890s had been hard on Roy and his siblings, starting with the death of their mother, Mary, Jacob's wife, on April 17, 1892, in San Francisco. She had died at age fifty after having borne nine children, six of whom survived her.

Her youngest child, Percy, remembered that their mother suffered greatly in her final months, writing in his memoir, "On her death bed, older brother Charles promised Mother he would take care of Roy (then fourteen), and sister Laura promised she would take care of me (then ten years of age), and Mother, relieved, turned over and died. Home was broken up and Father stored the furniture."

"With all the bad luck I had through life," her husband, Jacob, wrote in his memoir, "that was the hardest blow on me … Truly there was the best wife that ever lived; it was worth more than one horse to find her! I chided myself so often that I did not listen to her counsel. If I had, I would have been worth over a million today. I did what I thought was best, but could not see so far ahead as she."

When Roy and Percy moved into their older siblings' households, they ascended several rungs on the social ladder. Both Charles Pike and Laura Fuller, who was married to William Parmer Fuller, were listed in the *San Francisco Blue Book* of socially prominent families. "It is well to know … those who are most conspicuous … by virtue of their social standing," noted the *Blue Book*, "which is to some extent a guarantee of respectability and merit. Society has its forces, equal or superior to the powers of mind or money. Success in life as often depends on social standing as on money or intellectual ability."

Laura's husband owned W. P. Fuller & Company, a large paint manufacturer headquartered in San Francisco. Percy immediately noticed differences in the Fuller household. "They were a wealthy family. Sister had a maid, nurse for son, and Chinese cook. I was compelled to bathe twice a week. Wednesday and Saturday, where formerly I had known only the Saturday-night bath time. Also was introduced to the toothbrush for the first time and compelled to use. Things were getting tough and how I kicked at the new regulations."

Roy's older brother, Charles Pike, was seventeen years his senior, married and the father of two young boys. Roy was a teenager now and without parental supervision—which might explain why he was sent away in the fall of 1893 to the Mount Tamalpais Military Academy in San Rafael, a boarding school just north of San Francisco.

NOTHING IN HIS LIFE would suggest any affinity between Roy and military discipline. He had grown up in the heart of San Francisco, one of the most cosmopolitan cities in the world. He was ten years old in 1888 when his family lost their home and moved to a Market Street loft opposite the luxurious Palace Hotel. Along with his two older brothers—Willis, then sixteen, and Tom, fourteen—Roy had freely roamed the city's streets and observed the highs and lows of urban life.

At the Mount Tamalpais Military Academy, discipline reigned supreme. "The purpose of the military training," explained the school brochure, "is not necessarily to make soldiers or to cultivate a desire for army life, but to form habits of punctuality, obedience and order, and at the same time to develop an erect and manly figure and carriage." A contemporary observer praised the school for its "daily contact and friendly association with men and women of education and refinement, and the small tables in the dining room, with a master or officer at each table to correct carelessness in behavior at meals."

Reveille sounded every morning at 6:40. Students attended chapel at 8:45. Every afternoon, students drilled on the parade grounds at 3:10. for fifty minutes. At night, taps signaled lights out at 9:45. Students were required to wear a uniform at all times while in attendance at school. Visits home were restricted to one day a month because, as the school catalog noted, "The weekly taste of unrestricted freedom at home makes the necessary restraints of school life more irksome and distasteful, and the student becomes discontented and restless."

Roy's first day of class was Tuesday, August 15, 1893. Four days later he placed two calls to his brother Charles lasting two minutes at a cost of $0.30 each ($8.43 in 2017 dollars). We might guess that the calls were an urgent plea to remove him from the school. Had he quickly found the regimentation too "irksome and distasteful"? Aside from these two calls and a family photograph of Roy in his military tunic, there is no record of the length of his attendance at the school. We might guess that he stayed less than a year.

AFTER LEAVING SCHOOL, Roy worked as a clerk for the next three years at two related lumber companies in San Francisco, Excelsior Redwood Company and C. A. Hooper & Company. In 1897 he found a job as a clerk at the Alaska Commercial Company, which operated a chain of stores in Alaska and Yukon Territory supplying natives, prospectors, and trappers.

On June 6, 1897, Roy boarded the steamship *Excelsior* for its annual trip to resupply the company's far-flung stores. News of the Klondike Strike had not yet percolated south. The ship's 2,850-mile passage north took it through the Aleutian Islands and the Bering Sea to St. Michael, Alaska, near the mouth of the Yukon River.

To the astonishment of the *Excelsior*'s crew, the shoreline of St. Michael Bay was crowded with dozens of newly rich gold miners waiting for transportation back to the continental United States. "There was gold in suitcases and leather grips," wrote historian Pierre Berton, "gold in boxes and packing-cases, gold in belts and pokes of caribou hide, gold in jam jars, medicine bottles, and tomato cans, and gold in blankets held by straps and cord, so heavy it took two men to hoist each one aboard." Most had been paupers only months earlier.

"Some had not seen civilization for years. Now each was worth a fortune. One, imprisoned in the Yukon for two years and reduced to a diet of half-raw salmon... was heading for civilization with thirty-five thousand dollars. Another had left Seattle the previous spring, impoverished and desperate, and now was worth more than one hundred thousand." (about $1 million and almost $3 million, respectively, in 2017 dollars.)

When the *Excelsior* arrived back in San Francisco Bay on July 14, the sight of these miners walking down the gangplank with bags of gold electrified the nation. By the end of the summer, tens of thousands of men (and some women) would be rushing to the Klondike.

ROY SPENT his summer on St. Michael Bay operating a gasoline-powered launch, ferrying passengers and cargo to and from steamships anchored offshore. He earned $40 a month ($1,220 in 2017 dollars). Growing frustrated by his meager pay, he submitted his resignation, but was persuaded to return by a manager who "told me I was hardly doing the best thing for myself & offered to send me to 40 M [Forty Mile], which I was very glad to accept."

Soon after, Roy boarded a paddle wheeler for the 1,700-mile journey up the Yukon River to Forty Mile. His salary would be raised to $65 a month. Roy's general store was a two-story log structure about thirty by sixty feet. It offered a wide variety of products, including food (beans, bacon, canned vegetables, dried fruits), mining gear (shovels, picks, pick handles, nails, rubber boots), and personal items (arctic socks, cigarettes, chewing tobacco).

Tom and Roy Pike, Dawson City, Yukon Territory, winter of 1898–1899.

ROY ARRIVED at Forty Mile in September 1897. A month later, the *Bella*, carrying the refugees fleeing Dawson, was forced to stop at Forty Mile for repairs. Sam Dunham, a passenger on the *Bella*, wrote, "The volume of ice increased to such a degree that it was absolutely necessary, in order to escape destruction, to make a landing, preferably at the mouth of the Fortymile River." (The river name was spelled differently than the town name.) Roy took a picture of the stern wheeler moored off a mudflat opposite the Alaska Commercial Company warehouse.

During the *Bella's* forced layover at Forty Mile, Roy met Dunham and a fellow passenger, Joaquin Miller, both literary witnesses to the hardships suffered by Yukon gold rushers. They gave young Roy a handwritten copy of Miller's poem "Comrades of the Klondike," which began:

> Have you, too, banged at the Chilkoot,
> That storm-locked gate to the golden door?
> Those thunder-built steeps have words built to suit,
> And whether you prayed or whether you swore,
> 'Twere one, where it seemed that an oath were a prayer,—
> Seemed that God couldn't care,
> Seemed that God wasn't there.

On November 18, 1897, the Yukon froze solid. Movement of people and goods ceased for the next six months—except by dogsled. To get drinking water, residents had to cut through four or five feet of ice to the water below. On November 29, the temperature dipped to sixty-seven degrees below zero. "Trees cracked like pistol shots with the freezing and expanding sap," wrote Berton. "Cooked beans turned hard as pebbles, and the touch of metal tore the skin from naked fingers." On Christmas Day there were four hours of weak daylight at Forty Mile with the sun rising at 11:30 a.m. and setting at 3:30 p.m.

JUST BEFORE the spring thaw in April 1898, Roy sent a plaintive letter to his boss, J. E. Hansen, in Dawson. "I deem my whole Forty Mile experience a most profitable one—mostly as I feel that I now have a grasp of what the details of an A. C. Co. [Alaska Commercial Company] post should be. I think I understand fully how the system, the books & cash, should be handled. I have been enabled to meet many, from whom I have learned much—both regards trading with In-

Roy Pike, about 1900.

dians & dealing with men of the many different classes we meet. And moreover, I have seen a good deal of the country and have learned to know good from bad traveling. And to know pretty much what one should and what one should not do in the Yukon in winter."

There were just two problems. He wanted to work in Dawson City, and he wanted a raise. The letter continued, "I felt that I should be paid $100.00 from Jan 1st, '98 & expect $125.00 from June 1st. I do not think 'tis too much at all to ask—& that if my services are worth much to the company—they at least are worth that. I do not wish to make any particular point of this now—& if a question is raised, I do not care to ask for the two changes in salary—but I surely expect to be paid $125 from June 1st."

WE DO NOT KNOW if Hansen replied to Roy's letter. The Alaska Commercial Company had far larger concerns that spring of 1898. During the previous winter, tens of thousands of stampeders had climbed the Chilkoot Pass and were poised to descend upon the town. When the ice broke in the first week of May, an armada of makeshift craft headed downriver, bringing a tsunami of hopeful prospectors, including an unknown writer named Jack London.

The new arrivals, *cheechakos* in the local vernacular, had virtually no chance of staking successful claims—now almost two years after the original Klondike Strike. Veteran miners, known as *sourdoughs*, had already scoured every possible river and stream in the region.

Jack London stayed less than a month before leaving "dreary, desolate Dawson, built in a swamp, flooded to the second story, populated by dogs, mosquitoes, and gold-seekers." The town was filled with all-night saloons, dancehalls, and gambling dens. But these required money to enjoy, and London had none.

On June 8, he and two friends set out in a small boat for the 1,750-mile trip downriver to St. Michael, passing Forty Mile on their second day. Although London did not stop, he memorialized the name of the town in one of his short stories, "The Men of Forty-Mile," in which the hero prevents a duel between two miners by threatening to hang the man not shot. London fled the Klondike dead broke, but rich in stories.

ROY SURVIVED another year in the Yukon. His brother, Tom, had joined him in May 1898, perhaps after climbing the Chilkoot Pass. The two brothers were finally able to move to Dawson in December where they operated the Klondike Steam Laundry that winter, which explains why one photograph of their one-room cabin showed the two brothers formally dressed with starched collars.

In the spring of 1899, they advertised themselves as "Pike Bros., Customs Brokers & General Transportation Agents." But none of their money-making schemes paid off, and in the fall of 1899, Roy retraced his route down the Yukon River to St. Michael where he boarded an ocean steamer home.

Roy did not return to San Francisco empty-handed. His two years in the Klondike had taught him a valuable social skill—how to spin a great yarn without necessarily adhering to all the facts. In the words of Jack London, "The Alaskan gold hunter is proverbial not so much for his unveracity, as for his inability to tell the precise truth. In a country of exaggerations, he likewise is prone to hyperbolic descriptions of things actual."

RETURNING FROM the Klondike in 1899, Roy found that his sister, Laura Fuller, had moved into the Palace Hotel as a permanent resident, occupying a large suite on the sixth floor. She and Roy shared a special bond of affection, and we can imagine that they spent many days together at "America's first luxury hotel." The seven-story, 800-room building dominated the skyline as the city's tallest. Five hydraulic elevators with mirror-faced walls whisked passengers to the upper floors. Its hotel dining room was 150 feet long, the largest in the West and the scene of numerous civic events.

In 1903 when Laura moved to a large estate in San Mateo, Roy followed. His brother, Percy, wrote in his memoir, "Roy had come into the household and was a great joy to Laura. He had an excellent singing voice and the ability to bring into the house nice social people." With his natural charm and new social pedigree, Roy reinvented himself as a leading man about town and a well-known business executive.

VAULTING TO THE TOP of the social pyramid, he was a guest at a New Year's Eve party hosted by M. H. de Young, publisher of the *San Francisco Chronicle* on December 31, 1903. "An exceedingly clever group of young society people," wrote de Young's own newspaper, "delighted the merry company bidden last evening to the residence of Mr. and Mrs. de Young on California Street...The guests comprised the companions of the young ladies of the household and a few married friends of the host and hostess, about 150 in all."

As part of the entertainment, Roy appeared in a play, *My Colorado Belle*, in the de Young's home theater. "A semi-musical absurdity in two acts, the play was the development of an idea conceived by Mrs. de Young while in New York recently. She thought her friends would enjoy hearing the latest popular music that all the Eastern people were humming." Playing the role of Jack Pott, "Roy Pike had plenty to do singing and dancing, but he will be remembered longest for the work he did in his duet, 'By the Sycamore Tree' with Miss Pearl Landers, who has a particularly sweet voice and naïve manner."

A week later, Roy's name again appeared in the *Chronicle* as a guest of the de Youngs at the Grand Opera House for a concert by Adina Patti, "the unquestioned mistress of her art who heard a storm of 'Bravas!' that climaxed in a burst of thousand-throated cheering...The house was, perhaps, the greatest and the most truly representative that has ever gathered here for a concert...including practically all the people prominent in society."

Under the headline, "A Magnificent Spectacle of Fashionably Dressed People," Roy's presence was documented as: "Left Box 1: Mr. and Mrs. M. H. de Young, Miss Constance de Young, Miss Mamie Deane, Roy Pike, William H. Smith, Jr." Two weeks later, Roy was again with the family, as "Mr. and Mrs. de Young formally introduced their second daughter, Miss Constance de Young, at a reception... at their California-street residence." He appeared as one of sixty dinner guests "seated at four tables set in the Chinese room."

Four years earlier, Roy had spent two winters with a rough cast of characters in the Klondike. Now he mingled with San Francisco's upper crust. We can guess that he captivated his audiences with colorful and dramatic tales of the Klondike—not too overburdened with facts.

NOTHING EPITOMIZED Roy's truth-spinning better than his tale of rescuing Enrico Caruso, the world famous tenor, on the day of the San Francisco Earthquake and Fire, April 18, 1906. The night before, Caruso had sung in *Carmen* at the Grand Opera House to rapturous applause.

In family lore, Roy recalled that he was jolted awake in his bed at the Palace Hotel. That he quickly realized, "This city is going to burn!" That he rushed to the

St. Francis Hotel where members of the opera troupe stayed. That he "organized trunks to get packed, closed, and man-handled down to the streets" because "the elevator shafts had been so twisted that the elevators could not be used."

That he "finally commandeered a dray for trunks and carriages for the people, including one for Caruso." That the cast went to the home of Asa Simpson at 2200 Pacific Avenue. (Roy had met the Simpson family a year earlier.) That "Caruso was absolutely terrified... [and] spent the day pacing up and down the living room, speaking to no one, trying to vocalize, in fear that he would lose his voice. Stroking his throat, he would, in a low voice, do his mi-mi-mi-me-me-me arpeggios."

What a wonderful blend of fact, fiction, and the unknowable. Other observers documented a different reality that day. Alfred Hertz, Caruso's conductor, saw him half-crazed in the lobby of the Palace Hotel, not the St. Francis, shortly after the quake. "Caruso... embraced me hysterically and, crying like a child, repeatedly insisted we were doomed." The singer did make his way to the relative safety of Union Square, a city park adjacent to the St. Francis Hotel, with a towel wrapped around his throat to preserve his voice.

Caruso's official biographer quoted a fellow singer, Antonio Scotti, who explained how he personally rescued Caruso. "I went looking for some sort of conveyance and found a wagon. I asked the driver how much he wanted to take some trunks and friends to the home of Arthur Bachman, whom Caruso and I knew. He insisted on being paid three hundred dollars (about $8,000 in 2017 dollars), and I agreed. Anything, I thought, to get to some place of safety... That night Caruso could not be induced to occupy a room in the house; he slept under a tree in the Bachman yard." The Bachmans lived at 2409 Scott Street, five blocks west of the Simpson home.

Edith Simpson, Roy's future wife, later blended these stories together and confirmed Caruso's presence, at least briefly, in her family's home. "This is the year 1906. The New York Opera Company is here and is playing *Carmen* complete with Caruso... Laura Fuller... has come up from her home in San Mateo, and both she and her brother [Roy] are at the Palace Hotel for the night... Roy was a real theater bug and knew a girl named Bessie Abbott [who sang the role of Micaela] ... He brought Bessie out to the Simpson house. It was looking for her that brought Caruso out to us later." The truth is buried somewhere in these divergent memories of that catastrophic day.

WITH HIS ENTERTAINING STORIES, Roy was a prized guest at dinner parties. "Possessed of a fine mind, an excellent singing voice, and a uniquely attractive manner," his nephew, Tom Pike, later wrote, "Roy was a popular and active club man and a leading social figure who was much in demand by San Francisco hostesses, due to his great charm." Roy possessed a "driving motivation to succeed in business and get to the top... His commanding personality, and his access to people of prominence and influence enabled him to secure the confidence and financial backing of many of the leaders of the California banking and business community."

By 1909, Roy's prominence was such that his name appeared in a business-page headline, "Pike Joins Pioneer Company." Beneath his picture, the *San Francisco Call* wrote, "Roy Pike, well known in financial and club circles, has become identified with the Pioneer Automobile Company." Pioneer represented the Thomas Flyer, which had won the prestigious New York to Paris Automobile Race the year before. The four-cylinder, sixty-horsepower car had been driven from New York to San Francisco (then across the Pacific by steamship) and from Vladivostok, Russia, to Paris, a total of 13,000 miles, in 169 days.

"In both business and social circles," the *San Francisco Chronicle* echoed, "Pike is one of the most widely known young men of this city... Pike will take hold of his new work with the experience which comes from handling large business enterprises." Magically, Roy's clerkship in the Klondike had morphed into this extraordinary statement: "Beginning his business career while still in his teens, Pike was interested in the *control of the telephone and steamship lines of the Upper Yukon*" (emphasis added). What a fantastical tale. We can picture Roy's audience listening to him in rapt attention and willingly suspending their disbelief, as he spun his tall tales about the frozen north.

A YEAR after joining Pioneer, Roy would marry Edith Simpson and drive a Thomas Flyer on their honeymoon. Unlike him, she was born into a life of wealth and privilege. We begin her story in New York City where she has been sent to an exclusive finishing school.

CHAPTER 12

A Western Princess

Edith, 1896–1919

TWENTY-EIGHT GIRLS, including fifteen-year-old Edith Simpson, my grand-mother, set out for their morning walk up Fifth Avenue to Central Park in New York City in September 1896. This brisk, forty-minute exercise for boarders at Miss Spence's School was a daily ritual before classes began at 9:00 a.m. Instructed to look straight ahead, to ignore passing school groups, and not to step out of line, they marched two by two, chaperoned by a teacher in front and one at the rear.

"In Central Park," one classmate recalled, "we were allowed to wander about a trifle, and then back in line down Fifth Avenue, directly to 6 West 48th [Street] for the opening of school. Of course, we all wore long skirts below the ankle. Our hair was dressed in high pompadours and kept in place by 'rats,' a pad used to puff out hair, and our heads were held very high with the boned collars we all loved. Our hats were quite complicated. We had definite walking partners, and no one really minded the parade, though there were complaints about our hours for walking, not being the chic time to be on the avenue."

Another student, Lucy James, who would become Edith's lifelong friend, re-membered their preparations for inclement weather. "We black our own stout calfskin boots. Inside the black boots we wear black merino stockings; outside, at the least suspicion of moisture, capable rubbers, and for snow, galoshes. Our skirts are down to a nice dampish length around the ankles. Our coats have full-weight mutton-leg sleeves. Our hats cling precariously to our topknots as we head into the north wind, and the line bends to it like the swaying of young trees."

Edith later explained why she was sent east to a finishing school. "Mother made up her mind that I was too Western or something. She took me to New York and, on the advice of Mrs. Whitelaw Reid, put me in Miss Spence's School where I stayed for four years without coming back [to San Francisco]. Mother always came for the summer vacations." Twenty-five years earlier, Mrs. Whitelaw Reid had been twelve-year-old Elisabeth Mills, Sophie's tutee, before Sophie's marriage to Asa Simpson. Now Elisabeth was the wife of Whitelaw Reid, the prominent editor of the *New York Tribune* and future ambassador to Great Britain.

THE SCHOOL BUILDING was a "typical brownstone," thirty feet wide and four stories tall over a full basement. "High ceilings, tall windows, and rooms opening one into another created a feeling of space in these narrow structures," according to a school history. "One climbed the high front stoop to enter the school. Miss Spence's office was straight ahead, located in what had been the butler's pantry. The front parlor, with connecting doors that opened into the next room, became the assembly room."

Chemistry was taught in the basement, while the top floor with high ceilings and good lighting housed art classes. "Every square foot was used. Larger rooms often contained three or four different classes reciting aloud at the same time. 'This,' Miss Spence claimed, 'taught concentration'...The girls studied a broad scope of literature, Greek and Roman mythology, English, French, American history, botany, chemistry, psychology, and art history. Much memorization and recitation facilitated the learning process."

Tuition and board totaled $900 per year ($27,100 in 2017 dollars). Miss Spence promised parents that class size would not exceed eight students. Edith and her fellow boarders lived at 43 West Forty-Eighth Street. "Our room is the usual back bedroom of an ordinary brownstone-front, with a stoop," Lucy James wrote. "In it, running down the east wall, head to foot, are two narrow iron beds; on the west wall, against the fireplace, a third bed. There are also three narrow chests of drawers with looking glasses...three wardrobes; three chairs, and a stationary wash-hand-stand. Every girl in the house washes her hair there. Supplementing the famous wash basin, we have one bath night a week."

DURING HER SUMMER vacations, Edith traveled extensively with her mother. Once to New England and Canada; once to Racine, Wisconsin, Sophie's home-town, to visit her sister; and once to Europe with Edith's brother, Edgar. After completing her senior year at Miss Spence's, Edith received her diploma in May 1900 along with twenty-six of her classmates. "You ought to have seen me leading in one line of graduates," she wrote to her brother, Edgar, "in a trailing white gown four yards long, before all the big bugs in New York who came to witness [the ceremony]."

Addressing the graduates as "My dear girls," Clara Spence challenged them "to awaken and to keep ever alert the faculty of wonder in the human soul... Are you well started on the right path towards a formed character, towards a noble, gracious womanhood? Do you possess this 'wonder,' this reverence, and interest to know more and more of the deep and beautiful things in the world and in life and in books?"

AFTER A FOUR-YEAR absence, Edith returned to San Francisco and the family's new home at 2200 Pacific Avenue at the northwest corner of Pacific and Buchanan. "Now began a delightful period of living at 2200, doing all the usual things. I remember mostly dancing. I must have danced at least around the world." Edith made her debut on December 7, 1900, at the Friday Night Cotillion.

"To the debutantes I'm sure it must have seemed like a beautiful dream come true," wrote Lady Teazle, the *Chronicle's* society columnist. "The girls all had pretty new frocks for the occasion, and the debutantes, without exception, were arrayed in white, some with a touch of gold trimming, to relieve the dead whiteness of the costume... it was hard to pick out the prettiest. There were three who seemed to win the most admiration, deservedly, I think. They were Edith Simpson, who was exquisite in white and gold, Marjory Gibbons, and Frances Allen."

IN THE SUMMER OF 1901, Edith and her mother traveled to Europe again. "We stayed at Brown's Hotel in London. We were at Canterbury Cathedral when news reached us of McKinley's death [on September 14]. We went by ship to Spain and Gibraltar where we saw the famous monkeys. In Tangiers we rode donkeys through narrow, walled streets to the market place. We crossed the Mediterranean to Amalfi, where mother got very sick. I always thought she never got wholly over it. We did the Italian mountain towns by diligence and visited the Blue Grotto in Capri."

Like any twenty-year-old traveling with her mother (this would be their fifth summer together), Edith longed for the absence of parental supervision. Writing

Graduating class at Miss Spence's School, New York City, 1900.

Edith is in the middle row, third from the right.

to her brother, Edgar, she described her family as "infernally queer and different," commenting that "Sophie, you know, has a sense of humor like a brick wall." Edith's fantasy was to return to Europe—unchaperoned—with Edgar. "When you get back from the sea, and before you get nailed down too tightly in the office [of Simpson Lumber], you and I together and alone are to come over here for a half year or so and bum."

She also fantasized that she might get a job, baring her soul in a fit of youthful angst. "Dinners, dances, and all the rest of the awful lot. How I would rather have stayed in Rome and studied...I surely was not meant to be a society girl, but because I have a straight nose and a figure not to be despised, that seems to be my lot in life...Ed, I'm thinking of taking up a career. Fact I am. I am so tired of enjoying myself. I think I shall take up the pastime of earning my living. Something ladylike, you know—like writing short stories for *Munsey's Magazine* or designing monograms for cigarettes."

EDITH PLOTTED her next adventure with two old Spence classmates—Lucy James and Helen Christian. "[We] decided that Japan was quite near, and we persuaded Mr. James [Lucy's father, Thomas] that we needed him to chaperone us." Thomas James's cousin, Edwin Dun, had been the American Minister to Japan and still lived there. The *San Francisco Chronicle* duly noted that "Miss Edith Simpson, a well-known member of society" sailed for Japan on April 23, 1903.

"We landed at Yokohama and stayed in the Grand Hotel for a long time. Went everywhere by rickshaw and did lots of shopping in funny little streets...We three girls took Mr. James' 'man' [his valet] and made the trip walking around the foot of Fuji. Took three days. We stopped at night in Japanese inns. We all took lots of similar trips into the country. We took a train one night, and I think that was the night we saw cormorant fishing by torchlight."

At lunch one day at the Grand Hotel, Edwin Dun introduced the party to Mr. F. M. Huntington Wilson, the Chargé d'Affaires (temporary ambassador) at the American legation. Sparks flew immediately between the young diplomat and Lucy. "I had a delightful talk with Lucy James," Wilson later recalled, "and discovered at once that, besides beauty, she had a high order of intelligence, a sense of humor, as well as excellent education and wide reading. She was very tall and slender, with a fine figure, big dark eyes, well-cut features, and a complexion of *matte* white."

The benefits of Wilson's pursuit of Lucy soon became apparent, as he arranged picnics, dinners, luncheons, and sightseeing tours for all three women. Edith wrote to Edgar about an expedition to the seashore. "We have fled the wickedness and frivolity of the town and are now rusticating at the seaside in a little paper house... Truly you would laugh to see three fastidious and luxurious young women in a Japanese house sitting on the floor and arranging their hair by the aid of a hand mirror.

"Of course, we have not a single article of furniture and have lived in stocking feet for so long that I really doubt if I shall ever be able to bear the restriction of shoes again. At night they bring in a little mat and spread our bedding thereon. Then I just slide back one side of our paper house and the stars stream in just as though one were sleeping out of doors. It really is a most adorable little place. We go in the surf twice a day and live a lazy life in kimonos the rest of the time."

Leaving nothing to chance, the ardent F. M. Huntington Wilson recalled, "I took along two servants to assure good food and to augment the resources of the little Japanese hotel. We used to swim before breakfast, and at the right moment Kiku would appear coming down the cliff with a tray of hot coffee. After the midday swim, he would bring cocktails and *hors d'oeuvres* to the beach. We were all young, and these simple pleasures, reinforced by walks in the country and endless conversation, made the days pass happily."

After six months of what must have been an exceedingly pleasant sojourn in Japan, Edith and her party sailed for home, arriving in San Francisco on December 23, 1903, eight months to the day after they left. In family lore, Edith would remain a lifelong admirer of Japanese culture.

Wilson's courtship of Lucy had succeeded, and Edith attended Lucy's wedding a year later in Baltimore on April 30, 1904. The *New York Times* reported that she and Helen Christian were the two maids of honor for the bride, who "wore a gown of white satin brocade trimmed with pearls. Her tulle veil was caught with pearls." In a sentence that leaves much to the imagination, Lucy's biographer wrote, "Lucy chose bridesmaids' gowns in the style of a Van Dyke painting and made it a lilac wedding after her favorite color."

EDITH TURNED twenty-three in 1904. Her father, Asa Simpson, turned seventy-eight. She enjoyed high society; he reigned over his business with an iron hand. She loved "balls, dances, and parties"; he considered San Franciscans "too cosmopolitan [with] ... nearly all addicted to the liquor habit." But no amount of righteous living could cover up the cracks spreading across his lumber and shipping empire.

"Simpson's fleet of lumber carriers—primarily designed for use on short, coast-wise routes," observed historian Thomas Cox, "was made up of vessels too small to compete on equal terms with the giant cargo ships being used by competitors on runs to distant markets…The size of ship that could call at some of his mills was severely restricted by the nature of the harbors on which they were located.

"Much of the captain's earlier investment had been in…mills located on harbors that…railroads had not reached. He had prospered because he had succeeded in getting lumber to market more inexpensively than his rivals. He had done so because he was better equipped than they for overcoming the challenges of the sea that confronted participants in the old cargo trade." Now, railroads were lacing the West together and his competitive advantage was evaporating.

Blissfully unaware of these tectonic changes, Edith lived a carefree life. "I seemed to go fairly frequently to Coos Bay…on one of Father's ships…Once when we came out of the bar to the ocean, down the coast came Eddy and the *Chehalis* in full sail. It was so beautiful; I shall never forget it. He had her so close to shore it looked as though he was on the shore—with the gold sand of the beach, the light there on the water and the full sun shining on every scrap of sail hoisted. It was an unforgettable sight. Alas! They are no more. Steamers came in and…the Modern Age and all its improvements began."

WHEN AND WHERE Edith met her future husband, Roy Pike, we do not know. They appear together for the first time in a family photograph dated 1905. Possibly they met as members of a wedding party for a mutual friend that year. She was a bridesmaid, and he was an usher at the marriage of Florence Bailey, a San Francisco socialite, and William Mohr, a "dashing New York clubman," on March 16. "Easily the most picturesque church wedding of the late winter," raved the *San Francisco Call*.

Roy led the six ushers down the aisle, followed by Miss Grace Spreckels, the maid of honor, and her "six bridesmaids—a stunning group of smart set maids—Miss Helen de Young and Miss Bessie Wilson in pink chiffon frocks, Miss Constance de Young and Miss Freda Mohr in pale primrose, and Miss Edith Simpson and Miss Lucie King in palest green, all carrying shower bouquets of roses." These were the daughters of great family wealth.

Edith Simpson in 1909, age twenty-eight. "I surely was not
meant to be a society girl, but because I have a straight nose and
a figure not to be despised, that seems to be my lot in life."

ONE YEAR LATER, Roy would guide Caruso to the Simpson home, or so he claimed, after the earthquake on April 18, 1906. Edith recalled the chaos of that fateful day. "About five in the morning I was awakened by the most terrific shake. The walls of my room seemed to come in and out. I don't remember noise, but there must have been much as every chimney pot [the top of a chimney] in the neighborhood crashed down. I sat up in bed and just waited to see what would happen—nothing did. So we all got up and dressed hurriedly. There were no lights and there was no water.

"Out on the streets on the curbs we gathered bricks from the chimneys and built little stoves to hold a pan. Several blocks from us there was a hilly park and on the top was a dwelling that had an artesian well [in today's Lafayette Park]. They were very generous and Edgar, who was living at home, used to go there and get buckets of water for cooking. He also dug a hole in the back garden and rigged up a couple of sheets, as we could use no toilets in the house."

AFTER FIVE YEARS of courtship, twenty-nine-year-old Edith and thirty-two-year-old Roy announced their engagement in the *San Francisco Chronicle* on April 26, 1910. "The delightful news will be heralded with pleasure by the many friends of the young people in this city. Miss Simpson is the daughter of A. M. Simpson and the late Mrs. A. M. Simpson, and has been prominent in all the social gayeties since her debut [ten years earlier] ... She is an attractive and accomplished girl, and her splendid education has been augmented by extensive travel."

Sophie Simpson had died on August 9, 1909. Could her mother's death have removed a roadblock to Edith's marriage? Did Sophie prefer a different suitor for her pampered daughter? Or did Edith wonder when Roy might be ready for marriage? On his thirty-fourth birthday, she would compose a poem to her husband that hinted at the latter explanation.

The poem pointedly described Roy's wandering ways: "There are some years within your life / Which make me very sad / Some years indeed wherein I fear / That you were very bad." After living on "seal broth," foraging for "booze," and "stealing squaws," Roy tired of the "endless snows" and returned to the "café lights" of the city. "And that was the time I met you / And I made you wait, because / It took five years to tame you down."

IN A CEREMONY "marked by an entire absence of ostentation" Roy and Edith were married on July 12, 1910, at St. Luke's Episcopal Church in San Francisco. "The quietude of the affair was due to the fact of bereavement in the Simpson household, the bride's mother having died a few months ago," noted the *Chronicle*. "The bride's gown, with its long, flowing lines and general appearance of simplicity, was of exquisite design and material. The white satin robe was made with a tunic of lace, embroidered with pearls, a long veil of real lace completing the costume, the bride carrying a bridal bouquet of gardenias and lilies of the valley."

Three days after their marriage, the *Chronicle* reported that the couple was enjoying their honeymoon in Mendocino County, "having made the trip by motor to Westport, where Mr. Pike owns extensive interests." A half-century later, Roy Jr. included this vignette in his memoir: "At that time dad was running the Star Lumber Company up in Mendocino County. They went up there on their honeymoon, having rented a Thomas touring car [from his dealership]. One can only imagine what the roads were like, especially going over the mountain passes in 1910! They sent horses up ahead and lived in a rustic cottage on the coast, ably cared for by a cook and mother's personal maid!"

NOW A FULL MEMBER of the moneyed class (by marriage), Roy set out to make his own fortune. He and Edith headed east to visit his great friend, Archibald S. White of White & Company, investment bankers in New York City. White owned a dozen power companies and streetcar lines in Kentucky and Ohio and had built the first electric railway in Cincinnati. He asked Roy to manage the Cincinnati Union Depot project, which was the development of a new central station for all railroads serving the city. Roy and Edith moved to Cincinnati for a year, but the project stalled and the investors lost all their money.

Next, White appointed Roy president of the Yolo Water & Power Company, based in Woodland, California. Yolo Power planned to build a dam and canals to irrigate 200,000 acres of prime farmland in Lake County and Yolo County. But the project was hugely controversial, forcing Roy to fight a series of legal battles over water rights along Cache Creek.

At one heated community meeting, Roy and his colleagues were labeled "a band of pirates [who] should be taken out and 'stood up against the wall to be shot at sunrise.'" The judge ordered a change in venue because local leaders had created the impression that Yolo Water & Power was a "great octopus unlawfully permitted in the lake and unscrupulously reaching out with its sinuous arms to take possession of every fertile valley in the county."

Next, White asked Roy to manage the Whitehall Estates, an 18,000-acre farm, near Tracy, California, primarily devoted to grain and livestock. A sugar refinery was under construction nearby for the Spreckels Sugar Company, so sugar beets were planted on thousands of acres to supply the mill.

WHILE WORKING on these large development schemes in the Central Valley, Roy always lived in San Francisco. There he led an active club life at the Bohemian, the Family, and the Burlingame Country Clubs. Roy treasured friendships above all else, and his social connections with fellow members would frequently blossom into business relationships.

Although they remained friends, nothing in the written record or in family lore suggests that Roy made any significant money managing White's schemes. Roy did record in great detail his day-to-day business and social activities from October 1912 to July 1917. But there were no year-end operating statements or balance sheets to document his income. Typed by his secretary, the four volumes of his diaries weigh almost six pounds and total 1,198 pages covering 1,743 days.

The daily entries range from the personal: "Edith and I went to [the] de Young's to a supper for Ethel Barrymore." (Oct. 24, 1912) To finance: "Received from New York $12,500 for Whitehall and $7,500 for Yolo Land. A.S.W. [Archibald White] wires that the golden fountain will be exhausted, if we do not arrange to take care of these needs locally." (Oct. 9, 1914) To farming: "…a man has offered to trade us 12 mules for the midget caterpillar. It appears that this will be a good thing for us to do. This caterpillar cost us $1,600 and does the work on the ranch of 8 mules only" (May 3, 1916).

"[Roy] was a promoter par excellence," wrote his nephew, Tom Pike. "He was enormously ambitious and dreamed great dreams. He was an indefatigable worker, putting in long days and often nights and weekends on his many enterprises. He took little time off… Here was a man! Roy Pike was a one-of-a-kind American free enterpriser. He was highly skilled in assembling the requisite capital, people, and management skills to launch pioneering, large-scale farming, water, and power enterprises in California."

ONE MONTH BEFORE his eighty-ninth birthday, Asa Simpson died on January 10, 1915. He had worked a full week, including Saturday, went to the hospital on Sunday, and died on Monday. "He slipped into a coma," Roy wrote in his diary, "at 5 a.m. [Monday] and never regained consciousness, which of course was a wonderful way for the splendid old Spartan to die, for he was really at the helm directing all of his forces right up to Saturday evening."

Edith received a quarter share of her father's probated estate, which was valued at $1,650,000 ($41.5 million in 2017 dollars). The inventory of Asa's assets ran for twenty legal-size pages: real estate properties ($275,000), stock certificates ($860,000), promissory notes ($270,000), ships ($15,000), and household furniture ($230,000). Two of the promissory notes for $10,000 each were loans from Asa to his son-in-law, Roy ($252,000 in 2017 dollars for each note).

A year later, Jacob Pike, Roy's father, died on March 30, 1916, at age eighty-four. For the last few years of his life, Jacob had lived in San Francisco with Roy's brother, Percy. Six-year-old Tom Pike, Percy's son, remembered Jacob's "gold-headed cane, his gold watch as big as a turnip... and the gold coins he jingled in his pocket, the four-wheel [street] coaster, and all the other loving gifts Grandad Pike showered on me."

Two days before he died, Roy wrote in his diary, "My Father took a sudden change last Saturday, and it appeared last night that he would only be able to survive for a few days. He is 84 years old. He is just gradually sinking away without any pain, although his lungs are beginning to show congestion." As his legacy, Jacob left a priceless memoir of his adventures in early California.

ASA AND JACOB had lived long enough to witness the birth of Edith's two children. Her first, Roy Jr., was born on January 10, 1913. A few months later, the *Chronicle*'s Sunday society page printed a full-page line drawing of mother and son, captioned, "Mrs. Roy Pike, who is one of the charming matrons of the smart set... Before her marriage several years ago, Mrs. Pike was Miss Edith Simpson, one of the most sought-after belles in the Greenway set." (Ned Greenway organized the San Francisco Cotillion for decades.)

The birth of my father, Peter Pike, followed on December 6, 1914, although not without some controversy about his name. On the day of his birth, Roy wrote in his diary, "Went to the hospital with Mrs. Roy at 2 a.m. Archibald White Pike was born at 5:48 a.m." But Edith revolted at that name and insisted that her second

Peter, Edith's favorite dog.

son be named after her favorite dog, Peter, an Alaskan malamute, as confirmed by a picture of Peter in a family album under which she wrote, "Peter Pike 1st." As pets generally do not have middle names, neither did the human Peter Pike.

IN THE LATTER half of the 1910s, Roy and Edith were in the prime of their lives. They were rich, thanks to Edith's inheritance. They lived in an elegant home at 2200 Pacific, into which they had moved after her father's death. Their two boys were raised by a governess, and two cooks prepared the family's meals. They socialized with their wealthy friends and saw their names mentioned frequently on the society pages of the *San Francisco Chronicle*.

Roy continued his frenetic pace of business promotion and travel, which led to a memorable "telephone dinner" hosted by Edith in 1916. Roy Jr. later documented the story in family lore. "Mother and Dad planned to give a large dinner party… Shortly before the date of the party, Father was called east suddenly on business. (Those were the days when it took five days by train to New York on the *Overland Limited*.) He was sure he could get back in time for the dinner party, but at the last moment he realized he could not.

"Was the dinner cancelled? Certainly not! Father got in touch with the phone company and leased a transcontinental line for half an hour. This line had only just been installed to connect San Francisco and New York for the first time. Then he

Edith Simpson Pike, about 1920, at "William Crocker's Ball."

had twelve telephones installed at the dining room table. So mother greeted her guests, and after the dessert and coffee were served, a call was put through to New York where Father had gathered some of his club friends and for the next half hour that two-way line was filled with songs and music and amusing repartee. Must have been quite an evening!"

AS NEW YEAR'S DAY dawned on January 1, 1920, Roy and Edith must have looked forward to the decade ahead. They had it all—youth, glamor, and wealth. What they could not have known was that they would never again be as rich as they were at that moment. Indeed, their financial fate had already been sealed by Roy's acquisition of El Solyo, a large ranch in the Central Valley, which would lead to their financial ruin.

Before we trace the rise and fall of El Solyo, we will rejoin my maternal grandparents whom we last saw as teenagers living half a continent apart, Alan Cline in St. Louis and Emilia MacGavin, always called "Dolly," in San Francisco. Their daughter, Catherine, would become Peter's future wife, but not before Dolly's surprise matrimonial detour.

CHAPTER 13

The Social Whirl

Dolly, 1899–1915

THE HEADLINE on the front page of the *San Francisco Chronicle* stunned society on Tuesday, February 22, 1910.

Marry Suddenly

And Surprise

Relatives

"Dolly" MacGavin and

Douglas Fry Are United by a

Justice of the Peace

Each Is Nineteen Years

Later a Religious Ceremony

Occurs at Home of the

Bride's Parents

Emilia "Dolly" MacGavin did marry twice on the same day. That much was true. But the couple's ages were only half true. Dolly was actually twenty-one, four days shy of her twenty-second birthday; Douglas Fry was nineteen. "For a long time parental objections, predicated upon the youth of the groom, prevented any thoughts of a wedding," reported the *Chronicle*. "Yesterday, however, the young people concluded to settle the matter for themselves by marrying first and explaining afterward."

149

At the conclusion of the morning ceremony, "Their happiness was too great to be kept to themselves, so they telephoned to the home of the bride, broke the news of their marriage as gently as possible to the astonished family, and then hung up the receiver."

Later they called again and heeded the pleas of her parents to have a religious service performed at their home at 2602 California Street. So at 9:15 that night, the Rev. R. J. Renison, rector of St. Paul's Episcopal Church, performed the second ceremony of the day before "a few immediate and very intimate friends."

Walter, her father, tried to put a positive spin on the event by fudging the truth. "I will confess that the marriage was unexpected and—yes, I might say, impromptu, but there was no elopement, for there was no reason for one. Feeling that the only obstacle was one of age, we immediately asked them to come to our home and have a religious ceremony performed in addition to the civil ceremony...They have our blessings and good wishes for both prosperity and happiness."

We can imagine that Kate, her mother, was less than pleased with her new son-in-law who would tell the census enumerator later that year he was a "Conductor for a Street Railroad," in other words, a streetcar conductor. Perhaps to soften the blow, a friendly society page editor at the *San Francisco Call* claimed that, when Fry reached his majority, he would inherit great wealth. "In his own name he already owns a ranch of several thousand acres in Sonoma County." What, if any, of this was true is lost in the sands of history.

Given its rocky beginning, we should not be surprised that the "runaway marriage" did not last. Within a year the couple had separated, and Dolly filed for divorce. She claimed that she had been deserted, a charge that Fry freely admitted in open court. On July 5, 1912, a divorce was granted after all property rights were settled. Dolly was a fierce archivist of her social life, leaving behind almost two dozen albums filled with thousands of family photographs, newspaper clippings, and personal ephemera. But there was not one picture of Mr. Fry, who was quickly erased from family lore.

(*Note: Dolly and her brother, Drummond, spelled their last name "MacGavin" to honor their great-uncle, Dr. Drummond MacGavin. Their parents, Walter and Kate, spelled their last name "McGavin."*)

ONE MEMORY that Dolly did preserve in dozens of pictures was the 1906 San Francisco Earthquake and Fire. When the quake struck on April 18 at 5:12 a.m., the McGavin family must have been shaken awake just like the Simpson family nine blocks away. We can imagine Dolly's sense of shock as she and her parents, along with the cook and the maid, scrambled in semi-darkness to get dressed and check for damage (there was none).

After sunrise at 5:31 a.m., the McGavins and their neighbors likely congregated on the street to see if anybody needed help. Walter would also have been concerned about the Wells Fargo Nevada Bank Building downtown. So after his family was settled, he made his way to work, passing streams of refugees heading in the opposite direction.

"The Nevada Bank opened for business at 9 a.m. the morning of the earthquake," wrote Frances Dinkelspiel in her history of the bank. "The building was not severely damaged, and most of the tellers had reported for work, as if it were just a routine day." Now in his twenty-sixth year at the bank, Walter McGavin was the assistant cashier. His boss was Frederick Lipman, the cashier and number two man under President Isaias Hellman.

"Lipman had been jolted out of bed by the earthquake, but had taken the ferry as usual from Berkeley that morning," Dinkelspiel noted. "From the boat, [he] could see smoke rising in a number of places, but was not greatly alarmed. He planned to attend the opera that night, so he had packed his dress suit in a suitcase."

Dolly MacGavin, about 1907.

Lipman recalled, "[When] the boat landed, I got off, carried my suitcase up to the bank, which was at Pine and Montgomery then, and we could see that the fire was spreading. I came up California Street and you could see where the fire was burning in places, but there was nothing in the way to keep me from getting through, although there were fires not so very far away." Walter approached the bank from precisely the opposite direction, walking east from his home twenty blocks away.

"At 10:30 a.m., the smell of smoke was noticeably stronger," wrote Dinkelspiel. "Business was slow, but the bank remained open. Suddenly the fire department rushed in and ordered everyone out…The clerks hurriedly put the bank's working books and ledgers into the massive brick and steel vault, which had been designed to withstand fire." Walter must have helped gather up these vital records in the hectic rush.

Lipman painted the final scene. "Just as I left my desk, I opened the drawer [and]…saw…my father's old watch that my mother had worn from the time of his death until she gave it to me, and it was saved…Of course we had to get out of the bank, and that was the last of that. The bank was burned during the day. There was nothing to do but go home."

As Walter made his way home, he might have shared the observations of Frank Leach, the director of the San Francisco Mint, who was also walking west through the burning city. "Great clouds of black smoke filled the sky and hid the rays of the sun. Buildings in the track of the rapidly spreading fire went down like houses of cardboard; little puffs of smoke would issue from every crevice for a brief time, to be suddenly followed by big clouds of black smoke…Great masses of flame would quickly take the place of the smoke and shoot up above everything, announcing the consummation of destruction, and then sweep on to the doomed one next in order."

WITH ITS BUILDING a smoking ruin, Wells Fargo set up temporary headquarters at 2020 Jackson Street, the home of Isaias Hellman's son-in-law, Emanuel Heller. Lipman remembered, "We got around the dining room table, and we dumped the mail that had been accumulating. The last business day we had was Tuesday. Wednesday morning the earthquake and fire occurred. It was Friday before the fire was under control. We had to go to little stationery stores for children's composition books and things of that sort to write on. All the stationery stores [downtown] were destroyed."

In the aftermath of the fire, bank safes could not be opened until they had cooled. Otherwise, oxygen entering a safe would have incinerated its contents. So for a month, only the memories of senior management, including Walter's, enabled the bank to settle its accounts. "We had no books. If people claimed they had accounts with us, we had to do the best we could in remembering it. We had nothing to go by. We paid everybody and our losses were nominal. I don't think we lost $200 in paying out thousands."

After the executives in the dining room certified a check as legitimate, a customer still needed a source of cash, and no banks had any cash until their safes could be opened. Only the surviving U.S. Mint at Fifth and Mission had cash, and, luckily, the heroic actions of Leach and his staff had saved the building as flames engulfed adjacent properties. At the height of the inferno, the Mint had been hit by "a tremendous shower of red hot cinders that fell on our building as thick as hail, and piled up on the roof in drifts nearly two feet deep," recalled Leach, whose team shoveled the cinders off the roof.

To access the Mint's cash, including $9 million in coin of Wells Fargo, the city's Clearing House Bank set up shop in the Mint, where "Walter McGavin ran the show," in the words of Wells Fargo historian Robert Chandler. The Clearing House Bank opened on May 1, just two weeks after the quake, with the authority to accept deposits and cash checks of up to $500 ($14,100 in 2017 dollars). With cash flowing, the wheels of commerce turned and the massive rebuilding of the city began.

FOUR WEEKS to the day after the quake, workmen pried open the Wells Fargo vault with a wedge and sledge hammer on May 16, 1906. Dolly accompanied her parents to watch the opening of the safe, recording the event in a family photograph. Dressed elegantly, including gloves and a striking hat, she watched from a scaffold next to the vault. Standing between Dolly and her mother stood "Marco" Hellman, the son of Isaias Hellman; behind them stood John Bigelow, a vice-president.

This was a critical moment in the history of Wells Fargo, and the senior leadership of the bank was front and center to witness the event. Miraculously, fifteen of sixteen massive Boston Ledgers had been saved. Employees removed bags filled with gold coins from the vault and loaded them onto a wagon for delivery to the Mint under armed guard.

Five days later, Wells Fargo opened for business downtown in the Union Trust Company Building at Market and Montgomery. "The interior of the bank's temporary quarters looked like it had during the gold rush. Unpainted planks had been laid down to form counters and desks. Smoke-stained and fire-scorched walls were hidden behind bolts of white cotton cloth."

The McGavin family had to wait longer for their household to return to normal.

For weeks, their cook, Fun Yuen, prepared meals curbside on a brick stove surrounded by wooden screens. Dolly included a picture of him at work, labeling it "Fun in our earthquake kitchen." Finally, on June 5, the family received an official red placard that read: "Chimneys in this house having been put in order, permission is given to use them until further notice."

THE YEAR 1906 marked the twenty-fifth anniversary of Kate McGavin's arrival in San Francisco, having spent the first half of her life in Paris (she was now fifty). Raised with a European appreciation of culture, fashion, and social status, Kate passed on to her daughter a fierce desire to be recognized in society. This must explain the untold hours that Dolly devoted to her collection of scrapbooks and photograph albums, documenting the minutia of her everyday life.

Dolly first appeared in the *San Francisco Chronicle* on June 29, 1905, when she was seventeen years old. The one-sentence paragraph in Lady Teazle's column read: "Miss Dolly MacGavin is visiting Miss Frances Martin at Ross." Frances Martin was a classmate of Dolly at Miss Murison's, a small private school, "which all the buds and belles of the past few years have attended," noted the *San Francisco Call*. Ironically, Miss Murison's was located at 2234 Pacific on the same block as the Simpson residence, and Edith had attended briefly before being sent east to Miss Spence's School. (The two did not attend Miss Murison's at the same time.)

A year earlier, Dolly pasted pictures in her album of Frances and her seated in a Victoria carriage behind a coachman, "driving" together, probably in Golden Gate Park. The girls were fashionably dressed in dark outfits with elegant, wide hats. Frances wore a white-flower lei, and Dolly wore a fur wrap. Both wore gloves. Quite a ladylike pair.

Before Miss Murison's, Dolly had attended the Pacific Heights Grammar School, a public school on Jackson between Webster and Fillmore, for grades three through seven (1899–1904). Demonstrating her early archival instincts, thirteen-year-old Dolly wrote down the names of all forty-three classmates in her fifth grade on the back of their class picture in 1901.

WHEN DOLLY'S MOTHER, Kate, had traveled to California to marry Walter in 1881, she arrived in a city only thirty years removed from the Gold Rush. "The town had not yet entirely outgrown its free-and-easy past," wrote the historian Oscar Lewis, "when to express curiosity about a man's antecedents was always bad form and sometimes downright dangerous. Of course there had been progress; men were no longer merchant princes one day and pushcart peddlers the next. Fortunes were reasonably stable and dozens of families had been prosperous enough to impress themselves and, occasionally, others."

Banker Walter McGavin and Kate, 1913.

Into this milieu stepped Edward M. "Ned" Greenway from Baltimore, an affable agent for Mumm's champagne who saw an opportunity to bring order to the city's social chaos (and not coincidentally to promote his own business). "The opening gun of his campaign was the organization of his Friday Night Cotillion Club," observed Lewis. "Ostensibly, its aim was to assemble a congenial and not too numerous group at a series of dances each winter. There were to be five dances, with refreshments, and the cost was twenty dollars per couple. In reality the club was the device by which Greenway planned to separate the authentic social leaders from the impostors." Greenway's first ball was in 1887, and, over time, an invitation to the Cotillion Club would become an important marker of social status in the city.

Debutantes and their escorts must have found Greenway a memorable character. His cotillions began at ten o'clock with a series of choreographed steps, more military drill than dancing. Greenway shouted out the commands "Grand Right, Grand Left!" "Royal Arches!" "Reversed Circle!" Each command was reinforced by a short toot on a small gold whistle that Greenway always carried. At three o'clock in the morning, he blew the final toot at the end of the last dance. A man of impeccable taste, substantial girth, and enormous energy, Greenway habitually danced all night, retired near dawn, and arose at four in the afternoon.

GREENWAY CHOSE Dolly as a debutante for the 1907–08 winter season. He would have based his choice on two criteria, wrote one social critic, "the money and achievements of the father and the 'social presentability' of the mother." Dolly's father would have qualified, as a senior banker at one of the city's largest banks, and her Parisian mother would have scored high on a scale of social presentability.

The *San Francisco Call* raved about her mother's social skills. "The McGavin home is a center not only for society's most exclusive young people whom the debutante daughter draws about her, but for the artistic, literary and musical people of the city. It has for many years been like a little salon, presided over by Mrs. McGavin, whose two children have grown up in an atmosphere that is very rare in these days of false standards and changing ambitions. So Miss Dolly takes her place quite naturally in the social world and has a poise and manner quite unusual to a debutante."

Later the *San Francisco Chronicle* echoed a similar theme. "Mrs. McGavin has been affording especial pleasure to her friends by her delightful rendering of old French chansons…Those who heard her were most enthusiastic in the praise of the exquisite charm of her singing. Miss Dolly MacGavin has been credited with being one of the most popular debutantes of the winter, and she also enjoys the distinction of having one of the most charming and attractive mothers, who has been untiring in her efforts to make the first winter 'out' of her daughter and her young friends a most memorable one."

BEFORE AND AFTER her debut, Dolly continued her voluminous documentation of San Francisco society. For example, in one large scrapbook, she covered 148 days on 102 pages (August 15, 1908 to January 9, 1909). A typical page might contain nine clippings from three daily newspapers of which six mentioned her name, always underlined.

On September 20, the *San Francisco Chronicle, Call* and *Examiner*—all noted the same small tea honoring a friend of Dolly who was departing for New York, a "pleasant little affair, which was informal in the extreme." (Her name appeared in all three articles.) Thus, Dolly recorded the rhythm of her daily life—tea after tea, luncheon after luncheon, reception after reception, dance after dance—as she archived thousands of articles over the years.

In addition to newspaper clippings and invitations, she frequently glued envelopes on the page with dried flowers that had been presented to her. One example: "October 31, 1908, Lilies of the Valley!!" above the calling card of one Mr. Archibald McNeal Johnson. She included advertisements for movies she saw and added the names of her companions. She attached programs of events that she attended, like "Buffalo Bill's Wild West Historical Sketches and Daily Review" on October 6 with five friends and the Big Game on November 14 with her brother, Drummond, a Cal grad (class of 1904). Stanford beat Cal 12–3.

AFTER THE SCANDAL of her brief marriage and divorce, Dolly bounced back quickly, at least judging from the numerous photographs of her with eligible-looking young men. In November 1911, she spent two weeks in Coronado, California, attending the wedding of a friend who was marrying a midshipman. Dolly seemed particularly enamored with another naval officer, Charles Felton Pousland, the best man, who appeared in many of her pictures. She wrote at the top of the page, "Taken the day I left Coronado. I *hated* to leave!!"

Dolly moved back into her parents' home at 2602 California Street and re-named herself "Mrs. Dolly MacGavin"—a construct guaranteed to confuse genealogical researchers a century later. Interestingly, her name did not appear in Lady

"Dolly and the dahlias for my tea." Smartly dressed
Dolly MacGavin, September 20, 1916.

Teazle's *Chronicle* society columns in 1914, 1915, or 1916, perhaps the result of the lingering stigma attached to her divorce.

IN 1915 DOLLY attended the World's Fair in San Francisco to celebrate the rebirth of the city after the earthquake and the completion of the Panama Canal. Built on the northern edge of the city (today's Marina District), the Panama-Pacific International Exposition was swarmed by 250,000 visitors on opening day. The fairgoers were dazzled by tens of thousands of displays celebrating technological progress and the advancement of civilization—led by the United States of America.

If Dolly was among the crowd that day, she might have ridden the Aeroscope, a two-story observation booth at the end of a long steel arm carrying riders almost 265 feet into the air before swiveling 360 degrees to provide panoramic views. "You get the thrill of aviation, without the danger—a bird-like, gliding sensation," one rider said.

Perhaps she later watched the Ford factory assembly line. "Twenty-eight mechanics worked the fifty-foot line from 2:00 until 5:00, completing eighteen cars daily, or about one every ten minutes…Each car started as an empty chassis, pulled along by a chain. Everything was attached on the line, including axles, wheels, engine, transmission, interior, windshield, and soft top, then gas was added" to drive the Model T off the line.

The only surviving building of the fair today is the Palace of Fine Arts, a semicircular gallery behind an open rotunda "embraced by graceful, arcing colonnades," in the words of one architectural historian. Inside were thousands of works of art, including John Singer Sargent's famous *Portrait of Madame Gautreau* (originally *Madame X*). Thirty-one years earlier, Sargent had exhibited his controversial painting at the Paris Salon of 1884, the same year that he painted his portrait of Dr. MacGavin.

DID DOLLY NOTICE a handsome visitor from St. Louis? In family lore, she did not, but she could have. His name was Alan Cline, and he had recently moved to San Francisco. Within two years, they would meet, and he would become the true love of her life.

CHAPTER 14

The Salesman and the Socialite

Alan and Dolly, 1905–1937

SEVEN YEARS after her ill-fated elopement, Dolly's name again appeared atop a *San Francisco Chronicle* headline—this time under far happier circumstances.

Mrs. Dolly MacGavin to Be
Bride of Alan Cline in July
San Francisco's Younger Set
Is Entertaining Lavishly in
Honor of Engaged Couple

"No more interesting piece of news has the smart set enjoyed for some time," wrote Lady Teazle on April 17, 1917, "than the announcement of the engagement of Mrs. Dolly MacGavin, daughter of Mr. and Mrs. Walter McGavin, and Alan Cline. Close friends of the attractive bride-elect were told of it yesterday, and good wishes and congratulations are being showered on the engaged couple.

"Mrs. MacGavin is one of the most popular members of the younger set and takes a leading part in its gayeties. Gifted with a distinctive personality, and with the same charm and magnetism for which her mother is famous, she has rightfully won her place in the affections of a wide circle of friends."

DOLLY'S INTENDED, Alan Cline, was a thirty-two-year-old native of St. Louis, the fourth son of Judge Frederick Cline and his wife, Frances Holmes. Alan had grown up in the Cline family home at 4321 Olive Street near the West End, an area known for its large estates surrounding Forest Park. Of Alan's education, we know nothing except that at age fifteen he was listed in the 1900 census as "At School." We do know that he did not attend college.

No doubt he must have found the 1904 St. Louis World's Fair more exciting than a classroom. Formally known as the Louisiana Purchase Exposition, the fair celebrated the acquisition of the Louisiana territory from France in 1803. As one critic noted, "For seven months in 1904, St. Louis became the most cosmopolitan city on earth."

Like the San Francisco World's Fair eleven years in the future, exhibitors displayed a dazzling variety of consumer goods, agricultural produce, and manufactured products in twelve white palaces ("the Ivory City"). Venetian gondoliers rowed guests across the Grand Basin between the palaces. Today only the Palace of Fine Arts remains as the St. Louis Art Museum in Forest Park.

IN 1905 ALAN'S NAME first appeared in the *St. Louis City Directory* as a "clerk," residing at his parents' address. In 1906 and 1907, he listed himself as a salesman at the Graham Paper Company in downtown St. Louis. In 1908 he found a job selling manufactured roofing materials for the Weatherproof Manufacturing Company, producers of "Roofing Materials, Building and Insulating Papers, Felts and Cement." Thereafter, he was listed as "traveling," meaning that he was a traveling salesman, probably for a roofing manufacturer.

From 1912 to 1916, he appeared in the *San Francisco City Directory* as a manager for the General Roofing Manufacturing Company, a producer of roofing shingles and building papers, headquartered in St. Louis. We can imagine Alan traveling for weeks at a time and living out of a suitcase while calling on customers and prospects across the west. When in San Francisco, he listed his residence variously as the Granada Hotel, an apartment house at 843 California Street, and the Hotel Plaza on Union Square.

California was a booming market for building products at the beginning of the twentieth century. Between 1900 and 1920, the population of the state more than doubled from 1,485,000 to 3,427,000. By 1917, according to its corporate history, General Roofing "had established itself as a leader nationwide in the production

Alan Cline, about 1905.

and distribution of 'asphalt roofing, insulating papers, paints, and varnishes.'" That year the company changed its name to Certain-teed Products Corporation, forming the name from its motto: "Quality made CERTAIN... Satisfaction GuaranTEED."

WE MIGHT GUESS that Alan and Dolly were introduced by his boss, Dutro Cale, the Pacific Coast manager for Certain-teed. Originally from St. Louis, Cale and his wife moved to San Francisco, probably in 1916, and in September that year, Mrs. Cale was an honored guest at a tea party given by Dolly. Within a year, Dutro Cale would serve as the best man at Alan and Dolly's wedding. (Her maid of honor would be her sister-in-law, Helen Baker MacGavin.)

Prior to their engagement announcement, neither family knew much about the couple's courtship. Alan's mother, Frances, was surprised, writing to Dolly from St. Louis. "It was all great news to us, as we thought Alan was only absorbed in his business." Dolly's aunt and namesake in Paris, Emilia Hinshelwood, also found herself in the dark. "I would like more details about the surprise [and] a description of your fiancé."

Regrettably, Alan's parents were struggling financially and could not attend the wedding. Frances blamed their difficulties on World War I, which the U.S. had entered on April 6, 1917. "My darling son," she wrote, "between the war depression, Liberty bonds & Red Cross that Papa had to help out, it has made us terribly short." As the wedding date approached, Frances wrote again, "Everything is so uncertain. Saw lots of soldiers & train loads of them going 'somewhere.'" Could these images have brought back painful memories of St. Louis during Civil War times?

Alan's younger sister, Isabel Cline Harney, also in St. Louis, wrote, "We all are

Dolly MacGavin and Alan Cline, June 3, 1917, a month before their marriage.

dreadfully disappointed not to be able to come out for the wedding, but I can't see how it is possible to do so." She had just had a child and "not having a nurse for the baby keeps me rushing from morning till night."

From wartime Paris, Aunt Emilia hoped that her niece and Alan would be "the two happiest youngsters in the world. You ought to be happy far away from all the troubles of Europe. If ever you think something is hard or difficult, think of all the hardships over in France, England, Russia, Germany, Italy, Romania, etc., etc. Think one second of all that & you will find your path strewn with roses in comparison."

Alan first appeared in a family photograph dated June 3, 1917. On that day, the whole clan had gathered in the backyard of her parents' new home at 2730 Broderick—Walter and Kate, Dolly's brother, Drummond, and his wife, Helen, and their two young children. (Drummond was now in his army uniform.)

ALAN AND DOLLY were married on July 10, 1917, in an evening ceremony at her parents' home. "No wedding of the year created more genuine interest," wrote the *Chronicle*, "the bride and bridegroom both being social favorites here and the bride one of the most popular members of the younger set of this city." Dolly wore "a handsome gown of white satin, completely veiled in real lace."

Nearly one hundred family members and friends attended the ceremony "in the drawing-room, beneath a bower of pink sweet peas and maidenhair ferns, the flowers completely covering a lattice work screen that formed the walls of the bower." One of the guests was Alan's uncle, eighty-three-year-old Colonel Chipman, who stood with Lincoln at Gettysburg.

But gloom reigned in St. Louis where Alan's mother, Frances, fretted about her decision not to make the trip to San Francisco. "I said this morning I felt almost like jumping on the train & going west—but I can't leave Isabel & the baby." His father, Frederick, was also downhearted thinking of his "baby boy." To brighten the mood, Isabel and her husband, Gerald Harney, hosted a dinner party. Everyone wrote silly verses on postcards, which, Frances worried, might give the McGavins the wrong impression. "Papa spelt 'Dolly's' name with the [alphabet letters] ... in the soup & we all tried to be as gay as possible."

FOR THEIR HONEYMOON, Alan and Dolly drove to Los Angeles in a Model T roadster, following the Pacific Highway (later U.S. Route 101). On July 17, they were photographed at Long Beach, standing on the sand dressed in formal attire—Alan in a three-piece suit and starched collar, Dolly in a long dress with a white ermine wrap.

When they returned to the city, the couple moved into an apartment at 2407 Fillmore Street. Judging by pictures in a family album, their apartment was comfortably furnished, perhaps with help from her parents. Walter and Kate must have been thrilled that their twenty-nine-year-old daughter was at last properly and happily married.

Naturally, Dolly carefully cataloged the deluge of wedding gifts in her scrapbook—"silver water pitcher," "large silver platter," "1 dozen salad plates," "platter & 1 dozen meat plates," "6 silver oyster forks," and a "silver candy dish," etc., etc. Knowing that his parents were hard-pressed, Alan tried to emphasize their frugal lifestyle in a letter home. But he could not conceal their extravagant wedding gifts. His mother replied, "Perhaps you can exchange some of the presents for something you really need...I am so glad you are both sensible & will try & control your expenses."

In the fall of 1917, Dolly joined Alan on a business trip to St. Louis via Salt Lake City and Pocatello (Idaho). She met his parents for the first time in St. Louis and wrote under one photograph, "End of a perfect visit Oct. 15, 1917."

A YEAR LATER, Catherine Holmes Cline, my mother, was born on October 25, 1918. The next day, Alan's mother sent him a congratulatory note. "We are greatly relieved that the darling baby had arrived safely & the dear little mother [is] doing well. It is such a dreadful ordeal to go through! That I have felt very anxious over Dolly. Of course, we all know it is nature, but that doesn't keep one from worrying."

Frances continued, "Do let us know the particulars & how she was taken, rushed to the hospital, etc. We know how nervous you must have been dear, particularly if you were present at the birth." Alan and Dolly had recently moved to 2501 Union Street, only two blocks from her parents' home. We can imagine the stress in the household with Dolly's mother, Kate, trying to comfort Dolly before rushing her to the hospital.

Two weeks later, Frances Cline wrote a long letter to Kate McGavin—grandmother to grandmother. "I don't wonder Alan likes to look at [Catherine] by the hour. Babies are the sweetest things in the world. How very fortunate it is that Dolly can nurse her & I hope it will last."

Frances also mentioned Dolly's brother, Drummond, then serving in the U.S.

Army in France. "How happy you will all be when your beloved son returns safely from France & I hope it won't be long now till this fearful strife is ended." Five days after the letter was postmarked, the Armistice ending World War I was signed on November 11, 1918. Drummond did return home safely.

A YEAR-AND-A-HALF LATER, the grandparents' concerns about childbirth returned during Dolly's second pregnancy. Sadly, their fears would be confirmed this time in a series of frantic telegrams from her brother, Drummond, and his wife, Helen, in San Francisco to Alan, who was away on business in St. Louis,

After Dolly experienced early labor pains on Monday, May 17, 1920, and was rushed to St. Francis Hospital, Helen immediately recognized the danger of a premature delivery and telegraphed Alan to come home immediately. The next day, Tuesday, she wired that Dolly had a baby girl and was doing fine, but that there was "not much hope" for the baby. A few hours later, Drummond advised Alan that the baby had "passed away."

Alan did not receive these telegrams until Wednesday, May 19, when he replied:

```
JUST RECEIVED THE SAD NEWS GIVE DOLLY LOADS OF LOVE
AND MUCH SYMPATHY PLEASE USE YOUR JUDGEMENT IN HANDLING
ANYTHING NECESSARY I CAN BE REACHED CARE CONDUCTOR
OVERLAND LIMITED NUMBER ONE OMAHA THURSDAY MORNING
OGDEN FRIDAY MORNING ARRIVING HOME SATURDAY AFTERNOON
```

Taking command, Drummond wired to Alan's train the next day, Thursday, May 20:

```
DOLLY IS GETTING ALONG SPLENDEDLY SHOULD BE OUT
OF HOSPITAL IN ABOUT A WEEK REALIZING YOU COULD
NOT BE HERE BEFORE FRIDAY EVENING WE DETERMINED
IT BEST TO HOLD FUNERAL TODAY AND BABE NOW RESTS
PEACEFULLY IN MOUNTAIN VIEW CEMETERY PIEDMONT
```

When she learned the terrible news, Frances Cline wrote directly to Drummond's wife, Helen, "We were much shocked & saddened by the news of the premature birth & death of the baby…I fear late hours & strenuous social affairs tired her out." The next week Frances tried to assuage the sorrows of her son and daughter-in-law, "My Dearest Children…The ways of God are strange, but we must believe for the best in the end … Our lives are full of sorrows as well as joys & we simply have to accept what comes—even if hearts ache & break."

DOLLY'S MOTHER, Kate, died on October 25, 1921, at age sixty-five, the same day that Catherine turned three. Two years later, Walter retired from Wells Fargo in 1923. Grateful for his long service, the bank's directors gave him a Patek Philippe gold pocket watch inscribed, "Walter McGavin from his Old Associates of the Wells Fargo Nevada National Bank, 1880-1923."

The *San Francisco Chronicle* recognized him with a two-column article headlined:

Banker, 70 Years Young,
Retires Today, Protesting
That He's 'Just Going Good.'

"In fact, when 'Walter,' as he is known from president to office boy was first approached concerning this retirement business, he filled the air with protests, contradictions, denials, dissents and otherwise poked a hole in the atmosphere with a varied assortment of syntax and prosody…'I have preached clean athletics all my life, lived them, love them, and I again protest at being retired like an old fire horse.'"

PROFESSIONALLY, Alan was thriving at Certain-teed, now as the district manager covering the Pacific States. In 1920 the company reported that "The demand for buildings of every kind and description—factories, apartments, theatres, hotels, schools, railroad stations, etc., etc., is at enormous figures. It seems impossible to catch up with this pressing demand for several years."

By 1926 the company could boast, "We believe that we have the most economical selling and distributing system … and we believe our products are sold in every county in the United States … about sixty percent of all the people live in agricultural or other small centers and towns under 10,000 population, and that they represent more than sixty percent of the purchasing power of our lines." Translation: Alan would spend most of his time on the road making sales calls, frequently in smaller cities.

When he was away, Dolly filled her scrapbooks with a meticulous record of every letter, postcard, and telegram that Alan sent home to his daughter, Catherine.

From Spokane, Washington, he sent her a picture of a fish and wrote, "Honey Bunch—I saw this fish. And caught him for you. He is a nice fish and very gentle. I asked him his name & he said 'Slippery Jim.' Now isn't that a funny name for a fish?"

From Portland, Oregon, he wished her happy birthday: "Seven years ago, you opened your eyes, And ushered yourself into the world with cries, A wonderful baby you were then, And soon you were crawling around in a pen." On a week-long sales trip to Chico (California), Seattle, and Portland, he wrote a poem to his hyperactive, nine-year-old daughter:

> Here's to my sweet little girl
> Whom I left all in a whirl
> So much to do has this little lady
> That it nearly makes her go crazy
> Up in the morning, hurry-hurry-hurry
> Eat down your food hurry-hurry-hurry
> Off to school she goes in a flurry-flurry-flurry
> Her mind must be in a blurry-blurry-blurry
> Boy she is alright this kid of mine
> She and her dad are good old pals
> He wouldn't trade her for all the other gals
> So again—here's to Daddy's girl
> Mind Mother and avoid a whirl

In January 1927, Alan combined business with pleasure taking his family to Hawaii, where Dolly and Catherine enjoyed the Moana Hotel on Waikiki Beach. On January 15, a Honolulu newspaper published a picture of Alan, sporting a tie and Hawaiian lei. "Alan P. Cline, Pacific Coast district manager of Certain-teed... will investigate local business conditions." Dolly archived every scrap of paper documenting their vacation, including passenger lists, menus, and a concert program of hula songs.

Alan's sales leadership was recognized by a visit from Certain-teed's New York headquarters in April. Robert M. Nelson, the treasurer of Certain-teed, told the *San Francisco Chronicle* that sales in Alan's district had "shown a larger increase in percentage than in any other district of the company."

Alan Cline and three-year-old Catherine on the beach in
Santa Monica, California, Fourth of July 1922.

Alan Cline, about 1925.

SADLY, Dolly's father, Walter McGavin, died on March 6, 1928, just a month shy of his seventy-fifth birthday. The appraised value of his estate filed in Superior Court was $96,000 ($1,370,000 in 2017 dollars), mostly in stocks and bonds. Presumably, Dolly took a lesser share of the securities in return for ownership of 2730 Broderick, across the street from her brother Drummond's house at 2701 Broderick. She and Alan remodeled the home and moved into it in the fall of 1928.

ONE YEAR LATER, the Clines' financial world was shattered. "Like an earthquake, the Stock Market Crash of 1929 cracked startlingly across the United States," wrote historian David Kennedy, "the herald of a crisis that was to shake the American way of life to its foundations."

From an all-time high of $61.50 a share in 1928, Certain-teed's stock fell almost 80% to $13.00 in December 1929. "The close of the year found buying at a minimum," the company stated, "with stocks reported throughout the country as being at unusually low totals... with building and consumer demand very inactive, although Federal and other authorities were calling meetings and discussing ways and means for improving business conditions."

The company's revenues continued to fall precipitously, 26% during the second half of 1930, and their stock plunged further to $2.00 a share. Still, 1931 would be even worse. Certain-teed reported that "All salaries and all labor rates of pay throughout the business have been reduced." In 1932 the company would hit rock bottom and report all wages and salaries had been reduced again. But, "in spite of these economies, the loss for 1932 was much greater than 1931." As 1933 began, Certain-teed's stock hovered slightly above a dollar a share.

With new home construction moribund during the Depression, Certain-teed emphasized the home repair market, and Alan wrote a motivational article for the *Pacific Builder* magazine in 1935. He described how Certain-teed had "conducted a school for salesmen...We helped dealers learn how to ring door bells by sending out field men specially trained in this work... if dealers went after this business, they got it [with] good, conscientious salesmanship... Modern merchandising methods are all that the building industry needs to put the wheels of production again in motion."

ALAN'S FATHER, Frederick Cline, had died unexpectedly on September 4, 1930, at age seventy-six in Los Angeles, where he and his wife had moved ten years earlier. Six months later, his wife, Frances Holmes, died at age seventy-three on March 5, 1931. Their son, Frederick Jr., wrote that his mother had "never recovered from the shock & grief" of her husband's death. Both Frederick and Frances were cremated and their ashes buried in the Holmes's plot at the Bellefontaine Cemetery in their hometown of St. Louis.

Despite the hardships caused by the Great Depression, Alan managed to accumulate some capital in the 1930s. In 1934 he and Dolly bought a larger house at 2490 Filbert Street. He even acquired an investment property, a three-story apartment building on the northwest corner of Bush and Jones Streets in 1936.

Dolly's enthusiasm for society was not diminished by the Depression, and she continued to be recognized on the society page. When she and her friends organized a series of dances for their daughters, the *Chronicle* referred to them as "patronesses where once they danced." When she and Alan moved into their new home on Filbert Street in 1934, they invited over two hundred guests for tea and that evening hosted a buffet supper party for sixty.

ALL THIS MADE their abrupt move to Los Angeles in 1937 even more startling. After a quarter century with Certain-teed, through good times and bad, Alan left to become the general sales manager for Schumacher Wall Board Corporation in Los Angeles, which manufactured drywall for building construction. Was there a corporate reshuffle at Certain-teed? Or did his new job simply pay more? In 1940 Alan told the census enumerator that his annual salary was $5,000 ($87,400 in 2017 dollars).

Dolly's last few weeks in San Francisco culminated in a whirlwind of activity. "It will be a very tired Mrs. Alan Cline," wrote the *Chronicle*, "who, on December 15, will bid farewell to her beloved San Francisco and take herself off, with all her worldly goods, for the city of angels. Few matrons in this city are as popular, and would be as sorely missed as Mrs. Cline—Dolly to her nearest and dearest." The weekend before their departure, she and Alan hosted two hundred friends at their home on Filbert Street, and, for the last time, their names appeared in a *Chronicle* headline on December 17, 1937, "The Alan Clines Bid Adieu at Gay Party."

Alan and Dolly could not have dreamed that their decision to relocate would lead their daughter to her true love. Four years later, Catherine would spend the Thanksgiving holiday with her parents in Los Angeles and meet her future husband, Peter Pike.

HIS PARENTS, Roy and Edith Pike, would lead quite different lives in the 1920s and '30s. Reaching for the stars, they would fall short, leaving behind a trail of grand plans and broken dreams.

CHAPTER 15

To the Manner Born

Roy and Edith, 1919–1941

BUOYED BY his wife's wealth and the esteem of his rich friends, Roy Pike set out to make his own fortune. "I determined in 1917 and '18 to give up any other business interests and major in agriculture ... I wanted to establish a farm or a ranch of four or five thousand acres." From experience, Roy knew that he could "horseback over" a ranch this size and monitor his workers on a daily basis. In 1919 he acquired five contiguous farms totaling 3,780 acres on the west side of the San Joaquin River near the town of Vernalis. Later, he added 540 acres, bringing the total acreage to 4,320. Roy named his ranch El Solyo, which he claimed meant "pike fish" in Spanish.

For decades, wheat and barley farmers had dry-farmed the west side of the San Joaquin Valley, meaning that they depended solely upon winter and spring rains to water their crops. Roy would be one of the first to irrigate this side of the valley. Neighboring ranchers questioned his judgment, even his sanity. "You can't irrigate the west side." "The west side is dry country. The land won't take water. It will run off!" "Pike is crazy." "Pike will ruin this country trying to put water on it."

Yet water was the key to Roy's vision, and his first priority was building an irrigation system that would allow him to plant a diversity of crops. This diversity would allow him to invest his capital and manage his employees more efficiently. Reflecting America's worship of mass production in the early twentieth century, Roy would farm on an industrial scale.

On May 1, 1920, three large pumps roared to life, drawing 20,000 gallons of water per minute from the San Joaquin River through three sixteen-inch pipes up to Pump

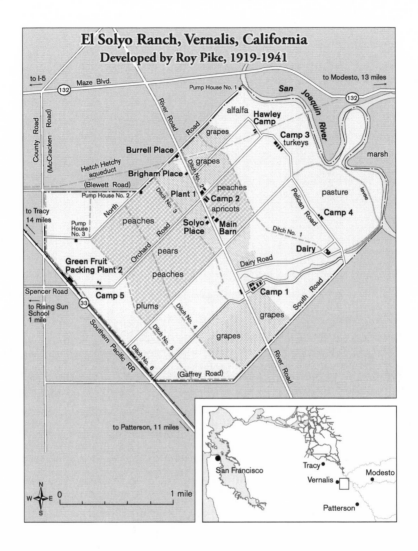

El Solyo Ranch, Vernalis, California
Developed by Roy Pike, 1919-1941

House No. 1 on El Solyo Ranch. From there, the torrent of water was pushed west-ward for a mile and a quarter through a forty-eight-inch redwood-stave pipeline to Canal No. 1, a thirty-foot-wide ditch running westward another half mile.

The ranch covered almost seven square miles in a rough rectangular shape. The eastern boundary of El Solyo ran two miles south from Pump House No. 1 along the river, and the northern boundary ran southwest three miles to the Southern Pacific Railroad tracks and later State Route 33. (Motorists today can still see Pump House No. 1 as they travel eastbound toward Modesto on State Route 132,

Maze Boulevard, just south of the bridge over the San Joaquin River.)

Canal No. 1 was built by teams of mules, each team of four harnessed to a "Fresno scraper," a curved metal blade that scooped up dirt. Roy's son, Peter, recalled, "The 'mule skinner' controlled the angle of the cut, the capacity of his bucket, and the weight of his load with one hand on a lever." With his other hand, he drove the mule team.

"A line was laid out on the ground and the Fresnos worked back and forth, digging in the center then dumping on the bank. Down the outside of the bank, turning, climbing the bank empty, down into the ditch, setting the angle of cut for the bottom, cursing the mules to pull like hell up the opposite bank loaded, dumping again, turning. Repeating, crossing, 50 Fresnos, 200 mules, dust almost impenetrable."

Surveyors stopped the action frequently to set up a transit to check the direction and depth of the cut. Peter remembered the supporting cast surrounding the ditch builders—backup mule skinners, "a blacksmith for shoeing, hay and grain for feed, relief teams of animals, water troughs, [and] water wagons with teams to haul water from the river."

BY THE MID-1920s, an aviator flying south over the Central Valley in the summer would have immediately spotted El Solyo Ranch, a patchwork quilt of various shades of green, surrounded by miles of dry, brown farms west of the San Joaquin River. Orchards covered 900 acres of the ranch with eighteen varieties of peaches, apricots, and plums. Vineyards were planted with 450 acres of Thompson table grapes and 150 acres of Carignan wine grapes. Vegetables covered 600 acres, mostly celery, lettuce, peas, carrots, and onions. Baby lima and mungo beans grew on 400 acres and alfalfa on another 300 acres.

Hundreds more acres were devoted to oats, millet, barley, rice, and sugar beets. Pastureland, totaling 300 acres near the river, was reserved for 120 milk cows. Each year the ranch incubated and matured 6,000–8,000 turkeys for Thanksgiving and Christmas. The turkeys were pastured in grain field stubble in the summer and in the vineyards later in bands of about 2,000 each.

Plant No. 1, a large dehydrating plant on River Road, dried raisins, apricots, and peaches, shipping 1,500 to 2,500 tons of dried fruit annually, marketed nationwide under the El Solyo brand. Plant No. 2, a fresh produce packing plant near the railroad, processed celery, lettuce, broccoli, onions, pears, and plums, and shipped between 600 and 1,000 rail cars of fresh vegetables and fruits each year.

EL SOLYO EMPLOYED a permanent work force of 250 who lived in housing provided by the ranch in a series of camps. Each employee was assigned to one of eleven departments (Sales, Dried Fruit, Orchard, Dairy, etc.), and all department heads reported directly to Roy as the general manager. During peak harvesting and packing times, another 500 seasonal workers would be added to the payroll.

In the early years, farm hands worked ten-hour days. Breakfast was served at 5:30 a.m. Morning work was from 6:00 a.m. to 11:30 a.m. before a midday break. Afternoon work was from 1:00 p.m. to 5:30 with the evening meal at 6:00 p.m. Trucks took workers back and forth between the fields and the camps. Roy marveled at the sight of "five or six trucks lined up, each with thirty or forty men on them, going to or from the fields at these times."

El Solyo reduced the workday in 1929 to nine hours because, as Roy explained, "Careful check over several years proved that large field crews deliver just as many working units per day in nine hours as in a ten-hour day. This is particularly true during the hot summer months." Breakfast was now served at 6:30 a.m., and the men left camp at 7:00 a.m. They returned "from the fields at 11:30 a.m. for mid-day dinner, going again to the fields at 12:30 p.m., working until 5:00 p.m. when they [were] again brought into the mess camps for 5:30 p.m. supper." A siren that could be heard around the ranch blew three times a day—at 7:00 a.m., noon, and 5:00 p.m.

Aerial view of El Solyo Ranch looking westward, December 1929. The Pike residence, El Solyo Place, is behind the trees across River Road; the El Solyo cottage is visible to the right. The large building in the center is the saddle barn with a tennis court to the left next to the road. An apricot orchard is in foreground, and a Thompson seedless vineyard is behind the Pike residence with a peach orchard beyond that. The Green Fruit Packing Plant is on the railroad line in the misty distance.

UNDER THE HEADLINE, "El Solyo Ranch Rivals Factory for Efficiency," the *Modesto News-Herald* bragged in January 1929, "The ranch, expected to be a model for the nation within a few years, is operated as a business, not as a sideline, and vast sums are being spent in its development. Costs and income are known to a fraction by every department of the ranch, and close check is kept on the work accomplished by the large crews employed."

Fifty miles of roads crisscrossed the ranch, tying the camps and fields together. Each department foreman and sub-foreman drove a Ford V-8 pickup roadster, averaging at least a thousand miles a month. But nobody drove more than the Water Master, who allocated water to the various fields and covered "65 to 100 miles every day," according to Roy.

The workers at El Solyo formed a close-knit community. The nearest towns were Patterson, thirteen miles south (population 905 in 1930), and Tracy, sixteen miles north (population 3,829). So the ranch showed its own films and held dances for residents. In February 1934, the *Patterson Irrigator* reported one such event: "Roy Pike and the staff of the El Solyo Ranch were hosts to a big assemblage Saturday night at one of the dances the ranch is famous for. The mess hall at Camp One was used for the occasion...A lavish supper was served at midnight, and the hosts exerted every effort to make the evening a success."

Decades later Tony Bronzan, who was first employed as a tractor driver and later as the equipment foreman, remembered Roy: "He was very kind—he helped me, pushed me along. He was a perfectionist far ahead of his time. He believed in good living quarters and good food—he thought a man couldn't work without them. Our quarters in the tractor department 'hotel' had curtains on the windows, rugs on the floors, and a flunky to clean. We had our own kangaroo court to keep the men in line. Mr. Pike didn't believe in fighting."

ROY PIKE lived in two worlds. On his isolated ranch he ruled over his domain as lord of the manor. In cosmopolitan San Francisco, he cherished the camaraderie of his clubs—the Bohemian, the Family, and the Burlingame Country Club. Nothing pleased him more than an evening of good fellowship over food and drink—unencumbered by Prohibition. (When Prohibition looked likely to pass Congress en route to its eventual ratification, he simply wrote in his diary, "Murder!!")

His fiftieth birthday celebration at the Bohemian Club on February 11, 1928, would be one of the highlights of Roy's life. In exquisite detail, he documented the evening in a 180-page folio, which today rests in the Bohemian Club archives. The idea of a celebration had "burst upon" him the previous Christmas, he wrote to his friends, "perhaps during one of those high moments born of the bloom of wine when the veil is lifted and the truth is momentarily known. Surely such an anniversary marks a milestone—a place to pause for a moment—to review—a time for stock taking."

The first hundred pages of the folio were copies of his invitation letters and responses of acceptance or regret. (Seventy-five were invited; fifty-four accepted.) Pages of documentation followed—the dinner menu, the seating arrangement, and a group picture with each person labeled. Fifty pages recorded the remarks of guests and the scripts of two original playlets written for the evening.

Attendees wore "dinner coats" (tuxedos), because the absence of women did not "justify tail coats." Dinner was served in the Jinks Room of the old club house (razed in 1932). To lubricate the festivities, Roy had promised to "sacrifice the balance of the old Pike Cellar." Fearful of the Prohibition law, the Bohemian Club barred the printing of a wine list on the menu itself. But Roy noted the beverages served as follows: Chateau Yquem with the Oysters, Sherry with the Turtle Soup, Riesling with the Striped Bass, Champagne with the Guinea Hen, and Brandy and Liqueurs with the Cheese and Black Coffee.

In opening remarks, Roy welcomed his guests to the festivities: "That we might, of a winter's night, gather as we so often do in the summer [at the Bohemian Grove], to know again the friendliness and delight of a hand-clasp—an occasional arm over a shoulder—the clink of glasses—the sparkle of eyes and humor and badinage, the lure of music—the satire or thrill of a play, and weaving through them all the sound of friendly laughter."

Then Roy spoke about the importance of friendship. "The statement to achieve Friendship is scarcely correct. It must be truer to say that one receives Friendship rather than achieves, for no matter what one gives, one receives so much more— so much that I sometimes pause and wonder. That, perhaps, is the experience of all of you. I think it is. It is one of the inalienable beauties of Friendship. In this room are most of the men who *have given color and character to my life*. I am largely the sum of you; just as I hope I am a small part of each of you as you also reflect the whole of us" (emphasis original).

THE EVENING CONTINUED with poetry, songs, and remarks, concluding with a short play about Roy titled *Pike in Nine Scenes*. Written in a humorous vein by his nephew, Parmer Fuller, the play displayed in bold relief two of Roy's, not always flattering, personality traits. In the first instance, he was portrayed as a charming ladies' man, if not a womanizer, frequently short of cash.

The sign at the beginning of Scene IV announces: "Roy's Salad Days, 1906 or so" (before his marriage to Edith). It opens with Roy in a hotel room tying his cravat and wearing "a ravishing bathrobe, or kimono." The telephone rings with a call from Mazie inviting him to lunch, to which he agrees at one o'clock, "my sweet one. Au revoir." He immediately calls the bellboy and orders two dozen American Beauty roses from the next-door florist for Mrs. Mazie Shanley to be charged to his account.

A moment later Lottie calls inviting him to dinner, to which he agrees at seven o'clock, "my sweet one. Au revoir." Again he instructs the bellboy to send two dozen American Beauties to Mrs. Lottie Parker. The final call is from Phoebe inviting Roy to a late supper at half after eleven, to which he agrees, "my sweet one. Au revoir." And again Roy orders the bellboy to send two dozen roses to Mrs. Phoebe Brown on his account. As the bellboy leaves, Roy calls out:

ROY:	Eddie (*Bellboy returns.*)
BELLBOY:	Yes, sir.
ROY:	(*With great poise.*)
	Eddie, could you lend me ten dollars?
BELLBOY:	Certainly, Mr. Pike, glad to help you out.
	(*He takes a bill from his pocket and hands it to Roy. As Roy pockets it, the bellboy speaks.*)
BELLBOY:	That makes sixty you owe me.
ROY:	(*Bored.*) You don't tell me.

Over the years, Roy's wide circle of friends also recognized him as a promoter of financial schemes, not always soundly conceived—his second unflattering trait. The sign introducing Scene VI reads, "Roy, the Promoter, 1910–1920." The scene opens in a room with a potential investor, Mr. Anybody, seated at a table. Roy is ushered into the room "perfectly garbed in morning coat, grey striped trousers, spats, gloves, silk hat and stick, flower in buttonhole, and handkerchief in breast pocket."

Roy presents his proposition to the investor. He is seeking assistance for a project that "cannot fail to make millions, not one million, but many. It is a ranching project, but of a most unusual kind. Large profits eventually are a certainty, but of course it will take some years of developmental work before we reach real production."

MR. ANYBODY:	Ranch you say! What are you going to raise?
ROY:	Bluebirds…The field is tremendous. No family should be without a bluebird. And there are none on the market nowadays except at a prohibitive price. We'll cover the world. "Pike's bluebirds are durable." "A bluebird in every home." "The last word: Pike's Bluebird."
MR. ANYBODY:	Where is this ranch going to be?
ROY:	At the end of the rainbow.
MR. ANYBODY:	Is property available there?
ROY:	Not right at that spot, but close by, just where the blue begins.

Roy asks for ten thousand dollars, to which Mr. Anybody quickly agrees, and Roy replies, "That's awfully good of you," and invites the investor to "lunch at the Club, say on Friday." As Roy is about to leave, the investor asks a final question:

MR. ANYBODY:	I say, Pike, how much money do you need to swing the entire deal?
ROY:	Four hundred and eighty thousand dollars.
MR. ANYBODY:	And how much have you got?
ROY:	Ten thousand.
MR. ANYBODY:	When that ten is gone, what are you going to do?
ROY:	Find somebody and get another ten.
MR. ANYBODY:	A very practicable system.
ROY:	It has always worked for me.

Roy and Edith Pike, October 11, 1929.

"WHEN NOT in San Francisco or Los Angeles," *Fortune* magazine wrote, "Pike lived rather feudally at the ranch. Hollywood stars and wealthy Easterners were his guests. The ranch house, Solyo Place, was comfortable rather than pretentious, but the gardens and lawns were lovely—three gardeners kept them up."

Roy's nephew, Tom Pike, disputed the word "feudal," but painted an elegant picture of life at the ranch. In 1925 fifteen-year-old Tom and a friend were invited to spend Easter week with Roy and Edith. After an arduous drive from Los Angeles, "We were warmly greeted by Aunt Edith and shown to our room. The residence was a two-story, four-bedroom, frame ranch house, designed and furnished tastefully, attractively, comfortably—not 'feudally,' as stated in the *Fortune* article. The gardens were beautifully planned and kept."

Edith labeled this photograph, "The Royal Family."
Roy Jr., Peter, Roy Sr., and Edith, at El Solyo, April 29, 1934.

Roy returned from the fields in time for dinner, "for which he changed to dinner suit and black patent leather pumps, which really impressed me. Edith wore an attractive long gown, and she was beautiful...I will never forget her warmth, courtesy, and genuine concern for her two young guests. Uncle Roy sang for us after dinner, and he was marvelous. He had a real flair in his voice and singing manner, and was every bit as good as I had heard."

The highlight of Tom's stay was "was riding with a pack of handsome hounds chasing rabbits. Whenever the hounds spotted a rabbit, they took off like a shot out of a gun in hot pursuit, and our horses did likewise. I hung on for dear life, scared to death, as my horse leaped over irrigation ditches and all other obstacles, until the hounds caught the poor rabbit, when everything finally slowed to a walk. [We] felt like English huntsmen of yore, engaging in the ancient sport of fox hunting, only hunting rabbits."

In fact, El Solyo did host fox hunts. "To combat rabbits wreaking havoc in the young vineyards," the *Stockton Record* wrote, "Pike imported a pack of greyhounds to run the rabbits out. This in turn led to a colorful form of entertainment on the ranch—formal foxhunts. Wealthy guests from the Peninsula and Hollywood rode to the hounds attired in the traditional red coats. Red foxes were imported for the hunts."

ROY JR. fondly remembered the repartee of the guests at his parents' weekend house parties. "These were all people prominent in their fields, fascinating and witty people—bankers and lawyers, friends from New York, men from Washington, D.C., with the latest gossip." In 1936 the *Patterson Irrigator* reported that "ex-President Herbert Hoover was the guest of Manager Roy M. Pike of El Solyo Ranch for a couple of days, adding another to famous notables who have inspected the big ranch."

When actors like "Billie Burke, Frances Starr or Grace Hamilton" appeared "in plays at the Curran or Geary Theaters," recalled Roy Jr., "on Saturday night, father would send the car down and fetch them after the performance and whisk them up to El Solyo for the weekend." He also remembered the Hollywood actors Melvyn Douglas and Helen Gahagan Douglas as "particularly sparkling people." Novelist Stewart Edward White and his wife, Betty, were frequent visitors, as were the publishers of the *San Francisco Chronicle*, George Cameron and his wife, Helen de Young.

Roy and Edith entertained Lady Anne Hunloke and her husband, Mr. Henry Hunloke, as houseguests on Thanksgiving Day in 1937. Lady Anne had a title, but her husband needed a job. Two days later, the couple was off to visit the Fred Astaires, where Mr. Hunloke was hoping to break into Hollywood. (He never did.)

CELEBRATING THANKSGIVING on the ranch was a special time of the year for the Pike family. Roy Jr. reminisced, "I can see the house now. A roaring fire in the fireplace with dogs lying peacefully on the carpet in front. The centerpiece on the dining table, a mass of small chrysanthemums and garlands of grape leaves.

"And the huge turkey was brought in (usually a 25 lb. one) and set on a small side table. And father would then carve and put slices on each plate, and candied yams covered with marshmallows were passed. And, of course, cranberry sauce and stuffing. And all of this topped off with pumpkin or mince pie. We boys sometimes sat at a side table, if there were too many for the big table. The grownups would indulge in much laughter and exciting conversation."

BASKING IN in the warmth of holiday cheer, Roy's family and friends remained blissfully unaware of El Solyo's true financial condition. Except for the host himself, no one seated at the table knew that the ranch had already decimated the family's fortune.

CHAPTER 16

"A Terrible Mistake"

Roy and Edith, 1919–1941

IT IS UNLIKELY that Roy's wife, Edith, paid much attention to the July 1935 issue of *Ford News*, published by the Ford Motor Company. So she probably did not read the first sentence of the article about El Solyo, which began, "The present manager of El Solyo Ranch says that he made a mistake when he was a young man by becoming interested in California ranching." It is even less likely that she read the "Story of El Solyo Ranch," a nine-page paper written by her husband, which began with exactly the same first sentence except that the word "terrible" was inserted before "mistake." Even if she had read both, however, she would not have learned the whole truth about El Solyo Ranch.

Roy traced the roots of his "terrible mistake" to a friendship in 1901 with an older rancher. He "envied this rancher's ability to…vacation at the end of the fruit harvest in September…The rancher then exercised his hobby for hunting and other lighter chores." Roy promised himself that "if he ever got his shoulders much above water, he would go in for California ranching and live that lovely sort of life with a good part of each year easily open for recreation."

Now Roy berated himself as a dreamer who "didn't realize that he would become a victim to the modern study of economics, extended into agriculture… which called for 'diversification.' Today…he has no chance for any vacations of any sort because the harvesting periods…run actively and under high pressure from the middle of May to the middle of January each year!!…To be an idealist…by no means connotes the technical ability to administer plans to make such Ideals or Dreams truly or quickly work out. That is the Rub of Life!"

THE WHOLE TRUTH begins with the purchase of the original five farms for $350,000 in 1919 by the El Solyo Land Company ($4.96 million in 2017 dollars). As the sole shareholder of the El Solyo Land Company and with no money of his own, Roy must have pledged his wife's inheritance to secure bank funding for the initial purchase. A year later, the El Solyo Land Company sold $350,000 of "First Mortgage 6% Gold Bonds," maturing over a ten-year period with equal annual redemptions of $35,000, starting in 1922.

The bond announcement in the *San Francisco Chronicle* on March 19, 1920, contained several exaggerations, if not outright falsehoods. "For a number of years," the notice began, "the entire ranch has been successfully farmed to grain, but as irrigation progressed the crops have been diversified. During 1920 practically the entire acreage will be planted to barley, rice, celery, cabbage, cauliflower, alfalfa and various garden [crops]."

In fact, "practically the entire acreage" could not possibly have been planted in 1920. Far from it. (The irrigation pumps did not even start until May 1 that year, six weeks *after* the announcement.) Testifying fourteen years later under oath, Roy presented a sharply different timeline. "I recognized that if one was to establish a great diversified agricultural project, it would take 10 or 12 years." Nor was it remotely possible that the ranch would have produced any positive cash flow, as projected in the announcement: "Net earnings for 1920 are conservatively estimated at over four times the interest charges on this bond issue."

After buying the land, Roy needed even more capital to develop the ranch—$150,000 for the irrigation system and $600,000 for buildings, equipment, and livestock—estimated *Fortune* magazine. So Roy secured an appraisal valuing the ranch at $960,000, based upon projected earnings. This higher appraised value facilitated more short-term borrowing. Yet El Solyo's demand for capital did not abate. After Edith's resources were depleted, Roy turned to an outside syndicate in 1924, placing a $200,000 second mortgage on the ranch. But he soon defaulted on this note too, and the syndicate moved to foreclose. By year's end, Roy was desperate.

IN PERFECT HINDSIGHT, we can see that Roy's ranching scheme was almost certainly doomed from the start. When he dreamed of acquiring El Solyo in 1917–18, agricultural prices were booming. America was the "breadbasket of the world" while Europe suffered the ravages of World War I. "The last year of any agricultural prosperity was 1920," wrote historian David Kyvig. "Thereafter farm income and land values would slide into a twenty-year depression and not emerge from that slump until World War II." Incredibly, farm prices fell by 43 percent alone between 1920 and 1921. Whatever revenues Roy had projected from his earliest harvests would have been reduced by almost half. As he later said in a gross understatement, "I came to very difficult financial times beginning in '21." Literally speaking, he had bet the farm and lost.

CALLING IT "A MIRACLE," Roy found his savior in a man named Allan C. Balch, a friend and fellow Bohemian. Balch owned controlling interests in San Joaquin Light & Power and the Southern California Gas Company, among many other utilities. When Pacific Gas & Electric (in Northern California) and Southern California Edison (in Southern California) acquired these interests, Balch became immensely wealthy.

He and his wife resided in a double-floor apartment in the newly built Biltmore Hotel in Los Angeles. They owned three Rolls-Royces, one for him, one for her, and one in Paris for their annual trip abroad. Roy Jr. remembered their visits to El Solyo: "Mr. Balch had one of the most beautiful Rolls-Royces I ever saw. It was a town car with the chauffeur up front in the open. The body was canary yellow with black top and black fenders. Mrs. Balch always arrived with her personal maid."

"Mr. Allan C. Balch came into the property at my request," Roy later testified. "[He] would buy the property in toto and asked me to remain in the management of it, and develop it along the lines which I originally conceived." In January 1925, Balch took over the first mortgage (the $350,000 in the bonds) and the second mortgage (the $200,000 debt to the syndicate). There was no equity. In family lore, most of Edith's fortune was wiped out. Henceforth, Roy would be paid a salary, plus his housing. That was the whole truth that only Roy knew.

ALTHOUGH LEGAL TITLE to the ranch had changed hands, little evidence of this shift was visible at El Solyo. Roy still ran the show as the general manager, and Balch, as an absentee owner, visited the ranch only infrequently. Roy spun a yarn to his wife that he had simply borrowed more money from him. To the family, Balch was an important, but perhaps transitory, figure.

When Roy extolled Balch's friendship at his fiftieth birthday celebration at the Bohemian Club, he spoke more honestly. He explained that Balch had said to him, "Roy, I won't let them do that to you," referring to the threat of foreclosure.

Balch then provided "an incredible amount" of capital within ten days and had continued to provide more funds "each year since—in faith and staunch courage—which I hope to repay."

El Solyo needed millions, and, as *Fortune* gently put it, "Balch proved to be an exceptionally durable angel." When Roy tallied the cost of El Solyo in 1934, it added up to the staggering sum of $3,542,000 ($64.8 million in 2017 dollars).

Of course, any repayment of Balch's investment was a pipe dream, especially when Roy told his guests that he "was not as well off materially at fifty as at forty." That is, he was worth less in 1928 than in 1918. Roy continued, "What then of the race? What then of some achievement? The answer to that is the glorious friendships I have known and which, in so many ways, continue to make each year a better one to live than the one past." (Balch was unable to attend the dinner.)

ANY FAINT HOPE that El Solyo would produce a profit was shattered by the Great Depression. No farm in the nation would escape a brutal plunge in demand for its crops. As historian David Kennedy wrote, "Nowhere did the Depression strike more savagely than in the American countryside. On America's farms, income had plummeted from $6 billion in what for farmers was the already lean year of 1929 to $2 billion in 1932."

Less income meant widespread unemployment, and Roy's son, Peter, remembered the result. "Daily 'boes' [hoboes] came through—bedrolls on their backs, walking miles and miles from one ranch to another looking for work or a meal. There were always tables in our large mess halls for the extra meals." Market prices fell so far that some of El Solyo's crops literally became worthless. Roy Jr. remembered that peaches in 1930 plunged to $15.00 per ton. "We just knocked them off to the ground and didn't pick them."

WHEN FARM labor wages declined, some agricultural workers formed unions. Strikes during the picking season were an existential threat to farm owners because a harvesting delay of even a few days could mean the loss of an entire crop. In 1933 that threat arrived at El Solyo when members of the Modesto Farmers and Workers Union struck growers in Stanislaus County. The *Modesto Bee* headlined, "Fruit Workers Strike for 30 Cents Per Hour."

The next day, picketers were sent to El Solyo. Ever the charmer, Roy invited the men to lunch. "Pike said the ranch recently increased its pay to 25 cents an hour and pays enough for picking [piece work] so the men can make more than 30 cents an hour. The men are fed for 75 cents a day, the amount not being raised when the wages were increased, and are given free living quarters. They are also transported to and from work." With his friendly manner, Roy defused a possibly tense encounter, and the picketers departed after lunch.

Elsewhere in Stanislaus County, the *Bee* noted, "Guns were reported pointed at men who have been on the picket lines…Pickets allegedly 'razzed' the workers, calling them 'yellow' and 'scabs.'" County-wide the strike did not appear successful. "Although many men and women have quit their jobs on ranches and at dry yards, work in most cases was reported going forward as usual." Strike discipline was impossible when many other migrants were willing to work for twenty-five cents an hour to put bread on the table.

EVEN UNDER Roy's benevolent rule, farm labor was tough work. Peter, his son, described the process of thinning fruit orchards in the spring. "In order to have fruit properly sized and the tree stay healthy and not lose branches with over-weight, the fruit has to be 'spaced.' Every single twig, branch or shoot of the tree must be looked at. Where double blossoms occurred, there would be double fruit. One of these has to be knocked off. Fruit growing closer than four or six inches has to be knocked off.

"This was done by maneuvering a 12-foot orchard ladder in and out and all the way around the tree, climbing to the top and working down each branch. By running your hand down every single branch or shoot and watching carefully, one learns when to close fingers and knock off a small fruit. The caution is that, if you knock off too many, the yield in tons per acre harvested is in jeopardy. To protect against this, inspectors come along with counters. They go over the tree you have done. Using hand counters and from their ladders, they would count the remaining fruit. If a man just willy-nilly stripped trees, he was fired. In the Depression, at 25 cents per hour, a man was damn cautious."

YEAR AFTER YEAR, the Depression rolled on with no end in sight. When President Roosevelt delivered his famous inaugural address on March 4, 1933 ("The only thing we have to fear is fear itself"), he pledged to take immediate action. "Our greatest primary task is to put people to work." To revive rural America, the nation should make "definite efforts to raise the values of agricultural products."

During his First Hundred Days, Congress passed two programs to achieve this goal—the National Reconstruction Administration (NRA) and the Agricultural Adjustment Act (AAA).

The NRA allowed industrial compacts to regulate the production of industries—for example, the production of peaches—and to control prices and wages, hopefully pushing them upward. The AAA authorized the government to collect taxes from agricultural processors to pay farmers for letting acreage lie fallow. The aim of both programs, in Roosevelt's words, was "to prevent unfair competition and disastrous over production."

Roy viewed these programs as grave infringements on his rights as a free American. Should the government have the power to regulate the tonnage of peaches that El Solyo delivered to canners? Could the government force him to pay higher wages? Why should the government tax him to pay another farmer not to grow crops? Although both the NRA and the AAA would be ruled unconstitutional by the Supreme Court, Roy would forever remain an implacable foe of President Roosevelt and the New Deal.

IRONICALLY, Roosevelt had swept the El Solyo precinct in the 1932 election, winning 83 percent of the vote (59 of 70 ballots cast). But for years to come, Roy would rail against government policies in letters to the editor, opinion columns, and public testimony. *Fortune* would describe him as "something of a pamphleteer against communism and the New Deal."

In January 1936, Roy published a broadside titled "Californians—Wake Up!" in the monthly magazine of the California Chamber of Commerce. He urged members to band together "to successfully combat communism, depression, excessive taxation, and the multitude of influences affecting the welfare of the country." Roy argued that all progress in America "has been developed by businessmen. Our America has been a nation of businessmen—small businessmen, big businessmen... No peasantry here!"

He warned of "an element in our midst... [who] would do away with our form of government which has the nearest approach to a classless society the world has ever known... because all avenues of life are reasonably open to the industrious and the meritorious... They would do away with our production for profit—even the tiniest profit to the dressmaker, the corner grocery man, the garage man, the little or big man."

EL SOLYO was the largest contributor to the Stanislaus County chapter of the Associated Farmers of California, a powerful statewide political organization allied with the Chamber of Commerce and other anti-New Deal groups. Although its name implied a broad-based coalition, the Associated Farmers reflected the big-business agenda of its major supporters, including Southern Pacific Railroad, Pacific Gas & Electric Company, and Holly Sugar Corporation.

A high priority of the Associated Farmers was the enactment of local anti-picketing ordinances to prevent strikers from blocking entrances and obstructing roads. Where these legal measures did not succeed, the group relied upon extra-legal methods to break strikes. In the words of one agricultural historian, these tactics included "deputizing hundreds of Associated Farmers' members," organizing and training "private armies ('pick handle brigades')," using "labor spies," and stockpiling "private arsenals."

The *Rural Observer*, a magazine supporting migrant labor rights, alleged that El Solyo had an "arsenal" that had been revealed to a committee of the League of Women Voters investigating housing and living conditions of California migrants. After Roy threatened legal action, the *Observer* published a semi-retraction by reprinting a letter from the League. "We were not shown a so-called 'arsenal room.' Nor was the word 'arsenal' used in conversation at that time. Four of us, however, were shown a table containing INDUSTRIAL MUNITIONS."

The *Rural Observer* did find evidence that El Solyo had purchased $847.68 of "Tear and Sickening Gas," which led to more questions. "If El Solyo ranch has no 'arsenal,' it would be interesting to know what Mr. Pike calls his array of defensive commodities. It would also be interesting to hear...what plans he had or has for using the 'industrial munitions' which the League of Women Voters' committee saw at El Solyo."

But the *Rural Observer* was no match for Roy Pike and his access to the mainstream press. With his good friend George Cameron listed on the masthead as publisher, Roy might well have ghostwritten the *San Francisco Chronicle* editorial himself on August 16, 1939. Titled "Mass Farm Production as a Fallacy," the editorial began, "Roy Pike of El Solyo Ranch says that the economy of mass production in agriculture is a myth... Mass production, he says, has proved unprofitable in comparison with the individual farmer's production."

Turning the world on its head, the *Chronicle* argued that farms like El Solyo were actually at a competitive disadvantage to small family farms. "Everything cost cash. There is no opportunity to use family labor. There is no such margin for economy cuts as in individual operations. Instead of being economical, large scale agriculture is extravagant by comparison...There is such a thing as bigness weakening the structure and getting top-heavy and out of hand."

ROY'S ADVOCACY for the Associated Farmers reached its zenith in December 1939 when he testified at the La Follette Committee hearing in San Francisco. Senator Robert La Follette chaired a subcommittee of the U.S. Senate that was investigating farm labor conditions in California. Earlier in the year, John Steinbeck's bestseller, *Grapes of Wrath*, had galvanized public anger about the plight of migratory farm labor. (In Steinbeck's book, the Associated Farmers became the fictitious "Farmers Association.")

In twenty-one pages of impassioned testimony, Roy sought to cast growers as blameless for the squalid conditions of migratory farm workers. He and La Follette sparred over the quality of accommodations available to migratory families.

> MR. PIKE: Farmers needing fifty or a hundred or more men at peak times generally have excellent bunkhouses, bathing and toilet facilities, good mess houses, and so forth.
>
> SENATOR LA FOLLETTE: You say that as a general rule?
>
> MR. PIKE: In Stanislaus County and many others, local ordinances provide that, when two or more family or other groups [are] working and living during harvest seasons on particular farms, that water service, toilet facilities, and so forth, must be furnished and operated under the inspection of the local health departments. We don't allow squatter camps.
>
> SENATOR LA FOLLETTE: Are those ordinances generally enforced, speaking of the State as a whole?
>
> MR. PIKE: Yes, speaking from our part of the district. The Associated Farmers have made it their business to see that the sheriff and the health department have strongly policed those conditions.

Furthermore, Roy argued, migratory labor was not really necessary because it represented only 30 percent of the harvest workforce. Senator La Follette drove home the fact that even 30 percent could be critical to a successful harvest.

SENATOR LA FOLLETTE: Could you harvest your crops and carry on your operations without these migratory workers?

MR. PIKE: It would be difficult. It would be that 15 or 30 percent difficult.

SENATOR LA FOLLETTE: You will be short what? Thirty percent?

MR. PIKE: Fifteen or thirty; maybe 25 percent...

SENATOR LA FOLLETTE: Yes; I understand that. But the point I try to make out is that I got the impression from your statement, as you read it, that the migratory [workers] were not important in your particular county.

MR. PIKE: That is correct. That is a correct statement.

SENATOR LA FOLLETTE: But you could not really function there without them, could you, if you had a 30-percent shortage of the actual labor needed? You would have to sacrifice some of your crops, would you not?

MR. PIKE: You would have to rustle hard. I don't know. I think they are necessary to that point, but not nearly the major item that some people think. That is all I want to register.

In conformity to the gender biases of his day, Roy argued that most of his female workers at harvest time were not looking for a living wage, but merely supplementing their family's income. They were actually permanent residents from nearby farms and towns.

MR. PIKE: Most of this female "part time" labor individually earn during harvest seasons from $100 to $300 per individual. This makes for "spending money" throughout the year... and is perhaps the reason for the operation of so many busy "beauty shops" throughout towns like Tracy, Modesto, Patterson, Merced, and so forth. Also why in these country packing plants and dry yards, one sees so many nice-looking women, young and old, who wear—as they come to work—so many good-looking dresses, shoes, and silk stockings.

THE CONSERVATIVE *San Francisco Examiner* praised Roy's testimony: "The importance and its effectiveness was manifested by the fact that it held the respectful attention not only of Senator La Follette and his aides, but also of the courtroom spectators whose attitude has been reflected time and again during the hearings here by boos and catcalls at other agriculturalists on the stand. To Pike, they gave rapt earnest attention, and no jeers."

But Roy had met his match. After twenty-eight days of hearings and hundreds of witnesses, the La Follette committee published its damning conclusion. The Associated Farmers had engaged in a conspiracy "designed to prevent the exercise of their civil liberties by oppressed wage laborers in agriculture, [which] was executed ruthlessly with every device of repression that anti-unionism could muster." Where Associated Farmers successfully implemented its policies, "local fascism was the result."

ROY'S PERSONAL fall from grace was precipitous. Eighteen months after his La Follette testimony, he suffered a stroke and resigned as the general manager of El Solyo in July 1941. Forced to leave the ranch, Roy and Edith never lived together again. He moved to the Bohemian Club, and she moved into a one-bedroom apartment in a seven-story building at 1850 Sacramento Street in San Francisco, near Van Ness Avenue.

In family lore, she was shocked by this turn of events. Roy spun a tale about Balch taking unfair advantage of him and reneging on some kind of a deal. For the rest of her life, she would believe that Balch had cheated Roy out of his rightful ownership. This was not true.

THE *PATTERSON IRRIGATOR* printed the truth on page one. "El Solyo has not been a money-making project... But it has paid big dividends in many less material things." Roy's biggest achievement was finding Balch, a "capitalist and philanthropist" with a "progressive spirit... [as] reflected in the records of El Solyo." Balch was willing and able to absorb the enormous losses required to develop "a model agricultural empire."

The *Irrigator* regretted Roy's departure due to his illness. "[His] infinite capacity for making friends drew ample capital into the project... Pike has likewise been a whirlwind worker in civic affairs. Almost single-handed, he has waged battle against San Francisco, Modesto, and Turlock to protect West Side water rights. And whether it's a Farm Center meeting, a Red Cross campaign, or a farm housing problem, El Solyo Ranch is always carrying its full share of responsibility and effort for the common good."

OBLIVIOUS to the family's financial woes, his sons, Roy Jr. and Peter, grew up proudly watching El Solyo become "the largest diversified ranch in its time." For them, the vast expanse of the ranch offered limitless opportunities for exploration, adventure, and rebellion.

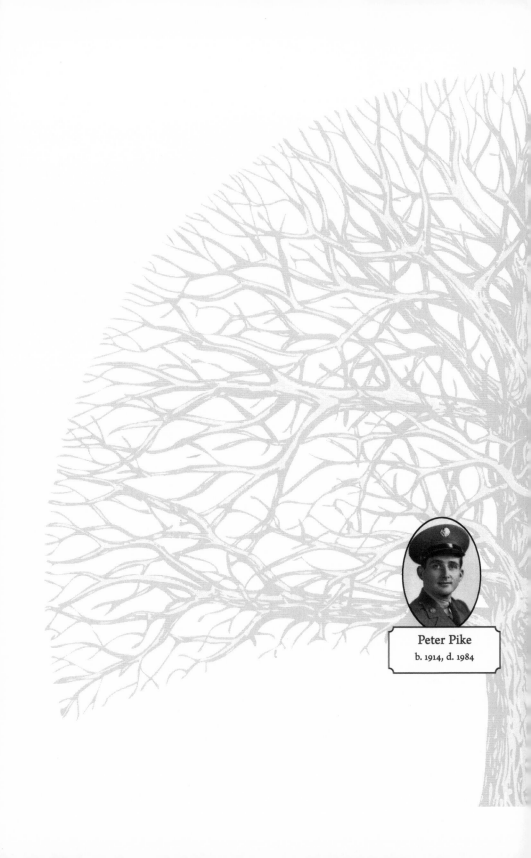

Peter Pike
b. 1914, d. 1984

Part Three

Parents

Catherine H. Cline
b. 1918, d. 1979

CHAPTER 17

Childhood on a Ranch

Peter, 1921–1928

THE TWO BOYS, Roy Jr. and Peter, spent their first summer on the ranch in 1921, looked after by their beloved English governess, Constance Taylor. Sixty years later, Peter still remembered meeting Connie for the first time. Unlike his old governess, Emily Ayling, who was "tall [and] thin with a sharp, authoritative voice," Connie was "short with a round happy face, dimpled cheeks, dark, almost black hair."

When Emily called Peter home to be introduced to Connie, he was playing across the street on a newly tarred and graveled garage roof. Emily "took one look at my dirty hands, became extremely cross and harshly told me to go wash them. Connie took hold of my hands and exclaimed, 'Why these are not dirty! These are little boy's hands!' At age six, I fell completely in love for the first time in my life."

That summer the boys and Connie shared a house at El Solyo with the ranch superintendent, Harry Blosser, a jovial corn farmer from Iowa. The two-story home, which also served as ranch headquarters, stood alone, surrounded by fields of grain. Peter remembered that the "land was flat as far as the eye could see, wheat or barley being the only crop. The heat was so strong that mirages appeared no matter what direction one looked and at almost any time of day."

Because in the early years all the roads were dirt, "We always knew when someone was coming by the dirt clouds rising in the distance that followed anything that moved." His brother, Roy Jr., remembered the ranch house was always full of dust "and the heavy grass-like carpets seemed to retain all the dust and dirt... Because of the proximity of the house to the barn, we were constantly plagued by flies. I can remember long pieces of sticky paper hanging from the back porch

The two Pike brothers—Roy Jr., ten, and Peter, eight—standing in a
newly planted peach orchard at El Solyo, May 13, 1923. Peter "always had
a remarkable affinity for collecting dirt," Roy later wrote.

ceiling to catch the flies. In spite of screened windows and doors, flies still got into
the house. There was always a fly swatter lying about within easy reach."

Upstairs were two bedrooms with brass beds. Downstairs a dingy hallway separated
the small living room from the dining room. Food was cooked on a big wood-burning
stove in the kitchen, and every morning the boys were awakened by the clanking sound
of the stove door being opened to remove ashes from the previous day.

Off the kitchen was "the cooler," a small room with three sides of wire screens.
Burlap sacks were hung over the screens, and water dripped down them soaking
the fabric. The evaporation of the water cooled the air in the room, which was
where the milk was kept. "Bringing the milk bucket back from the morning milking," Peter remembered, "meant that we could skim the cream from the top of the
milk that had settled the night before."

There was an icebox, but the nearest ice vendor was in Tracy, sixteen miles

away. Anytime anybody went to Tracy, that person always brought back a block
of ice. "However, there was not a lot of ice left from a 50-pound block after traveling home in the 100-degree valley heat in the back of a Model T pickup, even
though covered with layers of gunny sacks. The dust from the dirt roads settled
on the sacks, making a nice mud paste at the end of an hour's trip. I am sure that
at age six, when I rode in the back, the mud paste gave me much more joy than
the remaining ice did to the rest of the family."

A windmill and detached tank house, accessible by ladder, were located behind
the house. When the wind blew, the tank filled with water, which was most of the
time. When there was no wind, water had to be hand pumped from the well for
the household and for the livestock.

FOR THE FIRST three years, the boys only spent summers at El Solyo. So their
bodies faced a painful period of adjustment from San Francisco's cool fog to the
intense heat of the San Joaquin Valley. Acclimating to the new environment, Peter
suffered painful sunburns with large blisters followed by peelings that made him
"feel like a snake shedding his skin."

He and his brother slept in a second-floor bedroom, "with every window and
door open, hoping for some slight breeze or movement of air." Having baked in
the sun all day long, the roof "would emit pent-up heat for hours after the sun
went down. Lying naked, covered with blisters in the evening heat, on just a sheet
on a mattress to the tune of mosquitos and other bugs that could crawl through
the screens sounds like suffering. Not so. This was the way of life in every farm
house in the valley, except they had tans not sunburns."

Every night at 9:00, lying in bed, Peter would hear the long "whoooeee" whistle
as the Southern Pacific *Owl* made its nightly run southbound from San Francisco
to Los Angeles. After a while he could tell which ranch crossing it was whistling at
miles away. At 6:00 the next morning, he would hear the northbound *Owl* whistle
at the same crossings.

The only other regularly scheduled train was a local one-car diesel called a "skunk"—
one third of the car for the engine, one third for passengers, and one third for freight
and mail. After leaving Tracy, the southbound skunk went through Vernalis every
day at noon and returned northbound at six o'clock. "It would stop anywhere it was
flagged—a crossroad, a cow path, anyplace. Pick up a person, a five-gallon container
of milk, drop off a freight shipment such as a plow or parts a farmer needed for repairs."

HARRY BLOSSER took Peter and Roy "in hand and introduced us to life on the land." Harry had the first Model T on the ranch, a pickup truck with no top, and he always left a sack of barley in the back for the boys to sit on if he had another passenger. Frequently, he would take them on his trips to Tracy. Almost every time, it seemed, they would have at least one flat tire.

"A flat in those days," Peter explained, "meant taking the steel rim off the wood-spoked wheel, breaking the tire off the rim, pulling it off, and getting the inner tube out. Using a clamp vise on the fender, a raw patch could be burned on the tube. The tire remounted and then hand pumped to proper pressure. Hand pumping to 30 pounds in the hot sun of a summer afternoon—we didn't need jogging for exercise in those days!"

If Connie joined Harry on the trip, the boys could look forward to a special treat. Their goal was the ice cream parlor, painted white with "a marble countertop running the length of the store and iron wire chairs and tables all sparkling white. And the best part of all, the booths opposite the counter had white lattice arches." Each arch bore the name of a town where the "skunk" stopped, including Vernalis. "To have an ice cream soda in the Vernalis booth was … my real excitement on a town trip. Even better than throwing pebbles at the sparrows on fence posts by the side of the gravel road while flat tires were being fixed."

One of the most amazing sights on the farm was a huge combine harvesting barley. The combine machine was pulled by a Holt 75 tractor with caterpillar treads, and together the two machines "looked almost as big as our house," Peter remembered, "as if two great monsters were about to collide in the middle of a great plain with nothing to interfere or stop them." Young Peter was allowed to ride high up on the deck of the combine where the sacks were sewn, so high up that he could look directly into his second-floor bedroom window.

Decades later, he painted a hair-raising picture of the combine in action. "The machinery to run an 18-foot cutting blade, elevators, spindles, shakers, screens, etc. was complex. At the time, there was no such thing as an auxiliary engine. The whole process was driven off the main wheel. Gears, chain drives, reduction systems, belt drives, etc. whirred, spun and rattled as soon as the combine moved forward and the main wheel turned. All of these gears, sprockets and drives were fully exposed, no safety cages or protective bars."

THE BOYS' NEAREST playmates were the Schaeffer children, Al, Noel, and Margaret, who lived four miles away in Vernalis. The entire town of Vernalis was a one building general store with a post office in one corner. The building was owned by the Schaeffer family, and Mr. Schaeffer was the postmaster. "The second floor was the Grange meeting hall where all community functions were held. Dance meetings, and church."

"Any time we wanted to play," Peter remembered, "we would throw a hackam around a pony's head and ride over. Sometimes Noel would have the same idea we would find each other along the way. Sometimes Mrs. Schaeffer would say he went to play with the Delphia kids.' The Delphias lived four miles in the direction up to the foothills where Interstate 5 now runs. So off to the Delphia we went. I'm still sure they had the biggest barns and haylofts in the county

THE WHOLE PIKE FAMILY moved permanently to El Solyo in the spring of 1924. "Looking back," Peter wrote, "I wonder what was in the minds of our group when we arrived. Father excited about what he was starting and building, mother dumped here from a lovely home on the peninsula which had a large and cool garden with shade trees and flowers, our English governess whose only previous experience in the country was [the] green, lush English countryside."

Trying to mollify Edith's unhappiness, Roy rebuilt the farm house. Walls were moved to make a large dining room; a new kitchen was built with an electric stove and a restaurant-size icebox, later a refrigerator; the second floor was pushed out, creating a new master bedroom and three guest rooms. A garden and lawns were planted around a crescent-shaped driveway leading to the road. Peter remembered that the remodeling continued for the next fifteen years. "Mother was always coming up with new ideas."

Although the family lived together, Peter had little memory of his parents at dinner or other meals. "Father was away a lot and so was mother…Connie was always with us. She was loving, warm, and very pretty." With his parents absent, she helped him write notes to them. Seven of these have survived, poignantly written in the hand of a young child.

"Dear Daddy…Miss Taylor [Connie] saw a skunk. I wish I had seen it. Are you having a good time in New York? Please send me a card. Love to Mother, Peter." On Mother's Day, he wrote, "Dear Mother, I miss you very much…When I'm a man, I'll always send you some flowers. Your *fils* [son] Pierre."

on April 20, 1924, in Stockton, Peter sat sulking in a front row pew, holding back tears. He recalled hearing others ask, "What's the matter with Peter?" Connie and Harry did live nearby and remained "an integral part of our lives" for a year or two before they left the ranch.

IN THE FALL OF 1924, the boys were sent to a one-room school, the Rising Sun Grammar School, three miles from their home. The school building was divided into two sections by a partition with four rows of desks in each half. One side of the room was for grades one through four, taught by Mrs. Garrett; the other side for grades five through eight, taught by her husband, Mr. Garrett. Peter was in the fifth grade, Roy in the sixth.

In the center of the room at the back was the furnace and coal bin, which led to a dilemma for Peter. "Should you be bad and get a desk in back where you could get warm, or be good and get a desk up front near the teacher but would be cold?" Outside there was a windmill for water for the horse trough and a drinking fountain. Toilet facilities were behind the building in an outhouse.

The boys often rode bicycles to school. But Peter preferred to ride his white pony, Dynamite, because he wanted to be like the other children who all rode bareback or walked from their farms. Besides, "if you had a horse tied up outside, you could get out earlier for recess and noontime to water your horse and take care of it."

The school day began with the eighteen students lining up in separate queues, one for girls and one for boys. Each line entered a door to an anteroom where the students hung up their coats and deposited their lunch bags. Then they filed into their proper row depending upon their grade. Each child had a slate at his or her desk. Mr. Garrett played his violin, and the children sang "The Star-Spangled Banner." If he was in a good mood, Mr. Garrett would play several more songs, including "Old Black Joe," "Billy Boy," and "Sweet Genevieve."

Peter remembered that white-haired Mr. Garrett wore open-collared shirts "showing white chest hair that came up to a distinct shaving line. His sleeves were always turned up at the cuffs, never rolled beyond the elbows, exposing a white-haired arm. I always remember the white hair on the back of his hand when he leaned down on my desk to demonstrate a point in penmanship or correct a sum on my slate."

We can imagine that moments of silence in a schoolhouse full of children aged six to thirteen would be rare indeed. However, Peter did remember a couple of times this happened. "In our classroom, if no one was talking, the only noise heard would be a grasshopper jumping or the windmill turning if there were a breeze or a horse nervously kicking against some flies."

That quiet memory stayed with him for life, as did another extraordinary experience. "A couple of times we heard a strange roar very faintly. Eyeing Mr. Garrett to get his reaction, we waited until it got louder. Then he smiled, got up, and started toward the door. We all ran out into the schoolyard, looked up in the sky and saw an airplane—a first for us all."

ON WEEKENDS Peter was out of the house like a shot and never back until evening. "My world was with the teamsters and mule skinners or climbing on one of our new tractors." His brother remembered Peter's fascination with one tractor in particular, a new Rumely. "It was not a long machine like the caterpillar tractors, but it had huge high wheels with spokes in back and smaller wheels in front. He was fascinated with this implement because it had a very high smoke stack, and he would climb down inside. He always had a remarkable affinity for collecting dirt. Within just a few minutes in that stack, he was covered with black from head to foot. Needless to say, he was not a welcome site when he came home, and he was thrown into a hot tub!"

Across River Road from the family's remodeled house, now called Solyo Place, lived Tom Graves, who was part Indian. He did chores for the family, like feeding the horses and chickens and milking the cows. In the early years, Peter rode with him over the pastures and river bottom lands, listening to story after story. "Like all Indians he knew horses as people…There was a sense of really knowing the land when riding pastures and fences with an Indian, listening to him, watching him roll a Bull Durham cigarette with one hand and never release the reins in his other hand." Eventually, Tom was fired after drinking too much and taking a shot at Harry Blosser. Peter missed his stories.

Another character who made an impression on Peter was named Santa Cataline. "He had a soft lilting Spanish accent and a smile that never left him. I still remember the soft gentle way he talked with the animals. Jumpy horses would calm right down, barking dogs would lick his hands. Without any obvious 'teaching' he would bridge the gap between my nervousness with a new horse or pony or dog as if he were a father introducing his son to the next door neighbor's son."

Santa Cataline lived quietly near the stables, never seeming to have friends. "From time to time he would disappear, always to come back again in a few months or once over a couple of years. He would turn up at the stables, with his sweet, gentle almost inaudible voice with a hand on my head or shoulder, as if I were one of his animals, and greet me…as if he had never been away." It was only later that Peter learned, after the repeal of Prohibition, that Santa Cataline had been "the biggest bootlegger in this part of the valley."

IN EARLY YEARS, El Solyo was as reliant on horse power as tractor power. So the blacksmith shop was important. Charlie Brown, a German immigrant with a heavy accent, was the head blacksmith. Peter remembered him always dressed with a black shirt and leather apron from his chest to the ground. "His only recognition of hot summer weather was to roll up his sleeves which then exposed his long-sleeved union suit [long underwear]. No wonder sweat poured like a flowing stream from under his brown floppy hat off the end of his nose."

Working in one hundred degree weather, Charlie could "lift up the leg of the heaviest Percheron, lay it across his knee, file the hoof, and nail on a hot smoking shoe as easily as if it only weighed a few ounces. Charlie chewed tobacco and it was always a mystery to me as a youngster how his mouth produced a constant source of nails while he was shoeing, when all I ever saw him put in it was a quid of tobacco."

Peter could sit for hours under the big eucalyptus tree outside the blacksmith shop, listening to the rhythm and ring of Charlie's hammer. Or he would watch the harness makers carving long strips of leather and listen to the crunching of their sharp knives cutting into the hides. For the rest of his life, he would remember the "smell of the oil as batches of harnesses were pulled out of the oil tank to hang and drain." Every once in a while, he was asked to hold something or fetch something. "What a thrill."

"I always left the house ... early in the morning ... [to] go down to the headquarters camp and pray that someone would have me doing something when Connie found me. [Then] I could prove I was important and could get out of going off with a governess [to] do children's things. Pitching hay from the hay loft down to the mangers was a wonderful job. I was doing something and at the same time able to hide."

THE BOYS RETURNED that fall to the Rising Sun School, Peter now in the sixth grade and Roy in the seventh. Peter remembered "the Garretts herding us through whatever level of 2+2=4 or C-A-T for cat that we had achieved by that year. Mr. Garrett's hairy arms bowing his violin for our morning's 'Star Spangled Banner' and each session ending with the Pledge of Allegiance." There was one big change, however. The Rising Sun was no longer a one-room school. There were now two classrooms and an auditorium.

This would be the boys' last year at Rising Sun. Edith decided that they needed "stricter studying" and hired a tutor, Bill Oliphant, to home school them. Oliphant, who was a recent graduate of the University of California, was paid $100 a month and lived in the small house vacated by Harry and Connie Blosser, who had moved back to Iowa. An upstairs room in the Tack House across River Road served as their classroom.

"Bill stayed with us for two years," Roy Jr. wrote, "and proved a welcome addition to the family." The boys studied Latin, learned algebra, and read Shakespeare's plays. Under Oliphant's tutelage, both completed their freshman high school subjects and would later enter high school as sophomores. Oliphant liked to write, and he and Edith collaborated on a play about the life of Voltaire.

Another welcome addition to the household was a young Bohemian Club friend of their father named Brosie Whitmer. A Stanford University graduate (class of 1921), Brosie was much in demand as a popular piano player around San Francisco. He gave piano lessons to the boys and must have entertained the family's frequent guests at El Solyo. "Through his lessons," Roy Jr. remembered, "he instilled in us a love of music and harmony."

The boys adhered to a strict daily schedule. "Peter would get up first, go down and practice the piano for a half hour," Roy wrote. "Then he would go up to mother's bedroom and have a French lesson. When mother rang for her breakfast tray, we both went down and had our breakfast in the pantry. After breakfast, we went over to our classroom." When the boys' daily lessons with Oliphant were finished in the afternoon, "Brosie would take over."

THESE WERE happy years for Roy Jr. and Peter. A new tennis court was built at El Solyo where the boys learned to play tennis. One summer, the family vacationed on Santa Catalina Island where Peter learned to sail. They made frequent weekend trips to Yosemite with Oliphant. Their mother, Edith, however, was not happy.

CHAPTER 18

Schools Abroad

Peter, 1925–1932

MAROONED ON A RANCH far from the nearest town, Edith imagined a different life for her children. Perhaps, like her own mother, she worried that her two boys would grow up "too Western," especially her younger son, Peter, who preferred to ride his horse, rather than a bicycle, to school. So in January 1925, she took ten-year-old Peter and twelve-year-old Roy Jr. to Europe for six months. In family lore, she explained to the boys that she wanted them "to learn French."

The *San Francisco Chronicle's* announcement of their trip abroad was filled with magical thinking. "Since leaving town Mr. and Mrs. Pike have gone into ranching on a large scale, their farm being one of the model ones of its kind…Mr. Pike, who formerly followed the usual pastimes of the San Francisco club man, has distinguished himself as a farmer, orchardist, and fruit-grower and, needless to add, loves the new life."

In fact, this would be the same month that Roy Sr. lost the ranch and the bulk of his wife's fortune. Blissfully unaware of the financial wreckage left behind, Edith and her boys boarded the *Overland Limited* on January 23, arriving in New York City five days later.

AT PENN STATION, they were met by Lucy James's chauffeur, who drove them to her apartment on Park Avenue. "Both Peter and I fell in love with Mrs. James," Roy Jr. wrote. "She was one of the most beautiful and regal ladies I had ever met." Lucy was sole heir to the fortune of her great uncle, Robert G. Dun, and would later become the largest individual shareholder of the merged Dun & Bradstreet

Corporation. (She had divorced her husband and reverted to her maiden name in 1915.)

The boys were "enthralled by all the tall buildings, and the general air of a thriving huge city." In a whirlwind week of sightseeing, they visited the Natural History Museum, Grant's Tomb, and the Woolworth Building (then the tallest building in the city). Jane Assur, Edith's friend from Cincinnati, arrived and joined the family as Edith's traveling companion in Europe. A week later the party of four sailed on February 4 aboard the luxurious SS *France*.

Young Roy was "impressed with the two-story-high dining room which was entered by an elegant divided staircase. At the bottom of the staircase was a large table covered in white linen and filled with heaping platters of all kinds of hors d'oeuvres and always in the center a beautiful ice sculpture." They crossed the Atlantic in seven days, arriving at Le Havre on February 11. The train for Paris was waiting at the dock, and they arrived in the city later the same day.

TWELVE-YEAR-OLD Roy Jr. recorded his impressions of the teeming metropolis. "The buildings were all different. There were a million and one cabs with their squeaky horns. There were crooked streets and wide boulevards and strange faces. Everything was wrapped in an environment totally different from what I had ever seen before." At their hotel, the elevators looked "flimsy and moved up and down very slowly...The WC was down the hall and you called the 'femme de chambre' to get your bath prepared."

After a few days of sightseeing in Paris, Edith and the boys set off for what would be two months of almost continuous travel. They started in Switzerland (Bern, Wengen, and Geneva), where Peter and Roy were introduced to winter sports—skiing, sledding, and skating—although not with great success. When they tired of the cold, they headed to the south of France (Avignon, Arles, Nice, and Monte Carlo), before looping back to Paris in early April.

Constant touring made it difficult for the boys to learn French. If they stayed in a town longer than a few days, Edith sometimes found a teacher to give lessons, and once she sent the boys to a Berlitz school for a week-and-a-half. But after two months on the continent, their French language skills were minimal. So Edith decided to immerse them in an all-French school.

ON APRIL 21, both boys were enrolled in the third grade at the Sainte-Marie School, an exclusive Catholic boarding school on Rue Monceau in the Eighth Arrondissement. (They were put back multiple grades because of their limited French.) "A great many of the students had the small 'de' in front of their names denoting they were from noble families," Roy Jr. remembered.

"Our first week or so at school made us feel very strange. Everything was so different, and not being able to speak much French, we were handicapped considerably. But it was surprising how much French we did learn during our stay there. Every day I would learn some new word." Third grade subjects included reading, arithmetic, penmanship, history, and geography. "Geography was very boring as we had to memorize all the departments of France with their 'county seats.' We had no blackboards and did our work in blank books."

Wakeup time was 6:00 a.m. for Roy Jr. and 6:30 a.m. for Peter. After getting dressed, the boys attended chapel for fifteen minutes, as they would again at the end of the day before bedtime. Roy wrote, "I'll never forget the hard benches, the cold, and the smell of incense. It was boring to us because we understood so little and most of it in Latin!" Even so, he soon learned to repeat the prayers "like a parrot."

Breakfast consisted of "a hunk of bread with no butter and a bowl of rich chocolate." "Meals were served in a dungeon-like basement, and we sat at tables of ten, always with a teacher to make us mind our manners... Most of the boys had glasses of diluted wine for lunch and dinner... [They drank] wine in preference to milk."

The boys' dormitories had rows of sleeping cots, each with its own night table and chamber pot. The lavatories were all outside in the courtyard and consisted of a row of closets "with two steps to stand on and a gutter of water running beneath. Fortunately, there was a proper toilet in the building, and with Mother's firm insistence, permission was granted for us to use it." The boys took showers once a week on the same day that they got fresh underwear.

"We marched everywhere in twos—to class, to meals, to bed. And I shall always remember the man who led us. He was tall in his black frock and had a funny red beard and moustache." "He had no hair to speak of on his head and had the largest and reddest ears of any human being." "We called him *Monsieur L'Ascenseur* [Mr. Elevator]. He was always saying '*Allez vous en*' [Let's go]."

EDITH FREQUENTLY VISITED the boys in the afternoon. "Never before did I ever miss Mother as I did then, and Peter felt the same way. We used to sit in the courtyard watching the front gate, and eagerly hoping that the next person to come through would be Mother. Some days she would not appear, and we were terribly disappointed."

They did spend Sundays with Edith, mostly sightseeing. They saw the *Venus de Milo* at the Louvre and *The Thinker* at the Rodin Museum. They climbed two-hundred-seventy-five steps to the top of the Arc de Triomphe and three hundred steps to the top of Notre Dame. They visited Versailles and the Petit Trianon. They attended the International Exhibition of Modern Decorative and Industrial Arts (where the term "Art Deco" originated), but they were "too young to appreciate it," Roy wrote later.

The boys hated to return to their school after their day of freedom. Looking back, Roy wondered how he and Peter ever managed to spend two-and-a-half months at the Sainte-Marie School. Finally, their summer break arrived. Roy wrote, "I don't believe any two boys were happier than we were when Mother came to the school on the afternoon of the third of July and said we were going to leave school."

A FEW DAYS LATER, Edith sent the boys off on July 5 to a summer camp run by Captain Chadbourn, an eccentric expat, and his wife. The Chadbourns hosted an American school and artistic salon at Chateau Neuvic, a sixteenth-century chateau in the Dordogne region south of Paris. Isadora Duncan was a frequent house guest. The chateau was located close to the town of Neuvic on the Isle River, about twenty miles from Périgueux to the east and sixty miles from Bordeaux to the west.

After a day of travel from Paris, the boys were met by Captain Chadbourn at the Périgueux train station and driven to the chateau. Their arrival was delayed when their car ran out of gas, perhaps an early indication of Chadbourn's relaxed attitude toward planning. "It was moonlight when we arrived," Roy wrote, "and the entrance to the Chateau gave onto a small dirt road. We went through two gates and up a drive which wound through a dark grove of trees. We came out suddenly into a clearing... and ahead of us... loomed the black walls of the Chateau."

A moat extended around three sides of the chateau with the Isle River behind it. At the corners of the building were towers, each with a spiral stone stairway circling to the top. There were fifty rooms on three floors, although the third floor was not occupied. The boys were shown to their room, which had two beds, a big fireplace, and large French windows opening onto the river below.

For the next six weeks, the boys enjoyed the typical routine of an American summer camp, although apparently without a great deal of adult supervision. There were fifteen boys between the ages of eight and sixteen. They took bicycle trips and slept in farmers' fields. They played tennis and rode horses. They paddled canoes and practiced target shooting.

The highlight of the summer was a "glorious river trip" on Chadbourn's jolly boat, a motorboat about twenty feet long. The two-week voyage took them one hundred miles down the Isle River to the Dordogne River, down the Dordogne to the Gironde Estuary, and out the Gironde to Point de Grave on the Atlantic Ocean. The boys alternated staying in the boat or riding bicycles on the nearby roads during the day. At night, half the boys slept on the boat and the other half ashore, usually in a farmer's field under a blanket.

WHEN THEIR CAMP ENDED in August, Peter and Roy Jr. reunited with their mother in Paris and sailed a few days later from Cherbourg on the *President Harding*. Arriving in New York on August 27, Edith took the boys to visit Lucy James at her lovely oceanside estate, "Normandie," in Newport, Rhode Island. Roy remembered that on one occasion, Lucy and his mother "went over to have tea with Mrs. Vanderbilt at 'The Breakers.'"

They returned to New York and left on September 9 for their cross-country journey home, interrupted only by a side trip to Racine, Wisconsin, the birthplace of Edith's mother, Sophie Smith Simpson. In Racine, the boys met Sophie's younger sister, their grand-aunt "Lizzie" and her husband, John Meachem, for the first time.

Returning to Chicago, they caught the *Overland Limited* for California. Arriving in Sacramento on September 15, they found their father waiting on the platform. "I'm sure that we never stopped talking about the trip until we arrived home at El Solyo," recalled Roy Jr.

FOUR YEARS LATER, Edith planned another six-month trip to Europe "for more French." This time Roy Sr. would accompany them for the first two months to explore new markets for El Solyo's dried fruit products. On January 4, 1929, the whole family boarded the *Overland Limited* in Oakland to begin their cross-country journey.

In New York City, they were again guests of Lucy James, who had just moved into a beautiful apartment on East Seventy-Ninth Street, just off Park Avenue. Edith called Lucy "the last of the Victorians," Roy Jr. remembered. "Tall, aristocratic, with a perfectly modulated, soft speaking voice, she moved quietly and with dignity. Her knowledge of history, music, and politics made me very envious."

The family sailed on January 12 aboard the *George Washington*, arriving at Cherbourg eight days later. After brief visits to Paris, Geneva, and Zurich, the boys were enrolled at the Walter School, run by Dr. Hans Walter, a Swiss German, and his American wife. Located near St. Moritz in the Swiss Alps, the school was situated in a forest of pine trees in a small valley.

There were twenty-six boys, including three Americans. Most students did not speak English, making it difficult for Peter and Roy to communicate with their roommates who spoke German and French. Naturally, most recreation involved skiing, skating, and ice hockey.

Roy Jr. maintained a detailed journal of their school days. The students were awakened at 6:50 to begin their day, starting with exercises in front of the school. Breakfast was at 7:40, and classes began at 8:10. The only academic subjects Roy ever mentioned in his journal were French, arithmetic, and German. Mostly, he documented an endless stream of outdoor activities and games.

When their spring break arrived on March 28, Peter and Roy set out to meet their mother for a three-week holiday in northern Italy. They traveled by train from St. Moritz to Colico, a small town at the north end of Lake Como, where they caught a ferry to Bellagio and met Edith at the Hotel Grande Bretagne. They visited Lugano and Milan, where they saw *The Last Supper*, before arriving in Venice on April 3. "How thrilling it was! As soon as we collected our bags, we got into a gondola and were rowed to the hotel. Pete was jabbering with excitement for the rest of the evening." They remained in Venice for two weeks of nonstop sightseeing.

After spring break, the Walter School reconvened on April 18 at its summer campus on the shore of Lake Geneva at Saint-Prex, west of Lausanne. Set on a five-acre estate, the school was "built in the English style with white plaster and green boards on the sides." A long gravel driveway led up to the main building, and the extensive grounds included a tennis court, a vegetable garden, and a boathouse on the lake.

Again, Roy rarely mentioned studying academic subjects in his journal. Much of the boys' time seemed to be spent outdoors, playing games, riding bicycles along country roads, and rowing boats on the lake. Competition between crews from nearby boarding schools was fierce. Once, the Walter School's boat briefly led a race. "We were all very excited, cheering them on. We had practiced some cheers, as none of the boys had ever done any cheering before." The Walter boat ultimately finished third.

WHEN THE SPRING TERM ended on July 6, the boys left with "high esteem for both Dr. Walter and the school." They returned to Paris to spend the last month of their sojourn with their mother. Almost every day the brothers went to "Sherry's" for an ice-cream soda with fresh strawberries, "the only place where one can get good old American drinks," Roy remembered. Other days they made excursions to Chartres, Saint-Malo, and Mont-Saint-Michel.

Happily, their uncle, Percy Pike, arrived with his family for a visit to the city. "Uncle Perce" took the boys and their cousins—Tom, Jack, Mary, and Wanda—to Davis Cup tennis matches at Roland Garros Stadium. He gave them each fifty francs to bet on horse races at Maisons-Laffitte and took them to "Paillards" where, Roy recalled, "we had a delicious dinner." They walked through "the Catacombs... lined solid from ceiling to floor with bones and skulls." Mary and Wanda were "tremendously impressed with [the boys'] ability to speak French."

Edith and her boys sailed from Cherbourg on August 1, 1929, aboard the *President Roosevelt*, arriving in New York eight days later. Bill Oliphant, their old tutor who now lived in New York, was waiting at the dock. A few days later, Peter and Roy headed west by themselves. Edith had stayed in New York to try to persuade George Arliss, a well-known British actor, to play the lead role in the play that she and Oliphant had written about Voltaire. (He read the play and declined.) When the *Overland Limited* arrived in Oakland on August 15, Roy Sr. was waiting on the platform for his boys.

ONE MONTH LATER, on September 17, Peter donned a uniform to start the first day of class at the Harvard School, a military academy in Los Angeles. "Military discipline," the school catalog explained, "is not intended to make good boys out of bad boys, but there can be nothing better for all boys than such training. They learn the regularity of habits, abstinence, obedience, promptness, precision, respect for self and respect for others... a fitting preparation for the future daily tasks of American life."

With a student body of almost four hundred students (grades six through twelve), the school operated under the auspices of the Episcopal Church and was "a distinctly Christian institution." Boys were required to attend daily chapel and a Bible study class every Sunday. Harvard was set on a ten-acre campus at the intersection of South Western Avenue and Venice Boulevard, west of downtown Los Angeles.

Peter's brother, Roy Jr., went off to the Montezuma Mountain School for Boys, a non-military, non-denominational school set on a rustic campus in the Santa Cruz Mountains above Los Gatos. Ernest Rogers, the founder of Montezuma, believed that his students should practice democracy at an early age. "The kids governed themselves," remembered one alumnus. "We had a government, just like a city, with a mayor, a police commissioner, a labor commissioner. It was all very idealistic."

By contrast, student life at the Harvard School, observed one teacher, largely consisted of "bugle calls, formations, roll calls, and inspections." This must have come as quite a shock to Peter after the relaxed atmosphere at the Walter School in Switzerland and before that his private tutelage from Bill Oliphant. Nothing in his peripatetic academic career suggested that he would have thrived under the discipline of a military academy. Nor did he.

At Harvard, literally every minute counted. Each new activity was announced by a distinct bugle call. First Call in the morning sounded at 6:35, summoning the cadets from their quarters to the parade ground. Eight minutes later, at 6:43, Reveille warned them that only two minutes remained before Physical Exercise. After fifteen minutes of calisthenics, students returned to their rooms to await Mess Call for breakfast at 7:15.

The grading system at Harvard used simple letter grades with no pluses or minuses. A and B signified "Recommended to College" and C signified "Passed without Recommendation." Peter did not appear to be college material. As a sophomore, he received Bs in French and Modern History and Cs in English and Geometry. As a junior, he received all Cs in English, Economics, Physics, and Penmanship. After two years at Harvard, he prevailed upon his parents to send him to a different boarding school for his last year of high school.

The Pike family at El Solyo Ranch, December 1929. Peter home from the Harvard School and Roy from the Montezuma Mountain School for Boys.

IN SEPTEMBER 1931, Peter and his brother, Roy, enrolled as seniors at the Menlo School in Atherton, California, thirty miles south of San Francisco. The school occupied a large estate covered by oak trees near the corner of El Camino Real and Valparaiso Avenue. The total student body numbered about one hundred.

The primary mission of Menlo was the development of "proper physical and mental hygiene," in the words of its president, Lowry S. Howard. "Since the time of the Greeks and the Romans, it has been considered the purpose of education to promote the development of a healthy mind in a healthy body." Moral character was more important than the acquisition of pure knowledge. This must have been a welcome message for Peter, who never thrived in a traditional academic setting, preferring instead extracurricular activities and the camaraderie of his classmates.

Peter joined the Menlo theatrical society, El Roble Players, described in the yearbook as "the largest, most active and most popular student organization in Menlo." We do not know what roles Peter played. Among the productions that year were three one-act plays: *The Valiant* (about a doomed prisoner), *Free Speech* (a humorous satire on parliamentary law), and *A Dweller in the Darkness* (a mystery thriller). Like his father, he would display a lifelong interest in the theater.

PETER LEFT NO written memories of Harvard or Menlo, but we can imagine that he was thrilled to finish high school in June 1932 at age seventeen-and-a-half. After graduation, he embarked on what today we might call a "gap year," although his year lasted a full decade. Before we trace his circuitous path through the 1930s, we return to Catherine Cline, his future wife, who blazed her own trail straight ahead at full speed.

CHAPTER 19

A Well-Documented Life

Catherine, 1922–1936

CATHERINE CLINE would not be a debutante. "Miss Cline has already announced to her family," wrote the *San Francisco News* on February 1, 1934, "that she plans to study medicine and hopes, in time, to be able to write M.D. after her name... Her mother, remembered as the popular Dolly MacGavin, had planned a debut as she herself had, but youth designs its own plan for life."

Fifteen-year-old Catherine had long cherished her dream, recalled Laura (Applegarth) Cresap, who grew up two blocks away. As children, Laura remembered "the many times we played together in her room with her 'doctor's bag.'" At age three, Catherine and Laura had been classmates at Miss Wafer's nursery school, where each had served a one-week term as the "Queen of May."

Dolly snapped a picture of Catherine's "coronation," preserving the photograph in a family album and documenting the ceremony with a newspaper clipping. "Miss Catherine Cline... led the little group through the May Pole dances and songs... She was a dainty little ruler in her abbreviated, fluffy, white frock, with a trailing veil of white tulle which was held in place by a crown of baby roses [and] she carried a scepter of baby roses."

Three months later on August 8, 1922, Catherine attended a children's birthday party, which must have reinforced Dolly's belief that her daughter was on the debutante track—even though she was not quite four years old. Dolly archived a newspaper clipping of the event headlined, "Society Folk of the Future Have a Party." True to its claim, the guest list of little people did include some names that would remain prominent in San Francisco society for decades to come: "Master

Henry Bowles, Master Peter McBean, and Miss Lurline and Master William Roth Jr."

Starting in the fall of 1924, Catherine attended first grade at Grant School, a public school on Pacific Avenue near Broderick. Dolly saved the school's monthly report cards, stating that her daughter had "been attentive to her work" and "not tardy." Catherine switched to Miss Fitch's, a small private school at 2564 Sacramento Street, for the second and third grades. Her second grade report card at Miss Fitch's would set the tone for her future academic career—straight As in Reading, Spelling, Arithmetic, Penmanship, and Deportment.

IN THE FALL OF 1927, Catherine was enrolled in the fourth grade at Miss Burke's School at 3065 Jackson Street, where she rocketed through elementary school, graduating from the eighth grade at the top of her class in June 1932. The school's motto, "He lives most who thinks most," fit Catherine perfectly (except for the gender).

Laura Applegarth was again a classmate and recalled, "She was a star, a top student, and very popular." "Of all the girls in our class, Catherine was the most even-tempered," remembered Juanita (Hill) Schurman. "She had a great sense of humor and everyone liked her. I don't have to say that she was very bright, but never made that a point, ever."

Kathleen (Thompson) Parrish remembered that Catherine was "serious, not as concerned about being popular (very important!) or having the right clothes, or hair-do…Catherine was not considered eccentric or odd, but she did stand out as somebody who knew what she wanted far above having her dance card filled." Virginia (Coghlan) MacLean thought Catherine one of the "sweetest, nicest girls" she knew, "always fun and generous." But she was not perfect.

Coghlan vividly recalled an amusing incident of misbehavior. "Four of us in the seventh grade at Miss Burke's School had been planning an outing for weeks. Catherine, Kay Thompson, Laura Applegarth, and I left school about 12:30 p.m. and walked to the Uptown Theater (the site of today's Winterland Ballroom)… After we got inside, we removed one cuff from our uniform so we'd be 'out of uniform.' (The top was a white blouse with wool detachable striped collar and cuffs.) We watched a Douglas Fairbanks movie, chatting happily throughout the film. Three of us—not Catherine—also smoked. What an outing!

"As the movie ended and we prepared to leave, a familiar voice boomed out from behind us: 'Girls, I expect to see you in my office first thing tomorrow morning.' It was Miss Burke. I can't remember what the punishment was, as we stood

This domestic scene of eleven-year-old Catherine Cline—beautifully dressed
and perfectly coiffed—masks her burning ambition. "Ever since I was
a very young child, it has been my desire to be a doctor."

before her the next morning, but I do recall Catherine saying, 'We deserved it,
Miss Burke.'"

IF CATHERINE MARCHED to a different drummer, her mother emphatically
did not. Dolly loved society, and, equally, she loved documenting the social life
of her daughter. She compiled thousands of personal ephemera into a dozen large
scrapbooks: party invitations, dance cards, birthday gift tags, calling cards, thank-
you notes, Christmas gift tags, municipal railway passes, luggage tags, dancing class
announcements, football programs, track meet programs, fashion show articles,
and symphony programs.

And there was more: theater playbills, opera programs, movie dates, ticket stubs,
dried corsages and bouquet remnants, dance invitations, Sunday school announcements, lists of debutantes and sub-debutantes, engagement party and wedding announcements, junior assembly dance invitations, and school graduation programs.

She retained schedules of all of Catherine's swimming lessons, horseback riding lessons, diving lessons, tennis lessons, gymnastics lessons, and art classes. No
scrap of information was too insignificant to be archived.

"Her mother was a very ambitious woman," Constance (Crowley) Bowles remembered, "and wanted Catherine to be an all-around person...Growing up, most of us girls were crazy about boys. Nothing worked unless there was a boy in the picture. Catherine, on the other hand, liked boys but wasn't crazy about them. She never had a big crush on somebody that I recall. Maybe she was young for her age and not ready for boys. She had other things that she wanted to do that she felt were more important."

Another Burke's classmate, Bonnie Hunter, remembered the colorful dinner and dance parties organized by her mother at the Cline home. "She was a patroness of parties, sponsoring formal parties throughout high school. She had different dreams for Catherine than...medical school, but Catherine didn't care about the social whirl. She knew she wanted to be a doctor from an early age."

Attuned to the social buzz, Dolly always made sure that Catherine's parties appeared in the *San Francisco Chronicle*'s society pages. In March 1934, she hosted "a large dancing party" for one hundred of Catherine's friends at their home on Filbert Street. In September, Dolly welcomed an impromptu party for Catherine at home attended by forty-eight of her friends dressed in "blue jeans" for an evening of dancing. In October, Dolly surprised Catherine on her sixteenth birthday with an afternoon party at home for twenty-four of her friends.

DOLLY'S METICULOUS scrapbooks provide a breathless record of Catherine's social activities. As an example, she documented thirteen days in April 1934 (from the 13th to the 25th) with *forty-seven* newspaper clippings pasted onto seven pages. On Friday afternoon (April 13) Catherine and three girlfriends went to the Warfield Theater to see Al Jolson in *Wonder Bar*. That night Frank Freyer took Catherine to see Charles Laughton in *The Private Life of Henry VIII*. The next day, Saturday, Stewart Barber and Catherine double-dated to dinner and then went to a party at her best friend Mary Louise Kiernan's home, next door to the Clines.

On Sunday Catherine and her mother went to a tea at the Alpha Phi sorority house at Stanford University in Palo Alto. The next week was equally busy. On Thursday Catherine and a date attended a dinner party hosted by her parents. Friday afternoon Catherine and Mary Louise Keirnan went to a tea honoring an author. That same night Catherine entertained three friends at dinner. Her date, Eddie Bryant, brought her a corsage of lilies of the valley, which Dolly dried and put in an envelope in the scrapbook.

On Saturday Catherine and two girlfriends went to the California–Stanford Track and Field Meet in Palo Alto. (Stanford won.) Sunday afternoon, Catherine and a girlfriend went to see Clark Gable and Myrna Loy in *Men in White* at the Warfield. The following Wednesday (April 25) Catherine and two classmates in costume were pictured over the caption, "Misses Laura Bride Applegarth, Catherine Cline, and Virginia Coghlan dressed as Spanish senoritas" assisting at a tea. Whew!

SQUEEZED INTO Catherine's busy social calendar were piano lessons and recitals. One recital in particular stands out as a monument to parental excess, even by Dolly's lofty standards. Documentation of the event started with a short newspaper clipping headlined "Recitalist Is Thirteen." On Friday, May 6, 1932, Malen Burnett, Catherine's piano teacher, sponsored her recital in a private home at 2160 Green Street.

Dolly recorded the event over five pages in a scrapbook with dozens of calling cards received from family and friends: "Catherine darling, congratulations and love," "Lots of love and many good wishes," "Love and congratulations! We're proud of you!" On many of the calling cards, Dolly carefully logged the receipt of flowers: "corsage of gardenias," "box of roses," "pink roses," "old fashioned bouquet," and "box of baby roses."

Catherine played selections from Bach (a gavotte), Mozart (a rondo), and Chopin (a mazurka). She also played classical songs sung by "Mrs. Percy Goode, Soprano." Dolly annotated many of her daughter's clippings using the first person as if she were Catherine. So above Catherine's recital program, Dolly wrote, "Recital I gave." On the final page documenting the event, Dolly listed 130 names of guests who apparently attended the event or sent best wishes.

Catherine's piano-playing skill was widely appreciated by her schoolmates too. Laura Applegarth remembered "graduation and other special occasions at Miss Burke's, when the piano was rolled into the courtyard where the student body was gathered, and Catherine played with such grace and collection of mind, intricate music with no mistakes."

SHE CONTINUED to shine academically at Miss Burke's High School. Her detailed freshman transcript included marks for each grading period, a total of fifty notations over two terms. Catherine's academic record was a blizzard of forty-seven straight As and three B+s in five subjects—English, History, Algebra, Latin, and French. Not surprisingly, she also received straight As for "Attitude."

We know little of Catherine's extracurricular activities that year, except that she was a member of the Drum Corps, as was her friend Virginia Coghlan. "We played the snare drums at the beginning of daily assembly when the flag was carried in. We played them badly, but loved it."

For reasons lost in the sands of time, Catherine switched to Galileo High School for her sophomore year and the first semester of her junior year. This represented a dramatic change from a small, all-girls, private high school to a large, coeducational, public school. Her freshman class at Burke's had totaled twenty-four; her sophomore class at Galileo numbered about two hundred students. At Galileo, she remained a star student, receiving straight As in English, History, Geometry, Latin, Botany, and Chemistry.

Just as mysteriously, she returned to Miss Burke's in December 1934 in the middle of her junior year. What might have explained her change of heart? Catherine wrote in her diary that her grammar and high school years "were not overcrowded with the intangible state of happiness...I was not very happy in school. I was interested in different types of things from most of my classmates—books, music, and older people's conversation, as opposed to playing, parties, and fooling time away."

Catherine did want a beau; she just didn't talk about it much. This longing she made clear in a poem written in her senior year titled "Happiness."

> A fleeting glance,
> A soft spoken word,
> The slight pressure of a hand;
> Trivial though they be
> May bring Happiness to my
> Aching heart

FRIENDSHIPS with classmates masked a sense of loneliness that Catherine felt in her own home. "As a young child," she wrote, "I spent most of my time either alone or with older people. I was seldom with children my own age." While her mother doted on her, her father traveled constantly on business. She missed him fiercely. As a ten-year-old, she had once sent her love to him via telegram. "JUN 16, 1929: ALAN P. CLINE, HOTEL BENSON, PORTLAND, ORE: KISSES HUGS TO THE DEAREST DADDY IN THE WORLD. CATHERINE."

She felt conflicted by her academic success. "One thing I wonder about myself," she wrote in her diary, "do I wish to surpass in all I do because of personal satisfaction in doing something perfectly? Or is it a desire to feel superior to other people?" Did her drive for perfection hide her insecurity? "In regard to an inferiority complex, I have one in respect to my appearance—my being overweight. I think the feeling of inferiority is because it is something which I should control. It is just a lack of willpower—I know it." This was a harsh self-assessment. Family and friends throughout her life would find it hard to imagine that Catherine ever lacked the willpower to do anything.

But as a teenager and in her early twenties, she battled excess weight. In the vernacular of her friends, she was "chubby." Her Class History, printed in her high school yearbook, even mentioned her weight and her intelligence in the same sentence when describing Catherine's arrival at Burke's in the fourth grade: "Our latest addition, chubby Catherine Cline [brought] an era of average-raisers. It's never happened again!"

AS SHE turned fourteen in October 1932, her family doctor, Dr. Russell Ryan, issued strict "dietary instructions" to control her weight:

Breakfast: Small glass of orange juice; 4 tablespoonfuls of apple sauce (with no sugar or cream); 2 pieces of dry toast; a cup of weak tea (no cream or sugar) or better still a cup of Sanka with a little milk (no cream) and a ¼ of one teaspoon of sugar.

Luncheon: 6 Stalks of asparagus (no butter and no sauce); a pineapple and cottage cheese salad made with one slice of either fresh or water-packed pineapple; 2 heaping tablespoonfuls of cottage cheese, and 2 leaves of lettuce, and one tomato sliced (no oil or other dressings); one broiled lamb chop and a glass of buttermilk.

Supper: One small slice of broiled fish with no butter, or other sauces or two broiled lamb chops, or one-half a slice of broiled or roast ham, with all fat removed, and cut thin; 3 heaping tablespoonfuls of spinach (no butter or other sauces); one baked tomato, and, if desired 2 or 3 radishes, and 2 or 3 green onions. A small bowl of Jell-O with no cream and a glass of buttermilk; one piece of dry toast, if desired.

What teenager would possess the willpower for such a diet?

IN HER SENIOR year at Miss Burke's, Catherine again found herself at the head of her class with As and Bs in English, History, Latin, Trigonometry, Chemistry, and Physics. Interestingly, her Attitude grades declined from A to B. Perhaps she suffered from "senioritis."

She was a member of the tennis team, her "favorite sport," and the treasurer of the senior class. She played the role of Viola in Shakespeare's *Twelfth Night*. The *San Francisco Call Bulletin* reported that her "determination to study medicine" made her the "busiest girl of her age in San Francisco." She volunteered four afternoons a week at Stanford Hospital (today's California Pacific Medical Center) to accustom herself "to the sights and sounds of her perspective milieu."

"Catherine was always tops in our class scholastically," recalled Joan (Ehrman) Avenali, "brighter than most of us but she also worked hard, while many of us were lazy. Often as you know, when one student always shines, there is a certain resentment on the part of others, but with Catherine this was never the case, or so it seemed."

Her high school yearbook, *Works & Days*, included a page titled "The Perfect Senior" that recognized in each girl a personal attribute—like Smile, Personality, and Sweetness. For Catherine it was Brains. Another yearbook page titled "Can You Imagine?" posed a series of questions for each girl that could not be answered "yes"—like "Can you imagine so-and-so not talking?" Catherine's question was "Can you imagine Catherine not conscientious?" Nobody could.

A final page asked each student "How she would like to appear?" Catherine's answer to the question was "Indifferently bright"—a concise summation of her internal dilemma. Whatever conflict she felt, her friends expected her to succeed. Of the twenty-two classmates who signed her *Memory Book*, seven of them recognized her determination and drive by including the word "doctor" in their farewell remarks: "I'll call you when I need a good doctor," "Don't work too hard when you're a doctor," and "Good luck in your doctor's career. You always were quite a cut up!"

The last two weeks of her senior year at Miss Burke's were devoted to final examinations woven into a string of "luncheons, teas, suppers, and dances," wrote society columnist Lady Teazle in the *San Francisco Chronicle*. Catherine and Kathleen Thompson hosted a luncheon at the San Francisco Golf Club.

Catherine and her classmates received their diplomas at a commencement ceremony on June 4, 1936. She was also presented with a silver cup for the highest

Catherine Cline, age seventeen, at her graduation
from Miss Burke's in 1936.

scholarship. Ten days later, the University of California sent her an acceptance letter. "We find your record satisfactory for admission to the University in freshman standing." At the time, admission to the university simply required graduation from an accredited high school with a B average in the required subjects. Cal would be the next step on Catherine's march toward a medical degree.

"EVER SINCE I was a very young child," she had written in her senior essay, "it has been my desire to be a doctor... Now that I am nearing my college days, this ideal is planted deeply in my soul... Many people attempted (and they do yet) to discourage me in my purpose to be a doctor with the common argument against women doctors. These people, in their attempt to dissuade me from my purpose, unconsciously spurred me on towards my goal."

CHAPTER 20

University of California, Berkeley

Catherine, 1936–1938

CATHERINE AND DOLLY checked into the Durant Hotel in Berkeley on Thursday, August 13, 1936, where they would stay during "rushing season" for sororities at Cal. Over the next two weeks, sorority members and prospective pledges would court each other at an endless stream of social events. By the end of rushing, Catherine would pledge a sorority—if she were invited. This was a high-stakes contest. There was no university housing for freshman women.

We can imagine Dolly marshaling her formidable social skills to support her daughter's quest. She would have made sure that Catherine wore the right clothes, displayed the right table manners, and mentioned the right names. The day after her arrival, Catherine entered the fray, visiting six sororities for tea, according to her mother's scrapbook.

Sunday's headline across the *Oakland Tribune's* society page read, "Sorority Maids Return to Campus for Initiation of Rushing Season." "To get ready for this strenuous program, active members of Alpha Phi have been devoting considerable time to swimming, bridge playing, and lunching around the Orinda Country Club during the last few weeks."

The article featured a photograph of four "Alpha Phi's" poolside at the Club, including "Catherine Cline." Of course, Catherine was not yet an Alpha Phi (although she would eventually pledge this house). Perhaps Dolly planted the story with a friendly society columnist, in this case, "Suzette" at the *Oakland Tribune*.

At the end of the two-week rushing season, all sororities held "preference dinners" for girls invited to pledge. Catherine accepted an invitation to pledge the

Alpha Phi sorority at 2830 Bancroft Way. She was one of fifteen pledges. Dolly must have been ecstatic.

At a formal dinner at the Alpha Phi house on September 1, Catherine received the Alpha Phi pledge pin with the Greek letters A Φ over a silver ivy leaf set in pewter and recited the Alpha Phi oath: "I pledge allegiance to Alpha Phi, who has chosen me to uphold her high ideals of womanhood, of scholarship, and of service, and to perpetuate her spirit of sisterly love and kindness."

After dinner, Catherine was handed a white paperboard sign with the Greek letters A Φ. She was instructed to wear this placard to the Channing Way Derby the next morning, her first rite of ritual hazing. On September 2 at 6:30 a.m., she reported for duty to the "Good Ship Sigma Chi" on Channing Way, which was blocked off between College and Piedmont Avenues.

Catherine was one of 276 pledges from twenty-two sororities signing onto the imaginary "ship" that morning. Sigma Chi fraternity members, posing as naval officers, trained the new "crew." Pledges scrubbed the asphalt "deck," ran a relay race with dead mackerels, and screamed "caw-caw" from a "crow's nest." After an hour of harassment witnessed by thousands of spectators, pledges scattered to their respective houses for breakfast and morning classes.

MIDWAY THROUGH rushing season, registration had begun for the fall term of the University of California on Thursday, August 20. Dolly, again, ghost-wrote in Catherine's scrapbook, "I went to register—big thrill." Over the next three days, almost 14,000 students registered for classes, including 3,500 freshmen. As a resident of the State of California, Catherine did not pay any tuition. But she did pay an "incidental expense" fee of $26 per semester.

Student counselors interviewed each new student immediately after registration and "put him in touch with those groups in which his interests and previous experience lie," wrote the *Daily Californian*. Every twenty minutes, orientation tours left Eshleman Hall. Incoming women were invited to an afternoon tea in faculty glade where they met Mrs. Robert G. Sproul, the wife of the president, and Miss Lucy Ward Stebbins, dean of women.

Freshmen boys were greeted rather less warmly. Sophomore boys warned freshmen that they would soon enforce the traditional rules governing freshman conduct. Freshmen had to wear "dinks," blue and gold beanies, at all times on campus. They could not smoke cigarettes, only corncob pipes. No "queening" would be allowed, meaning that freshmen could not speak to coeds on campus, except in classrooms.

Enforcement of these rules would be by a committee of fifty sophomore vigilantes, "wearing blue arm bands with gold 'Vs' on them." To prevent injuries, the *Daily Californian* noted, "all punishments would be inflicted in the presence of at least five members of the Senior Peace Committee."

Perhaps this is why President Robert G. Sproul penned a stern letter to all students. "The State of California offers you the opportunity for sound university training on this campus; but it cannot force you to take advantage of that opportunity. How well you do in your studies and the value you derive from them depend almost entirely upon your own attitude and industry. Here, as everywhere, you will be exposed to distractions which, if not resisted by the exercise of willpower, may prove overwhelming."

Sproul need not have worried about Catherine, who set out for her first day of classes as a pre-med student on Monday, August 24. Three of her courses—English 1B, German 1A, and Chemistry 1A—satisfied the pre-med curriculum; the other two were electives—History 4A (Western Europe) and Art 19 (Appreciation of Art). She carried a full load of fifteen-and-a-half units, which included a half unit of Physical Education.

CATHERINE'S GREAT friend and pre-med classmate, Allen Barbour, remembered the academic atmosphere on campus in the late 1930s, "They were the exciting years of Robert Gordon Sproul and his marvelous spirit and booming voice. We just loved those days. They were very exciting, and there was a lot of sharing of intellectual activity." In 1936 there was only one University of California and one president, Sproul, who reigned over Berkeley, the Davis Farm (later UC Davis), the Los Angeles Campus (later UCLA), and the San Francisco Medical Center (later UCSF).

"We took Physics 2A from E. O. Lawrence himself," Barbour recalled. "He was still teaching an undergraduate course. He had just presented his crazy idea of making electrons go around in a circle to the Physics Department, and they all thought it was crazy, but said, well—give him a chance. Let him play with his toy for a while.

"Those were the peak days of Joel Hildebrand who had a great influence on the university. If I recall correctly, [Melvin] Calvin and Joel [Hildebrand] and

Catherine Cline and Allen Barbour (r.), at U.C. Berkeley in June 1937.

[Willard] Libby were all section leaders in Chemistry. They were all wonderful people. Little did we know that all three would get Nobel Prizes before too much longer." Barbour was right on two out of three. Libby won the Nobel Prize in Chemistry in 1960, and Calvin won the following year. Hildebrand was awarded the Priestley Medal, the highest honor conferred by the American Chemical Society, in 1962.

In the second semester of her freshman year, Catherine enrolled in Psychology 1A, early evidence of her lifelong interest in the human mind and mental health. Like every teenager, she sometimes wrestled with conflicting feelings of happiness and sadness. At age seventeen, she wrote a whimsical poem about death that began, "Perhaps I shall die tomorrow / Perhaps in one year and two months / Perhaps in one hundred years and two months." She did not know how far she would travel or what she might accomplish. But she would make the world a better place, and "On my lips I shall leave a smile!"

ALWAYS LURKING under the surface of her private writings was a longing for a husband, and, in this sentiment, she would have been completely in synch with her sorority sisters. Catherine wrote about a boy for the first time in her diary in June 1937. When studying for a summer school final exam, she had been reluctantly dragged downstairs in the Alpha Phi house to meet a mutual friend. Wearing her "most peculiar India print pajamas and with her hair done up in a bandana," she intended to stay for only five minutes with him, but ended up spending three hours. After he left, she stayed up until 3:30 a.m. studying for her exam.

Her visitor was handsome, "medium height, curly-blondish hair, blue eyes, with an extremely engaging twinkle, and a smile which warms the very cockles of your heart with its sincerity and kindliness." A week later she wrote a poem about him:

> We found the lost chord—
> The chord we both needed
> To complete our first bar,
> The bar that was ended
> When our lives came together.

However, two weeks later she had still not heard from him, and Catherine was regretting that she had "built up gigantic castles in the air of a married life with a good-looking chap." Now he was just "another fellow with a good line...thank Heavens we didn't indulge in a kiss...I actually wore my ring on my left hand, instead of my right, in his honor, but tonight it's back where it belongs."

Three months later, Catherine's mood brightened dramatically when she met John Sneed Schmidt, a U.S. Naval Academy graduate, class of 1937, and All-American halfback. "Sneed" was the assistant navigator on the battleship USS *Idaho*, anchored in San Francisco Bay. "He is good looking, but not exactly handsome—such a good, kind, wholesome face. He is very fond of opera and symphony and books, particularly poetry...He plays several musical instruments and likes to sing away, like I do."

Catherine wrote this at 3:45 in the morning of August 9 in the afterglow of their first date. A launch had taken the couple out to the battleship for dinner and a movie in the ship's theater. They saw *Café Metropole*, starring Loretta Young and Tyrone Power. After returning ashore, Catherine and Sneed went to the Mark Hopkins Hotel, where they danced until closing time. When he left her at her parents' home on Filbert Street, she wrote, "Away went my dearest, and there I was standing tearfully at the door. Of course, Mom would come down and jabber, which bothered me intensely."

Even though she was enthralled by her naval ensign, she ended her diary entry on a note of realism. "I like Sneed very, very much—more than anyone on such short acquaintance. I so look forward to seeing my dearest again. But I wouldn't be a good navy wife, so I mustn't let myself get serious. God bless that dear boy."

A week later, Sneed was still very much on her mind when she day-dreamed, "One night I was in paradise. My spirit danced on the most delicate of wings and the arms of another were about me. We danced together with our hearts rushing out to one another...We were in paradise one night—and never met again."

Two months later, Sneed was still on her mind. "I am fat and seem to have little will-power. I must get thin, for I have lost my own self-respect, as well as a lot of other people's, I guess...For [Sneed] I shall be slim, beautiful, and good... By my affection for Sneed, I shall stick to my diet till Xmas. I shall be strong for him, good for him, and beautiful for him!" Unfortunately, that entry was the last time his name would appear in her diary. Her romance was over.

CATHERINE LIVED in two worlds, the rigorous academic world of a pre-med student and the social whirl of her sorority. Although she excelled academically, earning mostly As and accolades from her professors, she berated herself for not doing more. "Well, tomorrow I shall be 19!" she wrote on October 24. "I don't feel festive at all...Looking back over this year it has been happy and interesting. I have done a lot, but not nearly all I could have done. I have learned a lot, but not nearly all I could have learned. And I do regret it—I have wasted so much time."

Mostly, she lamented the distraction of living in a sorority. "Activities & social 'doings' (the House, etc.) take up so much time, too much." The curriculum of her sophomore year would have left her little free time. First semester: German, Chemistry, Physics, and Social Institutions (sociology). Second semester: German, Physics, English, and Zoology. Long days and nights in lecture halls and laboratories left little time for her sorority obligations. Soon the differences between her two worlds would become irreconcilable.

Catherine did make time to attend a lecture by the internationally renowned author Thomas Mann on March 30, 1938. Self-exiled from his native Germany, Mann spoke to an overflow crowd in Wheeler Auditorium. "He made a splendid talk," she wrote in her diary, "with his fine carriage, his European graciousness, and his marked German accent, lending force to a truly stimulating lecture."

"In tones of almost desperate sincerity," the *Daily Californian* reported, "Thomas Mann, sworn enemy of dictators, last night called upon Democracy to institute broad social reforms upon itself and prepare to defend its ideals against the totalitarian states of the world. Mann's electric personality held more than 1,200 persons tense as they listened to his sharp contrasts between Democracy and Fascism."

IN LESS THAN FOUR MONTHS, Catherine would see fascism with her own eyes, as she drove through the heart of Europe on the brink of war.

CHAPTER 21

European Adventure

Catherine, 1938

"MISS CLINE is leaving on May 15 with Mrs. Margaret Barber of Pasadena for a two-month motor trip through Europe," noted the *Los Angeles Times'* society columnist in April 1938. Who was Mrs. Barber and how did Catherine meet her? We do not know. She may have been a friend of her parents. All we know for certain is that Mrs. Barber was a forty-nine-year-old widow who owned a 1935 Dodge sedan.

Catherine documented their grand adventure in a two-hundred-page travel journal. She and "Mrs. B" (as Catherine called her) drove three thousand miles from Los Angeles to Baltimore where they put their car on a ship and crossed the Atlantic. Arriving at Le Havre, they traced a three-thousand-mile loop through France, Switzerland, Italy, Austria, and Germany, before visiting southern England. Homeward bound, they sailed to New York and drove home to Los Angeles—a 15,000-mile odyssey across two continents and one ocean, all in just ninety days.

THEIR FIRST DAY on the road, Mrs. B and Catherine followed U.S. Route 66 three hundred miles east through Barstow and Needles to Kingman, Arizona. Despite the desert heat that reached 105 degrees, Catherine was enchanted by the landscape. "The Joshua trees writhe and twist as people tortured and in agony, standing on vast burial grounds. The whitish boulders lie about amongst the scrubby bushes like the skulls and bones of a vanished race." Catherine tallied the expenses for the day as $5.48 for gas and oil, $0.75 for food, and $1.90 for lodging.

Driving across New Mexico the next day, Catherine noted that the speed limit was set at "Reasonable and Proper." Their six-cylinder Dodge "reasonably averaged

62 miles per hour!" she wrote. The roads were excellent, and there was "very little traffic." This lack of traffic made it easier to coordinate their trip with another car, driven by Mrs. B's friend, Mrs. C. Temple Murphy and her daughter, Betty, also from Los Angeles. The Murphs (as Catherine called them) drove a 1935 Dodge convertible coupe, affectionately known as the "Green Bug." Betty was a year ahead of Catherine at Cal and a member of the Kappa Kappa Gamma Sorority.

Crossing the country, the foursome stayed in "tourist camps" or "auto camps," the forerunner of today's motels. Often they boasted folksy names, like "Kozy Korner Kabins" or "U Pop Inn." On the third night, Catherine wrote, "We are staying in a slick little cabin overlooking a pretty lake just outside of Oklahoma City. It is most comfortable and welcome after 548 miles." The next night, near Lebanon, Missouri, she wrote, "Tonight our auto camp is comfortable, but not as roomy as last night…We four have lots of fun together."

A contemporary article in the *New York Times Magazine* described a typical tourist camp after dark. "A main house of logs in a noble grove; a street of small log cabins…Lights gleaming from doorways and windows. Automobiles sheltered for the night under shed roofs, each car beside its driver's cabin. Dim forms in bathrobes and slippers, with towels and soap dishes in hand, making for the main house. Clean linoleum on the floor, a rocking chair, another chair, a table… a washbowl with running water; a Franklin stove with firewood in the box; and beds with modern mattresses…The advertised hot and cold baths are at the main house. They consist of a common shower for the men and another for the women."

Leaving U.S. Route 66 at St. Louis, the two cars headed due east on U.S. Route 60 through the Midwest. Catherine wrote, "Illinois (southern part) was so pretty—wide fields of wheat and oats—a real prairie state…Indiana (southern) was gorgeous with its rolling green hills covered with lovely trees…The blue grass of Kentucky is waving over sloping hills, and everywhere one sees handsome thoroughbred horses." They arrived in Richmond, Virginia, where Catherine stayed with her cousins. "Though I have admired other states, Virginia is by far the loveliest…The Virginians are so polite and charming—the true gentlemen of America."

After visiting Williamsburg and Mount Vernon, Catherine and Mrs. B blazed through Washington, D.C., in thirty-six hours, visiting the Lincoln Memorial, the Washington Monument, the Library of Congress, and the Smithsonian.

"I poked around in the White House and inspected portraits of the Presidents and wives, a fine-looking bunch on the whole, but oh, what a change when Eleanor gets here. There is a room full of stuff given to Franklin D—pictures of himself and Eleanor, a vulgar display, I thought—poor taste." Perhaps her negative view of President Roosevelt and his wife, Eleanor, reflected the Republican politics of her businessman father, despite her two years at Cal, even then a hotbed of political activism. (In later life, she would be a staunch Democrat.)

She was even less impressed with Congress. "I saw both the Senate and the House in session which was most interesting. The congressmen look like a bunch of shyster lawyers—to think our destiny is in the hands of a bunch of that sort of men. They rant and rave, argue and are rude. Most of them sit and read papers while the others talk—they aren't even trying to be attentively polite…What a government we have!"

TWELVE DAYS after leaving California, Catherine and Mrs. B boarded the *City of Hamburg* in Baltimore. Operated by the Baltimore Mail Steamship Company, the *City of Hamburg* carried mail, freight, and eighty passengers on its regular trans-atlantic run. Both Mrs. B's car and the Murphs' car were loaded as cargo. Known more for inexpensive fares than speed, the *City of Hamburg* stopped a day later at Norfolk to load freight before making its ten-day passage across the ocean.

At sea Catherine quickly acclimated herself to the wind and the waves and the ship's rolling. She played shuffleboard, deck tennis, and ping-pong and was asked to play the piano at the Sunday service. Over their long days at sea, she and her fellow passengers bonded together—a "cute little round French professor," "two naval commanders," a "lank, long-nosed Czech," and "a middle-aged flapper…with the mind of an eighteen-year-old." Her new Czech friend predicted there would be war "next summer, after the harvest!…The Germans were the cause of the last war and will be the cause of the next." Sadly we know in hindsight that his prediction would come true.

On the evening of June 5, the *City of Hamburg* docked at Le Havre. Catherine and Mrs. B got passes to go ashore. She wrote, "Oh, how thrilled I was. It all seemed a dream—it is a dream, but a dream come true. Everywhere in the little city of Le Havre one travels on cobblestones. We walked on them beneath a lovely moon on a warm starlit night—our first solid ground in 11 days." The next day a giant crane plucked their car out of the hold and deposited it on the dock. "After saying goodbye to all our shipboard friends, new and old, we set out on our way."

Driving toward Rouen, they passed through "neat little fields making a jigsaw

Wearing a stylish hat, Catherine Cline debarks
in Le Havre, France, on June 6, 1938.

pattern of different colors. And, oh, the lovely little thatched houses and barns everywhere!...Words cannot express what I have seen, such was the beauty and atmosphere...Everything is tranquil, quiet, and peaceful—the old and established way of living seems to be permanent here. One doesn't feel the nervous hurried tension of America. The sense of values of these people seems so real."

En route to Paris, she and Mrs. B stopped at Giverny for lunch. "Here in Giverny was one of the loveliest sights I have ever seen, the beautiful, colorful garden and charming low house of Claude Monet. We passed through lovely country—vast velvet green carpets of grass dotted with red poppies—tiny little houses, their gray colors forming bouquets of tiny communities—houses built into the chalky cliffs as the cave dwellers did."

ENTERING PARIS ON JUNE 8, they drove under "the stately Arc De Triomphe" and down the "lovely Champs Élysée" to the Hotel d'Ecosse ("Hotel of Scotland"), located near the Gare du Nord (Saint-Lazare on the Paris Métro). After checking in, Catherine wrote in her journal, "I walked alone through the streets and enjoyed the thrill of 'being in Paris.'"

That evening they drove across the Seine to the apartment of "Little Auntie," Emilia Hinshelwood, the sister of Catherine's grandmother, Kate (Hinshelwood) McGavin. "She is a tiny, dainty little person with a crown of white hair, sharp dark eyes and brows and pink cheeks. She is graceful and so gracious and sweet—May I be as she is at 85...Auntie's apartment is charming, lovely pink satin walls and such pretty furnishings. The French often cover their walls with cloth rather than paper—a pretty custom." Little Auntie lived at 7 Rue Sédillot near the Eiffel Tower in the 7th Arrondissement.

Over the next week, Catherine ran a tourist marathon, visiting all the iconic shrines of Paris, including Notre Dame, the Louvre, the Cluny Museum, and Versailles. Documenting her daily excursions, she filled twenty single-spaced binder pages in her journal with gushing superlatives. "Today was an experience I shall never forget—all my ideas of the beauty of Notre Dame came to a full and greater realization than I had dared hope." The next day: "I spent a priceless morning in the wonderful Louvre! I was glad to be alone with a guidebook for I could linger where I wished."

If she carried *Paris for Everyman*, a contemporary tourist guide, she might have followed the detailed directions for navigating the Louvre. "We pass on to the Grand Gallery of Nineteenth Century French Art. Over the door is a Henri Renault (*Portrait of General Prim*). On the right wall are a Millet (*The Gleaners*), a Delacroix (*Algerian Women in Morocco*), a Géricault (*The Raft of the "Méduse"*)" and the names of another nine paintings. "One could spend a lifetime here," Catherine wrote. "There is so much to see, study, and enjoy...The *Mona Lisa* is superb—its gorgeous blue green background, enigmatic expression, and matchless hands."

Saying a sad goodbye to Little Auntie, Catherine and Mrs. B headed off to Chartres. "We went to the Cathedral...words cannot tell of it. It is an unparalleled memory of beauty—the matchless blues of the many exquisite windows, the 'frozen-lace' of statues about the choir stall, the detail and grandeur of the massive interior."

In Tours, Catherine watched a group of children leaving a church. "A confirmation service had just taken place and the little girls, dressed as diminutive brides and the little boys with white satin ribbons on their arms were most picturesque." Stopping at a nearby restaurant for lunch, she noted the cost—"7 francs (about 20 cents), including ½ bottle of wine, ½ loaf of French bread each, veal (tender), peas, potato salad, meringue, and apricots!" Curiously, she noticed that the restaurant's "steady customers kept their napkins in a rack … It was France as the French know it and, therefore, most interesting."

MEANDERING EAST through small towns and villages—Chenonceaux, Avallon, Dijon, and Gex—they crossed the Swiss border on June 20. Stopping briefly in Geneva, they visited the League of Nations, where they watched the International Labor Council in session. Catherine was impressed by the "modernistic and lavishly furnished" buildings, the "social and health departments," and the simultaneous translation of "numerous different languages," concluding that "the League, if ineffectual, is well organized!"

That afternoon they drove along the north shore of Lake Geneva to Chillon Castle, immortalized in Lord Byron's poem, *The Prisoner Of Chillon*. "Words can't tell how lovely this old castle is … It is so real and yet unreal." They spent the next three days in the Swiss Alps—Gstaad, Lucerne, and Interlaken—before heading to the Italian Lake Country.

Climbing the 6,000-foot Gotthard Pass, they suffered their worst car trouble of the whole trip, probably a case of vapor lock. "When we were nearly at the top we stopped while I tramped in the snow and took photographs. When we got back into the car, we got a little way up the hills, and then the car gave up the ghost! The Murphs dashed up and down looking for tow-cars, but none to be had. So Mrs. Murph jumped into our car, and, presto, it started, and up and over we went."

AFTER CROSSING the border into Italy, "All along the road, nearly all the children large and small gave us the Fascist salute." As they drove south toward Rome, they passed "carefully cultivated farmland, woeful little houses, millions of bicycles, and very few cars, signs of Il Duce [the Italian dictator Benito Mussolini] and lovely little towns and deserted fortresses perched on hills … There are so many soldiers about … and quite a few barracks scattered amongst the towns."

In Milan, Catherine saw Leonardo da Vinci's *Last Supper*. "To me this fresco is almost ethereal in its unbelievably beautiful color and masterful composition." Naturally, they had to stop in Pisa to see the Leaning Tower—"an amazing and really a beautifully designed tower." In Rome, Catherine attended an outdoor performance of Beethoven's Fourth Symphony in the Roman Forum. "Never have I had such a wonderful experience. Gorgeous music played by a fine orchestra on a starlit night amidst those noble old ruins."

The foursome—Catherine, Mrs. B, and the Murphs—continued south to the Isle of Capri and the famed Blue Grotto—"a world of glorious blue, the ceiling of jagged rock was a silvery blue, and the color of the water was indescribable." They had reached the southern tip of their driving loop. Backtracking northward, they retraced their route up the Amalfi coast—"Words can't tell of this scenery. It is one of the most beautiful drives in the world."

Passing through Rome again, they drove on to Florence, where Catherine praised Michelangelo's *David*—"The expression, the latent power, the pride of self-confidence—all make this statue a supreme work of art." Also in Florence, she recorded a rather more bizarre sight. "One interesting thing we saw today was a window full of gas masks for sale—50 lira per! A household commodity, I guess."

When visiting the graves of Galileo, Michelangelo, and Machiavelli at the Basilica of Santa Croce, she recorded more evidence of Italian fascism. Amidst the ancient graveyard was a newly built memorial inscribed, "To those who have died for the Empire and the Fascist Revolution in Spain." Mussolini had sent tens of thousands of troops to North Africa to conquer Ethiopia and to Spain to fight in the Spanish Civil War. The names of the Italian dead were listed in small bronze letters in an adjacent room, where the uniforms of the fascist guards "stood out black against the white marble."

Despite these warning signs, she met a Fiat engineer who had worked in Detroit and who thought that war would be avoided. "The Italians dislike England because of the trade sanctions and hate France for they feel she looks down upon them. Germany is fine with them as long as she behaves." Unfortunately, his rosy prediction of peace would not be true.

In Venice, the four women stayed at the Hotel Monaco on the Grand Canal. Catherine was enthralled. "We glided along amazing canals—the spacious Grand Canal and the enchanting 'piccolo' canals, which I adored even more. One can't describe Venice for one can't grasp her reality—she is a feeling, a myth, a memory…What fun it was to awaken to the lapping of water and canal sounds!"

CATHERINE AND MRS. B crossed into Austria on July 11, 1938, four months after the Anschluss, Nazi Germany's occupation and annexation of the country. On the highway to Innsbruck, she wrote, "One sees loads of soldiers here, as in Italy, and each one seems to have a different uniform...A large bunch of tanks and other army equipment went clattering by—an ominous procession driven by fine-looking young soldiers."

The Tyrolean dress of Austrians startled her. "Everywhere one sees colorful native costumes—boys and men, young and old, wear short leather pants. Even great tall hairy-legged creatures show their knees! The gay suspenders, colorful feather-decked hats, 'socks-around-the-calves-only' mark the men. The women wear bright skirts with aprons, white blouses, and black velvet bodices. They are sweet, but the men are a panic!"

That evening she enjoyed listening to two yodelers in a tavern where "beer and song prevailed." After midnight, she went dancing with a "charming" Austrian who held decidedly racist views. "He seems to feel quite strangely against the Jews, though he admitted the higher class is fine. He feels they took away business and 'spoiled things' for others."

Her new dance partner told her that "90% of the Austrians wanted Hitler to come into Austria." In this assessment of the Anschluss, her partner echoed the words of one historian who wrote, "Church bells pealed and loyal addresses were read in front of cheering crowds. Men saluted and bellowed '*Sieg Heil.*' Women wept for joy and uttered thanksgivings. Girls garlanded steel-helmeted troops as though they were an army of liberation." But the enthusiasm was not universal. Harsh persecution of Jews began immediately.

On July 12 the women entered Germany, passing dozens of "Strength Through Joy" buses (*Kraft durch Freude*), a state-sponsored German tourist organization. Stopping for lunch at a roadside inn outside Munich, Catherine remarked that "Everyone here is so friendly and kind. The people seem happy and certainly are cheerful in their appearance. Everywhere there is a smile and a wave."

Today we know that there was nothing innocent about Nazi Germany in the summer of 1938. Yet American tourists remained oblivious to the Nazi threat, as Andrew Nagorski wrote in *Hitlerland: American Eyewitnesses to the Nazi Rise to Power*, "One factor that encouraged such blindness was how, when it came to people-to-people contact, young Americans found Germans friendly and welcoming."

In Munich, Catherine visited the Honor Temples (*Ehrentempel*), a shrine to

Nazi party members killed in a failed coup attempt in 1923. "Two motionless soldiers stand guard, and as everyone goes up the steps, he gives the Nazi salute. I
gave it too for, after all, this is their country, and that's their custom. There is no
roof, but a colonnade and the rain beat down on the bronze coffins...This was one
of the most impressive sights I have ever seen. The rain glistened on the stone and
the ribbons of the wreaths lay wet on the ground where the red swastikas had run."

In Heidelberg, Catherine toured the university and had coffee "at a fine luxurious café, the Café Schafheutle." This café, she noted pointedly, was "a gathering
place of the intellectuals, not of the Nazis. I wonder how long it will last?" In a
hotel in Wiesbaden, she saw a sign, "Jews are not allowed in these rooms," and in
nearby little towns were signs, "Jews are not wanted here."

Driving north, Catherine and Mrs. B followed the Rhine River to Belgium.
"We passed through 'unreal' towns, unbelievable groups of quaint old buildings,
old walls, ancient towers, wonderful houses, seasoned by the years and lovely old
churches." They spent two nights in Bruges, where Catherine drew a crude map
of her favorite walk. "This quiet, meditative little canal scene is as lovely a place
as I can ever hope to see. Heaven can't be far away from here."

SHE AND MRS. B. took a cross-channel ferry from Ostend to Dover. Approaching
the English coast, Catherine wrote, "Oh, the thrill of first gazing upon the white
cliffs of Dover!" Once they cleared customs, they drove ("on the wrong side of
the street!") straight to Canterbury Cathedral. "To me the most impressive thing
about this cathedral is the gigantic sweep of its Gothic arches."

The next two nights they stayed at nearby Chilham Castle as guests of Sir
Edmund Davis and Lady Davis. "We drove up to the door after the gates were
opened by the gatekeeper. Sir Edmund came out to meet us with formality...He is
a tiny well-padded little man of about five-feet—rather bald with a long beak-like
nose and an air of silence and reserve.

"The interior of the mansion is magnificent—priceless paintings of the old
masters, handsome antiques and fine carved stone and woodwork...One could
just walk about the rooms for hours looking at all the exquisite paintings—Van
Dycks, Gainsboroughs, etc....There is a fine swimming pool on the ground floor
and seemingly endless living quarters for the servants."

When Catherine returned to her room, the maid had already unpacked her bag
and laid out her evening dresses on the bed. "I dove into a bath and dressed in a

pesky old formal and then on to dinner. There were just the four of us in tuxes and formals—like little puppets. Sir Edmond says little and is perfectly frank—wow! He asked me why I wore 'all that glass on my arm'—referring to my beloved rhinestone bracelet. No answer seeming adequate, so I took it off & said 'I didn't know why.' There's no use quibbling with a Sir… Dinner was delicious, and afterwards we had coffee in the drawing room and undertook a somewhat stiff conversation."

The next morning Catherine was awakened by "Hearst," the maid, who brought her hot tea and was accompanied by a dachshund puppy. Sir Edmond later walked the castle's grounds with her. "He has greenhouses and raises about everything imaginable—peaches, cherries, plums, tomatoes, currants, and all kinds of vegetables, etc. We went down to the lovely little lake while Sir E. fed his ducks—of every possible variety. Then Sir E. and I wandered through his raspberry and gooseberry vines, which are covered with netting. He looked so droll with his thin hair all mussed up by rubbing on the low netting. We gobbled down berry after berry—it was such fun."

After dropping off their car in Southampton, they piled "12! pieces of luggage into the baggage car" and took a train to London where they stayed at the Regent Palace Hotel at Piccadilly Circus. Catherine spent her last five days in England in a manic drive to consume every possible tourist experience—Trafalgar Square, Westminster Abbey, the House of Commons, Madame Tussauds, Harrods, Covent Garden, the Tower of London, the Tube, double-decker buses, and the changing of the guard.

She spent "an unforgettable afternoon wandering around the endless halls" of the National Gallery. "It is heartbreaking to hurry through this gallery for every painting is wonderful. I particularly enjoyed the paintings of Constable, Gainsborough, Goya, Rembrandt, Cezanne, Monet, and Degas. I didn't leave until about 7."

EXHAUSTED AND ELATED, Catherine and Mrs. B boarded the *Manhattan* on July 29, 1938, homeward bound to New York. Unlike the plodding *City of Hamburg*, the *Manhattan* was a thoroughbred passenger liner, carrying over 1,200 passengers. In 1936 the *Manhattan* had carried the U.S. Olympic Team to Germany. Perhaps this athletic connection explained why "Champ," the gym instructor, called Catherine "chubby." He "wore me out every day—I bicycled miles, rowed, played with weights, played with a punching bag, with no success, etc. Boy, that swimming pool felt good."

Landing in New York on August 4, she was assaulted by the heat. "It is absolutely sweltering, a veritable Turkish bath. You take a shower, get dry and in 2 minutes you're à la Turkish bath again." After a summer touring the glories of the Old World, sightseeing in New York City produced culture shock. "Times Square is so exciting—so vital, so confused, and so American. The huge, wildly colored neon signs, the movies, shops, and skyscrapers hover over the busy little square. Everyone is in a hurry, probably going nowhere. They'll all land in the same place anyway, probably via the lunatic asylum."

ON AUGUST 7 they picked up their car and raced home to Los Angeles. From there Catherine headed north to start her junior year at Cal and to move into her new residence, International House.

CHAPTER 22

Blazing Her Trail

Catherine, 1938–1941

"MISS CLINE is a very superior person who should be allowed to escape to International House from the regimentation of a sorority." So wrote Joel Hildebrand, Catherine's freshman chemistry professor. "She is an A student and has an unusually buoyant personality, sound character, and an interest in intellectual matters...I recommend her most heartily."

International House (referred to as "I-House") described itself as "a residential center, free from barriers of race, creed, and nationality, appealing primarily to the mature student who desires inspiring and broadening associations." Catherine was accepted as a resident member at the beginning of her junior year. She would be one of five hundred students at I-House, half American and half foreign.

SHE WAS on an academic fast track. Undergraduates, like Catherine, who majored in Medical Sciences and completed the prerequisites by their junior year, could apply to the University of California Medical School and, if accepted, count their first year of medical school as their senior year of undergraduate study. (At the time, all medical students spent their first year on the Berkeley campus and the last four years at the Medical Center in San Francisco.)

The first semester of Catherine's junior year began on Monday, August 20, 1938. She carried thirteen units: Zoology 100 (Vertebrate Embryology and Microscope Technique), English 117E (Shakespeare), Psychology 165 (Clinical and Abnormal Psychology, Mental Deficiency), and Philosophy 104A (Ethics).

For her spring semester, she took her last prerequisite, Chemistry 8 (Organic

247

Chemistry). She filled the rest of her class schedule with liberal arts electives: Philosophy 136B (Aesthetics), Art 1B (History of Medieval, Renaissance, and Modern Art), Sociology 1B (Progress and Civilization), and Oriental Languages 172 (The influence of Buddhism on Far Eastern Civilizations).

Her one extracurricular activity that year was volunteering at the Little Theater, Cal's drama club. Perhaps she worked in the ticket office or moved props around. With no actual theater on campus, all productions were staged in Wheeler Auditorium, a large lecture hall. As a result, "everything on stage—sets, props, and so forth—had to be stored in a nearby classroom so that the daytime lectures could proceed undisturbed."

In family lore, Catherine watched a young actor named Eldred Peck, later Gregory Peck, on stage. In March 1939, Peck starred in the Little Theater's production of *Anna Christie*, Eugene O'Neill's poignant drama of a prostitute, Anna, who falls for a dashing sailor, Matt Burke (Gregory Peck), whom she and her father had rescued from drowning.

"Peck's handsome face and muscular frame," wrote Peck's biographer, "created a buzz among the female theatergoers, all the more so…because he appeared naked to the waist for part of the performance." The *Daily Californian*, however, was less impressed. "Eldred Peck…almost endangered the success of the production with his exhibition of inexperienced acting technique. Lack of restraint was his chief fault." The play sold out its two nights.

WAS DOLLY worried about her daughter's heavy workload? She glued a newspaper article into a scrapbook, headlined "U.C. Students Warned Against Overworking." A school psychiatrist advised students "against giving all they have in a strenuous effort to attain a goal which is too high for them. A too great desire to better one's lot causes a worker to strive in a nervous atmosphere which is exhausting and handicaps the usefulness he should find in his own sphere." If Catherine ever saw the article, she paid no heed.

But Catherine must have been stressed by international events. How could she not be? She had just driven through the heart of Europe where she witnessed young children giving fascist salutes in Italy, convoys of Nazi troops in Austria, and anti-Semitic signs in Germany. At I-House, she was surrounded by politically aware students concerned about conflict in their homelands. Japan and China had been at war since 1938.

After Prague fell to the Nazis, history professor Robert J. Kerner issued a dire warning in the *Daily Californian* on March 17, 1939. "Hitler's annihilation of the Czechoslovakian state has exposed the sham of his so-called policy of self-determination of Germans wherever they live. He used this policy as a screen for the advance of German imperialism to complete domination of central and Eastern Europe."

Two days later, Catherine wrote a poem expressing her heartbreak witnessing the desperate state of world affairs.

> People are dying in Europe;
> People are dying in China;
> People like you and me;
> Not by ones,
> Not by twos,
> By thousands,
> By ten-thousands,
> We laugh
> They cry
> We live
> They die
> Why?

Her emotional connection to the wider world galvanized her commitment to medicine, as she had written in high school. "The work of a doctor seems to me to be the most beneficial of all the professions. I hope that I shall have the privilege of studying and practicing medicine, and that someday I shall be able to help alleviate the suffering of mankind."

CATHERINE DID earn this privilege when she was accepted into the University of California Medical School at the end of her junior year. Her senior year as an undergraduate would be her first year of medical school, and her first day of class would be August 28, 1939.

Catherine reveled in the moment. "Well, a week of medical school has passed, and I have worked extremely hard and loved doing it. The first day's gross lab we four girls 'glowed' as we stripped the skin off our cadaver's back—a nice dainty operation for four specimens of femininity, I thought. Our little 'subject' is quite a mystery to us as to nationality, as we haven't yet unveiled his black bearded face (on fear of desiccation). He is evidently of a dark-skinned race, with straight black hair."

Her first semester of medical school was brutal. She spent seven hours a day in class starting at 8:00 a.m. and ending at 4:00 p.m. with a one-hour break at lunchtime. Of the thirty-five hours of classroom instruction per week, eight were in the lecture hall and twenty-seven in the laboratory. She took only two courses— Anatomy 101 (Histology and Microscopic Organology) and Anatomy 105 (Systemic Human Anatomy), respectively six and eleven units, for a total of seventeen. At night there was more study.

"I study surrounded by books & bones," Catherine wrote, "and my little neighbors look quite abashed to enter the room as I sit with a vertebral column on my lap, a shoulder-blade by my side...Carrying a microscope and a slide box and an armful of books up the hill from the Life Sciences Building is no fun. I think I'll buy a pack horse!" As the course catalog emphasized, "*A student will not be permitted to begin work in the Medical School unless he has a microscope.*"

We can be certain that the use of the male pronoun, "*he*," bothered Catherine, who was one of only five women in her class of sixty-one. Although she left no written example of discrimination, in family lore she clearly felt that women were not recognized as the equal of their male colleagues. Indeed, we can imagine that this prejudice further spurred her to excel.

Catherine's lifelong friend and I-House neighbor, Anne Waybur, remembered visiting with Catherine at night. "I'd come home late, see the light under her door and knock. She always invited me in, welcoming the chance to take a break from studying. She'd be sitting cross-legged at the head of her bed, dressed in a night-gown or sweat suit and surrounded by books... She was enchanted with medical school. She ate it up, talking about how exciting it was. She was thrilled to be involved in the study of the human body and linked this with her profound commitment to 'do good.' I think the latter was an ethical compulsion, not a burden but a mission that she cherished."

ON SEPTEMBER 1, 1939, exactly five days after Catherine started medical school, Germany invaded Poland, starting World War II. She recorded her despair in her diary. "War has been declared, with all its devastating implications which we talk about and cannot feel or realize. How tragic that the elemental greed and jealousy of man should ever stay with him, after centuries of appalling examples of its futility and barbarous wastefulness. We all feel we should do something about it.

"We make treaties and send ultimatums and utter commanding pleas, and, when the dreadful calamity arrives, everyone feels empty and blank and useless. Men will die, fine young men, who have loved ones and high ambitions, for a cause they do not understand and yet feel is hopeless and false…That is the height of tragedy."

But she had no time to dwell on her sorrow. Her immediate priority was to succeed in medical school. The law required all medical students to complete 4,000 hours of classroom instruction and laboratory work in four years, plus untold more hours working with clinical patients and a fifth year internship at a hospital.

The second semester of her first year of medical school (and the last semester of her senior year) was no easier. Her two eight-unit courses, Physiology 101M (Human Physiology) and Biochemistry 101M (Basis of Life Processes), featured interlocking schedules. Although there were a few holes in the middle of the week, each day began with an 8:00 a.m. lecture and each afternoon, except Thursday, ended with a lab until 5:00 p.m.

CATHERINE GRADUATED from the University of California on May 25, 1940, receiving her Bachelor of Arts degree with Honors in Medical Sciences, and she was elected to the Phi Beta Kappa Society. We can imagine her parents, Alan and Dolly, beaming with pride as Catherine crossed the stage in her cap and gown. She may not have been a debutante, but she was recognized by society.

President Robert Sproul delivered an inspirational address, emphasizing the vital role of universities in making the world a better place. "If the peace that follows the war now raging in Europe is to be anything more than a gestation period for subsequent wars, the social values and the human ideals which are inherent in democracy must be given greater clarity in the minds of men."

Sometime that summer of 1940, Catherine moved to San Francisco for her second year of medical school. She rented an apartment at 556 Roosevelt Way near Twin Peaks with sweeping views of the city to the east. Her apartment was about a mile from the San Francisco Medical Center at 533 Parnassus Avenue. Anne Waybur remembered visiting her apartment and seeing a "lovely jade goddess of compassion" by the front door. Perhaps the piece was an acquisition of her father, who was a frequent patron at antique auctions.

As a second-year medical student for the academic year 1940–41, Catherine again found her days filled with a constant stream of lectures and laboratories, starting most days at 8:00 a.m. and finishing at 5:00 p.m. She carried nineteen units both semesters and took introductory courses in a wide variety of medical fields, including bacteriology, pathology, psychology, pharmacology, surgery, and obstetrics. She had no time to write in her diary.

Starting her third year of medical school on August 25, 1941, she would have been excited. At last she could focus on pediatrics, her chosen field. The school catalog outlined her curriculum: "The work consists of clinical exercise and case studies on the diseases of infancy and childhood in the wards of the San Francisco Hospital. Students have intimate charge of patients and follow them under proper supervision... Students are required to submit complete records and studies of assigned cases."

WEARING HER WHITE COAT and carrying a stethoscope, Catherine was living her dream. In hospital wards and clinics, she was providing care and understanding to her little patients and their parents. To quote her words, she was helping to "alleviate the suffering of mankind."

Even better, she would soon meet the love of her life, Peter Pike, on Thanksgiving Day, just a few months away. We now circle back to Peter eight years earlier as he is about to embark on an ill-starred voyage to Alaska.

CHAPTER 23

Alaskan Adventure

Peter, 1933

BEDROLL ON HIS BACK and suitcase in hand, Peter Pike climbed the gangplank to board the SS *Chirikof* at 6:00 a.m. on the morning of May 16, 1933. Pandemonium reigned ashore at Pier 50 in San Francisco with crowds shouting and steam winches grinding to load last-minute cargo. Bound for Alaska, the crew and passengers aboard the *Chirikof* would spend the brief northern summer fishing and canning salmon in Bristol Bay for the Alaska Packers' Association.

After signing the ship's papers, Peter was gruffly directed to his quarters two decks below. He found a cabin twelve feet by twelve feet with three rows of pipe berths for nine men. The room had steel walls, a steel deck, and a steel ceiling. There was one porthole. He found a small spot for his suitcase and returned topside.

Back on deck, Peter decided to go ashore one last time. But before he took two steps down the gangplank, he was roughly accosted by "a man, seemingly twice my size, with hands the size of baseball gloves." He "grabbed my shoulder and literally threw me back on board, landing me in the scuppers. 'Nobody goes ashore once on board,' he growled and went back to his post." This was his first warning that the summer ahead would not be the adventure that he had imagined.

AFTER GRADUATING from Menlo in 1932 with no immediate plans to attend college, Peter spent a miserable winter working in the Tractor Shop at El Solyo Ranch. "Winter in the San Joaquin was cold…The temperature was always just around freezing with weeks on end of no sun—just fog. Cement floors wet with mud and rain. Open sides with wind breaks for protection. Jerrybuilt kerosene stoves for what warmth they could give, hopefully near the work you were doing."

For years Peter had listened to his father spin yarns about life in the Klondike during the Gold Rush. So when he heard about a summer job in Alaska, he jumped at the opportunity. The day before the *Chirikof* sailed, Peter's mother, Edith, came up from the ranch to say goodbye to her eighteen-year-old son, perhaps sensing the hard knocks that lay ahead. She took him to lunch and to see a movie, *Madame Butterfly*, based on the opera, starring Sylvia Sidney and Cary Grant. This would be Peter's last hint of culture for many months.

THE *CHIRIKOF* cast off its dock lines and headed out the Golden Gate. Perched along the rail and gazing at the rocky coastline, Peter noticed a man standing next to him "easily as big as the man who knocked me down earlier. He stared down at me and said, 'First time away from home, kid?' I wouldn't dare admit the truth, so I tried to look big and seasoned by saying that I had a job as a 'catskinner' in the San Joaquin Valley." (A catskinner was an operator of a caterpillar tractor.)

"He stared silently at my face as I answered and, after a while, asked me, 'What are you doing here—deck, stewards, or black gang?' I eagerly answered, 'Wiper here and cannery hand in Alaska.' (This being the first time I had ever heard the engine room crew called the 'black gang.') Another silence followed, and he finally turned and said, 'Jesus Christ, you poor kid!'" This was Peter's second warning.

Peter knew not a soul among the 600 men aboard and wrote that "loneliness set in quite early." He did notice that the men broke down into several distinct groups "who spoke their own language, stayed by themselves, and never crossed their group lines." The Norsemen—Norwegians, Swedes, and Danes—made up the ship's crew both above decks and below.

The Italians were the fishermen and "were given full respect and deference from all segments. They were catered to, given room on deck for their work, and had the best accommodations and food. Any day that was clear, the decks were covered with their nets, which they repaired... After all, their success meant the whole success of our trip."

The only men that Peter never saw on deck were the Chinese, who would work in the cannery and were quartered in the forecastle. "Our only contact with them was on 'opium watch.' Every hour one of us had to go up to the foc's'le and walk through the rows of bunks checking to see that no one had gone to sleep with a burning opium pipe, which could set the ship on fire. The stench of an enclosed foc's'le housing around a hundred humans and no ventilation meant we practically ran on our rounds."

PETER REPORTED to the engine room for his first watch at eight bells, twelve noon. "That first descent down the iron ladder to the bottom of the engine room, combined with the heat, the noise, and the rolling of the ship gave a sensation of descending into hell." The ship's triple expansion steam engine was over two stories high and drove a twenty-four-inch propeller shaft. "The engine had a stroke of about ten feet, each piston's connecting rod going to the crankshaft, which had enormous counter-weighted bearings revolving in large pits. Passageways of iron grating laced through the connecting rods to give access for cleaning and oiling."

Peter's watch schedule would be four hours on and eight hours off, so he would next report for duty at midnight. Over the coming days, he would lose all track of time because his working hours below deck meant he rarely saw the light of day.

Near Unimak Pass through the Aleutian Islands, the *Chirikof* was buffeted by gale-force winds and heavy seas. To prevent the propeller from spinning uncontrollably when the stern came out of the water, the engine room crew spent hours standing by two levers, one for steam and the other for forward or reverse. Depending upon the motion of the ship, they would push or pull one or both levers. "From the bottom of the engine room ... there was obviously no sightline outside, and the entire process was done with feel and balance."

EIGHT DAYS after leaving San Francisco, the *Chirikof* dropped anchor on the night of May 24, completing a passage of 2,380 nautical miles. Because of the shallow depth of Bristol Bay and the extreme tidal range, the ship was miles from shore. "We anchored in the black of a moonless night somewhere," Peter wrote, "and all I knew was that the seas were still fairly high. Hatches opened, cargo winches steamed up, and shore-type pandemonium broke out again."

A tug towing a barge pulled up along the lee side of the *Chirikof*. With the ship's deck lights illuminating the scene, cargoes were immediately hoisted from the holds of the ship and lowered onto the barge. "Loaded cargo nets swayed willy-nilly with the roll of the ship. As the ship rolled, the barge alongside was either against us or away from us. The [cargo] nets had to be dropped the last five or six feet timed to the movement of both ship and barge."

The cannery crew and the fishermen were on their own. "We had to go over the side with our gear and get onto the barge in between cargo swings." Peter jammed his suitcase into a cargo net, hoping to find it once aboard the barge. He climbed down a rope ladder. "As the ship rolled, the ladder would swing out, only to come back again with a slam. The jump from the ladder had to be timed with the swing of the barge along with the roll of the ship." He made it safely.

SOMETIME AFTER MIDNIGHT a tugboat towed the barge up the Kvichak River "many miles" to the Alaska Packers' cannery, which was built on stilts above the tundra "at what was once an Aleut Village called Kogiung." The cannery and its outbuildings of bunk houses and mess halls had been mothballed over the winter.

"We were the first crew in and our task was to put everything together... and to get ready for 'the season.' This phrase became the goal. Every move, every job, every thought was to get ready for 'the run'—even to the point of a continuous threat." This was his third warning.

Peter and his crew fired up the boiler, which was "the total source of all energy, heat, and light. Every pipe spreading throughout the compound had been taken apart at each joint and greased the previous fall so that they would drain and not freeze and split during the winter. Every electrical line had to be traced out to see that an icicle hadn't chafed it, so that it would fire up when the juice was turned on." Supplies continued to come ashore by barge, and, after all the tin plate had been unloaded from the ship, the crew started the machines to make tens of thousands of cans for the salmon catch.

Just before the season started, Peter and a friend were assigned a job to repair some outside machinery at the dock. "The wind coming off the polar ice and across the vast, flat frozen tundra was constant and howling and indescribably cold. Time of day under these conditions gets lost because the sun never goes down. It just sinks to the horizon and seems to follow along that line and rise up again further to the east."

But the time of day really did not matter anyway. The cannery workers were paid ten cents an hour for a ten-hour day, plus room and board. No overtime was ever paid. At a dollar a day, the most a worker could hope to earn that summer would be $86 ($1,630 in 2017 dollars) for the eighty-six days from the day of departure to the day of return to San Francisco—assuming the worker spent no money at the company store. A young friend told Peter that this would be "the only money his mother, father, and brother had earned in the last two years."

THE COMPANY STORE attracted a small community of "Wintermen" (trappers) and their native wives who built a temporary settlement nearby. "Their only currency was furs—fox, martens, mink, and some wolf. Our store looked like any frontier general store. It was stocked with everything imaginable that Wintermen would need—traps, guns, sacks of flour, sugar, coffee, clothing, boots, tools, and some cloth for the squaws, although they dressed in fur parkas mostly. This was during Prohibition, but there was a thriving business in whiskey. Standard price was $5.00 for a coke-bottle full."

"Cigarettes, soft drinks, candy, extra gloves, work clothes, etc. were all available. A large accounting book was at the cash register. If you didn't have cash, the amount was put in the book to be taken out of your pay at the end of the trip. On payday in San Francisco in the fall, it seemed there was, in many cases, more money owed to the commissary than due a man." (If so, the man had to work another season to pay off his debt.)

ONCE THE twenty-one-day fishing season for sockeye salmon started, Peter was assigned to a "filler" machine. After the fish bodies were gutted and the heads and tails cut off, the filler machine inserted a fish into a can, cut and trimmed the superfluous pieces, put a lid on the can in a vacuum chamber, and sealed it. Cans were fed from the second floor "around 200 cans a minute."

Decades later, Peter vividly recalled the manic conditions during the season. "After the first few days, I noticed that the bosses began carrying side arms. Not too conspicuous, but noticeable. I could feel the tension mounting. We had been away from San Francisco for over a month-and-a-half. Already there were some threats by some to quit. There had been no mail (and never was) and no news or communication of any kind (and never would be).

"A standard way to handle a quitter was to say, 'Five dollars a day to stay till we go back and then a charge for passage (several hundred dollars). Or, leave now and work your way up to Iliamna Lake with some Indians and hopefully get someone to take you south to the coast with a dog sled when the snow comes.' That generally ended the argument but the man was watched very closely from then on. A hand on the holster of a side arm could be very persuasive." (Peter did not report any actual violence.)

"We were awakened every morning at 3:00 and canned fish until around 9:00 or 9:30 at night. Then the whole operation had to be washed and cleaned down.

Any part of the entire line that the fish passed through during the processing had to be steam cleaned. A live steam gun under high pressure makes a noise that is deafening. No ear plugs, no ear cups as we use today. After finishing the steaming, it might be thirty minutes before we could hear again.

"Obviously, after steaming, every part had to be oiled and greased again. Those parts that contacted the fish had a special lubrication of fish oil. Petroleum-based oil can't be used on parts touching edible products. The cleaning job took until about midnight. Up again at 3:00 a.m. Twenty-one hours a day! No overtime pay! No breakfast between 3:00 a.m. and regular breakfast time at 6:30 a.m. Out of your bunk and onto the machine... After fourteen days at twenty-one hours a day, my exhaustion caught up. I passed out one night and slept through for a solid eighteen hours."

When the fishing season ended, the pace of the cannery hardly slowed. The cans had to be labeled, put in cases (four dozen cans to a case), and ferried out to the *Chirikof.* As the month of July wore on, the sun would dip below the horizon and the day finally came when the cannery closed. "Everything had to be undone... Each pipe disconnected to drain and the wiring protected. The process converged back on the boiler plant where we had started months before."

As his barge was towed down the Kvichak River on August 1, Peter looked back at the cannery. "The whole complex standing on its stilts above the tundra seemed as forlorn and deserted as if no one had been there for years. It was hard to believe that, just moments ago, it was teeming with the lives and activities of over 600 people scrambling to make a whole year's income out of just twenty-one days of fishing."

When his barge arrived at the *Chirikof,* Peter scrambled back up a rope ladder and over the side, "but at least this time it was daylight." The next morning, August 2, less than three months after leaving San Francisco, the *Chirikof* was homeward bound. The captain ordered the anchor raised at 5:07 a.m. and full steam ahead at 5:34 a.m. "The whistle blew and all on deck sent up a cheer." Eight days later, the *Chirikof* entered San Francisco Bay late at night.

PETER CHOKED UP as the ship slid past the lighted Ghirardelli sign atop the chocolate factory. "This was the symbol that anyone at sea, the world over, recognized as 'port at last.' It stood out clearly, no background then of lights and buildings. And an unending stream of auto lights up and down the hills... It was so big and so bright that from the dark sea, it seemed almost magic.

"I truly don't remember what the others on deck said or did, I can only re-member my own reaction which was one of being unable to speak or wanting to speak ... As we slowly steamed around the waterfront, weaving our way through the ferry lanes, and looking at the beauty of San Francisco in the full moon, the whole summer seemed to vanish."

As he gazed at the city, he thought, "Who might there be watching us? Who knew of our trip? Our lousy food, the Artic cold, the tundra, the twenty-one-hour work days? Who knew our holds were filled with 132,000 cases of canned salmon packed at ten cents an hour and no overtime, fished by men pulling nets to ex-haustion to bring home the only money that a family in the Depression would see until next year? Who knew that if you slipped going over the side at Bristol Bay, the barge could have crushed you to oblivion?" At 10:05 p.m. on August 10, Peter wrote, "the *Chirikof* was warped into the same pier where we had left. No one could ever again say 'you poor kid.' I could now get papers and ship out, if I wanted to."

BUT A LIFE at sea for Peter was not to be. In a complete turnabout, he was off to college six days after his ship docked.

CHAPTER 24

Finding His Way

Peter, 1933–1941

PETER REGISTERED for a two-year course at the Davis Farm, a campus of the University of California, on August 16, 1933. This non-degree curriculum in the College of Agriculture was "designed primarily for young men and women who desire a good practical training in agriculture in order that they may be better prepared for the business of farming." Upon completion of their coursework, they would receive a Certificate of Graduation from the University of California in the College of Agriculture.

Most students at Davis, like Peter, registered for the certificate program, not the academic program (227 non-degree versus 140 degree students). Of the total student body of 367, seventeen were women, a fact celebrated by the student newspaper, the *California Aggie*, under the awkward headline, "Agricultural Education at University Farm Attracts Gorgeous Creatures."

Regardless of classification—degree or non-degree—all first-year students were called freshmen, and the boys were subject to harsh rules published in the *Cal Aggie*. "1. Frosh shall NOT walk on the grass; 2. Frosh shall NOT go on the campus without their dinks [beanies]."

Peter lived in the North Hall dormitory where, the *Cal Aggie* reported, "freshmen...were stripped to the waist and 'dobbed-up' in very fine style" with red stripes on their foreheads and cheeks. After enduring the brutal conditions at the Alaskan cannery just weeks earlier, what must Peter have thought of this hazing ritual?

PETER SPECIALIZED in agricultural engineering. No records have survived of his coursework, but he probably took Agricultural Engineering 2 (Farm Equipment and Its Relation to Agriculture), a two-unit course that met once a week for a one-hour lecture and a three-hour lab. Never happy in a classroom, Peter's most enjoyable hours must have been working on all types of farm machinery in the recently completed Agricultural Engineering Building.

If class was boring, the campus drama club was not. Peter joined the California Aggie Players and was cast as a "fast-stepping college boy" in a November production of *Nightie Nite*, a "three-act, rollicking comedy." In his second semester, he was a little boy who delighted in playing with machinery (sounds perfect) in his parents' basement in *The Show-Off*.

That same spring Peter also performed as a female impersonator in a comedic review, which was covered by *Dingleberry*, the campus humor paper. Under the headline, "Fan Dancers of Repute," a picture of Peter's head with lipstick and penciled eyebrows appeared above a line drawing of his naked body fan dancing with a man similarly attired. The satirical poem below began, "There is a guy we don't all like / His name is Peter Pansy Pike."

PETER RETURNED to Davis for his second year in the fall of 1934 and was elected Song Leader of North Hall. That semester he performed in the Aggie Players' production of *Dulcy*, a comedy by George S. Kaufman. He played Vincent Leach, a screenwriter, described in the script as *"young, very languid, a bit effeminate, and with a modesty that admits he's great."*

"Vincent Leach," the *Cal Aggie* touted, "has no doubt about the ability of Vincent Leach... All women in the play, including the not too intelligent Dulcy, just love him. Members of his own sex have an impulse to annihilate him. The Aggies will be treated to a lesson in love-making on a high plane, and the coeds are sure to appreciate it. Using subtleties, he is most convincing as a lover." Sample dialogue of Leach romancing a house guest named Angela:

LEACH: I was afire—afire with love for you, Angela!

ANGELA: Why, what are you saying?

LEACH: Oh, those deep burning eyes! The mystery of your hair! Angela, you're wonderful! I love you! Almost from the first moment I saw you, I've loved you—wanted you—longed for you! To be with you is to breathe the perfume of exaltation. Angela!

ANGELA: (*Breathlessly.*) Vincent!

On November 13, the Players presented *Dulcy* to an audience of "some two-hundred-fifty to three-hundred people who enjoyed the play a great deal," wrote the *Cal Aggie*. "Peter Pike in the part of Vincent Leach gave some interesting points on the art of love making." *El Rodeo*, the college yearbook, included a picture of the entire cast of *Dulcy* on stage. Dressed in a dark suit, Peter sits in a chair with his head tilted upward and a confident smile on his face, looking just the part of a charming rogue.

This would be his final role as a Cal Aggie. Peter dropped out of Davis at the end of his third semester in December 1934, the same month that he turned twenty. Why? Perhaps because he became aware of the truth about El Solyo, not the whole truth, but enough to realize that his father was struggling financially.

Roy Sr. had promised both boys that he would pay them $1,000, if they did not smoke or drink until they turned twenty-one ($18,300 in 2017 dollars). This they did. But when Roy Jr. turned twenty-one in January 1934, his father was unable to pay him. "Poor father went broke," Roy Jr. lamented, "and couldn't afford to give us the whole amount." The message was clear. El Solyo Ranch was not a profitable enterprise. Peter would never be a farmer. So why would he need a Certificate of Graduation from the University Farm?

PETER MOVED to San Francisco, where he made his way into society with confidence and charm—assisted by his father's reputation as a clubman and his mother's connection to old money. "We got invitations to all of the debuts and private parties in Burlingame and San Francisco," his brother remembered. "In those days, 'society' was rather exclusive, and Father and Mother knew all the old families—the Spreckels, the Crockers, the Camerons, etc."

In February 1936, Peter attended the Mardi Gras Ball at the Palace Hotel, dressed as a harlequin drawing Pierrot and Pierrette on a float around the ballroom. The *San Francisco Chronicle* hailed the event as "one of the most brilliant social functions of the season" with dancing from 11:00 p.m. to 4:00 a.m. In May, he appeared in *L'Eternelle Histoire* (The Eternal Story) presented by the Salon Français, a French literary society. The *Chronicle* described the production as a "vertiginous farce abounding with 'esprit,' 'folie,' and other French qualities." Peter played a young boy.

In November, Peter was a supernumerary (in family lore, "a spear carrier") in a famous production of *Tristan and Isolde* with Lauritz Melchior and Kirsten Flagstad as the lead singers and Fritz Reiner conducting. Alfred Frankenstein, the music critic for the *Chronicle* gushed about the opera. "To say that this completely over swept the memory of all other 'Tristan' performances is to deal in superlatives, but there are times when even superlatives are as inadequate to convey a meaning as an unnoticed spark is inadequate to portray the sun."

Peter signed up for classes in bookkeeping at Heald College, a business college in San Francisco. Heald featured his name and picture in an advertisement for the school with the caption, "The Heald-Hadley Training Insures a Position for You!" Peter was described as an "accountant and office assistant with the Federal Pitter Company in Vernalis, California." In reality, his father probably owned Federal Pitter or, maybe more accurately, Mr. Balch did, and Peter preferred to spend most of his time in San Francisco, not pipsqueak Vernalis. (Pitter machines automatically pitted peaches.)

LIKE HIS FATHER, Peter was a great raconteur and never afraid to embellish a story. While his servitude in the Alaskan cannery might have been a bit grim for dinner table conversation, Peter did have one excellent tale to tell—crossing the Golden Gate Bridge on catwalks as the cables were being spun. For San Franciscans in the depths of the Depression, the idea of spanning the Golden Gate was an epic story. In the words of California historian Kevin Starr, it was "a marvel of engineering construction … and a testimony to the skills, resilience, inventiveness, and courage of the American worker."

Peter was joined on his escapade by Tommy Magee III, another society man about town. In family lore, Peter and Tommy bluffed their way onto the bridge by flashing a coin to a watchman. Supposedly, the coin resembled an official badge, and they were allowed to pass. By comparing Peter's photographs with construction pictures of the bridge, we can roughly date their trespass to January 1936.

After construction of the north and south towers of the bridge was completed in 1935, work could begin on spinning the enormous suspension cables. The first step was to suspend footbridges from the towers parallel to the future cables between San Francisco and Marin County. Then spinning machines drew thousands of miles of thin wire between the two gigantic anchor blocks on the opposite shores. As these wires were strung, they were first tied into strands, and later the strands were

Peter Pike and Tommy Magee on the Golden Gate Bridge, January 1936.

compacted into the suspension cables that support the roadway today.

Peter and Tommy walked up the catwalk from the San Francisco anchorage to the top of the south tower and down the arc to the midpoint of the bridge. There they somehow managed to scramble onto the completed strands of wire above the catwalk and had their picture taken, presumably by a nearby worker. On the back of this photograph, Peter wrote, "Walking on cable, very dangerous. Cable laid and bound in those small bundles. If walked on, they swayed. The rest speaks for itself in the line of risk."

BY 1939 PETER had found a way to marry his passion for music and opera to a source of income—at least that was his hope. He and his friend, Harry de Witt, would open a classical records store. The two lived on Telegraph Hill, which was then becoming an attractive neighborhood for the younger set according to an article in the *San Francisco Chronicle* headlined, "High Life Revolves Around Coit Tower."

"Up until only a handful of years ago the only abodes on the hill were modest, unassuming, and too often nondescript. Recently, streamlined, chromed, and plate-glassed abodes have been built on the ridges, and, with the event of bathtubs on the hill, came a flock of the carriage trade… A snug establishment on Calhoun, an alley which runs parallel to Montgomery, houses two young men about town, Harry de Witt and Peter Pike."

Their store was called the Music Album, located at 14 Tillman Place off Grant Avenue near Sutter Street in downtown San Francisco. Their slogan: "For classical records…It's the Music Album." Although we do not know details of their venture, we can guess that Peter invested little, if any, capital. Most likely, he committed only his time, while promising to deliver his wealthy friends as customers. If true, he was marching in his father's footsteps—promoting a scheme that combined business connections with social cachet.

Before they opened their store, the pair needed to acquire an inventory of records and that meant a transatlantic voyage to meet with record distributors. Most classical recordings sold in America during the 1930s came from England, which explains their quick visit to London over sixteen days from December 19, 1938, to January 4, 1939.

While making the arrangements to purchase their inventory, they stayed at the Regent Palace Hotel, the same hotel that Peter's future wife, Catherine, had stayed in five months earlier at the end of her European tour. After their whirlwind visit, Peter and Harry booked passage home in third-class, a big step down from Peter's elegant voyages in the 1920s with his then wealthy parents.

Back in San Francisco, the duo prepared to open their store. We do not know the exact date, but they placed their first display advertisement in the *San Francisco Chronicle* on February 9, highlighting a recording by a well-known Welsh pianist, named Alec Templeton—"You have read about him in *Time, Esquire* and the *New Yorker*, now for the first time in San Francisco."

All classical records at the time were recorded at 78 rpm, which played four to five minutes per side. Longer musical pieces, therefore, like a symphony, needed a set of multiple discs, hence a music album. Individual twelve-inch records sold for $1.00 ($17.60 in 2017 dollars). To generate more sales, albums had to be discounted, as the store advertised in the *Chronicle*—"Columbia Masterworks Records as much as ½ off."

Still, even fifty cents for a classical record was much more than the thirty-five cents typically paid for a recording of popular tunes. The Music Album targeted a niche market of affluent record collectors who wanted to build a library of fine music. Were there enough such collectors in San Francisco to support their store? Apparently not.

When the census enumerator visited Telegraph Hill and knocked on the door of 37 Calhoun in April 1940, he did not find Peter. Instead Harry de Witt lived alone and was the sole proprietor of the record store. Peter was now a clerk at Decca Distributing Company, a record distributor. We can guess that their business simply did not generate enough income for the two partners, and Peter needed a steady salary.

EVEN THOUGH his record shop was not a success, Peter thrived as a man about town. At the Finnish-Polish relief ball in January 1940, he portrayed White-Hat McCarthy (a well-known saloon character) in a pageant celebrating Old San Francisco. He appeared in another French comedy, *Léopold le Bien-Aimé* (Leopold the Beloved) in May at the Ferrier French Theater of Art. On election night in November, Peter attended the Motion Picture Research Council party at the Palace Hotel dressed as one of the past U.S. presidents, although the social pages differed as to whether he portrayed Zachary Taylor or John Adams.

Outside San Francisco, Peter appeared in the Mountain Play, performed on the slopes of Mount Tamalpais in Marin County. He played a cricket in *The World We Live In* by Josef and Karel Čapek, a play known as "The Insect Comedy." "Scores of players," wrote the *Chronicle*, "representing butterflies, moths, ants, and beetles will dance, fight, make love, and exterminate one another, in behavior analogous to that of human beings, in this Czecho-Slovakian satirical fantasy."

A picture of Pamela Wright, the female cricket playing opposite Peter, shows her dressed in a leotard wearing light fabric wings. Peter must have worn a similar costume. Unfortunately, their insect lives were short-lived. According to the program notes, "Act II contains the story of gentle crickets, who are to meet death through the rapacious Ichneumon fly [part of the wasp family]."

The Mountain Play was presented on one day only, May 19, 1940, shortly after Germany launched its blitzkrieg invasion of France, Belgium, and Holland and less than a month before the German army would occupy Paris. The state of the world must necessarily have looked dire to the thousands who attended the outdoor theater that day.

Successful in his avocation of acting, Peter joined the Bohemian Club as an artistic member, a class of membership available to "persons proficient in Literature, Art, Music, Drama, or Science." As an artistic member, most of his club fees would have been waived in return for active participation in the club's theatrical productions.

WHILE PETER searched for a sense of direction in San Francisco, he must have felt the emotional turmoil between his parents, still living at El Solyo. After years of deception, his mother, Edith, had finally grasped the dire reality. Her husband, Roy, did not own the ranch and never would. Her fortune was mostly gone, and she would now be forced to live in reduced circumstances.

Edith never wrote about her shock at this turn of events. But Joan Didion probably captured her mood when she wrote, "California is a place in which a boom mentality and a sense of Chekhovian loss meet in uneasy suspension; in which the mind is troubled by some buried but ineradicable suspicion that things had better work out here, because here, beneath that immense bleached sky, is where we run out of continent."

Peter felt the shock, too. From an early age, he had lived a privileged lifestyle with a governess, trips to Europe, and a private tutor. He had watched his parents entertain Hollywood stars, business leaders, and political luminaries. He had witnessed the development of El Solyo into "the largest diversified ranch in the world." He had followed his father's footsteps into San Francisco society and been recognized as a charming man about town. But as he turned twenty-six in December 1940, he had yet to find his *métier* (one of Peter's favorite French words).

FOR THE FIRST time in his life, he alone would be responsible for his fate. What to do? Where to go? It was time to start anew. He resigned his membership in the Bohemian Club and headed to Southern California to search for a job. He had not yet run out of continent.

He had always liked machinery on the ranch and had studied agricultural engineering at Davis. He had thrilled when a plane passed over his one-room school and the students stared up in amazement. Why not look for a job in the booming aviation industry in Los Angeles?

In March 1941, Peter found work at Lockheed Aircraft in Burbank, where he was one of 18,000 employees working in two huge plants building P-38 fighters for the U.S. Army (the Air Force did not yet exist) and Hudson light bombers for the British Royal Air Force. He worked as an "expediter" in the Engineering Division, although we do not know precisely what he meant by the term. With thousands of parts for hundreds of planes moving down the assembly line, delivering components in the right sequence at the right time was critical. Perhaps Peter helped coordinate a step in this process.

The outbreak of World War II in Europe and the rearmament of the United States had produced a huge backlog of orders for aircraft manufacturers.

"Lockheed Goes on War Footing," headlined the *Los Angeles Times* on March 19. "Lockheed Aircraft Corp. was placed on a war footing yesterday and dedicated first and foremost to the production of its deadly P-38 interceptor for national defense." The president of Lockheed warned that the slightest "indication of loitering, slackness, and fooling around...will be cause for immediate and positive dismissal."

Six months later, a *Chicago Tribune* reporter visited Burbank in September 1941. Under the headline "Warcraft Pouring Out," he described the frantic pace of activity at Lockheed's plant. "Benches, machines, lathes, drills, and crews of workers riveting sheets to skeleton metal structures, are crammed as closely as possible. Space inside the plant is at such a premium that employees must mount to lofts suspended from the ceiling girders to wash their hands or get a drink of water."

The massive plant stretched through "five or six hangers" constructed side-by-side with their walls removed. Inside, two assembly lines snaked nearly 2,000 feet through the facility. "From wings on each side of these main lines come small subassembly parts to be joined to a constantly growing structure that before the eyes of watchers becomes a whole airplane." He noted that the workforce in September was 35,000 people, double the March number of employees.

Lockheed would build a total of 1,538 planes in 1941, almost four times the production of the previous year. Aviation employment in Los Angeles County shot up from 13,000 men and women to 113,000 between January 1939 and December 1941. *Fortune* described the industry as the "arsenal next door to Hollywood... making dive bombers in the Land of Oz."

PETER DEVELOPED his own connection to Hollywood through his friendship with a Hungarian movie director and his actress wife—Andrew and Jarmila Marton. How Peter met the Martons is lost in the sands of time. Andrew would later become well known as the director of *King Solomon's Mines* (1950) and the chariot race in *Ben-Hur* (1959). Both films were nominated for Best Picture Academy Awards with the latter winning.

The Martons lived in Laurel Canyon, even then a popular spot for the motion picture industry. Jarmila invited Peter to a cocktail party on Thanksgiving Day at a neighbor's home on Lookout Mountain Avenue. So it was that Peter Pike and Catherine Cline met each other that fateful holiday, November 20, 1941. (President Roosevelt had moved Thanksgiving up a week to extend the holiday shopping season to stimulate the economy.)

CHAPTER 25

Romance in Wartime

Peter and Catherine, 1941–1942

WHEN CATHERINE saw Peter and Jarmila Marton enter the room, her first thought was "There is my greatest disappointment. If only I could have met him before he was married." After they were introduced a few minutes later, she realized that he was not married. "I guess from that time on, Peter was a 'dead pigeon.' We stood in front of the fireplace and chatted about something-or-other, and I was never happier."

The feeling was entirely mutual. Peter told Jarmila that night that he had met the girl he would marry. Two days later, on Saturday, November 22, 1941, he went to Catherine's parents' house at 460 N. Las Palmas for cocktails. Peter and Catherine walked to a nearby restaurant where they talked of their "dearest wishes in life—the things we felt were the most worthwhile." The next day, the love-struck couple parted until the Christmas holidays, Catherine north to San Francisco to finish the fall semester of medical school and Peter back to the Lockheed plant in Burbank.

Two weeks later on Sunday, December 7, 1941, Japan launched a surprise attack on the U.S. Pacific fleet at Pearl Harbor. The next day, the United States declared war on Japan. Fear and paranoia swept the Golden State. As Kevin Starr wrote, "Was Pearl Harbor the beginning, Californians asked, of an assault on the American mainland itself: an assault that would turn California into a battleground?"

The *San Francisco Chronicle* stoked that fear with its December 9 headline, "JAPAN PLANES NEAR S.F." After a blackout was ordered at 2:31 a.m. that morning, the *Chronicle* reported, "Almost immediately the roar of planes was heard—particularly in Marin County, in Berkeley, and in San Francisco."

Brigadier General William Ord Ryan said, "There was an actual attack. A strong squadron was detected approaching the Golden Gate. It was not an air raid test. It was the real thing." In fact, there were no Japanese planes off the California coast, and the unknown aircraft were probably U.S. naval planes on patrol. But the shock of the Japanese attack on Pearl Harbor had made it easy to believe such a story.

TWELVE DAYS after Pearl Harbor, Peter and Catherine reunited in Los Angeles on Friday, December 19. She documented their dramatic conversation that evening at her parents' home. After Alan and Dolly had retired for the night, she and Peter sat on a couch in the living room looking "long, deeply, and silently into each other's eyes."

She remembered that the silence lasted about five minutes, before Peter took her hand and said, "I love you." With this declaration, Catherine boldly responded, "Gee, but I hope that we can be married soon." "So do I," replied Peter. Thus, "in about two minutes, we settled our whole life course together. So on this third meeting of such old friends, we became engaged." They kept their engagement a secret.

Catherine must have been ecstatic that holiday season. She had met her true love and would celebrate Christmas with him. Under a picture of her family's Christmas tree, she proudly wrote, "The tree we trimmed—our first together." We can imagine that Peter would have experienced conflicting emotions. He, too, would celebrate Christmas with the person he loved. Yet it would be his first Christmas after the loss of El Solyo Ranch, his family's lodestone.

Always the raconteur, Peter would have been a charming guest at Christmas dinner, spinning yarns about his life and travels—a welcome break from the alarming war news. Just that morning, the *Los Angeles Times* had published a full-page headline, "TWO MORE SHIPS TORPEDOED." "Japanese submarines disabled two American lumber schooners yesterday in daring daylight raids off the California coast. One man was killed and 33 were rescued from the 409-foot lumber ship *Absaroka*, while hundreds on the shoreline watched the spectacular whish of two torpedoes through the water."

Peter and Catherine at her parents' home in Los Angeles in
December 1941. "Engaged and so happy, but nobody knew!"

PETER AND CATHERINE announced their engagement to her parents on New Year's Day 1942. "We were amazed that they were surprised, after having seen the two of us together for two weeks. My Peter had some bad moments telling Daddy—rather trying to—after I had taken a graceful exit. On returning in ten minutes (Peter swears it was two), the news was still untold, so we told him together, which was much more fun anyway. Such joy!"

For the first time in years, Catherine and her mother could embrace the social whirl together. Dolly would look forward to months of preparation for her daughter's wedding and reception—reserving a church, finding a florist, selecting a caterer, and sending invitations. Catherine would pick out a wedding dress and a honeymoon trousseau. Her father, Alan Cline, would proudly walk his daughter down the aisle of a church filled with their wide circle of friends.

On January 4, 1942, Peter and Catherine drove north to San Francisco to meet his mother, Edith. If they took U.S. Route 99 up the Central Valley, they would have passed under Modesto's archway with the city motto, "Water Wealth Contentment Health." For Peter, this would have triggered a flood of childhood memories of El Solyo Ranch, just fifteen miles away. After turning west on U.S. Route 50, they would have driven through Tracy past his favorite ice cream parlor where he and his brother had coveted the booth labeled "Vernalis."

"Never were two people so on edge," Catherine wrote in her bridal diary. "After a day of dismal war news, Mummie [Edith] had the shock of hearing that I was to be her 'daughter' and at our first meeting! Peter said to Mummie, 'You see in front of you two of the most frightened children in the world,' and indeed he was right." Peter, who had turned twenty-seven the day before Pearl Harbor, sounded like he was still yearning for his mother's love.

Reconnecting with the *San Francisco Chronicle*'s society editor, Dolly secured a five-column headline announcing their engagement. "Catherine Cline and Peter Pike Are Planning a Spring Wedding." "Miss Catherine Cline," the article began, "will be getting her MRS. before she receives her M.D." Their mothers, Dolly and Edith had both been debutantes, so the social editor wrote, "The marriage will serve to unite two prominent California families."

The *Chronicle* story ended with a real whopper, "The future bridegroom attended Harvard and also studied in France and Switzerland"—true, but not the whole truth. Peter had attended the Harvard School, a military academy, and had "studied" in Europe as a fifth and ninth grader. There was no mention of his time at the Davis Farm.

Alan and Dolly hosted an engagement dinner at the Palace Hotel on January 9. Both of Peter's parents, Edith and Roy Sr., who was in declining health, attended. This gathering might have been the only time that her parents met his father. The families agreed that a spring wedding would take place in Marin County at St. John's Episcopal Church in Ross, followed by a reception at the home of the bride's godfather, Dr. Russell Ryan, on Upper Toyon Drive, also in Ross.

ON JANUARY 14 Peter enlisted in the United States Army Air Forces (shortened to AAF), the predecessor to the U.S. Air Force, which was not formed until 1947. Now Peter's immediate fate would be in the hands of Uncle Sam.

For almost a month, ever since their secret engagement on December 19, the couple had been inseparable. Under one contemporary photograph of Peter with his hands clasped together, Catherine had written, "Peter—holding hands with himself for a change."

Peter was inducted as a private in the AAF at the Monterey Presidio, 115 miles south of San Francisco. Catherine drove down to see him on Sunday, January 18, and recorded his transformation in two photographs, which she annotated, "Peter—unmercifully foreshortened!" (referring to his haircut) and "Cats—very proud of her 'soldier-boy.'" The next day she began her spring semester classes at the University of California Medical Center.

After his induction, Peter was sent to Hamilton Field in Marin County. How happy he must have been to be based so close to his fiancé. We do not know what training he received during his first weeks in the AAF. But we can imagine that Peter's natural mechanical skills and his previous experience in aircraft manufacturing made him a valuable enlisted man at a time when the ranks of the AAF were swelled by tens of thousands of raw recruits monthly.

Hamilton Field played a critical role early in World War II as the official point of departure for all aircraft moving into the Pacific theater. After the Pearl Harbor attack, the army had rushed a company of ground troops and an artillery battery to defend the airfield. Seventeen tanks and gun emplacements were positioned around the perimeter of the base to protect against low-level attacks.

As AAF units were organized, reorganized, and rotated into and out of the base, Hamilton Field hosted tens of thousands of transitory personnel and thousands of planes. According to one history, life became "crowded, frenzied, and emotionally harried for all personnel. Nighttime blackouts were required and previously gleaming

Peter Pike, engagement photograph, January 1942

Catherine Cline, engagement photograph, January 1942

whitewash on the base buildings was blotted out with dark camouflage paint... Netting was hung between the hangars and covered with camouflage to hide the aircraft."

IN FAMILY LORE, Peter learned that his unit was about to be shipped overseas. Whether this was a rumor or an actual order was never clearly explained. Whatever the circumstances, he believed the information to be true, and he desperately wanted to be married before he left. Wartime security prevented him from telling this directly to Catherine. But the tone of his voice apparently conveyed that message in his early morning telephone call to her on Tuesday, February 3, 1942.

"I awakened sleepily, as usual," she recorded in her diary, "never dreaming this was to be our wedding day. Peter phoned at 7:30 a.m., saying something very important had come up and to please come over at 7:30 p.m. He wouldn't tell me what the news was, but I had a premonition it was bad. Off to school I went at 8:00 a.m., just as usual, but with, oh, such a preoccupied mind. Not a word I heard penetrated my poor, worried old head. So at 1:00 p.m., I gave up the fight, and left school—a worried little girl.

"To while away the long hours before 7:30 p.m., I decided to get our marriage license. So I wandered into the county clerk's office about 4:00 p.m. The dear little county clerk told me that Peter had phoned him and the chaplain had phoned him and to rush over and to have Peter sign the papers so he could issue the license right away, as a lot of the boys were being sent overseas the next day.

"With my heart in my boots, I fled to Hamilton Field, and finally caught up with Peter, who had tried to find me all day. He told me the news and the bottom of my world dropped out, to think of being apart from him for so long. I tore back to San Rafael, and the clerk had waited to issue our license. So there I stood waiting for my marriage license with a tear now and then dropping on the desk—a happy bride. I looked at the calendar, between tears to see the date, for I thought I had better find out on what day of the year we'd celebrate our anniversary."

Wedding license in hand, Catherine raced back to Hamilton Field and fell into Peter's arms, overwhelmed with feelings of happiness and sadness—joy that she was getting married and sorrow that she would soon be parted from her husband. "From about 6 to 7 the bridegroom's shirt was damp with the bride's tears! But about 7 the idea of being married in a dirty shirt without a girdle, with a wedding dress and trousseau just across the bay, made me giggle. So we began to recover our battered senses of humor."

Catherine would never wear her "white satin wedding dress, white satin slippers, and veil" that she and Dolly had chosen. Nor would she wear her patriotic honeymoon outfit: "Navy blue and white print dress and jacket (elephants for good luck), red straw hat and veil, navy shoes, red purse, and white gloves."

Soon the two other members of the wedding party arrived—Peter's mother, Edith, from San Francisco, and Jack Ward, his army buddy from the base. Off the four went to "an adorable little blacked-out wooden chapel with candles on the altar," where Carlton W. Harrod, Chaplain, U.S. Army, waited to perform the ceremony.

"The front of the chapel was partitioned off to form a library, and several of the boys, who had never seen a wedding, asked if they could watch. So several little soldiers, whom we had never met before were our 'wedding guests'... One little soldier sang 'Oh Promise Me' before the wedding."

> Those first sweet violets of early spring,
> Which come in whispers, thrill us both, and sing
> Of love unspeakable that is to be;
> Oh, promise me! Oh, promise me!

"The boy who played the organ was a concert pianist so it was beautiful. We had a double ring ceremony—but no wedding rings—so we used my engagement ring (which Peter couldn't get on my finger) and Peter's seal ring. It was a beautiful, simple little ceremony."

The wedding party adjourned to the parking lot for the "'reception' in the pouring rain, drinking champagne in the car!" (According to the next day's *San Rafael Independent*, it rained two-and-a-half inches that night.) To the surprise of the bride and groom, the chaplain had managed to get Peter a ten-hour leave, enough for a "wee honeymoon." Peter's mother insisted that the couple spend their wedding night in her apartment, while she moved to her women's club.

From Edith's apartment in San Francisco, the bride and groom finally called her parents in Los Angeles to deliver the sudden news. "They were wonderful and understood our marrying without them perfectly. So we came to the end of a day full of the sorrow of impending separation, but still the happiest day of our lives. For now we belong to each other forever."

The *San Francisco Chronicle*'s social page headlined their elopement as "The Pikes' Romantic Fait Accompli." "Miss Catherine Cline and Peter Pike," Lady

Teazle wrote, "were married on Tuesday! That is the surprise announcement which is rattling coffee cups at breakfast tables all over town this morning."

On the day after their wedding, February 4, Catherine wrote in her wedding diary:

> *Peter does not leave.* (emphasis added)

With this news bombshell, her parents' understanding became somewhat less than perfect, and, in family lore, they never did forgive Peter for concocting a scheme to marry their daughter in a mad rush. (For the duration of the war, he never would be sent overseas.)

Catherine gave Peter his wedding ring, and the next day wrote:

> Peter gives me my wedding ring—Our rings are inscribed
> —Peter and Catherine, Feb. 3, 1942—Forever

THUS, THE ARCS of three generations intersected ninety-two years, almost to the day, after eighteen-year-old Jacob Pike stepped ashore in San Francisco on the night of February 4, 1850. We have bound together my great-grandparents and grandparents into a single California couple—my parents, Peter and Catherine Pike. Our journey is complete.

EPILOGUE

CATHERINE GRADUATED from the University of California Medical School on February 7, 1943, adding M.D. to her name and fulfilling her childhood dream. On graduation day she was three months pregnant with me. She moved to Sacramento to join Peter, who was stationed at McClellan Field (later McClellan Air Force Base). I was born on July 29, 1943, and named Peter Pike Jr. Like my father, I was not given a middle name.

For most of World War II, Peter remained at McClellan. He was trained as an airplane instrument mechanic, specializing in the maintenance and repair of bombsights and autopilot controls. Later he was promoted to technical sergeant and instructed other personnel.

Their second son, Alan Cline, was born in Sacramento on February 3, 1945. After the war, Peter and Catherine moved to San Rafael and later Ross in Marin County where Catherine was one of the first women pediatricians. Even fifty years later, I would occasionally meet one of her young patients (now a senior citizen) who fondly recalled being treated by "Dr. Pike." Two more sons followed: Drummond MacGavin on October 11, 1948, and Bruce Simpson on May 19, 1951.

Over the years, Catherine became more interested in mental health issues and did graduate work in psychiatry at the University of California in San Francisco. She refocused her medical practice on pediatric counseling and converted a bedroom into an office at her home on Thomas Court in Ross. She loved playing on the floor with her young patients and asking them to tell her stories, using children's toys.

After the war, Peter bought two automotive parts warehouses in San Francisco and Oakland, renaming the business Pike Services. In the early 1960s, he finally found his true *métier* as a mutual fund salesman and stockbroker in San Francisco. The pinnacle of his career was working for Kidder Peabody & Company on the thirty-second floor of the Bank of America Building. A born raconteur like his father and grandfather before him, Peter loved working in the Financial District and lunching at the Merchants Exchange Club. He always preferred to wear a bow tie.

Peter taught his four sons how to sail, and we spent endless days on his beloved *Runa IV*, a narrow, thirty-six-foot Danish sloop with a low freeboard, making it one of the wettest boats on San Francisco Bay. Each summer he sailed *Runa* up the coast to Tomales Bay, where we boys would spend weeks living with the Dudley Miller family at Shallow Beach, rowing and sailing and playing on the beach. I was allowed the use of a ten-foot catboat that I sailed around the shoreline and into nearby coves. Years later when I sailed across the Atlantic solo, I still remembered the thrill of singlehanding my first boat at Shallow Beach.

Sadly, Catherine died at age sixty in a traffic accident in Holland in 1979. Although she lived to see the birth of four grandchildren, the oldest, Caitlin, was just four when she died. Caitlin has only the faintest memories of her grandmother, who took her to the Children's Playground at Golden Gate Park and taught her how to make a necklace of dandelions. Absolutely nothing would have pleased Catherine more than spending time with her grandchildren as they grew up.

After Catherine's death, Peter married Henri van Minnen Wolfe in 1980. With Henri's encouragement, he sold *Runa* to buy *Oceana*, a Westsail 32, which was more comfortable for senior sailing. He and Henri enjoyed the opera and traveling to Europe frequently. He died in 1984 at the age of sixty-nine after a long battle with lymphoma. Henri died in 2011 at age ninety-seven.

IN 1944 Peter's father, Roy Pike Sr., was declared an "incompetent person ... [who] by reason of weakness of mind and other causes is unable, unassisted, properly to manage and take care of himself." A guardian was appointed, and Roy remained under institutional care for the rest of his life. No evidence has survived that Peter ever visited his father before his death in 1949. But Roy was remembered warmly by his friends. A. P. Giannini, the founder of the Bank of America, wrote Edith a note of condolence, and a mutual friend recounted a conversation with Mr. Giannini about Roy. "No one could have spoken with higher praise of one man's ability, charm, and contribution to agriculture of California." Allan Balch, Roy's benefactor whose money made the development of El Solyo possible, had died six years earlier in 1943.

Edith, or ESP (Edith Simpson Pike) as she was always called, was the grande dame of the family and treated with great deference by her two sons. To earn extra income, she worked for years at Peter's Oakland warehouse in a drafty office with a floor heater, keeping the books of Pike Services. She died in 1977 at age ninety-five. Her niece, Katherine Pike, echoed the thoughts of many: "Edith Simpson Pike [was] a heroine to me…because she accepted adversity as well as prosperity with courage, with élan, with dignity, with humor, and with grace."

Until her death, Edith was sharp as a tack, filling out the double-crostic puzzle in the *Saturday Review* each week. She lived with Roy Jr. in an apartment at 2702 Union Street in San Francisco, and they traveled extensively. Roy Jr., who never married, died in 1995.

CATHERINE'S FATHER, Alan Cline, died in 1955 after a life in retirement and endless games of Canasta with Dolly and their friends. When I stayed overnight in their apartment at 2164 Hyde Street on Russian Hill, I remember listening to the bells of cable cars. Unlike my parents, my grandparents never enforced a specified bedtime. Visiting our home in Ross, Alan would call out for my mother's attention in a loud voice, "Cats!"

Her mother, Dolly MacGavin, remained a social butterfly to the end. Nothing pleased her more than our family joining her for brunch at the Fairmont Hotel on a Sunday morning. I remember, maybe about age seven, that I hated to dress up in short pants for the occasion, but I do recall liking the Eggs Benedict. Dolly drove a powerful Chrysler New Yorker and must have been a danger on the road as she grew older. After she developed dementia, my parents donated her car to a civil rights group in the South. She died in 1968.

AFTER THE PASSING of my parents and grandparents, my wife, Dyan, and I became the older generation. Since then, two more generations have followed—our children and grandchildren. Decades hence, they will have the same questions that I had of my parents and grandparents. How did Dyan and I meet? What role did chance and calculation play in the decisions that we made? How did historical events alter our lives? I can hear their questions. It is time to start writing my answers.

ACKNOWLEDGMENTS

We are all outsiders to the past. Visiting the worlds of my ancestors has been like foreign travel. Some of the journey has been physical, much of it has been intellectual and emotional—like the exploration of new lands. For the past seven years, I have devoted many (my wife might say most) waking hours to this book.

I started by visiting the birthplaces of my great-grandparents and the towns and cities where they lived. I drove thousands of miles across the country and flew to cities in Europe, visiting dozens of libraries, archives, and historical societies to gather local information. Plotting my research itineraries with precision, I timed my visits to arrive during open hours at each facility, sometimes limited to one day a week.

Constrained by a tight schedule, I practiced "research triage." What information was vital to my story? What details would add color to it? And what miscellany would be nice—if I had the time? After listening to the reasons for my visit, librarians and archivists at local libraries and historical societies uniformly welcomed me and helped me navigate their collections. They are the unsung heroes of my project.

One of the most electrifying moments of my journey happened at the National Archives in College Park, Maryland, when I found an account of the 1849 mutiny aboard Jacob Pike's sailing ship, the *Nathaniel Hooper*. Buried in a large journal of the U.S. Consul at St. Catherine's, Brazil, were several pages of sworn testimony from the captain, crew, and passengers. Their testimony perfectly matched Jacob's description of the event in his memoir.

I experienced a different thrill on my visit to the historic Dalgarven Mill in Ayrshire, Scotland, when Robert Ferguson, whose family once owned the mill, opened the millrace and set the waterwheel in motion. Inside the three-story millhouse, the machinery sprang to life, spinning the grinding stone and creating a thunderous sound. This scene would have been familiar to young Walter

McGavin, who watched his father, the town miller, practice his trade at Green Mill in the 1850s and '60s.

At the Library of Congress in Washington, D.C., I requested bound volumes of *Galignani's Messenger*, the most popular English language newspaper of its day in Paris. As I carefully turned the brittle, yellowed pages, originally printed in 1893, tiny shards of paper unavoidably fell onto the table. Searching for a mention of Dr. MacGavin, Kate Hinshelwood's beloved guardian, my eyes scanned page after page of faded newsprint. Finally, "Eureka!" An article about his funeral service. "We mourn one today whose kindness and skill have brightened many a home and eased many a shoulder—one whose presence inspired confidence, and whose cheery words ever gave encouragement and hope."

Although the spiritual home of Asa Simpson's lumber and shipping empire was Coos Bay, Oregon, his business operations would today be located in the city of North Bend, which was founded by his son, Louis Jerome ("L.J.") Simpson, in 1908. Judith and Richard Wagner, authors of *The Uncommon Life of Louis Jerome Simpson*, kindly introduced me to the area and drove me around the site of Asa's sawmill, shipyard, and company town, now known as Simpson Heights.

Scanning a microfilmed newspaper at the St. Louis Public Library, I was stunned to learn that Frederick Cline had graduated from Yale College in 1874. This was a detail that had completely vanished from family lore. A century later, two of his great-great-granddaughters (our daughters, Caitlin and Sarah) graduated from Yale in 1997 and 2000.

En route from St. Louis to Russellville, Arkansas, I stopped in St. James, Missouri, where Edith Simpson Pike's great friend and traveling companion, Lucy James, was born. Johanna MacPherson and Lynn Wilson met me at the James Memorial Library, one of the many St. James civic works endowed by Lucy. A sketch of her by John Singer Sargent hangs over the main reading room. We visited Maramec Spring Park, originally the Maramec Iron Works owned by the James family; Trinity Episcopal Church, to view the stained glass window, which she donated; and the St. James Cemetery with its lovely urn containing her ashes.

At the Russellville Library in Arkansas, I found a local history of Mary Howell's family, "a well-known name in the annals of Pope County." Noticing Howell Road on the map, I drove down it, passing farmlands along the Arkansas River that must have been owned by one of her relatives. Later, I followed U.S. Highway 50 west through Kansas, roughly tracking the Arkansas River and the Cherokee Trail across the Great Plains, the route followed by ten-year-old Mary and her family in a covered wagon in 1852. Farther west in Nevada, I stopped several times to take pictures of trail ruts close to Interstate 80 where the California Trail paralleled the Humboldt River. Crossing the Sierra Nevada, I pulled off California State Route 88 to hike a steep section of the rock-strewn trail up Carson Canyon, the final hurdle that the Howell family faced at the end of their two-thousand-mile trek.

Back in California, I drove to Patterson in the Central Valley and met with Shane Donlon, who spent hours driving me around El Solyo Ranch, explaining how the farm was organized and how the irrigation system worked. The acreage of El Solyo is now owned by many individuals, including Shane, who grows almonds. Shane once served as a director of the El Solyo Water District, and he led me to original documents and maps in the district's archives.

Ron Swift at the Patterson Township Historical Society was enormously supportive of my research. As a past publisher of the *Patterson Irrigator*, he is steeped in the lore of El Solyo. In January 2013 Ron arranged a luncheon for me to meet older Patterson residents who remembered El Solyo, including ninety-eight-year-old Mae Belle Rogers.

Mae Belle was the widow of Eddie Rogers, a foreman at El Solyo and occasional chauffeur for Roy Pike. When she and Eddie drove Roy to San Francisco, she remembered that he would fall asleep in the back seat. After arriving in the city, Roy would give them theater tickets and money to spend around town. Mae Belle recalled Roy's great kindness after she suffered from appendicitis in 1937. He paid for her to go to the Good Hope Clinic in Los Angeles for an operation.

At my home computer, I spent countless hours researching the historical context of my ancestors. "History," Steven C. Levi has written, "is not a re-creation of the past. It's an assessment of the past based on documents provided by people in archives and museums who will answer your letters." By this wry standard, I was blessed with numerous email exchanges with librarians and archivists at the many institutions listed below:

In California, the Bancroft Library at the University of California, Berkeley; the Peter J. Shields Library at the University of California, Davis; the Seaver Center for Western History Research at the Los Angeles County Museum of Natural History; the McHenry Museum & Historical Society in Modesto; the Hamilton Field History Museum in Novato; and the Craemer Family Collections & Research Facility of the Marin History Museum in Novato.

The California Genealogy Society in Oakland; the Oakland History Room at the Oakland Public Library; the California History Room at the California State Library in Sacramento; the California Historical Society in San Francisco; the San Francisco Maritime National Historical Park Research Center; the San Francisco Museum and Historical Society; the San Francisco History Center at the San Francisco Public Library; the UCSF Archives and Special Collections at the University of California, San Francisco; Wells Fargo Historical Services at Wells Fargo Bank in San Francisco; the Anne T. Kent California Room at the Marin County Library, San Rafael; and the El Solyo Water District Archives in Vernalis.

In Arkansas, the David W. Mullins Library at the University of Arkansas in Fayetteville and the Katie Murdoch Genealogy Room at the Pope County Library in Russellville. In Connecticut, the Cowles Reference Center, Sterling Memorial Library, at Yale University. In Washington, D.C., the Law Library, the Newspaper Room, and the Special Collections Room at the Library of Congress.

In Maine, the Maine Maritime Museum in Bath; the Pejepscot Historical Society in Brunswick; the Bowdoin College Library in Brunswick; the Peavy Memorial Library in Eastport; the Harpswell Historical Society in South Harpswell; and the Maine Historical Society in Portland.

In Missouri, the James Memorial Public Library in St. James; the Missouri History Museum Library in St. Louis; the St. Louis County Library; and the St. Louis Genealogy Society. In Nevada, the California Trail Center, Bureau of Land Management, in Elko; and the National Automobile Museum, The Harrah Collection, in Reno.

In Oregon, the Columbia River Maritime Museum in Astoria; the Coos County Museum in Coos Bay; and the Oregon Historical Society in Portland. In Utah, the Church History Museum of the Church of Jesus Christ of Latter-day Saints and the Family History Library, both in Salt Lake City. In Washington, the Polson Museum in Hoquiam and the Washington State Library in Tumwater. In Wisconsin, the University of Wisconsin-Parkside Archives in Kenosha; the Wisconsin Historical Society Library in Madison; and the Racine Heritage Museum Research Center in Racine.

In Canada, the Klondike History Library & Archives in Dawson City, Yukon Territory. In the United Kingdom, the British Library's Newspaper Library at Colindale; and the Sibbald Library, Royal College of Physicians of Edinburgh, in Scotland.

Many relatives and friends played supporting roles in the creation of this book. Sometimes they found long-buried photographs and personal papers. Sometimes they clarified my memory of family lore. Sometimes they simply encouraged my writing when we met at family gatherings. Sadly, some passed on before the book was finished. I want to recognize Stephen Dow Beckham, John Dickey, Kate & Sanford Dickey, Susan & Dennis Fujita, Jeanie & Bill Graustein, Susie & Dirk ten Grotenhuis, Barbara McCarthy, Mark & Sara McCarthy, Martha Simpson McIntosh, Isabel Mullin, Alan Pike, Bruce Pike, Drummond Pike, Jody Pike, Ronald Rogers, Andy Simpson, Katie Simpson, Meade & Tessie Simpson, Michael & Sarah Simpson, Michael Simpson Jr., Ann Dickey Thompson, Jim & Sydney Wigle, Anne Waybur, Wendy & George Weiler, and Hep & Cyndi Wilkins.

My wife, Dyan, contacted a dozen of my mother's Miss Burke's School classmates after Catherine's sudden death in 1979. She wanted to pass on their memories to our two young daughters when they were older. Some she interviewed in person, others over the phone, and others by mail. Thirty-seven years later, her notes greatly helped me to paint a more complete picture of Catherine's childhood and education.

Sometimes Dyan joined me on my research forays—visiting old family addresses, walking through graveyards, and taking pictures. Gently applying her excellent editing skills to numerous written drafts, she made this a far better book than otherwise. I could not ask for a better traveling companion in life.

NOTES

Frequently cited works are listed in the Bibliography.

Chapter 1: Gold Rush Voyage

1 *Nathaniel Hooper*: Jacob Pike's handwritten memoir identified his ship as the *Nathan Hooper*, which was later incorrectly transcribed in his printed memoir as the *Nathan Hopper*. The correct full name was *Nathaniel Hooper*.

1 "The crew rose": Quotations of Jacob Pike in this chapter are from his memoir published as the *Memoirs of J. M. Pike and Percy Mortimer Pike*, unless otherwise noted.

1 300,000 feet of lumber: *Alta California*, Feb. 23, 1850, 3.

1 "The line between": Bunting, *Live Yankees*, 39. See also Elmo Paul Hohman, *History of American Merchant Seamen* (Hamden, CT: Shoe String Press, 1956), 25.

2 "came out of the forecastle": *U.S. Consular Records for Santa Catarina, Brazil, compiled 1834–1874 from Records of the Foreign Service Posts of the Department of State*. National Archives, Record Group 84, Entry UD 795, vols. 3 and 5. Testimony from passengers and crew of the *Nathaniel Hooper* was taken on or after Aug. 21, 1849.

3 Jacob Mabee Pike: In family lore, the spelling of Jacob's middle name has remained elusive. His gravesite in the Woodlawn Cemetery in Colma, CA, spells it "Maybe," but Jacob registered to vote in California on numerous occasions giving his middle name as "Mabee." (San Francisco County Voter Registers: 1869, 1872, 1876, 1880, 1882, 1886, 1888, 1890, 1892; Stanislaus County: 1896.)

3 middle child: Jacob Pike's four siblings were Samuel Tuttle (b. 1826, d. 1915), George K. (b. 1828, d. abt. 1875), William (b. 1834, d. unk.), and Helen Ann, also known as Celia (b. 1837, m. George H. Paine, abt. 1854, d. 1929).

3 Captain William Pike: Jacob incorrectly wrote in his memoir that he was seven and his father thirty-five when he died. Actually, he was five and his father thirty-three. Death notice in the *Columbian Centinel* (Boston): "Pike, William, Capt., of Eastport, lost overboard from fishing schr. *Swiftsure*, in Little River, Oct. 25th,

age 33 (C.C. Nov. 5, 1836)." Source: Ancestry.com: U.S., Newspaper Extractions from the Northeast, 1704–1930 / Massachusetts / *Columbian Centinel* / Death / Surname: Pabodie-Roane / page 409 of 924. Little River is a headland on Passamaquoddy Bay, near Eastport, ME.

3 "Mr. Pike": Bunting, *Live Yankees*, 37.

3 "We arrived off ": In his memoir Jacob said that a "southeast" gale forced the *Nathaniel Hooper* south. But he must have meant a southwest gale. The prevailing winds at Cape Horn are westerly, which is why rounding from east to west is so difficult.

4 February 4, 1850: Jacob Pike remembered a different date, Feb. 10, 1850. But the *Daily Alta California* reported that the *Nathaniel Hooper* arrived on Feb. 4, 1850, under Captain "Griffin, 235 days from New York, with 5 passengers." *Daily Alta California*, Feb. 5, 1850, 3. Although registered in New York, the ship sailed from Maine.

4 805 vessels: Delgado, *To California by Sea*, 78.

4 storeships: Ibid., 61.

4 steamer route: George H. Tinkham, *History of Stanislaus County, California with Biographical Sketches* (Los Angeles: Historic Record Co., 1921), 809.

4 "was the thoroughfare": Delgado, *Gold Rush Port*, 58. Today the Central Wharf would be located on Commercial Street, running east from Montgomery Street, which was the original shoreline of San Francisco Bay. The Embarcadero Center would cover the last four blocks.

4 The population: Delgado, *To California by Sea*, 53.

4 "Gambling here": Lewis, *Sea Routes to the Gold Fields*, 274.

5 Thousands of miners: Mildred Brook Hoover, et al., *Historic Spots in California*, 5th ed., rev. by Douglas E. Kyle (Stanford: Stanford University Press, 2002), 551.

5 "Here were real": Holliday, *Rush for Riches*, 119.

6 "Humbug!": Ibid., 171.

6 The rocker was: Ibid., 66.

7 "Beef, pork, beans": Johnson, *Roaring Camp*, 107.

7 "I have seen purer": Delgado, *Gold Rush Port*, 109.

7 "This country cannot": Johnson, *Roaring Camp*, 138.

9 The handmaiden: Catherine Coffin Phillips, *Coulterville Chronicle: The Annals of a Mother Lode Mining Town* (San Francisco: The Grabhorn Press, 1942), 129.

9 "We made a party": Handwritten manuscript by Jacob Pike, "Trip to Yosemite Valley in the Spring of 1857," written about 1912.

9 "Vernal Fall": Jacob identifies the waterfall as Nevada Fall, but it was certainly Vernal Fall, which lies below Nevada Fall.

10 "a pair of elongated": Hank Johnston, "Yosemite's Vernal Fall Ladders," *Sierra Heritage*, Apr. 2013.

10 The charge: James Mason Hutchings, *Scenes of Wonder and Curiosity in California* (San Francisco: J. M. Hutchings & Co., 1862), 114.

11 "Dreadful Affair": *San Joaquin Republican* (Stockton), Aug. 7, 1858, 2. Contradicting Jacob's account, the newspaper referred to the offending miners as "Frenchmen," not "Italians," and stated that the posse leader mortally wounded was "Mr. Chas. McKenny," not "George Warren."

12 new gold strike: Mace, *Between the Rivers*, 93.

12 New Diggings: Ibid., 93.

12 "Pike and his associates": Willard P. Fuller Jr., Judith Marvin, and Julia G. Costello, *Madam Felix's Gold: The Story of the Madam Felix Mining District, Calaveras County, California* (Calaveras County, CA: Calaveras County Historical Society and Foothill Resources, 1996), 18.

Chapter 2: By Covered Wagon from Arkansas

13 "One-half of it": Holmes, *Best of Covered Wagon Women*, 99.

13 four youngest children: We cannot be certain about the names and ages of the Howell children. The U.S. Censuses for 1850, 1860, and 1870, contain conflicting information on their names and birthdates. See also *Memoirs of J. M. Pike and Percy Mortimer Pike*, 36–37.

13 "We had candles": Royce, *A Frontier Lady*, 53.

14 "As we advanced": Holmes, *Best of Covered Wagon Women*, 101. See also Harold Curran, *Fearful Crossing : The Central Overland Trail through Nevada* (Las Vegas, NV: Nevada Publications, 1982), 181.

14 The Howell family: *History of Pope County, Arkansas* (Winston-Salem, NC: Pope County Historical Association and Hunter Publishing Co., 1979), 278.

14 the value of E.J.'s: Boyett, *Hardscrabble Frontier*, 139.

15 "became embroiled": *History of Pope County, Arkansas*, 278.

15 "whole of California": McArthur, *Arkansas in the Gold Rush*, 13.

15 "HO! FOR CALIFORNIA": Ibid., 19. See also Ruth B. Mapes, *Old Fort Smith: Cultural Center on the Southwestern Frontier* (Little Rock, AR: Pioneer Press, 1965), 21–27.

15 "We had our work": McArthur, *Arkansas in the Gold Rush*, 137.

15 "thousands would most": Ibid., 139.

16 "overwhelming characteristic": Ibid., 198.

16 "From what we can learn": Fletcher, *Cherokee Trail Diaries*, 15.

16 "the spring grass": Meldahl, *Hard Road West*, 13.

16 a company of families: Fletcher, *Cherokee Trail Diaries*, 29.

16 "sixty wagons": Ibid., 20, *Cherokee Advocate*, May 8, 1852.

18 "100 pounds": McArthur, *Arkansas in the Gold Rush*, 37.

18 Cherokee Trail: Broadly speaking, the trail ran northwest from Fort Smith, Arkansas, through Oklahoma (Sallisaw, Tulsa) and west through Kansas (Wichita, Dodge City), roughly tracking U.S. Route 50 across the Great Plains. After veering north, parallel to Interstate 25 through Colorado (Pueblo, Denver, Fort Collins), the trail turned west crossing the Rockies south of Interstate 80 to Fort Bridger, Wyoming. See Whiteley, *The Cherokee Trail*. See also Bieber, *Southern Trails to California in 1849*, 325–350. The best map of the Cherokee Trail is *Western Emigrant Trails, 1820–1870: Historic Trails, Cutoffs, and Alternates* (Western Emigrant Trails Research Center, 1999).

18 "Once women got over": Myres, *Westering Women and the Frontier Experience*, 105.

18 "The marching itself ": Brands, *The Age of Gold*, 144.

18 "Rise before dawn": Ibid., 144.

18 Twin Groves: Named after two groves of aspen trees. Whiteley, *The Cherokee Trail*, 9, 18, and 26. Twin Groves today is located 26 miles south of Rawlins, WY. See U.S.G.S. map #330434, *Divide Peak Historical Map, 1961*, Meridian: Wyoming (6th Principal Meridian), Township – Range: 016N – 087W, Section 15. http://nationalmap.gov/historical/

19 "seeing the elephant": McArthur, *Arkansas in the Gold Rush*, 47.

19 "I would make": Meldahl, *Hard Road West*, 16.

19 "I was never": *Journal History of the Church of Latter Day Saints*, Jul. 5, 1852.

19 "At this point": Royce, *A Frontier Lady*, 29.

20 California Trail: The iconic Oregon–California Trail followed the North Platte River across the Great Plains from Independence, Missouri, through modern Kansas, Nebraska, and Wyoming. After crossing the Continental Divide, the trail split—north along the Snake River in Idaho to Oregon and south to Nevada, the Humboldt River, and California.

20 "One can get": Meldahl, *Hard Road West*, 214.

20 "Livestock, desperately": Ibid., 215.

20 "Its water was": Ibid., 243.

20 "sheer-walled": Ibid., 259.

20 "the wildest hallooing": Ibid., 259.

20 "The route—thickly": Ibid., 262.

21 state's first census: Jackson, *Gold Dust*, 327.

21 160 acres: Two contiguous parcels: Meridian: Mount Diablo, CA; Township – Range: 001N – 013E [1 North – 13 East], Section 8: S1/2 SW1/4, and

Section 17: N1/2 NW1/4, Calaveras County, California. James Howell formally acquired title on July 30, 1873, Document #4918. Source: The Bureau of Land Management, General Land Office records, at https://glorecords.blm.gov/. He paid $200 ($1.25 per acre).

21 Central Ferry Road: The Central Ferry Road and the Central Ferry crossing appear on *Copperopolis, California, 1916*, U.S.G.S. map #301224 at http://nationalmap.gov/historical/. See also the "O'Byrnes and Central Ferry" web page at http://www.calaverashistory.org/post/obyrnes-and-central-ferry.

21 very steep hill: Jacob's horse had reason to balk. The Stanislaus River was at the bottom of a canyon, and the road rose abruptly 500 feet in the first half mile, a gradient of almost 20 percent.

23 "First come the": Barker, *More San Francisco Memoirs 1852–1899*, 107.

23 "The Oriental was": Neville, *The Fantastic City*, 72–73.

24 "Facing me was": Ibid., 38–39.

24 "A gambler in those days": Ibid., 41.

24 Thursday's show: *Daily Alta California*, Nov. 29, 1860, 6.

24 "His garb was": Robert Ernest Cowan, Anne Bancroft, and Addie L. Ballou, *The Forgotten Characters of Old San Francisco, including The Famous Bummer & Lazarus and Emperor Norton* (Laguna Beach, CA: Ward Ritchie Press, 1964), 45–46.

25 "Pony Express": In November 1860, cross-country news traveled fastest by Pony Express. Eastern dispatches were telegraphed to Fort Kearny, Nebraska Territory (near modern Kearney, NE), where they were put into pouches and carried by Pony Express riders fifteen hundred miles through the future states of Nebraska, Wyoming, Colorado, Utah, and Nevada to Fort Churchill, Utah Territory (thirty miles east of modern Carson City, NV), where they were telegraphed to San Francisco. The completion of the transcontinental telegraph on October 24, 1861, put the Pony Express out of business.

25 "A leading merchant": *Daily Alta California*, Nov. 26, 1860, 1.

Chapter 3: Boom and Bust

26 "Pike and Brothers": Mace, *Between the Rivers*, 76.

26 "It is astonishing": Ronald H. Limbaugh and Willard P. Fuller, *Calaveras Gold: The Impact of Mining on a Mother Lode County* (Reno, NV: University of Nevada Press, 2004), 77.

26 founding families: Stone, *The Tools Are on the Bar*, 11.

26 first postmaster: Jacob Pike was appointed postmaster of Copperopolis on December 19, 1861.

26   Wells Fargo agent: Chandler, *Wells Fargo*, 21–32, and Dinkelspiel, *Towers of Gold*, 231–232.

27   "By 1858, Wells": Fradkin, *Stagecoach*, 27.

27   "This community": Limbaugh, *Calaveras Gold*, 78.

27   Jackass Hill: Identified by two California Historical Landmarks (#124 and #138) near the intersection of Jackass Hill Road and State Route 49. If Clemens crossed the Stanislaus River on the Central Ferry and followed the Central Ferry Road, he would have walked past James Howell's farm.

27   "D—n Copperopolis": Frederick Anderson, Michael B. Frank, and Kenneth M. Sanderson, eds. *Mark Twain's Notebooks & Journals*, vol. 1, 1855–1873 (Berkeley: University of California Press, 1975), 82.

27   "Groceries and": *Copperopolis Courier*, Jun. 17, 1865, 3.

27   Grand Marshall: *Copperopolis Courier*, Jun. 14, 1865, 2.

27   "few could sleep": *Copperopolis Courier*, Jul. 8, 1865, 2.

28   all-time high: Mace, *Between the Rivers*, 78.

28   Jacob was bankrupt: *San Francisco Bulletin*, Mar. 13, 1868, 3.

28   California and Oregon: *Bancroft's Guide for Travelers by Railway, Stage, and Steam Navigation in the Pacific States* (San Francisco: H. H. Bancroft & Co., Jul. 1869), 84.

28   Concord stagecoach: Fradkin, *Stagecoach*, 44–46.

29   The average speed: Chico to Shasta, 74 miles, 14.5 hours, 5.1 miles per hour. Portland (heading south) to Jacksonville: 295 miles, 63 hours, 4.7 miles per hour. *Bancroft's Guide for Travelers*, 84. Regarding stagecoach drivers, see Oscar Osburn Winther, *The Great Northwest: A History*, 2nd ed. (Westport, CT: Greenwood Press, 1981), 199. For a passenger's perspective, see Frances Fuller Victor, "A Stage Ride in Oregon and California," *The American Publisher* (Hartford, CT) Aug. 1871, vol. 1, no. 5, 2, and no. 6, 3.

29   "When a driver": Fradkin, *Stagecoach*, 43.

29   "Various devices": Oscar Osburn Winther, *The Transportation Frontier: Trans-Mississippi West 1865–1890* (Albuquerque, NM: University of New Mexico Press, 1964), 66.

30   Weil & Co.: See advertisements in the *Daily Alta California*, Oct. 17, 1867, 4, and Aug. 21, 1868, 1.

30   "We take pleasure": "San Franciscans at Salt Lake," *Daily Alta California* Jul. 13, 1870, 1, reprinted from the *Salt Lake Herald* of Jul. 1, 1870.

31   Woodward Gardens: Berglund, *Making San Francisco American*, 70–80.

31   "It covered a sloping": Neville, *The Fantastic City*, 177.

31   Childhood mortality: Susan Craddock, *City of Plagues: Disease, Poverty, and Deviance in San Francisco* (Minneapolis: University of Minnesota Press, 2000), 66.

32   "rapid growth": Berglund, *Making San Francisco American*, 16.

32   adult white males: *San Francisco City Directory 1872*, 11.

32   "Clerks, bookkeepers": Lloyd, *Lights and Shades in San Francisco*, 63.

32   "sixty thousand dollars": Historic dollars were adjusted to current dollars at MeasuringWorth. https://www.measuringworth.com/uscompare/

32   "Perhaps the most popular": Lloyd, *Lights and Shades in San Francisco*, 64.

32   "A fine schooner": *Daily Alta California*, Dec. 3, 1875, 1. The *Laura Pike* was a 146-foot long, two-masted schooner. See the *Record of American and Foreign Shipping* (New York: American Shipmasters' Association, 1877), 622. After suffering financial losses in 1877, Jacob must have sold his interest, probably in 1878. See the *Daily Alta California*, Mar. 17, 1878, 2. The *Laura Pike* foundered crossing the Humboldt Bar with the loss of all hands later in 1878. See the *Daily Alta California*, Nov. 24, 1878, 1.

32   *Laura Pike*: After Jacob Pike's death in 1916, a misleading brass plaque was attached to the frame: "*Laura Pike*, A Belgian clipper ship named for Laura C. Pike, sister of P.[Percy] M. Pike, painted by W. A. Coulter in Brussels, 1877." Emphatically, the vessel was American, not Belgian, and a schooner, not a clipper ship. At the time, Coulter was studying marine painting in Europe and must have taken a sketch of the *Laura Pike* with him. He painted the vessel sailing off the California coast and probably sent the canvas back to Jacob in San Francisco.

33   We can plot: *Travelers' Official Guide of the Railway and Steam Navigation Lines in the United States and Canada, September 1874* (Philadelphia: National Railway Publication Co.). Railroad references are by the number symbol (#), not by page numbers; search for rail lines by #. From San Francisco to Omaha, Nebraska, on the Central Pacific #305 and Union Pacific #304 (1,029 miles, four nights); from Omaha to Kansas City, Missouri, on the Kansas City, St. Joseph and Council Bluffs Railroad #400 (204 miles, one night); from Kansas City to St. Louis on the St. Louis, Kansas City and Northern Railroad #317 (275 miles, one night); from St. Louis to Little Rock on the St. Louis, Iron Mountain and Southern Railroad #430 (345 miles, one night); and, finally, from Little Rock to Russellville on the Little Rock and Fort Smith Railroad #412 (74 miles). Total: 1,927 miles. The guide is online at http://books.google.com/.

33   In 1876 railroads: Stover, *American Railroads*, 143–146 and 153–155.

33   Russellville's population: Encyclopedia of Arkansas History and Culture, "Russellville, Pope County." http://www.encyclopediaofarkansas.net/encyclopedia/entry-detail.aspx?entryID=963

34   Reconstruction Era: Encyclopedia of Arkansas History and Culture, "Civil War through Reconstruction, 1861 through 1874." http://www.encyclopediaofarkansas.net/encyclopedia/entry-detail.aspx?entryid=388

34   tourist guide: *Tourists' Pictorial Guide for Washington, D.C., Containing Information for the Use of Strangers* (Issued by the Philadelphia, Wilmington & Baltimore Railroad, 1876), 2–7.

34 "Persons simply wishing": Robert Curtis Ogden, *Boston to Washington: A Complete Pocket Guide to the Great Eastern Cities and the Centennial Exhibition* (New York: Hurd and Houghton, 1876), 244.

34 International Steamship Co.: *Portland, Maine, City Directory 1875*, 340, and *Boston City Directory 1876*, 1176.

35 The population: John "Terry" Holt, *The Island City: A History of Eastport, Moose Island, Maine* (Lewiston, ME: Penmor Lithographers, 1999), 101.

35 "Catching and curing": George J. Varney, *Gazetteer of the State of Maine* (Boston: B. B. Russell, 1881), 211.

35 Jacob had reserved: Dorothy Gondos Beers, "The Centennial City, 1865–1876" in *Philadelphia: A 300-Year History*, Russell F. Weigley, ed. (New York: W. W. Norton, 1982), 467.

35 Centennial International: Robert W. Rydell, John E. Findling, and Kimberly D. Pelle, *Fair America: World's Fairs in the United States* (Washington, DC: Smithsonian Books, 2000), 18–25.

36 "A panic in mining": Cross, *Financing an Empire*, 370.

38 "power to dispose": *San Francisco Chronicle*, Jan. 20, 1888, 8.

38 "Father lost the home": Percy M. Pike, *Memoir*, 41–42.

Chapter 4: Lumberman and Shipbuilder

39 Telltale breakers: *Directory for the Pacific Coast of the United States* (Reported to the Superintendent of the U.S. Coast Survey by George Davidson, 1862), 84. https://catalog.hathitrust.org/Record/012104881

39 "this river is practicable": *Sailing Directions for The West Coast of North America: Embracing the Coasts of Central America, California, Oregon, Fuca Strait, Puget Sound, Vancouver Island, and the Other Islands and Rocks Off the Coasts of Central America and California* (London: James Imray, 1853), 124. https://catalog.hathitrust.org/Record/011536768

39 "I made port": Quotations of Asa Simpson in this chapter are from interviews conducted by researchers for Hubert Howe Bancroft's *Chronicles of the Builders of the Commonwealth* on Jan. 29, 1890, and Jul. 7, 1891. Biographical materials relating to A. M. Simpson, Bancroft Library, University of California, Berkeley, BANC MSS C-D 957.

39 Twenty-five years: Cox, "Lumber and Ships," 20. In 1876 Simpson Lumber cut 12.5 million board feet of lumber at two mills near Gardiner on the Umpqua River and shipped fifty-four cargoes, mostly to San Francisco.

40 "Professor Pike": Alfred Washington Pike. See George Thomas Chapman, *Sketches of the Alumni of Dartmouth College: From the First Graduation in 1771 to the Present Time, a Brief History of the Institution* (Cambridge, MA: Riverside Press, 1867), 178.

40 Pleasant Street Seminary: George Augustus Wheeler and Henry Warren Wheeler, *History of Brunswick, Topsham, and Harpswell, Maine, including the ancient territory known as Pejepscot* (Boston: Alfred Mudge & Son, Printers, 1878), 476 and 480.

41 *Birmingham*: The *Daily Alta California*, Sep. 1, 1850, 5, lists the *Birmingham* at 507 tons. This agrees with William Avery Baker, *A Maritime History of Bath, Maine, and the Kennebec River Region*, vol. 2 (Bath, ME: Marine Research Society of Bath, 1973), 826. Year Built: 1836; Tonnage: 507; Length: 129'10"; Beam: 29' 3 1/2"; Depth: 14' 7 3/4."

41 "400 thousand feet": *Eastern Argus* (Portland, ME), Nov. 6, 1849.

41 "We were all well": Asa M. Simpson to Eliza (Elizabeth A. Pennell) Simpson, the wife of his brother, Robert W. Simpson, Jun. 16, 1850. Harpswell Historical Society, South Harpswell, ME.

41 "It is with the greatest": Ibid.

42 *H. T. Clay*: *Portrait and Biographical Record of Western Oregon* (Chicago: Chapman Publishing Co., 1904), 231.

42 One fire alone: Delgado, *Gold Rush Port*, 79–81.

43 On a second trip: Beckham, "Asa Mead Simpson," 263.

43 "with painted and tattooed": *Portrait and Biographical Record of Western Oregon*, 231.

43 decimated by years: Nathan Douthit, *A Guide to Oregon South Coast History* (Corvallis: Oregon State University Press, 2009), 17.

43 "The object of building": Beckham, "Asa Mead Simpson," 263.

43 Tragically, the *Quadratus*: Wagner, *The Uncommon Life of Louis Jerome Simpson*, 1. Regarding dangers of crossing the Coos Bay Bar, see George Baxter Case, "The History of the Port of Coos Bay 1852–1952," (master's thesis, Pan American University, Edinburg, TX, Aug. 1983), 10, 11, and 19.

43 "Mr. McDonald": *Oregon Statesman* (Salem), May 13, 1856, 4.

44 "She was deeply": Wright, *Lewis & Dryden's Marine History*, 42.

44 Asa recovered: *Portrait and Biographical Record of Western Oregon*, 232.

44 "Very little power": Robert E. Johnson, "Schooners Out of Coos Bay" (master's thesis, University of Oregon, Jun. 1953), 26–27.

44 He even recruited: Edwin Van Syckle, *The River Pioneers: Early Days on Grays Harbor* (Aberdeen, WA: Pacific Search Press, 1982), 126.

45 "During the next forty-odd": Emil R. Peterson and Alfred Powers, *A Century of Coos and Curry: History of Southwest Oregon* (Portland, OR: Binfords & Mort, Publishers, 1952), 106.

45 *Fearless*: Wright, *Lewis & Dryden's Marine History*, 75. Specifications: "about 80-feet long, 24-feet beam, and 9-feet [deep]."

45 Numerous shipwrecks: Ibid., 176–177.

45 "The country is indebted": *The Oregonian* (Portland), Aug. 1, 1868, 3.

45   fleet of sixteen vessels: Cox, "Lumber and Ships," 20.

47   Slosson Brothers: Address: 501 Folsom. Mrs. Kelsey's address: 503 Folsom. *San Francisco City Directory 1869*, 350, 566.

47   "reposes in": Lloyd, *Lights and Shades in San Francisco*, 451.

47   "Living in a first-class": Barker, *More San Francisco Memoirs 1852–1899*, 234.

48   Second Annual: Sophie D. Smith, "Compositions & Etc.," 82.

48   "was a grand gala": Neville, *The Fantastic City*, 212.

48   "Perhaps in no other": Barker, *More San Francisco Memoirs 1852–1899*, 179.

48   "The fun was kept up": *Daily Alta California*, Feb.18, 1871, 1.

Chapter 5: An Educated Woman Heads West

50   The posse crept: Jackson, *Finding Freedom*, 40.

50   Glover's capture: Ibid., 43.

50   Summoned by: Ibid., 45.

50   three blocks away: The *Racine City Directory of 1850*, listed Eldad Smith at 93 Barnstable, which was later renamed Pearl Avenue and finally College Avenue in 1871. The Smith residence was at the northeast corner of College Avenue and Eighth Street.

50   Meanwhile in Milwaukee: Jackson, *Finding Freedom*, 44.

50   "One universal expression": Ibid., 48–49.

51   "Put back": Sophie D. Smith, "Compositions & Etc.," 68.

51   "sounding notes of woe": Ibid., 67. This passage is found on page 6 of her essay "Painting and Sculpting."

51   "jeweled frame of words": *Racine Advocate*, Jul. 6, 1864. A copy of this article was found in the archives of the Racine Heritage Museum.

51   Wisconsin Territory: Fanny S. Stone, ed., *Racine, Belle City of the Lakes, and Racine County, Wisconsin: A Record of Settlement, Organization, Progress and Achievement*, vol. 1 (Chicago: The S. J. Clarke Publishing Co., 1916), 109.

51   village of Racine: Eldad was appointed postmaster by President Zachary Taylor in 1849. At the time, postmaster jobs were awarded to party loyalists, which meant that Eldad was a Whig. Northern Whigs, like Abraham Lincoln, were abolitionists. Eldad served as postmaster for three years and thereafter was listed in the *Racine City Directory* as an insurance agent.

51   Sophie graduated: Even ten years later in 1870, only 2 percent of all seventeen-year-olds graduated from high school, 7,000 boys and 9,000 girls. *Historical Statistics of the United States, Colonial Times to 1970, Part 1* (Washington, DC: U.S. Bureau of the Census, 1975), 379. http://catalog.hathitrust.org/Record/000707742

51 "It is your country": Frank L. Klement, *Wisconsin and the Civil War* (Madison, WI: The State Historical Society of Wisconsin, 1963), 88.

51 "knitted mittens, scraped lint": Ibid., 89.

52 Camp Utley: Civil War military training post in Racine located along the lake shore south of Sixteenth Street.

52 "We marched along": Klement, *Wisconsin and the Civil War*, 89.

52 "We had cold turkey": Ibid., 90.

52 "This was Civil War": Edith Pike, "Early Years," 2.

52 "Nearly half the dead": Faust, *This Republic of Suffering*, 267.

52 "the unknown fate": Ibid., 170.

52 "I was anxious": Dictation of Sophie (Smith) Simpson on Jul. 24, 1891, 9. Biographical materials relating to A. M. Simpson, Bancroft Library, University of California, Berkeley, BANC MSS C-D 957.

53 Pacific Mail Steamship: F. N. Otis, *Isthmus of Panama: History of the Panama Railroad and of the Pacific Mail Steamship Company* (New York: Harper & Brothers, 1867), 161. See also *A Sketch of the New Route to China and Japan by the Pacific Mail Steamship Co.'s via the Isthmus of Panama and San Francisco* (San Francisco: Turnbull & Smith, Book and Job Printers, 1867).

53 the *New York*: John Haskell Kemble, *The Panama Route, 1848–1869* (Berkeley: University of California Press, 1943), 236, and Robert J. Chandler and Stephen J. Potash, *Gold, Silk, Pioneers & Mail: The Story of the Pacific Mail Steamship Company* (Palo Alto, CA: Glencannon Press, 2007), 7.

53 "male and female": Kemble, *The Panama Route, 1848–1869*, 149.

53 "It prostrates": Caughey, *Hubert Howe Bancroft*, 20.

53 Arriving at Panama: Otis, *Isthmus of Panama*, 161.

53 "Never shall I forget": William Frederic Badé, *The Life and Letters of John Muir* (Boston: Houghton Mifflin Co., 1924), reprinted in *John Muir: His Life and Letters and Other Writings* with an introduction by Terry Gifford (Seattle: The Mountaineers, 1996), 95.

53 "Seen as I saw": Barker, *More San Francisco Memoirs 1852–1899*, 191.

54 "I have a little": Sophie D. Smith, "Compositions & Etc.," 71.

54 Major Dallas: Major Alexander James Dallas served at Fort Vancouver during the Civil War. I am indebted to historian Stephen Beckham for this information.

54 *Cascade*: Wright, *Lewis & Dryden's Marine History*, 123.

54 sixty-five-mile: *Bancroft's Guide for Travelers by Railway, Stage, and Steam Navigation in the Pacific States*, 22.

55 "Millbrae": E. S. Carr, "The Rural Homes of California," *The California Horticulturist and Floral Magazine*, vol. 3, no. 3 (Mar. 1873), 69–72.

56 "You yourselves": Sophie D. Smith, "Compositions & Etc.," 65.

56 "The method of instruction": Catalogue of the Académie Parisienne 1873, 17. Antonio F. Coronel Papers, List dated 1/2/2013, Item 715, the Seaver Center for Western History Research, Los Angeles County Museum of Natural History.

56 "The church was": *Racine Weekly Journal*, Jun. 30, 1875.

58 "The whole street": Barker, *More San Francisco Memoirs 1852–1899*, 199. "At the peak of San Francisco's gaudiest period in 1890, that city accommodated more than 3,000 licensed saloons (one for every 96 inhabitants) and perhaps as many as 2,000 *un*licensed drinking places." Source: Kenneth D. Rose, *American Women and the Repeal of Prohibition* (New York: New York University Press, 1996), 17.

58 "As places for family": Lloyd, *Lights and Shades in San Francisco*, 391.

58 "A large square": The Simpson family occupied the northern half of the city block bounded by Grove, Sixteenth, Castro, and Fifteenth Streets.

58 Kellogg house: Charles W. Kellogg, NW corner Fifteenth and Grove Streets. *Oakland City Directory 1876*, 239.

59 "My Dear Wife": Sophie D. Smith, "Compositions & Etc.," 84.

59 "My Dear Wife—Sunday": Ibid., 86.

60 Miss Dyer's: *Oakland Tribune*, Jul. 10, 1883, 3.

60 Miss Horton's: *Oakland City Directory 1888*, 31, and *Oakland Tribune*, Jul. 25, 1888, 7.

61 train to Cloverdale: *Bancroft's Official Railway Guide Of The San Francisco And North Pacific Railway Company, San Francisco To Ukiah, California*, vol. 2, no. 5 (May 1890), 14.

62 "attended strictly to": Dictation of George R. Sanderson, Jul. 31, 1891, 1. Biographical materials relating to A. M. Simpson, Bancroft Library, University of California, Berkeley, BANC MSS C-D 957.

62 "twenty days for crossings": Jeffrey Steinbrink, "Why the Innocents Went Abroad: Mark Twain and American Tourism in the Late Nineteenth Century," *American Literary Realism*, vol. 16, no. 2 (Autumn, 1983), 284.

62 Emergency Passport: Source: Ancestry.com: U.S. Passport Applications, 1795-1925 / Emergency Passport Applications (Issued Abroad), 1877-1907 / 1886-1890 Volume 003 / Italy to West Indies / page 37 of 602.

62 Between 1880 and 1890: Google search for Excel file: "Historical Census Populations of Counties and Incorporated Cities in California"

63 "build a house": See picture in "Adams Point Property, Oakland, Cal.," Lake Shore Land Co. (San Francisco: Press of H. S. Crocker Co., 1897?), 26, Oakland Public Library. Caption: "1893: House built by Asa Simpson at the corner of Vernon and Perkins in Oakland. The photograph was taken sometime after 1895, when the residence was owned by Charles M. Cooke of Honolulu. To the right is the mansion of ex-Governor Perkins."

63 "Mrs. A. M. Simpson": *Oakland Tribune*, Nov. 25, 1895, 5.

Chapter 6: Building an Empire

64   "The spirit": Bancroft, *Chronicles of the Builders of the Commonwealth*, vol. 4, 448. Although Bancroft spelled Asa's middle name, "Mead," without an "e" at the end, his family always spelled his middle name, "Meade." Asa registered to vote multiple times in Oakland and San Francisco variously spelling his middle name with and without the additional "e."

64   "stood in the lead": Ibid., 437.

64   "In the midst of reverses": Ibid., 439.

64   "From the pattern": Caughey, *Hubert Howe Bancroft*, 314.

64   Asa paid $1,500: Harry B. Hambly, "List of Subscribers to Chronicles of the Builders of the Commonwealth, Stating Amount Subscribed and Paid," 3, Bancroft Library, University of California, Berkeley, BANC MSS C-D 957.

64   twenty-one-page chapter: Bancroft, *Chronicles of the Builders of the Commonwealth*, vol. 4, 428–449.

66   only clipper ship: Cox, "Lumber and Ships," 20.

66   "No sailing vessel": Wright, *Lewis & Dryden's Marine History*, 219. The cover painting of the *Western Shore* by John Alcott is in the Columbia River Maritime Museum, Astoria, OR. Its plaque reads: "'The Full-Rigged *Western Shore*.' The only full-rigged ship ever built in Oregon, and one of only three ever built on the West Coast, the *Western Shore* is shown here running before a gale, with all hands furling canvas on the fore upper topsail yard. She was built for Simpson Lumber in 1874 by J. Kruse in North Bend, Oregon." For the position of a furled upper topsail yard, see Harold A. Underhill, *Sailing Ship Rigs and Rigging* (Glasgow: Brown, Son & Ferguson, Ltd.), 84-85. I am indebted to Steve Priske for the measurements of the *Western Shore*.

66   562 miles: *Ocean Passages for the World*, 2nd ed. (London: British Admiralty, 1950), 168.

66   "The disaster": *San Francisco Chronicle*, Jul. 11, 1878, 3.

67   "Year by year": Cox, "Lumber and Ships," 17.

67   "More than a quest": Ibid., 20.

67   "even his sons": Beckham, *The Simpsons of Shore Acres*, 18.

67   "A. M. Simpson, a very": Robert E. Johnson, "Schooners Out of Coos Bay" (master's thesis, University of Oregon, Jun. 1953), 6.

68   "Stovepipe" Simpson: Jack McNairn and Jerry MacMullen, *Ships of the Redwood Coast* (Stanford: Stanford University Press, 1945), 57.

68   a character inspired: At a lunch in 1957, Peter B. Kyne told Michael Simpson, the grandson of Asa, and his new wife, Sarah (Hayne) Simpson, that the Cappy Ricks character was inspired by Asa Simpson. Note: Cappy Ricks was also modeled on the career of Captain Robert Dollar, a San Francisco lumber and

shipping baron. See the *Sunday Oregonian*, Jun. 6, 1947, Section Three, "Cappy Ricks Was a Webfoot," by Arthur W. Priaulx: "Cappy Ricks was really two men. Those who knew Robert Dollar intimately saw much of this shipmaster in Kyne's hero. And they were right, for at times Ricks was Dollar. Mostly though, Kyne built his character around fabulous Captain Asa M. Simpson and his exploits as early Oregon's big-time sawmill operator and ship owner."

68   "[Kyne] saw Captain": Ellis Lucia, *Head Rig: The Story of the West Coast Lumber Industry* (Portland, OR : Overland West Press, 1965), 133.

68   "A psychologist would": Peter B. Kyne, *Cappy Ricks, or The Subjugation of Matt Peasley* (New York: Grosset & Dunlap, 1916), 9.

69   Ralph E. Peasley: Born in Jonesport, Maine, May 30, 1866; died in Aberdeen, Washington, Dec. 15, 1948, at age 82. Peter B. Kyne dedicated *Cappy Ricks, or The Subjugation of Matt Peasley* to Captain Ralph E. Peasley among others, noting that he "skippered the first five-masted schooner ever built, brought her, on that first voyage, through the worst typhoon that ever blew..." See also Peasley's name in Edgar Simpson's, "Captain's Log, 1903–1907," 113, and Lucia, *Head Rig*, 133.

69   "a rangy Yankee": John C. Hughes and Ryan Teague Beckwith, eds., *On the Harbor: From Black Friday to Nirvana* (Aberdeen, WA: *Daily World*, 2001), 63.

69   Captain Rudolph Smale: Born Aug. 1, 1865, Koenigsberg, Prussia; died Apr. 27, 1956, Berkeley, California.

69   "I succeeded": Smale, *There Go the Ships*, 242–243.

69   "The vessel, now lying": Ibid., 264–266.

70   "Sailing ships": Ibid., 243–244.

70   Their dispute: Cox, "Lumber and Ships," 24.

70   "the day of sawing": Ibid., 25.

70   "throwing a large": Emerson to Asa Simpson, Hoquiam, Apr. 21, 1897. University of Washington Library, Special Collections, North Western Lumber Co., Accession Number: 4287-002, Reels: 6–8.

70   "I consider that": Emerson to Asa Simpson, Hoquiam, Feb. 20, 1899.

71   "Dear Sir": Emerson to Asa Simpson, Hoquiam, May 2, 1899.

71   "Captain Simpson's well": Nathan Douthit, *The Coos Bay Region 1890–1944: Life on a Coastal Frontier*, 2nd ed., rev. (Coos Bay, OR: Coos Bay Historical Society, 2005), 36.

72   "The ladies of the Free": *Oakland Tribune*, Dec. 1, 1888, 7.

72   Mary Simpson Sperry: Born Jun. 3, 1833, in Brunswick, Maine; married Nov. 6, 1862, Stockton; died. Apr. 12, 1921, in San Francisco, age 87.

72   After her husband's: Bancroft, *Chronicles of the Builders of the Commonwealth*, vol. 4, 491.

73   "a fine businesswoman": Dictation of Asa Mead Simpson, Sep. 10, 1891, 3. Biographical materials for Austin Sperry, Bancroft Library, University of California, Berkeley, BANC MSS C-D 315.

73   Mary was the prime: Ida Husted Harper, ed., *The History of Woman Suffrage*, vol. 6, 1900–1920 (New York: National American Woman Suffrage Association, 1922), 52. See also regarding the Susan B. Anthony Club, *San Francisco Chronicle*, Dec. 22, 1912, 26.

73   "My dear Mrs. Hearst": Mary (Simpson) Sperry to Phoebe Hearst, Sep. 30, 1911. Phoebe Hearst Papers, Bancroft Library, BANC MSS 72/204 Box 47.

73   "Prominent society woman": *San Francisco Call*, Mar. 29, 1912, 1.

Chapter 7: St. Louis Roots

74   column of Union: Third Regiment of the U.S. Reserve Corps. See map in Winter, *The Civil War in St. Louis*, 41.

74   Thousands of German: Goodheart, *1861*, 239.

74   "They were Germans": Winter, *The Civil War in St. Louis*, 42.

74   United States Arsenal: Today Lyon Park, at the corner of South Broadway and Utah Street, occupies part of the grounds of the old Arsenal.

74   Camp Jackson: Roughly bounded today by North Grand Boulevard, Lindell Boulevard, Olive Street, North Compton Avenue, and Laclede Avenue.

74   "Could anything equal": Francis Grierson, *The Valley of Shadows* (London: John Lane, 1913), 227. http://catalog.hathitrust.org/Record/006539568

75   Eight thousand Union: Winter, *The Civil War in St. Louis*, 34–55.

75   no one ever knew: Gerteis, *Civil War St. Louis*, 107–109.

75   "The fighting in St. Louis": Bruce Catton, *The Coming Fury* (London: Phoenix Press, 1961; paperback edition, 2001), 381.

75   his great-grandfather: *The History of Warren County, Ohio: Containing a History of the County; its Townships, Towns, Schools, Churches, etc.* (Chicago: W. H. Beers & Co., 1882, Reprinted Mt. Vernon, IN: Windmill Publications, 1992), 971. https://catalog.hathitrust.org/Record/006793250

75   "exactly what they": Goodheart, *1861*, 237.

75   "One need only walk": Ibid., 237.

75   "Monday, Tuesday": J. Joseph Mersman, *The Whiskey Merchant's Diary: An Urban Life in the Emerging Midwest* (Athens, Ohio: Ohio University Press, 2007), 217.

76   "distilled it a second": Ibid., 2–3.

76   family moved to: Early *St. Louis City Directories* list the following addresses for George W. Cline: south side Chestnut, between Third and Fourth (1853); east side 6th, north of Morgan (1854); 33 south 15th (1857); 46 south 14th (1860);

15th near Clark Ave. (1864); 46 South 15th between Walnut and Clark Ave. (1865); and 46 South 15th (1866).

76 "a city in motion": Primm, *Lion of the Valley*, 154.

76 average of 2,675: Louis C. Hunter, *Steamboats on the Western Rivers: An Economic and Technological History* (Cambridge, MA: Cambridge, 1949), 661.

76 "mile of steamboats": Primm, *Lion of the Valley*, 165.

77 "steamboats brought": Ibid., 169–170.

77 Although slavery: Ibid., 186.

77 father witnessed: William C. Jamison and Geo. W. Cline. http://cdm.sos.mo.gov/cdm/ref/collection/CivilWar/id/9302

77 Deed of Manumission: "Deed of Manumission signed by Walker D. Shumate, agent of the Missouri State Colonization Society and of St. Louis County, Missouri, April 29, 1856," Missouri History Museum, Collection Number: A1518.

77 South Fifth Street: Early *St. Louis City Directories* list the following addresses for Robert Holmes: southeast Walnut & 5th (1857), 5th and Elm (1858), 32 south 5th (1859), 30 south 5th (1860), 32 south 5th (1864 and 1865). Robert Holmes first appeared in the *St. Louis City Directory* in 1842, 65. His name was incorrectly spelled Holms; the spelling was corrected in the *St. Louis City Directory* 1845, 84.

77 "prominent citizen": *St. Louis Globe-Democrat*, Aug. 18, 1904, 5.

77 Holmes's residence: Deborah H. Isaacs, "Ante-Bellum Days in St. Louis," *Glimpses of the Past*, vol. 5, nos. 10–12 (Oct–Dec, 1938), 144.

77 "angry secessionists": Winter, *The Civil War in St. Louis*, 63–64.

78 Second Presbyterian: *St. Louis Globe-Democrat*, Aug. 18, 1904, 5.

78 contributed $100: James Peckham, *Gen. Nathaniel Lyon, and Missouri in 1861: A Monograph of the Great Rebellion* (New York: American News Co., 1866), 38.

78 "Almost a thousand": Lucy M. Schwienher, "Public Schools in Civil War Days," *Bulletin of the Missouri Historical Society*, vol. 13, no. 1 (Oct. 1956), 17.

78 "When hostilities": Paul C. Nagel, *Missouri: A Bicentennial History* (New York: W. W. Norton & Co., 1977), 129.

78 "Missouri would": Goodheart, *1861*, 265.

78 "During the Civil": *St. Louis Globe-Democrat*, Aug. 18, 1904, 5.

78 "Unionist refugees": Primm, *Lion of the Valley*, 260–261.

79 "Soldiers' families": L. P. Brockett and Mary C. Vaughan, *Woman's Work in the Civil War: A Record of Heroism, Patriotism and Patience* (Philadelphia: Zeigler, McCurdy & Co., 1867), 638.

79 Belle Holmes married: *Daily Missouri Republican*, Feb. 1, 1865, 2.

79 Civil War hero: Jeffery A. Hogge, *Norton Parker Chipman: A Biography of the*

Andersonville War Crimes Prosecutor (Jefferson, NC: McFarland & Co., 2008), 38, 40.

79   stood on the platform: Ibid., 79. After the Civil War, Chipman was the lead prosecutor at the Andersonville war crimes trial. William Shatner played Col. Chipman in *The Andersonville Trial*, a 1970 TV movie.

79   started public school: William Hyde and Howard L. Conard, eds., *Encyclopedia of the History of St. Louis, a Compendium of History and Biography for Ready Reference*, vol. 4 (New York: The Southern History Co., 1899), 2016.

79   school board: Howard L. Conard, ed., *Encyclopedia of the History of Missouri: A Compendium of History and Biography for Ready Reference*, vol. 5 (New York: The Southern History Co., 1901), 524.

79   "bright scholars": Hyde, *Encyclopedia of the History of St. Louis*, 2017.

79   Smith Academy: *Biographical Record with Report of the Triennial Meeting of the Class of 1874 in Yale College* (New Haven: Tuttle, Morehouse & Taylor, Printers, 1879), 59. "Frederick Addison Cline was prepared for college at the Preparatory Department of Washington University." See also Ralph E. Morrow, *Washington University in St. Louis: A History* (St. Louis: Missouri Historical Society Press, 1996), 38, 92.

79   "This system has": Morrow, *Washington University in St. Louis: A History*, 100.

80   "Here the daily routine": Ibid., 108.

80   "It was a protracted": Ibid., 105.

Chapter 8: Eastern Schools and Western Lives

81   At nine in the morning: Frederick Cline, Obituary File, Manuscripts and Archives, Cowles Reference Center, Sterling Memorial Library, Yale University.

81   "an examiner approaches": Bagg, *Four Years at Yale*, 543.

82   William Chauvenet: Morrow, *Washington University in St. Louis: A History*, 48, 103.

82   September 1871: Yale Calendar 1871–2, *Yale Banner 1871* (New Haven: Hoggson & Robinson, Printers, 1871), inside cover.

82   "They jump": Bagg, *Four Years at Yale*, 62.

82   Kappa Sigma Epsilon: Frederick joined three societies at Yale: Kappa Sigma Epsilon (freshman), Phi Theta Psi (sophomore), and Delta Kappa Epsilon (junior). Note: His societies were not the same as senior societies at Yale today. Source: Frederick Addison Cline Obituary File, Manuscripts and Archives, Yale University. See also Bagg, *Four Years at Yale*, 53, 90, and 107.

82   90 York Street: The Old Campus was bounded by Chapel, College, Elm and High Streets. See map in Reuben A. Holden, *Yale: A Pictorial History* (New Haven: Yale University Press, 1967), between illustrations 48 and 49. Frederick

moved onto Old Campus his last two years: 9 South (3d Floor, S. Middle Entry) and 8 South (2nd Floor, South Entry). Source: *Yale Banner 1871, 1872, 1873*.

82   He probably paid: Bagg, *Four Years at Yale*, 238.

82   "The steward": Ibid., 238–239.

83   Yale's school day: Ibid., 551.

83   All students attended: Ibid., 571.

83   new sophomores: William Henderson, "A Retrospect," *Biographical Record of the Class of 1874 in Yale College, Part Sixth, 1919–1924*, ix–xiv. Manuscripts and Archives, Yale College.

83   total enrollment: *Yale Banner 1871*: freshman 131, sophomores 137, juniors 135, seniors 129.

83   "The reciter is": Bagg, *Four Years at Yale*, 552.

83   "It was before the days": Wood, *College Days*, 31.

83   "Isocrates": Bagg, *Four Years at Yale*, 560.

83   "The regular time": Ibid., 251.

83   "A red devil": Ibid., 64.

84   "barbaric era": Wood, *College Days*, v.

84   "Hazing, the terror": *Statistics of the Class of Seventy-four in Yale College* (New Haven: Printed by Tuttle, Morehouse & Taylor, 1874), 3–4.

84   "The heads of ": Wood, *College Days*, 75–76.

84   "An entire class": Bagg, *Four Years at Yale*, 557.

85   Class Odist: *Statistics of the Class of Seventy-four in Yale College*, 31.

85   "Once more we meet": Program: Class Day, '74, Exercises in the College Chapel, at 11 A. M., Tuesday, June 23, 1874. https://repository.library.brown.edu/studio/item/bdr:293879/

85   123 graduates: *Statistics of the Class of Seventy-four in Yale College*, 5. Later updated to 124 graduates: Henderson, "A Retrospect," ix.

85   "Women's seminaries": Louise L. Stevenson, *Miss Porter's School: A History in Documents, 1847–1948*, vol. 1 (New York: Garland Publishing, 1987), v, viii.

85   "exclusively emphasized": Ibid., iv.

85   Chemistry, Composition: Ibid., 24.

86   Practicing domestic: Ibid., vi.

86   "Bed clothes laid": Ibid., 30.

86   "During May, the early": Ibid., 17–18.

86   "During the last year": Ibid., 19–20.

87   "I don't wonder": Ibid., 173.

87   "They behaved just": Ibid., 164.

87   "Avoid slang expressions": Ibid., 33–36.

87   40 percent: *Statistics of the Class of Seventy-four in Yale College*, 13.

87   St. Louis Law School: Not to be confused with the modern Saint Louis University School of Law.

87   "LL.B. curriculum": Morrow, *Washington University in St. Louis: A History*, 54.

88   Frederick graduated: *Catalogue of Graduates of Washington University Law School* (St. Louis: Washington University, 1911), 3.

88   "the prize for best": *Biographical Record with Report of the Triennial Meeting of the Class of 1874 in Yale College*, 59.

88   was admitted: *St. Louis Daily Globe Democrat*, Mar. 10, 1876, 7.

88   Cline, Jamison & Day: *St. Louis City Directory 1877*, 210.

88   Frederick married: *St. Louis Daily Globe Democrat*, Feb. 5, 1880, 5.

88   2712 Chestnut: *St. Louis City Directory 1880*, 242.

88   "Frederick A.": *St. Louis Post-Dispatch*, Sep. 4, 1880, 4.

89   Alan Purnell: Alan P. Cline was born at 3039 Locust.

90   Muench & Cline: *St. Louis City Directory 1887*, 131.

90   "NEW JUDGES": *St. Louis Post-Dispatch*, Nov. 11, 1894, 18.

90   A woman contested: *St. Louis Post-Dispatch*, May 5, 1896, 7.

90   A church declined: *St. Louis Post-Dispatch*, Mar. 11, 1895, 7.

90   Judge Cline seated: *St. Louis Republic*, Sep. 29, 1897, 9.

91   "The judiciary, both": *St. Louis Post-Dispatch*, Nov. 11, 1902, 1.

91   "illegal registration": *St. Louis Post-Dispatch*, Dec. 12, 1902, 1.

91   "ballots in the boxes": *St. Louis Post-Dispatch*, Jun 17, 1903, 4.

Chapter 9: City Lights and Country Life

93   The first Prussian: Horne, *The Fall of Paris*, 212.

93   "psychological moment": Kranzberg, *The Siege of Paris*, 133.

93   The daily bombardment: Horne, *The Fall of Paris*, 213.

93   four thousand British: Ibid., 169.

93   Flour and corn: Howard, *The Franco-Prussian War*, 320.

93   "Fresh meat": Hill, *Elihu Washburne*, 83.

94   Fresh vegetables: Howard, *The Franco-Prussian War*, 327.

94   Compounding the city's: Kranzberg, *The Siege of Paris*, 122–123.

94   Neuilly-sur-Seine: David H. Pinkney, *Napoleon III and the Rebuilding of Paris* (Princeton: Princeton University Press, 1958), 168.

94   Most visibly: Horne, *The Fall of Paris*, 23.

94   "the great boulevards": McCullough, *The Greater Journey*, 208.

95   A vast elliptical: Horne, *The Fall of Paris*, 4.

95   "The displays of novel": McCullough, *The Greater Journey*, 248.

95   fifteen million: Horne, *The Fall of Paris*, 13.

95   At age fifteen: Addison, W. Innes, *The Matriculation Albums of the University of*

Glasgow from 1728 to 1858 (Glasgow: James Maclehose and Sons, 1913), 413. http://www.archive.org/details/matriculationalb00univuoft

96   M.D. in 1844: W. Innes Addison, *A Roll of the Graduates of the University of Glasgow from 31st December 1727 to 31st December 1897* (Glasgow: James Maclehose and Sons, 1898), 370. https://archive.org/details/rollofgraduateso00addiuoft

96   Glasgow Lunatic: Ormond, *John Singer Sargent*, 124.

96   Montrose Lunatic: "Report of the Directors of the Montrose Lunatic Asylum, Infirmary and Dispensary (instituted 1782) for the Year Ending 1st June, 1849" (Printed by David Hodge, 1849). Wellcome Library, London, U.K.

96   Royal College of Physicians: *Historical Sketch and Laws of the Royal College of Physicians of Edinburgh from Its Institution to December 1865* (Edinburgh: Printed for the Royal College of Physicians, 1867), 12. http://www.archive.org/details/historicalsketch00roya

96   "He is highly": Dr. Ramsay to the Royal College of Physicians of Edinburgh in 1859. Sibbald Library, Royal College of Physicians of Edinburgh.

96   10 Rue des Saussaies: Dr. MacGavin's medical practice was listed in K. Baedeker, *Paris and Its Environs: Handbook for Travellers* (Leipsic: Karl Baedeker, 1874), 40. Kate's mother, Margaret Mary Coker, died at this address in 1876.

96   Legion of Honor: See Dr. MacGavin's death record: Paris Archives: État Civil; Registres d'actes d'état civil (1860–1902); Type: Acte de décès; Arrondisement: 8e; Date: 19/04/1893 / Page 11 of 31. Accessed at http://archives.paris.fr/. Also see obituary for Dr. MacGavin, *British Medical Journal*, 1893; 1: 864 (Apr. 22, 1893). The Legion of Honor building was burned by The Commune on April 24, 1871. All of its records were destroyed; consequently there is no modern acknowledgment of Dr. MacGavin's medal, which remains in the family.

96   "Every single tree": Horne, *The Fall of Paris*, 320. See also Roger Wahl, *Essai d'une Histoire Illustrée de Neuilly-sur-Seine "la Perle de la Banlieue"* (Neuilly-sur-Seine: Chez L'Auteur, 1935), 89.

96   tens of thousands dead: "Reliable French historians today seem more or less agreed on a figure of between 20,000 and 25,000 [dead]." Horne, *The Fall of Paris*, 418.

96   "The reign of The Commune": Hill, *Elihu Washburne*, 204.

97   "The parish is partly": *The New Statistical Account of Scotland 1834–45*, vol. 5 (Edinburgh: William Blackwood & Sons, 1845), Old Cumnock, Ayrshire, 475–478. http://www.nls.uk/family-history/local-history

97   "Little are the inhabitants": Robert Wilson, *Guide to the South-Western Railway and Surrounding Neighbourhood in Ayr and Dumfriesshires* (Glasgow: Thomas Murray & Son, 1852, reprinted by Grimsay Press, 2010), 23.

97   "The scenery down": Ibid., 18.

97   By 1861, the year: John Strawhorn, *The New History of Cumnock* (Cumnock,

Ayrshire: The Town Council of Cumnock, 1966), 223.

97   The bustling town: Ibid., 71–72. John McGavin was listed as John M'Gaan, baker, in *The Ayrshire Directory 1851–52*.

98   Gas lighting: John Warrick, *The History of Old Cumnock* (London: Alexander Gardner, 1899), 349.

98   Walter McGavin first: Note: McGavin was misspelled McGarrie.

98   On this day, students: Warrick, *The History of Old Cumnock*, 270.

98   Cumnock celebrated: Strawhorn, *The New History of Cumnock*, 72–73.

98   the town miller: *The Ayrshire Directory 1851–52* (Ayrshire: Ayr Advertiser Office, 1851), 139. The directory listed Walter's grandfather, William M'Gavin, Senior, as "farmer and miller," and his father, William M'Gavin, Junior, as "miller." The *1851 Scotland Census* listed the age of William Sr. as 75, and William Jr. as 39.

98   "The central importance": Enid Gauldie, *The Scottish Country Miller 1700–1900: A History of Water-powered Meal Milling in Scotland* (Edinburgh: John Donald Publishers, 1981), 1.

98   Above all, farmers: Ibid. See chapter 13: "The 19th Century Miller," 219–233.

98   Green Mill: James Pearson Wilson, *The Last Miller: The Cornmills of Ayrshire* (Darvel, Ayrshire: Ayrshire Archeological and Natural History Society, 2000), 25–26. Evidence of the mill was still visible in 1944: "The old lade, although filled in, could still be traced from the intake to the mill in a straight line, the tailrace continuing in the same straight line to rejoin the Lugar and cutting through a loop of the river of a good many acres in extent. The mill stood on a level field and a full view of the buildings could be observed. The buildings were unusually extensive for a country mill."

99   1857 Ordnance Survey: Survey date: 1857; Publication date: 1860; *Ayr Sheet XXXV.11 (Old Cumnock)*. http://maps.nls.uk/view/74937707

99   "I am here, returning": Warrick, *The History of Old Cumnock*, 231–232.

100 "Ambition begat discontent": Bolitho, *James Lyle Mackay*, 13.

100 Smith, Fleming: Munro, *Maritime Enterprise and Empire*, 255. Although we cannot be certain of Walter's employment at Smith, Fleming & Co., the arc of Walter's business life strongly corresponds to the trajectory of this firm in London and W. Nicol & Company in India. Both companies were at least partially owned by John Fleming, a Scotsman from Glasgow.

100 17 Leadenhall Street: The full letterhead address was 17 & 18 Leadenhall St., London, E.C. [Eastern Central]. Letter from Smith, Fleming & Co. to James Taylor, Esq., Secretary to the Chamber of Commerce, Bombay, dated Feb. 28, 1873, contained in the *Report of the Bombay Chamber of Commerce for the Year 1872–73* (Bombay: "Bombay Gazette," 1874), 113. Accessed at http:// books.google.com/ with search string: "Smith, Fleming & Co" "Bombay Chamber."

100 "As postal communications": Ibid., 83, 117.

100   "Traffic jams": Picard, *Victorian London*, 31.

100   "This was not the mud": Jackson, *Dirty Old London*, 27.

101   "had the benefit of straw": Picard, *Victorian London*, 38–39.

101   "Pedestrians feeling": Jackson, *Dirty Old London*, 230–231.

101   "top-hat-and-black": Picard, *Victorian London*, 117.

101   "The Victorian middle": Ibid., 201–202.

103   British Charitable Fund: *British Medical Journal*, 1874, vol. 1 (May 16), 655.

103   "The display of female": *Galignani's Messenger*, Apr. 29, 1874, 3.

103   Whether by serendipity: "Walter McGavin Celebrates 40th Year With Bank," *San Francisco Chronicle*, Jan. 30, 1920, 6.

103   He carried: *The Holy Bible: Containing the Old and New Testament, By His Majesty's Special Command* (London: George E. Eyre and William Spottiswoode, undated).

Chapter 10: Scotland Woos Paris

104   Disembarking in: *The Times of India*, "Arrival of the Overland Mails of Nov. 12," Dec. 1, 1875, 2.

104   "A tide of seething": Edwin Arnold, *India Revisited* (London: Trübner & Co., 1886), 55–56. https://archive.org/details/indiarevisited00arnogoog

104   "British metropolitanism": Gillian Tindall, *City of Gold: Biography of Bombay* (London: Penguin Books India, 1992), 172.

104   Mail was delivered: *Handbook of the Bombay Presidency with an Account of Bombay City, Second Edition* (London: John Murray, Albemarle Street, 1881), 115. http://catalog.hathitrust.org/Record/001266769

105   "largely the work": Munro, *Maritime Enterprise and Empire*, 15.

105   modern countries: Lawrence James, *Raj: The Making and Unmaking of British India* (New York: St. Martin's Griffin, 1997), 304, 312.

105   "At his invitation": Ibid., 316.

105   "It was a perennial": Tindall, *City of Gold*, 151.

106   "All Comers": *The Times of India*, Aug. 4, 1876, 3.

106   tennis doubles: *The Times of India*, Sep. 18, 1878, 3.

106   "During the forty odd": *The Times of India*, Sep. 30, 1878, 2.

106   "It produced": "The Monetary Crisis Yesterday," *The Times of India*, Oct. 5, 1878, 2.

108   "The light thrown": Munro, *Maritime Enterprise and Empire*, 255.

108   Mackinnon Mackenzie: Ibid., 139–140, 262.

108   "I found the work": Bolitho, *James Lyle Mackay*, 33.

108   returned to Bombay: *The Times of India*, Oct. 29, 1878, 2.

109   Baedeker's: K. Baedeker, *Paris and Its Environs: Handbook for Travellers* (Leipsic: Karl Baedeker, 1878), 45–46.

109 appointed physician: Ormond, *John Singer Sargent*, 124.

109 Silver Kings: The four owners of the Consolidated Virginia Mines were James C. Flood, William O'Brien, John Mackay, and James G. Fair.

109 "had no qualms": Dinkelspiel, *Towers of Gold*, 136–137.

109 "Mackay commuted": Nancy L. Green, *The Other Americans in Paris: Businessmen, Countesses, Wayward Youth 1880–1941* (Chicago: University of Chicago Press, 2014), 8.

110 Walter's obituary: Dolly (Emilia) Cline, Scrapbook, 1908–1930, vol. 3. California Historical Society, MS OV 5022, and *San Francisco Chronicle*, Mar. 8, 1928, 10.

110 January 29, 1880: "Walter McGavin Celebrates 40th Year With Bank," *San Francisco Chronicle*, Jan. 30, 1920, 6.

110 As he entered: Dinkelspiel, *Towers of Gold*, 137.

110 longest serving: "Banker, 70 Years Young, Retires Today," *San Francisco Chronicle*, Oct. 6, 1923, 5.

110 Almost two years: The marriage was performed at the Trinity Episcopal Church at the northeast corner of Post and Powell by Rev. Alfred Todhunter. In family lore, the date of the marriage was Dec. 1, although the marriage certificate in the family's possession includes other dates as well, Nov. 30, Dec. 5, and Dec. 17 (the recording date). The original records were destroyed by the 1906 Earthquake and Fire.

111 "Mrs. McGavin contributed": *San Francisco Chronicle*, Apr. 22, 1884, 2.

111 "Each participant": *San Francisco Chronicle*, Nov. 23, 1886, 6.

111 In May 1886: *San Francisco Chronicle*, Mar. 23, 1886, 6, and Sep. 28, 1886, 6.

111 4 Rue St. Philippe du Roule: *Galignani's Messenger*, Oct. 1, 1883, 2.

111 "Dr. MacGavin stands": *Galignani's Messenger*, Nov. 14, 1884, 1, "A Letter from Dr. MacGavin."

111 medical research: Steven Johnson, *Ghost Map*, 57–79, 191–207.

112 "the whole scientific": "The Cholera in Paris," *British Medical Journal*, 1884;2:1029 (Nov. 22).

113 waist-high portrait: Ormond, *John Singer Sargent*, 124.

113 "father of lawn": *San Francisco Chronicle*, Mar. 8, 1928, 10.

113 "This tie [match]": *San Francisco Chronicle*, Jul. 1, 1880, 5.

114 "Why Lawn Tennis": *San Francisco Chronicle*, Sep. 25, 1887, 8.

114 "only old-timer": *San Francisco Chronicle*, Nov. 11, 1889, 5.

114 "alleged judges": *San Francisco Chronicle*, Oct. 6, 1890, 6.

114 Pacific Coast Championship: *San Francisco Chronicle*, Aug. 13, 1904, 7.

114 On their first: *San Francisco Chronicle*, Mar. 23, 1890, 6.

116 passed through Chicago: *San Francisco Chronicle*, Oct. 27, 1890, 8, and Nov. 3, 1890, 8.

116 She made hurried: *San Francisco Chronicle*, Apr. 20, 1893, 3.

116   "one of the oldest": *Galignani's Messenger*, Apr. 20, 1893, 2.

116   Reverend H. E. Noyes: *Galignani's Messenger*, Apr. 22, 1893, 2. Noyes served as chaplain to the British Embassy 1891–1907. See also H. E. Noyes, *Seventeen Years in Paris: A Chaplain's Story* (London: Baines and Scarsbrook, 1910) at http://catalog.hathitrust.org/Record/007668808.

Chapter 11: A Go-Getter Seeks His Fortune

121   "Go! Go! Flee": Berton, *Klondike*, 166.

121   "For those who have": Dunham, *The Alaskan Gold Fields*, 41.

121   population of Dawson: Ibid., 39.

121   Within a year: Ibid., 25, 27. Dunham estimated that prospectors had extracted three million dollars of gold ($91.5 million in 2017 dollars). Claims were "five hundred feet long, as a rule measured in the direction of the general course of the stream, and extending in width from base to base of the hill or bench on each side."

121   Forty Mile: So named for its location forty miles downstream from Fort Reliance, an early Alaska Commercial Co. trading post.

121   "a collection": Harry De Windt, *Through the Gold-Fields of Alaska to Bering Straits* (London: Chatto & Windus, 1898), 139.

122   "On her death bed": Jacob Pike and Percy Pike, *Memoirs*, 42.

122   "It is well to know": *The San Francisco Blue Book, 1892* (San Francisco: The Bancroft Co., 1892), page a.

123   "The purpose of": *Mount Tamalpais Military Academy Catalog, 1894–1895* (San Francisco: The Traveler, 1894), 8.

123   "Daily contact": Colin MacGregor, "Mt. Tamalpais Military Academy," *Overland Monthly,*, vol. 44, no. 2 (Aug. 1904), 195.

123   Roy's first day: *Marin Journal*, Aug. 17, 1893, 3.

123   Four days later: Chits for two telephone calls from "Mr. Pyke" to San Francisco 1380. Mount Tamalpais Military Academy archives, Marin History Museum, Craemer Family Collections & Research Facility, Novato, CA. Telephone listing for "San Francisco 1380": Pike, Chas. W., Shipping and Commission Merchant, 124 California. *Pacific States Telephone and Telegraph Company Directory*, Jan. 1894, 88. https://archive.org/details/sanfranciscotele1894paci

124   "There was gold": Berton, *Klondike*, 90.

124   He earned $40: Roy M. Pike to Captain J. E. Hansen, Forty Mile, dated Apr. 2, 1898. Roy wrote on the envelope: "Copy of personal letter sent to J. E. Hansen, April 3, 1898." Handwritten draft in the family's possession.

125   two-story log structure: Gates, *Gold at Fortymile Creek*, 74.

125   variety of products: Samuel P. Johnston, ed. *Alaska Commercial Company 1868–1940* (San Francisco: 1940), 34.

126   "volume of ice": Dunham, *The Alaskan Gold Fields*, 45. Roy Pike misidentified the *Bella* as the *Alice*, writing under his picture: "Steamer 'Alice' edged into smooth water of Forty Mile River with stern wheel just clearing the first ice running in Yukon, Oct. 1, 1897. Yukon all had jammed below... 10 days later it [the ice] cleared and she was able to proceed 200 miles downriver to Circle City where there was plenty of food. She wintered in a back water slough there." Source: Roy Pike Picture Album, 1896–1930, 25.

126   "Comrades of the Klondike": This poem is written on a large folded ledger sheet and is in the family's possession. On the front is the word "POMES!!" perhaps a play on the word "poems." Written in pencil below is "1898, Dawson – Yukon Territory." This may be an incorrect date. Or, if accurate, this would indicate that Miller gave it to Roy after their initial meeting at Forty Mile in October 1897.

126   Have you, too: Sam C. Dunham, *The Goldsmith of Nome and Other Verse* (Washington, DC: The Neale Publishing Company, 1901), 11. The published version includes the notation "Circle City, Oct. 19, 1897," where Dunham and Joaquin Miller spent the winter after the Yukon River froze and trapped the *Bella*.

126   "Trees cracked": Berton, *Klondike*, 171.

126   "I deem my whole": Pike to J. E. Hansen, Forty Mile, April 2, 1898.

128   "dreary, desolate Dawson": Franklin Walker, *Jack London & the Klondike: The Genesis of an American Writer* (San Marino, CA: The Huntington Library, 1978), 161.

129   "The Alaskan gold": Earle Labor, *Jack London: An American Life* (New York: Farrar, Straus and Giroux, 2013), 109.

129   America's first luxury: Lewis, *Bonanza Inn*, 26–27.

129   when Laura moved: The *San Mateo Directory 1907*, 69, lists the location as "Santa Inez Avenue, west of El Camino Real." Today the property may be located in the City of Hillsborough, which was incorporated in 1910.

129   "Roy had come into": Jacob Pike and Percy Pike, *Memoirs*, 46.

129   "An exceedingly": *San Francisco Chronicle*, Jan. 1, 1904, 28.

130   "the unquestioned": *San Francisco Chronicle*, Jan. 8, 1904, 9.

130   "Mr. and Mrs. de Young": *San Francisco Chronicle*, Jan. 24, 1904, 36.

130   "This city is going": Peter Pike, "Caruso and the San Francisco Earthquake," sent to the Metropolitan Opera Association Jan. 8, 1979. Copy in the family's possession.

131   "Caruso...embraced": Lewis, *Bonanza Inn*, 332.

131   "I went looking": Pierre V. R. Key, *Enrico Caruso: A Biography* (Boston: Little, Brown, and Company, 1922), 228–229.

131   "Arthur Bachman": Bachman lived at 2409 Scott Street, five blocks from 2200 Pacific Avenue. *San Francisco City Directory 1905*, 218.

131   "This is the year": Edith Pike, "Early Years," 9.

132   "Possessed of a fine": Thomas P. Pike, "A Profile of Roy M. Pike's Diaries, 1912–1917."

132   "Pike Joins Pioneer": *San Francisco Call*, May 30, 1909, 48.

132   "In both business": *San Francisco Chronicle*, May 30, 1909, 32.

Chapter 12: A Western Princess

133   Twenty-eight girls: Edmondson, *Profiles in Leadership*, 6, 28.

133   "In Central Park": Ibid., 6.

133   "We black our own: Ibid., 9.

133   "Mother made up": Quotations of Edith Simpson in this chapter are from her short memoir, the "Early Years of Edith Simpson Pike."

134   "High ceilings": Edmondson, *Profiles in Leadership*, 4–9.

134   Tuition and board: Ibid., 10, 13.

134   "Our room is the usual": Ibid., 9.

135   "You ought to have": Edith Simpson to Edgar Simpson, undated.

135   "My Dear Girls": These words began Clara Spence's address to the class of 1913. They were posted at the school's website under "Retrospectives" in 2015, but are no longer accessible online.

135   "To the debutantes": *San Francisco Chronicle*, Dec. 9, 1900, 10.

138   "infernally queer": Edith Simpson to Edgar Simpson, Europe, mistakenly dated the "Spring of 1901," but clearly written in the summer.

138   Edwin Dun: Edwin Dun, *Reminiscences of Nearly Half a Century in Japan* (typed manuscript, 1919), 75–76. https://archive.org/details/CAT10899295 DunReminiscences

138   "Miss Edith": *San Francisco Chronicle*, Apr. 23, 1903, 12.

138   "I had a delightful": F. M. Huntington Wilson, *Memoirs of An Ex-Diplomat*. (Boston: Bruce Humphries, Inc., 1945), 111.

139   "We have fled": Edith Simpson to Edgar Simpson, Toyolkwan, Haragama near Nakamura, Iwaki-ken, Japan, undated.

139   "I took along two": Wilson, *Memoirs of An Ex-Diplomat*, 112.

139   arriving in San Francisco: *San Francisco Chronicle*, Dec. 23, 1903, 31.

139   two maids of honor: *New York Times*, May 1, 1904, 7.

139   "Lucy chose bridesmaids": *Lucy Wortham James* (New York: The James Foundation, 1971), 36.

140   "Simpson's fleet": Cox, "Lumber and Ships," 25–26.

140   They appear: Album of Edith Simpson Pike 1881–1929, 56.

140   "dashing New York": *San Francisco Call*, Mar. 16, 1905, 9.

142   "The delightful news": *San Francisco Chronicle*, Apr. 26, 1910, 3.

142   Sophie Simpson had died: *San Francisco Chronicle*, Aug. 10, 1909, 16.

142   "There are some years": "To Roy, Feb. 10, 1912," Edith Simpson Pike, *A Memory of Edith Simpson Pike*.

143   "marked by an entire": *San Francisco Chronicle*, Jul. 13, 1910, 18.

143   "having made the trip": *San Francisco Chronicle*, Jul. 15, 1910, 7.

143   "At that time dad": Roy Pike Jr.'s addendum to Edith Pike's "Early Years," 12. He incorrectly wrote Humboldt instead of Mendocino County.

143   Archibald S. White: *Distinguished Successful Americans of Our Day* (Chicago, IL: Successful Americans, 1912), 498.

143   Cincinnati Union: *Cincinnati Enquirer*, May 17, 1912, 2, and May 19, 1912, 8.

143   investors lost: Roy M. Pike Diary, vol. 4, Feb. 7, 1917.

143   Yolo Water: *Woodland Daily Democrat* (Woodland, CA), Oct. 5, 1912, 1.

143   "a band of ": Roy M. Pike Diary, vol. 1, Nov. 13, 1913.

143   "great octopus": *Woodland Daily Democrat* (Woodland, CA), Feb. 5, 1916, 1.

144   Whitehall Estates: *Woodland Daily Democrat* (Woodland, CA), Aug. 29, 1914, 1, and Sep. 6, 1916, 1. *San Francisco Chronicle*, Dec. 10, 1916, 62.

144   The daily entries: Roy M. Pike Diary, vol. 1, Oct. 4, 1912 ("Edith and I"); vol. 2, Oct. 9, 1914 ("Received from"); vol. 3, May 3, 1916 ("a man has").

144   "[Roy] was a promoter": Thomas P. Pike, "A Profile of Roy M. Pike's Diaries, 1912–1917."

145   One month before: *San Francisco Chronicle*, Jan. 11, 1915, 14.

145   "He slipped into": Roy M. Pike Diary, vol. 2, Jan. 10, 1915.

145   probated estate: San Francisco Probate #18480 D 1915.

145   Two of the promissory: Roy M. Pike Diary, vol. 1, Dec. 9, 1913.

145   "gold-headed cane": Thomas P. Pike, *Memoir*, 4.

145   "My Father took": Roy M. Pike Diary, vol. 2, Mar. 28 and 30, 1916.

145   "Mrs. Roy Pike": *San Francisco Chronicle*, May 24, 1914, 13.

145   "Went to the hospital": Roy M. Pike Diary, vol. 2, Dec. 6, 1914.

146   "telephone dinner": *San Francisco Chronicle*, Aug. 6, 1916, 15. This dinner party must have occurred during Roy's trip to Chicago and New York between Jun. 25 and Jul. 30, 1916. Roy M. Pike Diary, vol. 4.

146   "Mother and Dad": Roy Pike Jr.'s addendum to Edith Pike's "Early Years," 13-14.

Chapter 13: The Social Whirl

149 Marry Suddenly: *San Francisco Chronicle*, Feb. 22, 1910, 1.

150 "In his own name": *San Francisco Call*, Feb. 22, 1910, 16.

150 "runaway marriage": *San Francisco Chronicle*, Jun. 14, 1912, 3.

150 all property rights: *San Francisco Chronicle*, Jul. 6, 1912, 5.

151 "The Nevada Bank opened": Dinkelspiel, *Towers of Gold*, 244.

151 "[When] the boat": Quotations of Frederick Lipman are from "Lipman Interview I – Earthquake," Frederick Lipman Papers, WF L-9-10, Wells Fargo Archives. He was later president of the bank 1920–1935.

152 "Great clouds": Frank A. Leach, *Recollections of a Mint Director* (Wolfeboro, NH: Bowers and Merena Galleries, 1987), 39.

152 2020 Jackson Street: Dinkelspiel, *Towers of Gold*, 252. Emanuel Heller married Clara Hellman, Isaias Hellman's daughter.

152 senior management: *San Francisco Chronicle*, Jan. 12, 1906, 14. The eight directors and officers of the Wells Fargo Nevada National Bank on Jan. 9, 1906: president, Isaias W. Hellman; vice-presidents, John F. Bigelow and I. W. Hellman Jr.; cashier, F. L. Lipman; assistant cashiers, George Grant, Frank B. King, W. McGavin, and John E. Miles.

153 "a tremendous": Leach, *Recollections of a Mint Director*, 47–48.

153 including $9 million: Dinkelspiel, *Towers of Gold*, 255.

153 "ran the show": Chandler, *Wells Fargo*, 117.

153 Miraculously, fifteen: Dinkelspiel, *Towers of Gold*, 256–257.

154 MacGavin is visiting: *San Francisco Chronicle*, Jun. 29, 1905, 7.

154 Miss Murison's: *San Francisco City Directory 1904*, 1355.

154 "buds and belles": *San Francisco Call*, Jul. 13, 1906, 8.

154 "The town had not": Lewis, *Bonanza Inn*, 255.

156 "The opening gun": Ibid., 256.

156 Greenway's first: Altrocchi, *The Spectacular San Franciscans*, 268.

156 "Grand Right": Moffat, *Dancing on the Brink of the World*, 71–75.

156 "the money": Altrocchi, *The Spectacular San Franciscans*, 256.

156 "The McGavin home": *San Francisco Call*, Dec. 29, 1907, 46.

156 "Mrs. McGavin has": *San Francisco Chronicle*, Mar. 22, 1908, 32.

157 large scrapbook: Dolly Cline Scrapbook, 1908–1930, vol. 1. California Historical Society, MS OV 5022.

159 "You get the thrill": Ackley, *San Francisco's Jewel City*, 250.

159 "Twenty-eight mechanics": Ibid., 154.

159 "embraced by graceful": Ibid., 25.

159 *Portrait of Madame*: Ibid., 230, 234.

Chapter 14: The Salesman and the Socialite

160   "No more interesting": *San Francisco Chronicle*, Apr. 17, 1917, 7.

161   West End: Primm, *Lion of the Valley*, 366–367.

161   he did not attend: Frederick Addison Cline, Yale College Class of 1874, Obituary file in the Manuscripts and Archives, Cowles Reference Center, Sterling Memorial Library, Yale University.

161   "for seven months": Primm, *Lion of the Valley*, 418.

161   Alan's name: *St. Louis City Directories*: 1905, 389; 1906, 351; 1907, 359; and 1908, 367.

161   listed as "traveling": *St. Louis City Directories*: 1909, 524; 1910, 461; 1911, 456; 1912, 467; 1913, 516; 1915: 467.

161   General Roofing: Tina Grant, ed., *International Directory of Company Histories*, vol. 35 (Detroit: St. James Press, 2001), 86–87.

161   weeks at a time: *Certain-teed Products Corporation Annual Reports*, Dec. 31, 1917, and Dec. 31, 1918.

161   Hotel Plaza: *San Francisco Chronicle*, Feb. 6, 1916, 38.

162   Dutro Cale: *St. Louis City Directory*, 1915, 412, and *San Francisco City Directory*, 1917, 461.

162   Mrs. Cale: *San Francisco Chronicle*, Sep. 19, 1916, 4.

162   "It was all great": Frances Cline to Dolly MacGavin, St. Louis, Apr. 18, 1917.

162   "I would like more": Emilia Hinshelwood to Dolly MacGavin, Paris, Apr. 21, 1917.

162   "My darling son": Frances Cline to Alan Cline, St. Louis, Apr. 18, 1917.

162   "Everything is so uncertain": Frances Cline to Dolly MacGavin, St. Louis, Jul. 14, 1917.

162   "We all are dreadfully": Isabel (Cline) Harney to Dolly MacGavin, St. Louis, May 27, 1917.

164   "the two happiest": Emilia Hinshelwood to Dolly MacGavin, Paris, Apr. 21, 1917.

164   "No wedding of ": *San Francisco Chronicle*, Jul. 15, 1917, S2.

164   "I said this morning": Frances Cline to Dolly MacGavin, St. Louis, Jul. 3, 1917.

165   "Perhaps you can": Frances Cline to Dolly MacGavin Cline, St. Louis, Jul. 14, 1917.

165   "We are greatly": Francis Cline to Alan Cline, St. Louis, Oct. 26, 1918.

165   "I don't wonder Alan": Frances Cline to Kate McGavin, St. Louis, Nov. 6, 1918.

165   serving in the U.S.: In family lore, Drummond MacGavin spoke excellent French and served as a liaison officer between the American Expeditionary Forces and the French Army.

166   After Dolly experienced: Telegrams are in the Scrapbook of Dolly MacGavin Cline 1917–1921.

166 "We were much shocked": Frances Cline to Helen MacGavin, St. Louis, May 19, 1920.

167 "Walter McGavin from": This watch remains in the family.

167 district manager: *San Francisco City Directory 1920*, 504.

167 "The demand for": *Certain-teed Products Corporation Annual Report*, December 31, 1919.

167 "most economical selling": *Certain-teed Products Corporation Annual Report*, December 31, 1926.

168 "Honey Bunch": Scrapbook of Dolly MacGavin Cline 1919–1929, 29.

168 "Seven years ago": Ibid., 61.

168 Here's to my: Ibid., 125.

168 "will investigate local": Ibid., 95. The Clines departed on Jan. 5, 1927 and returned Jan. 25, 1927.

168 Robert M. Nelson: *San Francisco Chronicle*, Apr. 6, 1927, 18.

171 The appraised value: "Inventory and Appraisement" of the estate of Walter J. S. McGavin, Probate No. 49,499, City of San Francisco.

171 "Like an earthquake": Kennedy, *Freedom from Fear*, 10.

171 "The close of the year": *Certain-teed Products Corporation Annual Report*, December 31, 1929.

171 the company's revenues: *Certain-teed Products Corporation Annual Report*, December 31, 1930.

171 "All salaries": *Certain-teed Products Corporation Annual Report*, December 31, 1931.

171 rock bottom: *Certain-teed Products Corporation Annual Report*, December 31, 1932.

171 "conducted a school": A. P. Cline, "Certain-teed Products," *Pacific Coast Builder*, Feb. 22, 1935. Catherine Cline Scrapbook, 1931–1939, vol. 2, California Historical Society, MS OV 5034.

172 "never recovered": Frederick Addison Cline, Yale College Class of 1874, Obituary file in the Manuscripts and Archives, Yale University.

172 three-story: *San Francisco Chronicle*, Mar. 14, 1936, 12.

172 "patronesses where": *San Francisco Chronicle*, Oct. 21, 1934, S1.

172 new home: *San Francisco Chronicle*, Feb. 26, 1934, 19.

172 Schumacher Wall: The family has a sheet of personalized Schumacher Wall Board Corporation note paper with a handwritten date of Dec. 11, 1937, for Alan P. Cline, General Sales Manager, Schumite Products, with two addresses: 557 Market Street, San Francisco and 5721 S. San Pedro Street, Los Angeles. See also advertisements for Schumacher Wall Board: *Building & Engineering News*, Jan. 7, 1922, 1, and Jul. 3, 1926, 1.

172 "very tired Mrs. Alan": *San Francisco Chronicle*, Dec. 4, 1937, 12.

172 "The Alan Clines": *San Francisco Chronicle*, Dec. 17, 1937, 17.

Chapter 15: To the Manner Born

173 "I determined in 1917": Testimony dated Nov. 2, 1934, in which attorney W. C. Sloss questioned Roy Pike, 1. Transcript in the archives of the El Solyo Water District, Vernalis, CA. Hereafter, "El Solyo Water District testimony."

173 five contiguous farms: Ibid., 3. The farms were the "Burrell, Brigham, Hawley, Meyers, and the old Oaklea [Oakley]."

173 "You can't irrigate": Quotations of Peter Pike in this chapter from "Childhood on a Ranch, 1921–1924."

173 Three large pumps: Picture album "El Solyo, 1920–21," #78. See also picture album "El Solyo Ranch, Stanislaus County, Calif. on West Side of San Joaquin River," picture No. 18 titled "El Solyo Ranch, July 15, 1921." See also picture album "El Solyo Ranch, Book 2, October 1929," picture titled the "Main Canal" in archives of the Patterson Township Historical Society, Patterson, CA.

175 incubated and matured: Roy Pike, "Story of El Solyo Ranch."

176 eleven departments: El Solyo Ranch Organization Chart, Jan. 1, 1935. Original in the archives of the El Solyo Water District.

176 ten-hour days: These were the working hours at Huston Farms, which Roy Pike managed. Roy M. Pike Diary, vol. 2, Sep. 4, 1914.

176 A siren: *Stockton Record*, Sep. 28, 1966, 72.

177 "El Solyo Ranch Rivals": *Modesto News-Herald*, Jan. 5, 1929, 15.

177 Ford V-8 pickup: "El Solyo," *Ford News*, Jul. 1935, 137.

177 its own films: *Modesto News-Herald*, Nov. 21, 1928, 6.

177 "Roy Pike and the staff ": *Patterson Irrigator*, Feb. 23, 1934, 3.

177 "He was very kind": *Stockton Record*, Sep. 29, 1966, 35.

177 "Murder!!": Roy M. Pike Diary, vol. 4, Nov. 7, 1916.

178 "The statement to achieve": "An Anniversary Dinner, Bohemian Club, February 11, 1928, Roy M. Pike," 115. Bohemian Club archives.

182 "When not in San Francisco": "The El Solyo Deal," *Fortune*, 149.

182 "we were warmly": Thomas P. Pike, "A Profile of Roy M. Pike's Diaries, 1912–1917."

183 "To combat rabbits": *Stockton Record*, Sep. 28, 1966, 72.

183 "These were all people": Quotations of Roy M. Pike Jr. in this chapter come from his short memoir "My Early Life."

183 "ex-President Herbert": *Patterson Irrigator*, Apr. 3, 1936.

184 Lady Anne Hunloke: *San Francisco Chronicle*, Sep 7, 1937, 23; Nov. 24, 1937, 15; and Nov. 27, 1937, 15.

Chapter 16: "A Terrible Mistake"

185 "The present manager": See the first sentences in "El Solyo," *Ford News*, Jul. 1935, 132, and Roy Pike, "Story of El Solyo Ranch," 1.

186 $350,000 in 1919: This figure is an estimate. In 1934 Roy testified that the land cost for El Solyo was $405,000. Source: "El Solyo Water District testimony," 11. But this included 540 acres of land added after the original purchase, which Roy recalled was 3,780 acres. Most likely, the original land cost was close to the El Solyo Land Company's 1920 bond offering of $350,000. Note: The original acreage was stated as slightly less at 3,738 acres in Thelma York's paper, "El Solyo Ranch," 4.

186 sole shareholder: "El Solyo Water District testimony," 13.

186 El Solyo Land: *San Francisco Chronicle*, Mar. 19, 1920, 18.

186 "I recognized": "El Solyo Water District testimony," 3.

186 $150,000 for the irrigation: "The El Solyo Deal," *Fortune*, 149.

186 So Roy secured: York, "El Solyo Ranch," 16.

186 $200,000 second: "The El Solyo Deal," *Fortune*, 149. See also *Modesto Evening News*, Dec. 21, 1923, 7.

186 "The last year": David E. Kyvig, *Daily Life in the United States, 1920–1940: How Americans Lived Through the Roaring Twenties and the Great Depression* (Chicago: Ivan R. Dee, 2002), 14. Note also, farm wages fell from $2.80 a day (with board and room) in 1920 to $0.90 a day in 1933 and did not reach their earlier peak until 1943. *Historical Statistics of the United States, Colonial Times to 1970, Part 1* (Washington, DC: U.S. Bureau of the Census, 1975), "Farm Employment, Wages, and Indexes of Man-Hours Used for Farmwork: 1866 to 1970," 468. http://catalog.hathitrust.org/Record/000707742

187 farm prices fell: The farm price index fell from 205 in 1920 to 116 in 1921. Frederick Lewis Allen, *Only Yesterday: An Informal History of the 1920s* (New York: Harper & Row, 1931), 139.

187 "I came to very": "El Solyo Water District testimony," 13.

187 "a miracle": "The El Solyo Deal," *Fortune*, 149.

187 Allan C. Balch: Justice Brown Detwiler, *Who's Who in California: A Biographical Directory, 1928–29* (San Francisco: Who's Who Publishing Company: San Francisco, 1929), 592.

187 "beautiful Rolls": Roy Pike Jr., "My Early Life," 15.

187 "property at my request": In 1924 Roy held title to El Solyo as the Central California Orchard Company. When Balch acquired the property in 1925, title passed to the Greenwich Investment Company and later to Meridian Ltd., both of which Balch controlled. El Solyo Water District testimony, 13–14.

187 salary, plus his housing: An employee named Howard Shideler remembered that in the 1930s the general manager (Roy Pike) was paid $200 per month. Source: *Manteca News*, Mar. 21, 1981, B3. Shideler was the assistant manager of the Farms Department in charge of turkeys at El Solyo in 1935. Source: El Solyo Ranch Organization Chart, Jan. 1, 1935, El Solyo Water District Archives. In the 1940 U.S. Census, Roy reported that his annual salary exceeded $5,000 (about $417 a month).

187 "Roy, I won't": "An Anniversary Dinner, Bohemian Club, February 11, 1928, Roy M. Pike," 117.

188 "Balch proved": "The El Solyo Deal," *Fortune*, 149.

188 tallied the cost: "El Solyo Water District testimony," 11–12. Land purchase ($405,000), Land development (leveling, soil work, orchard planting) ($1,950,000), Irrigation system (pumps, pipes, power house) ($325,000), Equipment (spray rigs, road-making machines, cultivators) ($172,000), Farm buildings ($200,000), Livestock (horses, mules, cows) ($30,000), Plants (dehydrator, shipping) ($239,000), Supplies (seeds) ($46,000), Salable merchandise (dried fruit, crops) ($100,000), Working capital (accounts receivable) ($75,000).

188 "Depression strike": Kennedy, *Freedom from Fear*, 163.

188 "Daily 'boes'": Quotations of Peter Pike in this chapter from his short memoir "Fall & Winter 1932–Spring & Summer 1933."

188 "We just knocked": Roy Pike Jr., "The Thirties," 1.

188 harvesting delay: Clarke A. Chambers, "A History of the Associated Farmers of California, Incorporated, 1934–1939" (master's thesis, University of California, Berkeley, Jun. 1947), 2.

188 "Fruit Workers Strike": *Modesto Bee*, Aug. 28, 1933, 1.

188 "the ranch recently": *Modesto Bee*, Aug. 29, 1933, 1.

189 "guns were reported": *Modesto Bee*, Aug. 30, 1933, 1.

189 "Although many men": *Modesto Bee*, Aug. 31, 1933, 1. See also *Patterson Irrigator*, Sep. 1, 1933, 2.

190 National Reconstruction: Kennedy, *Freedom from Fear*, 151.

190 Agricultural Adjustment Act: Ibid., 204.

190 "to prevent unfair": Ibid., 151.

190 83 percent: *Modesto News-Herald*, Nov. 9, 1932, 18.

190 "pamphleteer against": "The El Solyo Deal," *Fortune*, 149.

190 "to successfully combat": "Californians—Wake Up!" Reprinted from the *California Journal of Development*, Jan. 1936.

191 largest contributor: "The El Solyo Deal," *Fortune*, 149.

191 Associated Farmers: Walter J. Stein, *California and the Dust Bowl Migration* (Westport, CT: Greenwood Press, 1973), 87 and 240.

191   "deputizing hundreds": Ibid., 238.

191   Roy threatened: *Rural Observer*, vol. 1 no. 8 (Jul.–Aug. 1938), 3–4. The *Rural Observer* was a bi-monthly publication of the Simon J. Lubin Society, a progressive organization fighting for farm workers' rights.

191   "Tear and Sickening": Ibid., 4.

191   "Mass Farm Production": *San Francisco Chronicle*, Aug. 14, 1939, 10.

192   La Follette Committee: Senate Subcommittee on S. Res. 266. Committee on Education and Labor. Hearings. "Violations of Free Speech and Rights of Labor. Part 48: California Agricultural Background, Marysville, Calif., Incident, May–July 1939," Spoken testimony: 17674–17695; written testimony: 17895–17908.

192   "Farmers needing fifty": Ibid., 17679.

193   "Could you harvest": Ibid., 17678–9.

193   "Most of this female": Ibid., 17678.

193   Roy's testimony: *San Francisco Examiner*, Dec. 15, 1939, 5.

194   "designed to prevent": Jerold S. Auerbach, *Labor and Liberty: The La Follette Committee and the New Deal* (New York: The Bobbs-Merrill Company, 1966), 187.

194   stroke and resigned: *San Francisco Chronicle*, Jul. 17, 1941, 12.

194   "infinite capacity": *Patterson Irrigator*, Jul. 11, 1941, 1.

195   "the largest diversified": Peter Pike, "Childhood on a Ranch," 1.

Chapter 17: Childhood on a Ranch

199   "tall [and] thin with": Quotations of Peter Pike in this chapter come from his short memoir, "Childhood on a Ranch."

199   house at El Solyo: Modern address: 3101 River Road, Vernalis, CA 95385

199   "and the heavy grass": Quotations of Roy Pike Jr. are from "My Early Life," 2.

201   intense heat: See caption under picture #164 in "El Solyo, 1920–21" picture album. "Jun. 20, 1920 – Temp is 121° in shade at noon, the hottest and longest day in the year."

204   At the wedding: Harry Blosser and Constance Taylor were married on Apr. 20, 1924, at the First Christian Church in Stockton, CA. "California, County Marriages, 1850–1952," database with images at FamilySearch. https://www.familysearch.org/search/ark:/61903/1:1:K82R-ZY1

204   Rising Sun Grammar School: The school appears on two maps in the USGS Historical Topographic Map Collection: (1) SOLYO, CA HISTORICAL MAP GEOPDF 7.5X7.5 GRID 31680-SCALE 1916 (Product Number: 299449) and (2) CARBONA, CA HISTORICAL MAP GEOPDF 15X15 GRID 62500-SCALE 1922 (Product Number: 300874). http://nationalmap.gov/historical/ Today the Patterson Joint Unified School District operates the Rising Sun Farm & Garden School at the site, providing "a life skill development

program for young adults with special needs, ages 18–22." Modern address: 2243 Welty Rd., Vernalis, CA 95385, at the northwest intersection of Welty Rd. and Spencer St.

207 Bill Oliphant: Willard E. Oliphant was twenty-six years old when he graduated from the University of California, Berkeley in 1926.

207 Brosie Whitmer: Wilson Ambrose Whitmer.

Chapter 18: Schools Abroad

209 "Since leaving town": *San Francisco Chronicle*, Nov. 8, 1924, 9.

209 "Both Peter and I": Roy Pike Jr., "Our Trip to Europe in 1925."

209 Robert G. Dun: *Lucy Wortham James* (New York: The James Foundation, 1971), 66–67. R . G. Dun & Company merged with the J. M. Bradstreet Company to form Dun & Bradstreet Corporation in 1933.

212 Captain Chadbourn: Chateau Neuvic was described by his son, Alfred "Chip" Chadbourn, a Maine artist, in "Alfred Chadbourn in Living Color" by Edgar Allen in *The Pied Cow*, The Chadbourne Family Association Newsletter, vol. 4, no. 1, Issue 8 (Fall 1986), 4. http://www.chadbourne.org/Piedcows/Issue08.pdf. Note: Alfred and his father spelled Chadbourn without an "e." For contemporary information on Chateau Neuvic, search online for Château de Neuvic, 24190 Neuvic-sur-l'Isle, France.

213 oceanside estate: "Normandie" was located at 228 Ocean Avenue, Newport, Rhode Island. See James Yarnall, *Newport Through Its Architecture: A History of Styles from Postmedieval to Postmodern* (Lebanon, NH: University Press of New England, 2005), 163: "The name 'Normandie' suggested the rural French Norman influence, seen particularly in the whitewashed brick surfaces, red tile roofs, and the round Romanesque archway of the gatehouse. From Ocean Drive, the gatehouse is the only part of the house visible, but through its archway the flagstone courtyard opens up to reveal a low-slung house hugging the rocky terrain of this dramatic stretch of the drive. Mrs. James originally called the house Cherry Creek Bungalow after a prominent estuary running through Cherry Neck, the name for this stretch of the south shoreline."

213 "Mrs. Vanderbilt": Alice Claypoole Gwynne Vanderbilt (1845–1934) was the widow of Cornelius Vanderbilt II (1843–1899), who built The Breakers.

214 "the Victorians": Roy Pike Jr., "My Early Life," 18, and Roy Pike Jr., "My Trip Abroad," Jan. 9–12, 1929.

214 from St. Moritz: Roy Pike Jr., "My Trip Abroad," Mar. 28, 1929. Thirteen-year-old Richard Kerry, the future father of U.S. Secretary of State John Kerry, traveled with Peter and Roy on the train as far as Colico.

215 "tremendously impressed": Thomas P. Pike, *Memoir*, 41.

215 George Arliss: He did play Voltaire in the movie *Voltaire* in 1933.

215 Harvard School: In 1938 the school moved to Coldwater Canyon. Today the school is the Harvard-Westlake School, a coeducational school, located at 3700 Coldwater Canyon, Studio City, CA 91604.

215 "Military discipline": *Harvard School Catalog, 1924–1925*, 43.

216 "a distinctly Christian": *Harvard School Catalog, 1930–1931*, 15.

216 "The kids governed": *San Jose Mercury News*, Jul. 10 1985, 13 (extra section).

216 "bugle calls, formations": Susan Wels, *Harvard-Westlake: 100 Years* (Los Angeles: Harvard-Westlake School, 2002), 26.

216 First Call: *Harvard School Catalog, 1930–1931*, 25. The U.S. Army posts the sounds of more than two dozen bugle calls at https://www.bands.army.mil/music/buglecalls/.

216 As a sophomore: Peter's transcript for his sophomore and junior years is in the Harvard-Westlake Archives. The transcript also includes his grades from Bill Oliphant, his tutor at El Solyo, for his freshman year coursework: English 9, 82, B; Algebra 9, 76, C; Ancient History, 78, C; Gen. Science, 85, B; French 1 & 2, B (no numerical average).

217 "proper physical": *Menlo Musketeer: Yearbook 1932* (Menlo School and Junior College: 1932), 4.

217 "the largest, most active": Ibid., 60.

Chapter 19: A Well-Documented Life

219 "Miss Cline": *The San Francisco News*, Feb. 1, 1934, 8.

219 "the many times": Conversation between Laura Bride (Applegarth) Cresap and Dyan Pike, Jan. 1993.

219 Miss Wafer's: Was located at 2682 Union Street, San Francisco, between Broderick and Divisadero.

219 Dolly snapped: Dolly Cline Photograph Album 1921–1922.

219 "Miss Catherine Cline": Dolly Cline Scrapbook 1919–1929, 6.

219 "Society Folk": Newspaper clipping dated Aug. 9, 1922, in the Dolly Cline Scrapbook 1919–1929, 7.

220 Grant School: Demolished in 1974, Grant School was located at 2940 Pacific Avenue, San Francisco, between Broderick and Baker Streets.

220 straight As: Dolly Cline Scrapbook 1919–1929, 60.

220 Miss Burke's School: In 1949 the Katherine Delmar Burke School moved the elementary grades to its current address at 7070 California Street, San Francisco, CA. In 1975 the high school closed, and the building at 3065 Jackson Street became University High School, a coeducational school.

220 "She was a star": Conversation between Laura Bride (Applegarth) Cresap and Dyan Pike, Jan. 1993.

220 "Of all the girls": Juanita (Hill) Schurman to Dyan Pike, Dec. 1992.

220 "serious, not as": Kathleen (Thompson) Parrish to Dyan Pike, Dec. 1992.

220 "Four of us": Telephone conversation between Virginia (Coghlan) MacLean and Dyan Pike, Dec. 1992. MacLean was the head of The Hamlin School from Sep. 1979 to Jun. 1984.

220 "It was Miss Burke": Barbara Burke became the head of Miss Burke's after the death of her aunt, Katherine Delmar Burke, the founder of the school, in 1929.

222 "Her mother was": Conversation between Constance (Crowley) Bowles and Dyan Pike, Feb. 1993.

222 "patroness of parties": Conversation between Bonnie Hunter and Dyan Pike, Mar. 1993.

222 "a large dancing": *San Francisco Chronicle*, Mar. 12, 1934, 17, and clipping in the Catherine Cline Scrapbook Jan. 1, 1934 to Sep. 22, 1934, 17. Scrapbook in the family's possession.

222 "blue jeans": *San Francisco Chronicle*, Sep. 12, 1934, 25.

222 Dolly surprised: *San Francisco Chronicle*, Oct. 26, 1934, 25.

222 On Friday afternoon: Catherine Cline Scrapbook, Jan. 1, 1934 to Sep. 22, 1934, 29–35.

223 "Recitalist is Thirteen": Catherine Cline Scrapbook, vol. 1, Jan. 11, 1931 to Dec. 31, 1933, California Historical Society, MS OV 5034.

223 blizzard of forty-seven: Transcript of Catherine Cline obtained from the Katherine Delmar Burke School on Mar. 2, 2016.

224 "were not overcrowded": Catherine Cline, Diary, Jul. 27, 1937.

224 "Happiness": Original in the family's possession.

224 via telegram: Dolly Cline Scrapbook, 1908–1930, vol. 4, California Historical Society, MS OV 5022.

224 "One thing I": Catherine Cline, Diary, Jul. 21, 1937.

225 "Our latest addition": *Works & Days 1936*, Miss Burke's School Yearbook (San Francisco, CA: Miss Burke's School, 1936), 18.

225 As she turned fourteen: Catherine Cline Scrapbook, vol. 1, Jan. 11, 1931 to Dec. 31, 1933, California Historical Society, MS OV 5034.

226 "favorite sport": Catherine Cline, *My Memory Book 1936*.

226 "determination to study": *San Francisco Call Bulletin*, Apr. 2, 1936, 10.

226 "Catherine was always": Joan (Ehrman) Avenali, Feb. 1993.

226 "The Perfect Senior": *Works & Days 1936*, 56, 59, 62.

226 "I'll call you": Catherine Cline, *My Memory Book 1936*.

226 "luncheons, teas": *San Francisco Chronicle*, May 24, 1936, S1, and Catherine Cline Scrapbook, vol. 4, Jan. 1, 1936 to Aug. 13, 1936, California Historical Society, MS OV 5034.

228   "We find your": Catherine Cline Scrapbook, vol. 4, Jan. 1, 1936 to Aug. 13, 1936, California Historical Society.

228   admission to: *University of California Bulletin*, General Catalogue, Published at Berkeley, California, vol. 30, Aug. 20, 1936, 25.

228   "Ever since I": Catherine Cline, "Women in Medicine," 1–2. The historical sections of Catherine's paper were largely based upon Dr. Louisa Martindale's *The Woman Doctor and Her Future* (London: Mills & Boon, 1922). https://archive.org/details/womandoctorherfu00martuoft

Chapter 20: University of California, Berkeley

229   "Sorority Maids": *Oakland Tribune*, Aug. 16, 1936, S1.

229   "preference dinners": *Oakland Tribune*, Aug. 30, 1936, S3.

230   "I pledge allegiance": "The Ivy Leaf: An Introduction to Alphi Phi" (Evanston, IL: Alpha Phi International, 2011).

230   Channing Way: *Daily Californian*, Sep. 1, 1936, 1, and Sep. 3, 1936, 1. See also Verne Stadtman, ed., *The Centennial Record of the University of California* (Berkeley: University of California Printing Department, 1967), 114.

230   Over the next three: *Daily Californian*, Aug. 20, 1936, 1, and Aug. 26, 1936, 1.

230   "incidental expense": *University of California Bulletin*, General Catalogue, Published at Berkeley, California, vol. 30, Aug. 20, 1936, 51–54.

230   "put him in touch": *Daily Californian*, Aug. 20, 1936, 1.

230   Freshmen boys: *Daily Californian*, Aug. 20, 1936, 10, and Aug. 21, 1936, 1.

231   "The State of California": *Daily Californian*, Aug. 20, 1936, 1.

231   "They were the exciting": Allen Barbour's remarks at Catherine (Cline) Pike's Memorial Service at the Marin Art and Garden Center, Ross, CA, Sep. 4, 1979.

233   "Perhaps I shall die": Untitled handwritten poem dated June 14–15, 1936.

233   We found the lost: Catherine Cline, Diary, Jun. 20, 1937.

234   John Sneed Schmidt: *Lucky Bag 1937*, U.S. Naval Academy Yearbook, 143. Schmidt won a Silver Star during World War II. http://valor.militarytimes.com/recipient.php?recipientid=56391

234   "He is good looking": Catherine Cline, Diary, Aug. 9, 1937.

235   earning mostly As: Transcript of Catherine Cline from the Registrar at the University of California, Berkeley.

235   "Well, tomorrow I shall": Catherine Cline Diary, Oct. 24, 1937.

235   "Activities & social": Ibid.

235   "He made a splendid": Catherine Cline Diary, Mar. 30, 1938.

235   "In tones of almost": *Daily Californian*, Mar. 31, 1938, 1.

Chapter 21: European Adventure

236   "Miss Cline is leaving": *Los Angeles Times,* Apr. 17, 1938, D2.

236   "The Joshua trees": All quotes of Catherine Cline in this chapter are from her "Travel Journal—U.S." and "Travel Journal—Europe."

237   Mrs. C. Temple Murphy: *Los Angeles Times,* Jun. 2, 1938, A5. Her daughter was Elizabeth P. Murphy.

237   "Kozy Korner": Warren James Belasco, *Americans on the Road: From Autocamps to Motel, 1910–1945* (Cambridge, MA: MIT Press, 1981), 138.

237   "A main house": *New York Times Magazine,* Aug. 12, 1934, 9.

240   Hôtel d'Ecosse: 26–28 Rue d'Edimbourg, 75008 Paris, France.

240   If she carried *Paris*: Arthur K. Griggs, *Paris for Everyman: Her Present, Her Past & Her Environs with Forty-Eight Coloured Maps* (Philadelphia, PA: David McKay Company, 1938), 116.

243   "Church bells pealed": Piers Brendon, *The Dark Valley: A Panorama of the 1930s* (New York: Vintage Books, 2002), 536.

243   "One factor that": Nagorski, *Hitlerland,* 224.

243   Honor Temples: In 1947 the *Ehrentempel* were destroyed by the U.S. Army as part of the denazification program.

245   Regent Palace Hotel: The Regent Palace Hotel was closed in 2006.

Chapter 22: Blazing Her Trail

247   "very superior person": Application for Admission to International House dated Apr. 20, 1937, from Catherine Holmes Cline.

247   Medical Sciences: *University of California Bulletin,* General Catalogue, Published at Berkeley, California, vol. 30, Aug. 20, 1936, Number 6, 86–87.

248   volunteering at: Application for Associate Membership to International House dated Feb. 19, 1937, from Catherine Holmes Cline.

248   "everything on stage": Gary Fishgall, *Gregory Peck: A Biography* (New York: Scribner, 2002), 46.

248   "Peck's handsome face": *Daily Californian,* Mar. 20, 1939, 4.

248   "U.C. Students Warned": Catherine Cline Scrapbook, vol. 6, Jan. 1, 1937 to May 1, 1937, California Historical Society.

249   "Hitler's annihilation": *Daily California,* Mar. 17, 1939, 2.

249   People are dying: Catherine Cline Diary, Mar. 19, 1939.

249   "Well, a week": Catherine Cline Diary, Sep. 3, 1939.

250   "A student will not": *University of California Announcement of the Medical School for the Academic Year 1940–41,* 53.

250   five women: Ingrid (Barany) Gifford, Edith (Rothenberg) Loewenstein, Jeanne

(Ingalls) Miller, Catherine (Cline) Pike, and Sumiko Matsumoto. All graduated except for Matsumoto, who was forced to leave medical school by Executive Order 9066.

250 "I'd come home late": Conversations between Anne Waybur and Dyan Pike, Sep. and Dec. 2001. Anne Waybur was Vice President of the ASUC (Associated Students of the University of California) in 1939–40.

250 "War has been declared": Catherine Cline Diary, Sep. 3, 1939.

251 The law required: *University of California Announcement of the Medical School for the Academic Year 1940–41*, 53.

251 "If the peace": *In Commemoration of Commencement Day 1936–41*. Bancroft Library, Call No. 308ic i 1936–41.

Chapter 23: Alaskan Adventure

253 "A man, seemingly": All quotations of Peter Pike in this chapter are from his short memoir "Fall & Winter 1932–Spring & Summer 1933."

254 *Madame Butterfly*: The movie played at the El Rey Theater. *San Francisco Chronicle*, May 15, 1933, 7. Peter wrote that he saw *One Night of Love* with Grace Moore, who sang a *Madame Butterfly* aria "Un bel di" [One fine day]. But this movie was not released until 1934.

254 *Chirikof* cast off: Engineer's and Mate's Log Books, SS *Chirikof*, 1932–33, Alaska Packers Association, Box 13, Folder 128 and 129, Historic Document Collection HDC 115, San Francisco Maritime National Historical Park.

256 Kogiung: See "The Fisheries of Alaska in 1906," U.S. Department of Commerce and Labor, Bureau of Fisheries Document No. 618, 38.

Chapter 24: Finding His Way

260 "designed primarily": *Prospectus of the College of Agriculture, 1934–35*, University of California Bulletin, Third Series, vol. 27, no. 5, September 1, 1934, 57.

260 "Agricultural Education": *California Aggie*, Aug. 23, 1933, 1.

260 "1. Frosh shall NOT": *California Aggie*, Aug. 23, 1933, 1.

260 red stripes: *California Aggie*, Sep. 6, 1933, 1.

261 Peter specialized: Agricultural Engineering was listed in his Separation Qualification Record from the Army of the United States, Peter Pike, Army Serial Number: 19 065 438, Date of Separation: Nov. 1, 1945, National Personnel Records Center, National Archives, St. Louis, MO 63138.

261 Agricultural Engineering 2: *Prospectus of the College of Agriculture, 1934–35*, University of California Bulletin, Third Series, vol. 27, no. 5, September 1, 1934, 80.

261 Agricultural Engineering Building: Ann F. Scheuring, *Abundant Harvest: The History of the University of California, Davis* (Davis, CA: Regents of the University of California, 2001), 57, and Dennis Dingemans and Ann Foley Scheuring, *University of California, Davis* (Charleston, SC: Arcadia Publishing, 2013), 26–27.

261 "fast-stepping college": *California Aggie*, Nov. 15, 1933, 1.

261 *The Show-Off*: *California Aggie*, Mar. 15, 1934, 1.

261 "Fan Dancers": *Dingleberry (California Aggie)*, Mar. 7, 1934, 1.

261 Song Leader: *El Rodeo 1935*, Yearbook of the College of Agriculture at Davis, 120.

261 *"young, very languid"*: George S. Kaufman and Marc Connelly, *Dulcy* (New York: Samuel French, 1921), 41.

261 "has no doubt about": *California Aggie*, Oct. 25, 1934, 1.

261 I was afire: Kaufman, *Dulcy*, 75–76.

262 "some two-hundred": *California Aggie*, Nov. 15, 1934, 1.

262 college yearbook: *El Rodeo 1935*, 56.

262 Peter dropped out: Robert Sibley, *The Golden Book of California* (Berkeley, CA: California Alumni Association, 1937), 1135.

262 "Poor father": Roy Pike Jr., "The Thirties," 6.

262 "We got invitations": Roy Pike Jr., "The Thirties," 3.

262 Mardi Gras Ball: *San Francisco Chronicle*, Feb. 25, 1936, 3.

262 "vertiginous farce": *San Francisco Chronicle*, May 22, 1936, 13.

263 "To say that this": *San Francisco Chronicle*, Nov. 3, 1936, 28.

263 "The Heald-Hadley": *San Francisco Chronicle*, Sep. 13, 1936, 13.

263 "a marvel of engineering": Starr, *Golden Gate*, 114.

263 Tommy Magee III: The day after Pearl Harbor, Magee was captured at the Battle of Guam on Dec. 8, 1941, and held as a prisoner of war in Japan for the duration of the war. When he went missing, Herb Caen wrote, "Is Lieutenant Tommy Magee III, a high-ranker in S.F. social circles, the first prisoner of war from here? He was sent to Guam several months ago, and no one has heard from him. (Magee left S.F. for Guam in style, incidentally—even took his own linen and silverware with him.)" *San Francisco Chronicle*, Dec. 20, 1941, 13.

263 By comparing: Original pictures in the family's possession.

263 After construction of: Cassaday, *Spanning the Gate*, 64, 85, and Starr, *Golden Gate*, 122–123.

264 "High Life Revolves": *San Francisco Chronicle*, Jul. 22, 1939, 6.

265 "For classical": *San Francisco Chronicle*, Aug. 11, 1940, 2.

265 Most classical recordings: Roland Gelatt, *The Fabulous Phonograph, 1877–1977* (New York: Macmillan, 1977), 263–264.

265 over sixteen days: Peter sailed on the *Georgic* from New York to Liverpool (Dec. 10 to Dec. 19, 1938) and from Southampton to New York on the *Paris* (Jan. 4 to Jan. 11, 1939).

265   Alec Templeton: *San Francisco Chronicle*, Feb. 10, 1939, 6.

265   "Columbia Masterworks": *San Francisco Chronicle*, Aug. 11, 1940, 2.

265   thirty-five cents: William Howland Kenney, *Recorded Music in American Life: The Phonograph and Popular Memory, 1890–1945* (New York: Oxford, 1999), 164.

266   clerk at Decca: *San Francisco City Directory 1941*, 1133.

266   White-Hat McCarthy: *San Francisco Chronicle*, Jan. 12, 1940, 3.

266   French comedy: *San Francisco Chronicle*, May 17, 1940, 8.

266   On election night: *San Francisco Chronicle*, Oct. 30, 1940, 12, and Nov. 6, 1940, 14.

266   He played a cricket: *San Francisco Chronicle*, Apr. 14, 1940, 70, and the Mountain Play Program, May 19, 1940, Anne T. Kent California Room, Marin County Library, San Rafael, CA.

266   "Scores of players": *San Francisco Chronicle*, May 12, 1940, 50.

266   female cricket: Elizabeth Ptak, *Marin's Mountain Play: 100 Years of Theatre on Mount Tamalpais* (Mill Valley, CA: Mountain Play Association, 2013), 97.

266   "persons proficient": Email from Matt Buff, Library and Archives, Bohemian Club, Jun. 30, 2016. Peter was an artistic member of the Bohemian Club from Jan. 25, 1940 to May 31, 1941.

267   "California is a place": Didion, "Notes from a Native Daughter," 172.

267   18,000 employees: René J. Francillon, *Lockheed Aircraft Since 1913* (Annapolis, MD: Naval Institute Press, 1987), 21.

267   "expediter": Peter Pike, Army Serial No.: 19 065 438, Separation Qualification Record, Army of the United States, Date of Separation: Nov. 1, 1945, National Personnel Records Center, National Archives, St. Louis, MO 63138.

268   "Lockheed Goes": *Los Angeles Times*, Mar. 22, 1941, 5.

268   "Warcraft Pouring": *Chicago Tribune*, Sep. 21, 1941, 10.

268   Lockheed would build: Francillon, *Lockheed Aircraft Since 1913*, 53.

268   Aviation employment: Starr, *Embattled Dreams*, 134. The major employers were Douglas Aircraft, Hughes Aircraft, Lockheed Aircraft, North American Aviation, Northrop Corporation, and Vultee Aircraft.

268   "arsenal next door": Ibid., 134.

Chapter 25: Romance in Wartime

269   "There is my greatest": Quotations of Catherine Cline Pike are from her album "Bridal Memories."

269   "Was Pearl Harbor": Starr, *Embattled Dreams*, 34.

269   "JAPAN PLANES": *San Francisco Chronicle*, Dec. 9, 1941, 1.

270   "The tree we": Peter and Catherine Pike album, 1941–1943.

270   "TWO MORE SHIPS": *Los Angeles Times*, Dec. 25, 1941, 1.

272   "Catherine Cline": *San Francisco Chronicle*, Jan. 9, 1942, 14.

273   St. John's Episcopal: *San Francisco Chronicle*, Feb. 6, 1942, 8.

273   Monterey Presidio: Today the Defense Language Institute Foreign Language Center (DLIFLC).

273   ranks of the AAF: Total USAAF personnel grew from 354,161 on Dec. 31, 1941, to 1,597,049 on Dec. 31, 1942.

273   Hamilton Field played: "Hamilton Field, Written Historical and Descriptive Data," HABS NO. CA-2398 (Historic American Buildings Survey, National Park Service, Department of the Interior San Francisco, California), 21.

273   "crowded, frenzied": Ibid., 19.

277   "an adorable little": Today the chapel is the Hamilton Children's Center, 531 Hamilton Parkway, Novato, CA 94949.

277   rained two-and-a-half: *San Rafael Independent*, Feb. 4, 1942, 1.

277   "The Pikes' Romantic": *San Francisco Chronicle*, Feb. 6, 1942, 8.

Epilogue

280   "incompetent person": "In the Matter of the Guardianship of the estate of Roy M. Pike, an Incompetent Person," Superior Court, San Francisco, No. 96565, Jul. 12, 1944.

280   A. P. Giannini: Giannini to Mrs. (Roy) Pike, San Francisco, Feb. 17, 1949. Original in the family's possession.

280   "No one could": Orville J. Taylor to Mrs. Roy Pike, Chicago, Feb. 1, 1949. Original in the family's possession.

Acknowledgments

282   Dalgarven Mill: Dalgarven Mill, Kilwinning, Ayrshire, Scotland.

283   St. James: Located in the foothills of the Ozark Mountains about 100 miles southwest of St. Louis off Interstate 44.

283   "a well-known name": *History of Pope County, Arkansas* (Winston-Salem, NC: Pope County Historical Association and Hunter Publishing Co., 1979), 278.

284   I stopped several: Richard K. Brock, ed., *A Guide to the California Trail Along the Humboldt River: From the Humboldt Wells to the Humboldt Sink* (Reno, NV: Trails West, 2007), 12–14, 21–24, 51–52, 66–68, 80–81, 84–85, 95, 105, 135–136, 138–141, 154–155.

284   Crossing the Sierra: Frank Tortorich Jr., *Gold Rush Trail: A Guide to the Carson River Route of the Emigrant Trail* (Pine Grove, CA: Wagon Wheel Tours, 1998), 14–22.

BIBLIOGRAPHY

Memoirs – Diaries – Personal Papers

Unless otherwise noted, these documents are in the family's possession.

Cline, Catherine (later Catherine Cline Pike). Diary 1937–1939.

___. "Travel Journal—U.S., May 15–25, 1938."

___. "Travel Journal—Europe, May 26–Aug. 10, 1938."

___. "Women in Medicine," 1–2. Catherine Cline Papers, MSS 79-12, University of California, San Francisco, Library Archives.

Pike, Catherine Cline. Bridal Memories, Nov. 20, 1941–Feb. 5, 1942.

Pike, Edith Simpson. "Early Years of Edith Simpson Pike," with an Addendum by Roy M. Pike Jr.

___. *A Memory of Edith Simpson Pike, 1881–1977.* A collection of poems privately printed by her sons, Roy Pike Jr. and Peter Pike.

Pike, Jacob M. "A Drumming Trip through Northern Oregon and Washington Territory, Now State of Washington [Winter of 1878]," handwritten in 1912.

___. "J. M. Pike's Memoirs," handwritten in 1912.

___. "Trip to Yosemite Valley in the Spring of 1857," handwritten in 1912.

Pike, Jacob M. and Percy M. Pike. *Memoirs of J. M. Pike and Percy Mortimer Pike.* Los Angeles: 1968.

Pike, Peter. "Childhood on a Ranch, 1921–1924."

___. "Fall & Winter 1932–Spring & Summer 1933."

Pike, Roy, M. Diary, vol. 1 (Oct. 1, 1912 to Jan. 2, 1914), vol. 2 (Jan. 4, 1914 to Oct. 31, 1915), vol. 3 (Nov. 1, 1915 to May 30, 1916), vol. 4 (May 31, 1916 to Jul. 9, 1917).

___. "Story of El Solyo Ranch," Apr. 1, 1935. Bancroft Library, BANC MSS C–I 16 Pt. I:58. Although the author's name does not appear, he refers to himself as "the present Manager of El Solyo Ranch," Roy M. Pike.

Pike, Roy M. Jr. "My Early Life."

___. "My Trip Abroad, Jan. 4–Aug. 15, 1929."

___. "Our Trip to Europe in 1925."

Pike, Thomas P. *Memoirs of Thomas P. Pike.* San Marino, CA: 1979.

___. "A Profile of Roy M. Pike's Diaries, 1912–1917," written in 1987.

Simpson, Edgar. "Captain's Log, 1903–1907."

Smith, Sophie D. (later Sophie Smith Simpson). "Compositions & Etc.," misc. documents scanned by Michael Simpson and saved as a Microsoft Publisher file.

Articles – Essays – Reports

Beckham, Stephen Dow. "Asa Mead Simpson: Lumberman and Shipbuilder," *Oregon Historical Quarterly*, vol. 68, no. 3 (Sep. 1967).

Cox, Thomas R. "Lumber and Ships: The Business Empire of Asa Mead Simpson," *Forest History*, vol. 14, no. 2 (Jul. 1970), 20.

Didion, Joan. "Notes from a Native Daughter," *Slouching Towards Bethlehem*, New York: Farrar, Straus and Giroux, 1968.

Dunham, Sam C. *The Alaskan Gold Fields*. Anchorage: Alaska Northwest Publishing Company, 1983, reprint. Originally published as *The Alaskan Gold Fields and the Opportunities They Offer for Capital and Labor* by Sam C. Dunham in *Bulletin of the Department of Labor*, No. 16, May 1898, pp. 297-425.

"El Solyo," *Ford News*, Jul. 1935, 132-33.

"The El Solyo Deal," *Fortune*, vol. 30, no. 2 (Feb. 1945).

York, Thelma. "El Solyo Ranch," A research paper for History 101 at Sacramento State College, submitted Jan. 2, 1961.

Books

Ackley, Laura A. *San Francisco's Jewel City: The Panama–Pacific International Exposition of 1915*. Berkeley: Heyday, 2015.

Altrocchi, Julia Cooley. *The Spectacular San Franciscans*. New York: E. P. Dutton and Company, 1949.

Bagg, Lyman Hotchkiss. *Four Years at Yale: By a Graduate of '69*. New Haven: Charles C. Chatfield & Co., 1871.

Bancroft, Hubert Howe. *Chronicles of the Builders of the Commonwealth, Vol. IV*. San Francisco: The History Company, Publishers, 1892.

Barker, Malcolm E., ed. *More San Francisco Memoirs 1852–1899: The Ripening Years*. San Francisco: Londonborn Publications, 1996.

Beckham, Stephen Dow. *The Simpsons of Shore Acres*. Coos Bay, OR: Arago Books, 1971.

Berglund, Barbara. *Making San Francisco American: Cultural Frontiers in the Urban West, 1846–1906*. Lawrence, KS: University Press of Kansas, 2007.

Berton, Pierre. *Klondike: The Last Great Gold Rush 1896–1899*. Canada: Anchor Canada, 2001.

Bieber, Ralph P., ed. *Southern Trails to California in 1849*. Glendale, CA: Arthur H. Clark, 1937.

Bolitho, Hector. *James Lyle Mackay: First Earl of Inchcape*. London: John Murray, 1936.

Boyett, Gene W. *Hardscrabble Frontier: Pope County, Arkansas, in the 1850s*. Lanham, MD: University Press of America, 1990.

Brands, H. W. *The Age of Gold: The California Gold Rush and the New American Dream*. New York: Doubleday, 2002.

Bunting, W. H. *Live Yankees: The Sewalls and Their Ships.* Gardiner, ME: Tilbury House, 2009.

Cassaday, Stephen. *Spanning the Gate: The Golden Gate Bridge.* Santa Rosa, CA: Squarebooks, 1986.

Caughey, John Walton. *Hubert Howe Bancroft: Historian of the West.* Berkeley: University of California Press, 1946.

Chandler, Robert J. *Wells Fargo.* Charleston, SC: Arcadia Publishing, 2006. .

Cross, Ira B. *Financing an Empire: History of Banking in California, Vol. I.* Chicago: S. J. Clarke Publishing Co., 1927.

Delgado, James P. *To California by Sea: A Maritime History of the California Gold Rush.* Columbia, SC: University of South Carolina Press, 1990.

____. *Gold Rush Port: The Maritime Archaeology of San Francisco's Waterfront.* Berkeley: University of California Press, 2009.

Dinkelspiel, Frances. *Towers of Gold: How One Jewish Immigrant Named Isaias Hellman Created California.* New York: St. Martin's Press, 2008.

Edmondson, Mary Dillon. *Profiles in Leadership: A History of the Spence School.* West Kennebunk, ME: Phoenix Publishing, 1991.

Faust, Drew Gilpin. *This Republic of Suffering: Death and the American Civil War.* New York: Random House, 2008.

Fletcher, Jack E. and Patricia K. A. Fletcher. *Cherokee Trail Diaries: Vol. III, 1851–1900, Emigrants, Goldseekers, Cattle Drives, and Outlaws.* Sequim, WA: Fletcher Family Trust, 2001.

Fradkin, Philip L. *Stagecoach: Wells Fargo and the American West.* New York: Free Press, 2003.

Gerteis, Louis S. *Civil War St. Louis.* Lawrence, KS: University Press of Kansas, 2001.

Goodheart, Adam. *1861: The Civil War Awakening.* New York: Alfred A. Knopf, 2011.

Hill, Michael. *Elihu Washburne: The Diary and Letters of America's Minister to France During the Siege and Commune of Paris.* New York: Simon & Schuster, 2012.

Holliday, J. S. *Rush for Riches: Gold Fever and the Making of California.* Berkeley: University of California, 1999.

Holmes, Kenneth L., ed. *Best of Covered Wagon Women.* Norman, OK: University of Oklahoma Press, 2008.

Horne, Alistair. *The Fall of Paris: The Siege and The Commune 1870–71.* London: Penguin Books, 1990.

Howard, Michael. *The Franco-Prussian War: The German Invasion of France, 1870–1871.* London: Routledge, 1989.

Jackson, Donald Dale. *Gold Dust.* New York: Alfred A. Knopf, 1980.

Jackson, Lee. *Dirty Old London: The Victorian Fight Against Filth.* New Haven, CT: Yale University Press, 2014.

Jackson, Ruby West and Walter T. McDonald. *Finding Freedom: The Untold Story of Joshua Glover, Runaway Slave.* Madison, WI: Wisconsin Historical Society Press, 2007.

Johnson, Steven. *Ghost Map: The Story of London's Most Terrifying Epidemic—and How It Changed Science, Cities, and the Modern World.* New York: Riverhead Books, 2006.

Johnson, Susan Lee. *Roaring Camp: The Social World of the California Gold Rush.* New York: W. W. Norton & Company, 2000.

Kennedy, David M. *Freedom from Fear: The American People in Depression and War, 1929–1945.* New York: Oxford University Press, 1999.

Kranzberg, Melvin. *The Siege of Paris, 1870–1871: A Political and Social History.* Westport, CT: Greenwood Press, 1950.

Lewis, Oscar. *Sea Routes to the Gold Fields: The Migration by Water to California in 1849–1852.* New York: Alfred A. Knopf, 1949.

Lewis, Oscar and Carroll D. Hall, *Bonanza Inn: America's First Luxury Hotel.* New York: A. A. Knopf, 1939.

Lloyd, Benjamin E. *Lights and Shades in San Francisco.* San Francisco: A. L. Bancroft, 1876.

Mace, Henry O. *Between the Rivers: A History of Early Calaveras County, California,* 2nd ed. Murphys, CA: Paul Groh Press, 2002.

McArthur, Priscilla. *Arkansas in the Gold Rush.* Little Rock, AR: August House, 1986.

McCullough, David. *The Greater Journey: Americans in Paris.* New York: Simon & Schuster, 2011.

Meldahl, Keith Heyer. *Hard Road West: History & Geology Along the Gold Rush Trail.* Chicago: University of Chicago Press, 2007.

Moffat, Frances. *Dancing on the Brink of the World: The Rise and Fall of San Francisco Society.* New York: G. P. Putnam's Sons, 1977.

Munro, J. Forbes. *Maritime Enterprise and Empire: Sir William Mackinnon and His Business Network, 1823–93.* New York: Boydell Press, 2003.

Myres, Sandra L. *Westering Women and the Frontier Experience, 1800–1915.* Albuquerque, NM: University of New Mexico Press, 1982.

Nagorski, Andrew. *Hitlerland: American Eyewitnesses to the Nazi Rise to Power.* New York: Simon & Schuster, 2012.

Neville, Amelia Ransome. *The Fantastic City: Memoirs of the Social and Romantic Life of Old San Francisco.* Boston: Houghton Mifflin, 1932.

Ormond, Richard and Elaine Kilmurray. *John Singer Sargent: The Early Portraits, Complete Paintings, Vol. I.* New Haven, CT: Yale University Press, 1998.

Picard, Liza. *Victorian London: The Life of a City.* London: Phoenix, 2005.

Primm, James Neal. *Lion of the Valley: St. Louis, Missouri.* Boulder, CO: Pruett Publishing Company, 1981.

Royce, Sarah. *A Frontier Lady: Reflections of the Gold Rush and Early California.* Lincoln, NE: University of Nebraska Press, 1977.

Smale, Rudolph. *There Go the Ships.* Caldwell, ID: The Claxton Printers, Ltd., 1940.

Starr, Kevin. *Embattled Dreams: California in War and Peace, 1940–1950.* New York: Oxford University Press, 2002.

____. *Golden Gate: The Life and Times of America's Greatest Bridge.* New York: Bloomsbury Press, 2010.

Stone, Rhoda and Charles A. *The Tools Are on the Bar: The History of Copperopolis, Calaveras, County, California*. Privately published, 1991.

Stover, John F. *American Railroads*, 2nd ed. Chicago: University of Chicago Press, 1997.

Wagner, Judith and Richard. *The Uncommon Life of Louis Jerome Simpson*. North Bend, OR: BYGONES, 2003.

Whiteley, Lee. *The Cherokee Trail: Bent's Old Fort to Fort Bridger*. Boulder, CO: Lee Whiteley, 1999.

Winter, William C. *The Civil War in St. Louis: A Guided Tour*. St. Louis: Missouri Historical Society Press, 1994.

Wood, John Seymour. *College Days: Or Harry's Career at Yale*. New York: The Outing Co., Limited, 1894.

Wright, E. W., ed. *Lewis & Dryden's Marine History of the Pacific Northwest*. Portland, OR: The Lewis & Dryden Printing Company, 1895.

PHOTOGRAPH CREDITS

All photographs are from family albums and collections except the following:

The steel-cut engraving of Asa Mead Simpson in chapter 6 is from Hubert Howe Bancroft's *Chronicles of the Builders of the Commonwealth, Vol. 4.*

The picture of Frederick Cline at Yale College in 1874 in chapter 8 is from Manuscripts & Archives, Yale University Library.

The aerial photograph of El Solyo Ranch in chapter 15 is from the Patterson Township Historical Society.

MAP CREDIT

Maps were created by Ben Pease, Pease Press, San Francisco.

INDEX

Page numbers in *italics* indicate photographs.
Page numbers followed by "n" indicate notes.

Continued >

Continued >